Schizophrenia
Comprehensive Treatment and Management

Schizophrenia
Comprehensive Treatment and Management

Marvin I. Herz, M.D.
Attending Psychiatrist
Department of Psychiatry
Strong Memorial Hospital;
Professor of Psychiatry
Director, Mental Health Services Research
University of Rochester School of Medicine and Dentistry
Rochester, New York

Stephen R. Marder, M.D.
Director
Veterans Affairs Desert Pacific Mental Illness Research, Education and
   Clinical Center
Veterans Affairs Greater Los Angeles Health Care System;
Professor and Vice-Chair
Department of Psychiatry
University of California—Los Angeles
Los Angeles, California

LIPPINCOTT WILLIAMS & WILKINS
A **Wolters Kluwer** Company
Philadelphia · Baltimore · New York · London
Buenos Aires · Hong Kong · Sydney · Tokyo

Acquisitions Editor: Charles W. Mitchell
Developmental Editor: Stacey L. Baze
Production Editor: Emmeline Parker
Manufacturing Manager: Colin Warnock
Cover Designer: Christine Jenny
Compositor: Lippincott Williams & Wilkins Desktop Division
Printer: Maple-Vail

Library of Congress Cataloging-in-Publication Data
Schizophrenia: comprehensive treatment and management / Marvin I. Herz, Stephen R. Marder
    p. ; cm.
    Includes index.
    ISBN 0-683-30709-6
    1. Schizophrenia.   2. Schizophrenia–Treatment. I. Marder, Stephen R., 1945- II. Title
    [DNLM: 1. Schizophrenia–therapy. WM 203 H582c 2002]
RC514.H465 2002
616.89′8206–dc21

Care has been taken to confirm the accuracy of the information presented and to describe generally accepted practices. However, the authors and publisher are not responsible for errors or omissions or for any consequences from application of the information in this book and make no warranty, expressed or implied, with respect to the currency, completeness, or accuracy of the contents of the publication. Application of this information in a particular situation remains the professional responsibility of the practitioner.

The authors and publisher have exerted every effort to ensure that drug selection and dosage set forth in this text are in accordance with current recommendations and practice at the time of publication. However, in view of ongoing research, changes in government regulations, and the constant flow of information relating to drug therapy and drug reactions, the reader is urged to check the package insert for each drug for any change in indications and dosage and for added warnings and precautions. This is particularly important when the recommended agent is a new or infrequently employed drug.

Some drugs and medical devices presented in this publication have Food and Drug Administration (FDA) clearance for limited use in restricted research settings. It is the responsibility of the health care provider to ascertain the FDA status of each drug or device planned for use in their clinical practice.

10 9 8 7 6 5 4 3 2 1

Dedicated to our wives,
Leslie and Paula,
for their inspiration, support, and love.

Marvin I. Herz
Stephen R. Marder

Contents

Introduction

Our primary purpose in writing this book is to provide clinicians with practical treatment recommendations for the optimal care of individuals with schizophrenia. We decided to write the book ourselves—rather than edit it with multiple contributing authors—in order to provide an integrated uniform approach for dealing with persons with this complex disorder. Our goal is to present "state-of-the-art" treatment practices that are based on scientific evidence, and when this evidence is not available, to provide expert opinion, including our own clinical experience. Case examples are used to illustrate particular treatment issues.

Although the book primarily targets clinicians who are mental health professionals, including psychiatrists, psychologists, nurses, social workers, and students and trainees in these professions, others may also find it valuable. These include primary care physicians, administrators, policy makers, and family members and patients, who, after all, are the consumers of mental health services.

The publication of this book coincides with major advances in the effectiveness of treatment, which, if implemented, offers great opportunities to improve the course and outcome of the disorder. Today, if advanced treatment methods are employed, individuals with schizophrenia can look forward to more independent, productive, and satisfying lives than seemed possible as recently as 10 to 20 years ago. No longer must a diagnosis of schizophrenia be considered the equivalent of a sentence of progressive deterioration in functioning, loss of contact with reality, alienation, and dependency.

The deficits associated with the disorder are multidimensional, involving an affected individual's thinking, feeling, and behavior. Therefore, in order to achieve maximal benefits, a comprehensive treatment approach is required, including psychopharmacological, psychotherapeutic, psychosocial, and rehabilitative interventions. Individuals with schizophrenia differ with respect to underlying personality, aspirations, motivations, clinical symptoms, functioning and coping skills, other personal assets, and social supports. Therefore, treatment planning should be individualized and flexible, with modifications made as the individual's clinical status and goals evolve over time.

We believe that optimal treatment requires active collaboration among the clinician/team, individuals with schizophrenia, and, whenever possible, their families. Treatment should be characterized by mutual respect and open communication. Continuity of care, with no time limits within a system of care, is vital. While our overall approach to treatment is empirically based, we use the stress-vulnerability model to guide our understanding and treatment recommendations. According to this model, individuals with schizophrenia have increased vulnerability to biological, psychological, and social stressors. Therefore, therapeutic efforts should aim to decrease both that vulnerability and the intensity of stress on the individual.

The existence of better treatments for schizophrenia does not mean that patients will receive them. A number of recent surveys have demonstrated that "state-of-the-art" psychosocial treatment programs are frequently not offered by service providers. The problem is also evident in medication-prescribing practices, where it is not uncommon for patients to receive a less-than-optimal choice of medication and incorrect dosing.

We view our mission as providing recommendations for the psychosocial and pharmacological treatment approaches that offer individuals with schizophrenia the greatest opportunity to achieve optimal benefits of treatment, which, in turn enable them to reach their full potential. Therefore, we do not discuss the costs of the practices we recommend. How does one measure the benefits versus the costs of achieving a better and more satisfying quality of life with minimal impairment for these persons? Furthermore, whenever cost/benefit analyses have been carried out, quality care is generally found to be no more costly than sub-par care. Because of the problem of stigma, the question of costs is frequently raised in limiting treatment of major mental illnesses, while on the other hand, it is infrequently raised for general medical disorders. Another major problem is that a large percentage of individuals with schizophrenia are treated in the public sector, where until recently they had little or no political clout to achieve more than minimal funding. However, aside from the funding issue, part of the problem lies with mental health professionals, many of whom have not yet implemented treatment approaches where efficacy based on solid evidence has already been established and where cost is not a factor. We hope this book will help remedy that situation.

The book is organized into the following sections and chapters:

Section I. General Issues in Treating and Managing Schizophrenia

Chapter 1: Neurobiology

This chapter presents information regarding etiology, including genetics, pathophysiology, neuroanatomy, neurochemistry, and developmental insults. It deals with theories of how medications work.

Chapter 2: Diagnosis, Course and Outcome, and Epidemiology

This chapter presents issues regarding diagnosis and differential diagnosis, including difficulties in establishing a diagnosis on first presentation. Studies of the long-term course and outcome are summarized, pointing out that course and outcome are widely variable. Epidemiological studies are summarized. Phases of the disorder—prodromal, acute, stabilization, and stable—are described.

Chapter 3: General Principles of Treatment and Management

This chapter presents our general, overall treatment philosophy, emphasizing the need for a biopsychosocial approach, integrating pharmacological with psychosocial treatment, and rehabilitation and the desirability of having a system of care in place to treat individuals over the course of their long-term disorder. The stress-vulnerability model is discussed as it relates to course, outcome, and treatment strategies. Aims and methods of treatment are presented for each phase of the disorder, including the importance of establishing a collaborative relationship with patients and family members. Issues relating to use of a team approach, which is used in most public settings, are discussed.

Chapter 4: Early-Intervention Prevention Programs

This chapter reviews published data dealing with: (1) prevention of the onset of the disorder through clinical intervention in the prodromal phase and ethical issues involved (primary prevention); and (2) prevention of relapse through early intervention in the prodromal phase for patients with established schizophrenia who are beginning the process of relapse (secondary and tertiary prevention). The roles of stress vulnerability, prodromal symptoms, psychoeducation, and early intervention treatment are discussed, along with recommendations for implementation.

Chapter 5: Pharmacological Treatment

Review of efficacy and appropriate use of commonly prescribed antipsychotic medications.

Section II: Treating and Managing the Phases of Schizophrenia
Chapter 6: Evaluation of the Acutely Psychotic Patient

This chapter deals with evaluation of acutely psychotic patients and immediate management concerns. It focuses on the diagnostic interview; differential diagnostic considerations, especially in patients without an established diagnosis, where it is important to rule out other disorders whose symptoms may mimic schizophrenia; laboratory evaluations; relevant history-taking (including issues involved in interviewing a psychotic patient); establishing rapport with psychotic and paranoid individuals; obtaining information and collaboration from collaterals, including family members and friends; and identifying and evaluating potential stressors that precipitate an acute episode.

Chapter 7: Management and Treatment of the Acute Phase of Schizophrenia

This chapter includes the following:

- Selection of settings for acute care, e.g.: hospitalization and alternatives to hospitalization, including day hospital, crisis home care, crisis residence, etc.
- Pharmacological management, including drug selection, dosing, and side effects
- Psychosocial treatment and management, including the optimal milieu for acute inpatient units
- Management of aggressive, assaultive, and suicidal behavior
- Dealing with uncooperative patients; attempts to establish rapport and legal issues
- Establishing a relationship with families and/or other collaterals, including support and family education
- Criteria for hospital discharge and the importance of continuity of care after discharge
- Management of treatment-refractory patients

Chapter 8: Stabilization Phase

This chapter deals with:

- Medication principles during this phase
- Ensuring continuity of treatment and maintenance of social supports, including adequate housing and income supplementation
- Limiting any potential stressors, since patients are highly vulnerable to relapse
- Psychosocial treatment

Chapter 9: Stable Phase

This chapter deals with:

- Pharmacological treatment, including dose, drug selection, side effects, and questions of dosage reduction

- Psychosocial treatments, including individual and group psychotherapy
- Cognitive behavioral treatment approaches
- Treatment approaches to prevent relapse and rehospitalization
- Family intervention, including psychoeducation and efforts to improve problem solving and communication within the family
- Treatment of negative symptoms
- Managing and preventing tardive dyskinesia
- Dealing with noncompliance and denial of illness
- Recognition and management of potential suicidal and/or aggressive behaviors

Chapter 10: Rehabilitative Approaches

This chapter deals with:

- Indications and methods of social skills training, vocational training, training to remedy neuropsychological deficits, and improving coping skills
- Goals of rehabilitation efforts should be arrived at in collaboration with the patient

Chapter 11: Community Intervention and Support

This chapter deals with:

- Types of case management
- Essentials of the Program for Assertive Community Treatment
- Varieties of residential options and their indications
- Involvement with advocacy and support groups

Section III: Special Issues in Treating and Managing Schizophrenia

Chapter 12: Management of First-Episode Psychosis Patients

This chapter deals with:

- The importance of establishing a diagnosis, ruling out disorders that may mimic schizophrenia
- Special issues in pharmacological treatment, including choice of medication, dosages, lowering doses over time, and possible drug discontinuation
- Early detection and treatment of individuals with previously undiagnosed schizophrenia who begin to demonstrate schizophrenic symptoms (secondary prevention)
- Psychosocial treatment involving patients and families
- Importance of ensuring continuity of care and setting realistic goals

Chapter 13: Treatment and Management of Dual-Diagnosis Patients

This chapter deals with patients who are chemical abusers, with optimal treatment calling for integration of psychiatric and substance abuse approaches, treatment and management of obsessive-compulsive disorder, depressive symptoms, and other comorbid conditions, including general medical disorders and polydipsia.

Chapter 14: Special Populations

This chapter deals with a variety of important issues related to treatment of special populations, including (1) homelessness; (2) special considerations regarding race and ethnicity; (3) differential issues in treatment of males and females (for example, in females, decisions about becoming pregnant and treatment during pregnancy and during the neonatal period); (4) special issues in treatment of elderly individuals with schizophrenia; and (5) interventions for individuals involved in the forensic system.

Appendices

Appendix 1

Describes empirically validated modules designed to teach those with serious and persistent mental disabilities the social and dependent living skills necessary to improve their functioning and quality of their lives. Each module provides a structured, user-friendly protocol.

Appendix 2

This appendix contains the NAMI Consumer and Family Guide to Schizophrenia Treatment, which provides patients and families information about treatment that has been shown to be effective.

Marvin I. Herz, M.D.
Stephen R. Marder, M.D.

SECTION I

General Issues in Treating and Managing Schizophrenia

1

Neurobiology

The idea that schizophrenia is a disease of the brain has attracted the attention of scientists for decades. Kraepelin viewed dementia praecox—or schizophrenia—as a disorder that resulted from a degenerative illness of the brain. It was clinically manifest in a dementia that emerged in youth and progressed in most cases to a terminal dementia. Later scientists were impressed that the experiences of individuals with schizophrenia resembled those of normals who had ingested a hallucinogenic drug. This led to the proposal that this disorder resulted from a circulating substance that caused psychotic symptoms. The search for this substance was vigorous but ended in failure.

A number of factors complicate the problem of finding the cause of schizophrenia. Perhaps the most important is the difficulty of defining the illness. Schizophrenia does not involve a pathognomonic lesion found in all individuals with the illness. Instead, its clinical features vary considerably among individuals. Moreover, schizophrenia cannot be localized to any area of the world where it can be associated with an environmental cause. Rather, the prevalence of schizophrenia is similar in nearly every population studied, whether in developed or developing countries, in urban or rural environments. The lack of an animal model of the illness also hampers the search for the cause of schizophrenia. In many other disorders an animal model provides convenient opportunities for understanding the factors that can cause the illness and for learning about treatments.

GENETICS

The evidence that schizophrenia can be inherited is compelling. The risk for schizophrenia worldwide is about 1%. This increases to about 8% to 10% if the patient has a first-degree relative, such as a sibling or a parent, who suffers from schizophrenia (1). If the patient has a dizygotic twin with schizophrenia, the risk is similar to that for a sibling. However, if the twin is monozygotic the risk increases to as high as 50% in some studies (2).

Since the concordance rate is not 100% in monozygotic twins it also suggests that other nongenetic factors contribute to the development of the illness. These environmental factors could be events that occur during fetal development or after birth. The possible role of nongenetic factors is also suggested by studies that focused on monozygotic twins who are discordant for schizophrenia. That is, researchers compared twins who are genetically identical but where one twin is diagnosed with schizophrenia and the other is not. These studies have revealed interesting anatomic differences, with the twin with schizophrenia demonstrating smaller hemispheric volumes and smaller anterior hippocampi (Fig. 1.1) (3).

Other studies have supported a genetic role in schizophrenia. Investigators in Denmark evaluated children who were adopted at birth. Since record keeping in Denmark is thorough, the researchers were able to compare the schizophrenia in the biologic and adopting mothers as well as the children. The findings indicated that there is an increased risk of schizophrenia in the adopted children of biologic mothers with schizophrenia. Similarly, there was a higher risk for schizophrenia in the biologic relatives of children who developed schizophrenia (4). This suggests that the risk for developing the illness is strongly related to genetic rather than to environmental factors related to the child's upbringing. A comparable study in Finland showed similar results (5).

More recent evidence suggests that the biologic relatives of individuals with schizophrenia are also at increased risk of developing schizoaffective illness, schizotypal personality disorder, and other nonaffective psychoses. This suggests that individuals inherit a vulnerability to develop a psychotic illness rather than just schizophrenia.

Despite the overwhelming evidence that schizophrenia is an inherited illness, a particular defective gene responsible for it has not been found. As a result, many researchers have abandoned the ambitious goal of discovering a "schizophrenia gene." Using recently developed gene maps, studies have focused on families where one or more individuals suffer from schizophrenia. Linkage studies attempt to locate genes that are associated with the presence of the disorder. Researchers have proposed a number of candidate genes (e.g., sites on chromosomes 5, 6, and 11), and findings have supported linkage. However, none of these genes have been consistently linked to schizophrenia.

Another strategy has focused on a search for abnormalities in particular genes that are hypothesized to be related to schizophrenia. For example, researchers have explored whether mutations on subtypes of dopamine and serotonergic receptors are related to schizophrenia. Studies have not yet located a mutation that is reliably related to schizophrenia.

Rather than supporting genes that are strongly associated with schizophrenia, an overview of the findings suggests a polygene model where multiple genes contribute to vulnerability for schizophrenia. In addition, the ob-

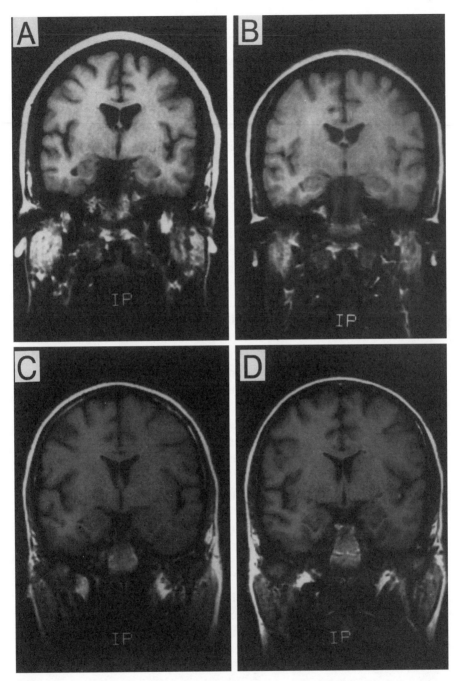

FIG. 1.1. MRI scans (coronal sections) of two sets of discordant monozygotic twins (**A** and **B** = set 1; **C** and **D** = set 2). For each pair, one has schizophrenia (**A** and **C**) while the other does not (**B** and **D**). For both pairs, the affected twin has larger ventricles than the unaffected twin, even though ventricular size appears to be within the normal range for the affected twin. (Courtesy of D Weinberger and EF Torrey.)

servation that the prevalence of schizophrenia is relatively uniform through-out the world suggests that it is unlikely that a single gene would explain the illness. That is, if a particular gene locus that is defective in schizophrenia exists, one would expect to find areas of the world where inbred populations have a high incidence of schizophrenia. The relative homogeneity of schizo-phrenia could be explained by an illness that is associated with combinations of relatively common genes.

CHILDREN AT RISK FOR SCHIZOPHRENIA

Children with at least one parent with schizophrenia, who are thus at high risk, have been found to have a number of abnormalities. Barbara Fish and her co-workers have found such children to have abnormalities of gait, pos-ture, and muscle tone (6). These children demonstrated early evidence of the disorder before they developed the full syndrome of schizophrenia. Walker used an interesting method for identifying early evidence of schizophrenia (7). Observers were shown home movies of siblings filmed before one of them developed schizophrenia. She found that observers could usually iden-tify the child who would later develop schizophrenia. These discriminations were most often based on impaired motor function in the twin who later de-veloped schizophrenia.

When these findings are taken together they suggest that schizophrenia is an illness that is inherited and begins to manifest some early signs during childhood in some individuals but does not appear until adulthood in others. The time of onset affects the person's development, with patients whose on-set began during childhood having more profound impairments in their so-cial functioning. As will be discussed later, individuals with an earlier onset are more likely to have neuroanatomic abnormalities.

NEUROANATOMY

Studies comparing the brains of individuals with schizophrenia with those of normals have uncovered a number of important differences. Although these studies have led to a consensus that anatomic abnormalities are associ-ated with schizophrenia, the overall results are somewhat unsettling, since no single pathognomonic abnormality is consistently found in the illness.

The most consistent neuroanatomic abnormality found in those with schizophrenia is an enlargement of the lateral and third ventricles. These ab-normalities were initially found with computerized tomography (CT) and have been confirmed using magnetic resonance imaging (MRI). A number of studies compared the images of patients with schizophrenia with those of normal individuals. Using "slices" that included the lateral ventricles, inves-

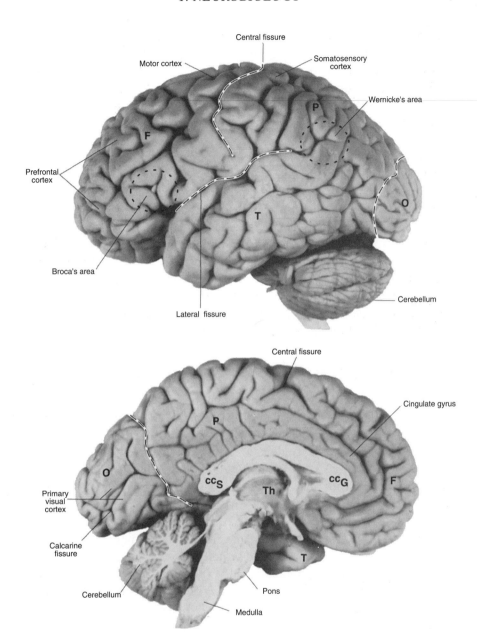

FIG. 1.2. Photographs of the lateral (top) and medial (bottom) of the left hemisphere of a human brain indicating the location of major surface land-marks. (Abbreviations: F; frontal lobe; O, occipital lobe; P, parietal lobe; T, temporal lobe; Th, thalamus; ccG, the genu of the corpus callosum; ccS, the splenium of the corpus callosum.)

tigators compared the area of ventricle to that of brain by computing a ventricular brain ratio (or VBR). Of the studies performed, nearly 80% found a higher VBR in those with schizophrenia. However, this is not a consistent finding because most investigators have found enlargement in only 15% to 30% of patients (8,9). This finding is also confusing because ventricular enlargement has been found in other disorders, including affective disorders (10,11).

The finding of ventricular enlargement in schizophrenia has been valuable because it revealed that the illness is associated with a loss of brain tissue. This raised a number of important questions about the nature of tissue loss: Is the loss of tissue due to an overall decrease in brain size, or are particular areas of the brain affected? Is the tissue loss present before the onset of the disease, or is the loss of brain tissue progressive (as Kraepelin might have predicted for dementia praecox)? Is the loss of brain tissue present in every case of schizophrenia, or is it characteristic of a particular subtype of the disorder. What biologic factors can lead to loss of brain tissue? Research addressing these questions has made an extraordinary contribution to our understanding of the biology of schizophrenia (Fig. 1.2).

MEDIAL TEMPORAL LOBE IN SCHIZOPHRENIA

Postmortem examinations of brains from individuals with schizophrenia have found reductions in the size of limbic brain areas, including the hippocampus, amygdala, periventricular gray and entorhinal cortex (12). Perhaps the most consistent finding is a reduction in the size of the hippocampus (13). These observations are supported by other studies that found a loss of neurons and disturbances in the usual alignment of neurons in some of the same brain areas (14–16). Since these disturbances in alignment did not also involve other signs of damage to these areas (e.g., loss of nerve cells or glia), they probably result from an abnormality in the development of these areas. For example, a failure of the normal migration of neurons during brain development would explain this finding. This remains a tentative finding since other groups (e.g., Benes) have failed to replicate the finding regarding cell alignment but have found other abnormalities in the hippocampus (17).

Stevens has pointed out that illnesses that are associated with much more serious abnormalities in these same brain areas are not associated with schizophrenia (9). Dwork has also emphasized that there are negative reports of differences between patients with schizophrenia and normal individuals in medial temporal areas and that some of the positive studies had relatively few subjects and possible methodological flaws (18). Despite these reservations a number of compelling findings implicate these areas.

Perhaps the most compelling line of evidence associates the anatomic observations of medial temporal abnormalities with the impairments observed in schizophrenia. The medial temporal areas are important for the processing of sensory information (reviewed by Bogerts) (19). Impairments in these brain areas could explain the distortions in the interpretation of external reality that are characteristic of schizophrenia. For example, the paranoid symptoms in schizophrenia could develop from the experience that events occurring in the environment are centered around the patient. Thus perceived events may be experienced as relating to the patient when these events are actually irrelevant.

PREFRONTAL CORTEX AND SCHIZOPHRENIA

Both anatomic and functional studies point to the prefrontal cortex as being affected in schizophrenia. This brain area is responsible for some of the most complex and highly evolved human functions. These functions include the integration of information from other cortical areas. The prefrontal cortex is largely responsible for the regulation of working memory, which involves maintaining information in temporary memory while that information is used for executive functions. This area is also involved in functions such as attention, which requires the filtering out of extraneous information from consciousness. Therefore abnormalities in prefrontal areas could explain the deficits in working memory and attention that are often present in schizophrenia. Also, the inferior parts of the prefrontal cortex are involved in emotional expression. Abnormal functioning in this region may account for the impaired emotional expressiveness or flat affect that is an important feature of schizophrenia.

A number of imaging studies have reported reductions in the size of the prefrontal cortex in patients with schizophrenia (20,21). The finding that individuals with schizophrenia demonstrate abnormalities in cerebral blood flow to their frontal lobes reinforces these anatomic studies. A number of studies have found that individuals with schizophrenia did not demonstrate the normal increase in blood flow to frontal lobes that occurs when individuals are asked to perform tasks that require frontal lobe activity (22). A subsequent study from this same research group compared the activation of the frontal lobes in monozygotic twins who were discordant for schizophrenia (23). They found that the twin with schizophrenia had greater impairment in performing the prefrontal task (which was the Wisconsin Card Sorting Task) and demonstrated less blood flow to this region when performing the task. Taken together, these findings suggest that individuals with schizophrenia are unable to mobilize frontal lobe circuits that may be useful for performing higher mental functions.

Another clue to the origins of psychopathology in schizophrenia comes from studies that found that patients who were experiencing auditory hallucinations demonstrated increased blood flow to Broca's area, a region of the inferior frontal lobe associated with language (24). This suggests that auditory hallucinations represent a form of internally experienced speech. As will be noted later in this chapter, individuals with schizophrenia may have a deficiency in a filtering mechanism that permits these internal experiences to reach consciousness and to be experienced as sensory inputs.

NEURODEVELOPMENTAL THEORIES

Recent evidence suggests that schizophrenia may be an illness that emerges during brain development. During fetal development, neurons migrate to appropriate sites in the developing brain. As they migrate they form connections with other neurons, and in the process they form functional neural networks. A failure of this process may lead to important abnormalities.

The important period of fetal development in schizophrenia appears to be the second trimester, when this migration is occurring in the cortex. Recent findings suggest that a number of factors may interfere with brain development during this period. The best studied is influenza virus. Mednick and his co-workers studied individuals who were born near the time of a serious influenza A epidemic in Helsinki in 1957 (25). These individuals were compared with control cases who were born before the epidemic. Individuals who were in the second trimester of development at the height of the epidemic were more likely to develop schizophrenia than control cases or individuals who were at a different state of development during the epidemic. Robin Murray from the United Kingdom was able to replicate this finding, although others did not find a relationship between prenatal exposure to influenza and an increased risk for schizophrenia (26,27). Although the relationship between viral infections and schizophrenia has not been proven, the Helsinki study suggests an interesting mechanism that can lead to the development of schizophrenia. The idea that viral infections during fetal development can increase the risk of schizophrenia is further supported by the finding that individuals who develop schizophrenia tend to be in the second trimester of development during the winter months, when viral infections are more likely (28).

Other evidence suggests that nutritional deficiencies during fetal development can also increase the risk of schizophrenia. During the winter of 1944 to 1945 there was widespread famine in the western Netherlands during the Nazi occupation. An interesting study found that the risk of schizophrenia was increased in individuals who were in early gestation during this period when compared with those in gestation at other times (29). This study provides further support for the neurodevelopmental theory that schizophrenia can be caused by factors such as infection or nutritional deficiency during fetal development.

The neurodevelopmental theories are also supported by studies indicating that the previously described decreases in brain volume in frontal and temporal areas are present in individuals who are experiencing their first episodes of schizophrenia (11,13,30). These observations suggest that individuals with schizophrenia have already developed brain abnormalities before the clinical onset of the disorder. However, another study suggests that if patients are followed for an average of 30 months, those with schizophrenia show a reduction in the size of their frontal lobes (31). Reductions in the size of the temporal lobes were seen in both patients with schizophrenia and controls, and may be age related. These findings suggest that patients with schizophrenia develop brain abnormalities before the onset of the disorder and that the process that leads to volume reduction continues after the illness emerges.

If the defect in schizophrenia is present at birth, how can one explain why the actual onset of the illness is delayed until adolescence or adulthood and why women have a later onset than men? The median age of onset for schizophrenia in men is about 21, whereas it is nearly 27 in women. A number of explanations have been put forth for this, including the possibility that estrogen may delay the onset of psychosis. Nevertheless, the delay in women has not been adequately explained and remains one of the important mysteries of schizophrenia.

NEUROCHEMISTRY AND SCHIZOPHRENIA

The search for understanding the neurochemistry of schizophrenia began as a search for abnormal substances in blood and urine. As mentioned earlier, these searches led to a number of false leads. The most important innovation in biologic studies of schizophrenia was probably the discovery that chlorpromazine has antipsychotic activity. The availability of chlorpromazine and other antipsychotic drugs permitted scientists to improve our understanding of the biology of psychosis by attempting to understand how these drugs work. Much of the focus has been on the activity of these agents on dopamine. For example, nearly all drugs that increase dopamine activity—particularly stimulants—can worsen schizophrenia. Similarly, nearly all drugs that decrease dopamine activity or block dopamine receptors improve schizophrenia. Moreover, the dose of an antipsychotic that is effective for treating psychosis is highly correlated with that drug's affinity for a particular subtype of dopamine receptors, the D2 receptor. Although other classes of dopamine receptors exist (e.g., D1, D3, D4), this close relationship to clinical potency exists only for D2. These and other observations are powerful evidence that the antipsychotics alleviate psychotic symptoms by their activity of blocking D2 receptors (32).

Although it is well established that blocking dopamine receptors improves psychosis, this does not mean that the dopamine system is abnormal in schizophrenic individuals. It is common in medicine that an illness can be treated through mechanisms that are unrelated to the etiology of the illness. The treatment of hypertension is a good example. Nevertheless, there has been a vigorous search for abnormalities in the dopamine system in patients with schizophrenia. The results have been largely negative. One group using positron emission tomography scanning found that patients with schizophrenia had more dopamine receptors than a control group (33). However, another research group failed to confirm this finding (34).

But even if schizophrenia does not result from a primary illness of the dopamine system, understanding the mechanism of action of antipsychotics has increased our understanding of the neurochemistry of the disorder. For example, schizophrenia is associated with anatomic abnormalities in prefrontal and certain brain stem areas. These areas have strong inputs from dopamine and other neurotransmitters.

It has been proposed that decreased activity in the prefrontal area may result from decreased dopamine activity, which, in turn, leads to negative symptoms. This decrease in dopamine activity could lead to an overall increase in dopamine activity to compensate. And the increased dopamine activity in the circuit could lead to increased dopamine activity in limbic areas, which could lead to positive symptoms of schizophrenia.

SEROTONIN AND SCHIZOPHRENIA

LSD, a drug that antagonizes serotonin (5-HT) in some models, can cause hallucinations that are similar to those in schizophrenia. This relationship led to the proposal that schizophrenia is related to a deficiency in serotonin (35). This hypothesis was subsequently changed to include the possibility that endogenous psychotogens could mimic the effects of LSD and that these effects were related to activity at 5-HT receptors. These theories never received substantial support and have not played an important part in recent thinking about the etiology of schizophrenia. A possible exception is recent interest in the possibility that a subtype of 5-HT receptors, the 5HT2A receptor, affects a subtype of glutamate receptors (i.e., the NMDA receptor), which in turn may have an important role in schizophrenia (36). The role of glutamate will be discussed in the next section.

GLUTAMATE AND SCHIZOPHRENIA

Although the dopamine theory of schizophrenia has dominated biologic research, other neurotransmitters have also been implicated. Interest in glutamate first emerged when it was found that phencyclidine (PCP) appeared to cause psychotic symptoms by binding to a site within the NMDA receptor complex. This binding interfered with the normal binding of glutamate to the NMDA receptor (37). This led to the theory that abnormal glutamate transmission or reduced glutamate levels were associated with schizophrenia.

The idea that abnormal glutamate function could cause psychosis is consistent with the observation that glutamate plays an important role in the modulation of dopamine activity. As a result, alterations in glutamate regulation would affect dopamine and vice versa. For example, destroying glutamate fibers increases an animal's sensitivity to dopaminergic drugs. Therefore decreased glutamate function would be manifest in a hyperdopaminergic state. Although investigators have found evidence of decreased glutamate levels in patients with schizophrenia, the results among studies have been inconsistent (38).

Drugs that affect the NMDA receptor complex affect schizophrenia. Ketamine, an agent that occupies NMDA receptors in a manner similar to PCP, can produce psychotic, negative, and cognitive symptoms in normal individuals (39). This indicates that antagonism at the NMDA receptor can produce symptoms in normals that have a striking resemblance to schizophrenia. In patients with schizophrenia, infusions of ketamine can cause a transitory worsening of psychotic thinking (40). Among these patients, the symptoms induced by ketamine resembled those of the individual's schizophrenic illness.

Other evidence suggests that there may be a role for glutamatergic drugs in the treatment of schizophrenia. Although a number of strategies have been proposed, most attention has focused on enhancing the activity at an NMDA receptor that can be modulated by glycine. For a component of this NMDA receptor, the Gly-B site, glycine is necessary to activate the site. This is supported by evidence that raising glycine levels can enhance the functioning of this receptor (41). More important, double-blind, placebo-controlled trials have supported the effectiveness of high doses of glycine in improving negative symptoms of schizophrenia (42,43). Other studies have found that d-cycloserine, a drug that appears to act as a partial agonist at the glycine site, is also effective for negative symptoms in schizophrenia (44). For both glycine and d-cycloserine, the findings are from relatively small trials and will need to be replicated by other researchers. Nevertheless, they confirm the importance of understanding the role of glutamate in schizophrenia.

ABNORMALITIES IN SENSORIMOTOR GATING

Individuals with schizophrenia often appear to have impairments in their ability to filter out irrelevant stimuli. This may appear as interpreting sounds or visual experiences as important when they are actually irrelevant. It may also appear as a type of sensory flooding where a patient with schizophrenia feels inundated by an excess of stimulation. These gating deficits are common in schizophrenia and have been used to explain the disorders of attention and reality testing that affect psychotic patients (45).

Information about gating disturbances has emerged from studies using evoked potentials. For these studies electrodes are placed on the surface of the scalp to measure electrical activity in the brain. Event-related potentials are changes in electrical activity that occur in response to a type of stimulation such as a noise or a visual stimulus. One of the productive areas of research has focused on the responses to two identical sounds that are administered within a very brief period of time. Each of these stimuli results in a response that can be measured as a waveform. The response to the second stimulus is normally suppressed through inhibitory mechanisms. The failure to suppress a particular part of the waveform, the P50, a response that occurs 50 msec after the sound, has been reported to be associated with schizophrenia (46). In addition, abnormal P50 suppression appears to be associated with the severity of neuropsychologic impairments and negative symptoms (47). However, the relationship between abnormal P50 suppression and psychotic symptoms is by no means clear. Jin et al. studied patient reports of perceptual abnormalities and found that individuals who reported more of these abnormalities were less likely to demonstrate abnormal P50 patterns (48).

Robert Freedman and his collaborators at the University of Colorado have studied abnormalities in P50 suppression and have found them to be genetically linked to schizophrenia. The abnormality is present in individuals with schizophrenia and in relatives who do not suffer from the illness (49). Their research suggests that abnormalities in P50 suppression in patients and their relatives may be related to altered expression and function of the gene that regulates the alpha7-nicotinic cholinergic receptor. They have theorized that abnormal activity of this receptor could be responsible for the deficits in the patient's ability to learn and for subsequent psychotic thinking and social impairment (50). Although a considerable amount of research is necessary to confirm this hypothesis, this work has demonstrated how research in genetics, psychophysiology, neuropsychology, and clinical psychopathology can be linked in a coherent theory.

This same sensory gating phenomenon has also been studied using a strategy that measures a subject's response to a startling response such as a loud noise. In these studies, the focus is on the reduction in the startle response that is associated with the presentation of a prestartle stimulus (e.g., a softer noise) that occurs 30 to 150 msec before the startling response. Termed *pre-pulse inhibition* (or PPI), the normal response is for the response to the louder sound to be diminished by the lower sound (or prepulse). Patients with schizophrenia tend to have a reduction in the response to the louder sound when a prepulse is presented (45,46). Moreover, the decrease in PPI has been associated with greater severity of thought disorder in schizophrenia (47).

These studies of gating deficits have also found that pharmacologic agents can affect these abnormalities. For example, dopamine blockers can reverse prepulse inhibition induced by dopamine agonists (48). Other studies have found that newer antipsychotics may be more effective than older agents for normalizing P50 in patients with schizophrenia (49,50).

BRAIN CIRCUITS IN SCHIZOPHRENIA

As mentioned earlier, it may be useful to approach the understanding of brain function by focusing on brain circuits rather than on a specific brain region. This approach appears to be useful for understanding complex behaviors that depend on the interactions of different areas that are organized to control complex mental process such as attention, memory, and information processing. Peter Liddle has proposed that reality distortions such as hallucinations and delusions are associated with abnormal functioning of a cortico-striatal-thalamic circuit (51). In his view, these symptoms are developed when individuals with the disorder experience external and internal events out of their normal context. The circuit connects cerebral cortex, striatum, and thalamus, and controls processes that regulate how the individual processes these stimuli. For example, if a signal is strengthened, this may indicate that the person is attributing greater importance or value to it. If the signal is weakened, this may indicate that a filtering mechanism in the brain is suppressing the signal; as a result, the person perceives this stimulus as irrelevant or unimportant. Liddle has data suggesting that the hippocampus connects with this circuit and controls this gating mechanism. In this model, the hippocampus determines which mental events are novel and important, and signals to the circuit that the signals from these events should be strengthened. Aberrant firing from an abnormal hippocampus in an individual with schizophrenia might lead an individual to evaluate mental events improperly.

This model, along with findings from studies of sensorimotor gating, suggests how impaired circuits can lead to reality distortions and impaired attention and perceptual processes. For example, an individual with schizophrenia may have difficulty organizing all the complex internal and external stimuli in the environment and determining which are important and require attention. This could lead to a failure to assign importance to novel events in the environment and therefore inability to adapt to important events. On the other hand, impaired functioning of this circuit could lead an individual to assign importance and value to irrelevant stimuli. For example, a patient may inappropriately evaluate a gesture by an individual in his or her visual field. This could lead to a belief that this gesture is aimed at the patient or, in other words, to an idea of reference. In a similar manner, patients with schizophrenia could be vulnerable to incorrectly assigning importance and meaning to internal and external events, which could lead to the development of false beliefs about the meaning or importance of these events. If the assignment of importance leads to the belief that the event pertains to them, this could result in suspicious ideas regarding occurrences in the patient's environment.

A deficit in the functions of these circuits could have more subtle manifestations. Individuals with an impaired ability to detect social cues could fail to learn appropriate responses and, as a result, could appear socially awkward. The social deficits in schizophrenia, according to this model, would originate in the person's inability to respond appropriately to social cues and to develop the social skills that develop from appropriately responding to these cues. Similarly, individuals with schizophrenia who are ineffective at scanning their internal and external environments and discriminating important stimuli may compensate by using other brain resources to accomplish the same purpose. However, they may be less efficient at doing this and their functioning may become impaired when the environment becomes complex or when the individual is under greater stress. In other words, impairments in these circuits may account for positive symptoms as well as for the social and cognitive deficits common in schizophrenia.

Liddle's formulation would also account for the responses of patients with schizophrenia to antipsychotic medications. Dopamine regulation in the striatum plays an important role in regulating the activity of this cortico-striatal-thalamic circuit. As a result, drugs that block dopamine receptors may be effective at regulating this system. Liddle's studies using functional imaging have found that risperidone reduces activity in the cortico-striatal-thalamic loop. He hypothesizes that this decrease is associated with the antipsychotic effect from these drugs. If Liddle's observations are supported by other studies, this would have profound implications for understanding schizophrenia and would explain a range of deficits from hallucinations and delusions as well as cognitive disturbances and impaired social skills. It would further suggest that a path to recovery in schizophrenia would include both regulating the dopamine system so that the patient can properly organize his or her external world and then teaching patients so that they can relearn social skills and readapt to their environment with optimal mental processing.

THE CONCEPT OF COGNITIVE DYSMETRIA

Nancy Andreasen has developed an interesting model that explains the phenomenology of schizophrenia based on an integration of findings from contemporary cognitive neuroscience (52). She views her model as an extension of the approach of Eugen Bleuler, the Swiss psychiatrist who first used the term *schizophrenia*. Bleuler viewed symptoms such as hallucinations and delusions as secondary manifestations of a more fundamental impairment in the processes of thought. The underlying process that explained the phenomenology of schizophrenia was the associational disturbance that clinicians frequently refer to as loosening of associations or an inability to carry out a logical train of thought. Andreasen suggests that the disturbance in thought processes described by Bleuler can be described in contemporary terms as a lack of normal coordination of mental activities or "cognitive dysmetria." This lack of coordination of mental processes parallels the lack of coordination of motor functions, which is referred to as dysmetria. Individuals with these dysmetrias have impairments in their abilities to smoothly carry out complex motor acts that require integration of sensory functions with motor acts. This coordination of activity is manifest in synchronous or fluidly coordinated motor acts, which can include ice skating or catching a ball. Cognitive dysmetria is manifest in an inability to coordinate the mental activities required for complex thought. This includes a lack of synchrony in coordinating mental functions such as memory, attention, word recognition, word retrieval, and recognition of social information. Individuals with cognitive dysmetria have difficulty using these functions to reply to questions or to solve a problem.

Andreasen's formulation of cognitive dysmetria may also be consistent with Liddle's notions. Both systems are regulated to an extent by the same biologic systems (including dopamine) that are affected by drugs that improve or worsen psychosis. Both also involve the coordination of complex neural circuits. Moreover, both of these models can accommodate to the complexity of schizophrenia and its complex clinical manifestations.

SUMMARY

The recent discoveries in schizophrenia have not uncovered the cause of this illness. However, they have reinforced a consistent view of the disorder. That is, they point to an illness associated with anatomic and functional abnormalities that affect different areas of the brain, particularly prefrontal and temporal areas. Fortunately, our understanding of the neurochemistry of schizophrenia has led to important innovations in the treatment of the illness. The future of therapeutics may involve combining an understanding of the biology of schizophrenia with an understanding of the mechanism of action of drugs that affect schizophrenia. This could lead to the development of pharmacologic strategies based on the deficits of individual patients.

REFERENCES

1. Kendler KS, Diehl SR. The genetics of schizophrenia: a current, genetic-epidemiologic perspective. *Schizophr Bull* 1993;19:261–265.
2. Kendler KS, Robinett CD. Schizophrenia in the National Academy of Sciences–National Research Council Twin Registry: a 16-year update. *Am J Psychiatry* 1983;140: 1551–1563.
3. Suddath RL, Christison GW, Torrey EF, et al. Anatomical abnormalities in the brains of monozygotic twins discordant for schizophrenia. *N Engl J Med* 1990;322:789–794.
4. Kety SS. The significance of genetic factors in the etiology of schizophrenia: results from the national study of adoptees in Denmark. *J Psychiatr Res* 1987;21:423–429.
5. Tienari P. Interaction between genetic vulnerability and family environment: the Finnish adoptive family study of schizophrenia. *Acta Psychiatr Scand* 1991;84:460–465.
6. Fish B. Infant predictors of the longitudinal course of schizophrenic development. *Schizophr Bull* 1987;13:395–409.
7. Walker EF. Developmentally moderated expressions of the neuropathology underlying schizophrenia. *Schizophr Bull* 1994;20:453–480.
8. Johnstone EC, Crow TJ, Frith CD, et al. Cerebral ventricular size and cognitive impairment in chronic schizophrenia. *Lancet* 1976;2:924–926.
9. Stevens JR. Anatomy of schizophrenia revisited. *Schizophr Bull* 1997;23:373–383.
10. Gross G, Huber G, Schuttler R. Computerized tomography studies on schizophrenic diseases. *Arch Psychiatr Nervenkrankheitern* 1982;231:519–526.
11. Andreasen NC, Ehrhardt JC, Swayze V II, et al. Magnetic resonance imaging of the brain in schizophrenia: the pathophysiologic significance of structural abnormalities. *Arch Gen Psychiatry* 1990;47:35–44.
12. Bogerts B, Meertz E, Schönfeldt-Bausch R. Basal ganglia and limbic system pathology in schizophrenia: a morphometric study of brain volume and shrinkage. *Arch Gen Psychiatry* 1985;42:784–791.
13. Breier A, Buchanan RW, Elkashef A, et al. Brain morphology and schizophrenia: an MRI study of limbic, prefrontal cortex, and caudate structures. *Arch Gen Psychiatry* 1992;49: 921–926.
14. Jakob H, Beckmann H. Gross and histological criteria for developmental disorders in brains of schizophrenics. *J Roy Soc Med* 1989;82:466–469.
15. Kovelman JA, Scheibel AB. A neurohistologic correlate of schizophrenia. *Biol Psychiatry* 1986;19:1601–1621.
16. Conrad AJ, Abebe T, Austin R, et al. Hippocampal pyramidal cell disarray in schizophrenia as a bilateral phenomenon. *Arch Gen Psychiatry* 1991;48:413–417.
17. Benes FM, Sorenson I, Bird E. Reduced neuronal size in posterior hippocampus of schizophrenic patients. *Schizophr Bull* 1991;17:597–608.
18. Dwork AJ. Postmortem studies of the hippocampal formation in schizophrenia. *Schizophr Bull* 1997;23:385–402.
19. Bogerts B. The temporolimbic system theory of positive schizophrenic symptoms. *Schizophr Bull* 1997;23:423–435.
20. Andreasen N, Nasrallah HA, Dunn V, et al. Structural abnormalities in the frontal system in schizophrenia: a magnetic resonance imaging study. *Arch Gen Psychiatry* 1986;43: 136–144.
21. Raine A, Lencz T, Reynolds GP, et al. An evaluation of structural and functional prefrontal deficits in schizophrenia: MRI and neuropsychological measures. *Psychiatry Res* 1992;45:123–137.

22. Weinberger DR, Berman KF. Speculation of the meaning of cerebral metabolic "hypofrontality" in schizophrenia. *Schizophr Bull* 1988;14:157–158.
23. Weinberger DR, Berman KF, Suddath R, et al. Evidence of dysfunction of the prefrontal-limbic network in schizophrenia: a magnetic resonance imaging and regional blood flow study of discordant monozygotic twins. *Am J Psychiatry* 1992;149:890–897.
24. McGuire PK, Shah GMS, Murray RM. Increased blood flow in Broca's area during auditory hallucinations in schizophrenia. *Lancet* 1993;324:703–706.
25. Mednick SA, Machon RA, Huttenen MO, et al. Adult schizophrenia following prenatal exposure to an influenza epidemic. *Arch Gen Psychiatry* 1988;45:189–192.
26. Torrey EF, Rawlings R, Waldman IN. Schizophrenic births and viral disease in two states. *Schizophr Res* 1988;1:73–77.
27. Done DJ, Johnstone EC, Frith CD, et al. Complications of pregnancy and delivery in relation to psychosis in adult life: data from the British perinatal mortality survey sample. *BMJ* 1991;302:1576–1580.
28. Wyatt RJ, Alexander RC, Egan MF, Kirch DG. Schizophrenia, just the facts: What do we know, how well do we know it? *Schizophr Res* 1988;1:3–18.
29. Susser E, Neugebauer R, Hoek HW, et al. Schizophrenia after prenatal famine: further evidence. *Arch Gen Psychiatry* 1996;53:25–31.
30. Shenton ME, Kikinis R, Jolesz FA, et al. Abnormalities of the left temporal lobe and thought disorder in schizophrenia: A quantitative magnetic resonance imaging study. *N Engl J Med* 1992;327:604–612.
31. Gur RE, Cowell P, Turetsky BI, et al. A follow-up magnetic resonance imaging study of schizophrenia: relationship of neuroanatomical changes to clinical and neurobehavioral measures. *Arch Gen Psychiatry* 1998;55:145–152.
32. Marder SR, van Kammen DP. Dopamine receptor antagonists. In: Kaplan H, Saddock B, eds. *Comprehensive textbook of psychiatry VII.* New York: Lippincott Williams & Wilkins, 1999:2356–2377.
33. Wong DF, Wagner HN Jr, Tune LE, et al. Positron emission tomography reveals elevated D2 dopamine receptors in drug-naïve schizophrenics. *Science* 1986;231:258–261.
34. Farde L, Hall H, Ehrin E, Sedvall G. Quantitative analysis of D2 dopamine receptor binding in the living human brain by PET. *Science* 1986;231:258–261.
35. Wooley DW, Shaw E. A biochemical and pharmacological suggestion about certain mental disorders. *Proc Natl Acad Sci* 1954;40:228–231.
36. Aghajanian GK, Marek GJ. Serotonin model of schizophrenia: emerging role of glutamate mechanisms. *Brain Res Rev* 2000;31:302–312.
37. Zukin SR, Javitt DC. The brain NMDA receptor, psychotomimetic drug effect, and schizophrenia. In: Tasman A, Goldfinger SM, eds. *American psychiatric press review of psychiatry,* Vol. 10. Washington, DC: American Psychiatric Press, 1991:480–498.
38. Goff DC, Wine L. Glutamate in schizophrenia: clinical and research implications. *Schizophr Res* 1997;27:157–168.
39. Krystal JH, Karper LP, Seibyl JP, et al. Subanesthetic effects of the noncompetitive NMDA antagonist, ketamine, in humans: psychotomimetic, perceptual, cognitive, and neuroendocrine responses. *Arch Gen Psychiatry* 1994;51:199–214.
40. Lahti AC, Koffel B, LaPorte D, Tamminga CA. Subanesthetic doses of ketamine stimulate psychosis in schizophrenia. *Neuropyschopharmacology* 1995;13:9–19.
41. Deutsch SI, Mastropaolo J, Schwartz BL, et al. A "glutamatergic hypothesis" of schizophrenia: rationale for pharmacotherapy with glycine. *Clin Neuropharmacol* 1989;12:1–13.
42. Javitt DC, Zylberman I, Zukin SR, et al. Amelioration of negative symptoms in schizophrenia by glycine. *Am J Psychiatry* 1994;151:1234–1236.
43. Heresco-Levy U, Javitt DC, Ermilov M, et a;. Efficacy of high-dose glycine in the treatment of enduring negative symptoms of schizophrenia. *Arch Gen Psychiatry* 1999;56:29–36.
44. Goff DC, Tsai G, Levitt J, et al. A placebo-controlled trial of d-cycloserine added to con-

ventional neuroleptics in patients with schizophrenia. *Arch Gen Psychiatry* 1999;56: 21–27.

45. Braff DL, Geyer MA. Sensorimotor gating and schizophrenia: human and animal model studies. *Arch Gen Psychiatry* 1990;47:181–188.

46. Adler LE, Pachtman E, Franks R, et al. Neurophysiological evidence for a defect in neuronal mechanisms involved in sensory gating in schizophrenia. *Biol Psychiatry* 1982;17: 639–654.

47. Erwin RJ, Turetsky BI, Moberg P, et al. P50 abnormalities in schizophrenia: relationship to clinical and neuropsychological indices of attention. *Schizophr Res* 1998;33:157–167.

48. Jin Y, Bunney WE Jr., Sandman CA, et al. Is P50 suppression a measure of sensory gating in schizophrenia? *Biol Psychiatry* 1998;43:873–878.

49. Freedman R, Adler LE, Bickford P, et al. Schizophrenia and nicotinic receptors. *Harvard Rev Psychiatry* 1994;2:179–192.

50. Light GA, Geyer MA, Clementz BA, et al. Normal P50 suppression in schizophrenia patients treated with atypical antipsychotic medications. *Am J Psychiatry* 2000;157: 767–771.

51. Liddle PF, Lane CJ, Ngan ET. Immediate effects of risperidone on cortico-striato-thalamic loops and the hippocampus. *Br J Psychiatry* 2000;177:402–407.

52. Andreasen NC. A unitary model of schizophrenia. *Arch Gen Psychiatry* 1999;56: 781–787.

2

Diagnosis, Course and Outcome, and Epidemiology

DIAGNOSIS

Before discussing current diagnostic criteria for schizophrenia, it is important to know the history of the development of the concept schizophrenia and limitations of our knowledge in establishing the diagnosis. It is widely agreed that schizophrenia probably consists of a group of disorders rather than a single disorder. Unlike many other medical conditions, at present no independent, non-interview-derived measures exist that can provide construct validity for the term *schizophrenia* (1). For example, there is no measure of biochemical, physiologic, or anatomic abnormality that is invariably present as a trait marker of schizophrenia. It has been traditionally defined as an illness characterized by the apparent clustering of specific signs and symptoms, which sometimes includes a typical course. Since the course and outcome of the disorder vary widely among individuals, it is likely that the characteristic signs and symptoms are the final common pathway for a variety of underlying etiologies. To use an analogy with a physical symptom such as a cough, the etiology may be viral, bacterial, fungal, or chemical, all of which can lead to inflammation of the lung and a cough.

History of Development of the Concept of Schizophrenia as a Psychiatric Disorder

Kraepelin studied a large cohort of individuals with serious mental illness over many decades and noted major differences in their course and outcome (2). He differentiated those patients whose illness started early in life and led to progressive deterioration compared with those who had an episodic course with reasonably good interepisode functioning. Those whose course was more episodic tended to have more prominent mood symptoms during their acute exacerbations. He called them manic-depressive. The progressive downhill course was called dementia praecox (early dementia). Although he believed that almost all these patients had a chronic course with a poor outcome, he recognized that a few could recover substantially. Whereas Krae-pelin emphasized diagnosis based on long-term course of the disorder, Bleuler emphasized cross-sectional symptomatology in establishing the di-agnosis (3). He used the term the *group of schizophrenias,* recognizing that schizophrenia was not a unitary diagnosis but rather a group of separate dis-orders. He focused primarily on signs and symptoms rather than on course and outcome, and attempted to identify the core symptoms of schizophrenia. For Bleuler the most important and fundamental symptom was a fragmenta-tion in the formulation and expression of thought, referring to it as "loosen-ing of associations." The disorder was renamed to emphasize this splitting of associations as the most fundamental feature of this disorder. He also de-scribed ambivalence, the inability to initiate and follow through on simple tasks; affective flattening, an extreme diminution of emotional expressive-ness; and autism, a great degree of social and interpersonal unrelatedness. Thus Bleuler focused on negative symptoms and thought disorganization rather than on the positive symptoms of schizophrenia, such as delusions and hallucinations, which can be found in other psychotic disorders. Another im-portant contribution to defining features of schizophrenia was Kurt Schneid-er's concept of "First Rank Symptoms" (Fig. 2.1) (4,5). Schneider attempted to identify characteristics that were highly specific to schizophrenia, but un-like Bleuler, he emphasized positive psychotic symptoms. His first-rank symptoms included bizarre delusions, such as thought withdrawal, thought insertion, thought broadcasting, and hallucinations in which voices talked

---

1. Hearing one's thoughts aloud.

2. Hearing voices describing one's activities.

3. Experience of having thoughts inserted by an outside agent.

4. Experience of having thoughts withdrawn by an outside agent.

5. Believing that one's thoughts are broadcast to others.

6. Experience that thoughts, affects, or motor activities are

   controlled by an outside agent.

FIG. 2.1. Examples of Kurt Schneider's first-rank symptoms.

about the patient or maintained a running commentary on the patient's behavior. These symptoms had as their basis the individual's loss of boundaries between self and outside world and internal versus external experiences. Schneider believed these symptoms were pathognomonic of schizophrenia, whereas other forms of hallucinations and delusions could occur in a variety of other disorders. However, later studies proved that first-rank symptoms were not specific to schizophrenia (6–10).

In the 1960s and early 1970s it became apparent that the diagnosis of schizophrenia by clinicians was very unreliable (i.e., when one clinician diagnosed schizophrenia, another would often not arrive at that diagnosis). Furthermore, it was noted that schizophrenia seemed much more common in the United States than in Europe. The U.S./U.K. study and the International Pilot Study of Schizophrenia clearly demonstrated that the American concept of schizophrenia was much broader than that prevailing in Europe, suggesting a need to narrow the concept in the United States (11–13). This narrowing involved eliminating nonpsychotic forms of schizophrenia and demonstrating that other disorders, mainly affective disorders, may have psychotic features. In addition, lithium had proven to be effective in the treatment of bipolar disorder, effective antidepressants became available, and there was a developing awareness of tardive dyskinesia as a side effect of antipsychotic medications. As a general rule, whenever effective treatment becomes available for a particular disorder, that disorder is diagnosed more frequently, as is the case with the narrowing of the concept of schizophrenia and the widening of the concept of affective disorders. As a result of these developments as well as recognition of the poor reliability of diagnosis, the *Diagnostic and Statistical Manual of Mental Disorders* (*DSM-III*) with operational criteria was developed, resulting in better reliability and a narrowing of the concept of schizophrenia (15). The negative side effect of the development of *DSM-III* was a belief that both reliability and validity were increased, when in fact validity remains a question. As stated previously, schizophrenia is probably a group of disorders rather than a single entity. Furthermore, the narrowing of the diagnosis did not improve the ability to predict the high prevalence in a family.

Current Diagnostic Features of Schizophrenia

The characteristic symptoms of schizophrenia have been classified into three broad categories: positive, negative or deficit, and disorganized. Positive symptoms include delusions and hallucinations. Disorganized symptoms include disorganized speech (thought disorder) and disorganized behavior and attention (15). Negative symptoms include affective flattening, decreased thought and speech productivity (alogia), loss of ability to experience pleasure (anhedonia), and decreased initiation of goal-directed behav-

TABLE 2.1. *Diagnostic criteria for schizophrenia*

A. *Characteristic symptoms.* Two (or more) of the following, each present for a significant portion of time during a 1-month period (or less if successfully treated):
   1. Delusions
   2. Hallucinations
   3. Disorganized speech (e.g., frequent derailment or incoherence)
   4. Grossly disorganized or catatonic behavior
   5. Negative symptoms (e.g., affective flattening, alogia, or avolition)
   Note: Only one Criterion A symptom is required if delusions are bizarre or hallucinations consist of a voice keeping up a running commentary on the person's behavior or thoughts, or two or more voices are conversing with each other.
B. *Social/occupational dysfunction.* For a significant portion of the time since the onset of the disturbance, one or more major areas of functioning, such as work, interpersonal relations, or self-care, are markedly below the level achieved prior to the onset (or when the onset is in childhood or adolescence, or when there is failure to achieve expected level of interpersonal, academic, or occupational achievement).
C. *Duration.* Continuous signs of the disturbance persist for at least 6 months. This 6-month period must include at least 1 month of symptoms (or less if successfully treated) that meet Criterion A (e.g., active-phase symptoms) and may include periods of prodromal or residual symptoms. During these prodromal or residual periods, the signs of the disturbance may be manifested by only negative symptoms or two or more symptoms listed in Criterion A present in an attenuated form (e.g., odd beliefs, unusual perceptual experiences).
D. *Schizoaffective and mood disorder exclusion.* Schizoaffective disorder and mood disorder psychotic features have been ruled out because either (a) no major depressive, manic, or mixed episodes have occurred concurrently with the active-phase symptoms; or (b) if mood episodes have occurred during active-phase symptoms, their total duration has been brief relative to the duration of the active residual periods.
E. *Substance/general medical condition exclusion.* The disturbance is not due to the direct physiologic effects of a substance (e.g., a drug of abuse, a medication) or a general medical condition.
F. *Relationship to a pervasive developmental disorder.* If there is a history of autistic disorder or another pervasive developmental disorder, the additional diagnosis of schizophrenia is made only if prominent delusions or hallucinations are also present for at least a month (or less if successfully treated).
   Classification of longitudinal course (can be applied only after at least 1 year has elapsed since the initial onset of active-phase symptoms):
   Episodic with interposed residual symptoms (episodes are defined by the reemergence of prominent psychotic symptoms); *also specify if:* **With prominent negative symptoms episodic with no interepisode residual symptoms continuous** (prominent psychotic symptoms are present throughout the period of observation); *also specify if:* **With prominent negative symptoms**
   Single episode in partial remission; *also specify if:* **With prominent negative symptoms**
   Single episode in full remission
   Other or unspecified pattern

ior (avolition) (16). Cognitive deficits, including problems with attention, memory, and concentration, are another important feature present in many individuals with schizophrenia.

According to *DSM-IV*, the essential features of schizophrenia are a mixture of characteristic signs and symptoms (both positive and negative) that have been present for a significant portion of time during a 1-month period (or a shorter time if successfully treated), with some signs of the disorder persisting for at least 6 months (criteria A and C) (Table 2.1) (17). These signs and symptoms are associated with marked social or occupational dysfunction (criterion B). In the differential diagnosis, it is important to rule out schizoaffective disorder or mood disorder with psychotic features, and symptoms should not be due to the direct physiologic effects of a substance or general medical condition (criteria D and E). In individuals with a previous diagnosis of autistic disorder (or another pervasive developmental disorder) the additional diagnosis of schizophrenia is warranted only if prominent delusions or hallucinations are present for at least 1 month (criterion F).

SCHIZOPHRENIA SUBTYPES

Subtypes of schizophrenia are defined by the predominant symptomatology at the time of evaluation and may change at subsequent evaluations. Not infrequently, the presentation may include symptoms that are characteristic of more than one subtype. The choice among subtypes depends on the following algorithmic sequence:

Catatonic type is assigned whenever prominent catatonic symptoms are present, whether or not other symptoms are present.

Disorganized type is assigned whenever disorganized speech and behavior and flat or inappropriate affect are present.

Paranoid type is assigned whenever there is preoccupation with delusions or frequent hallucinations are prominent.

Undifferentiated type is a remaining category describing presentations that include prominent active-phase symptoms not meeting criteria for catatonic, disorganized, or paranoid types.

Residual type is for presentations in which there is continuing evidence of a disturbance but the criteria for the active-phase symptoms are no longer met (18).

See Table 2.2 for *DSM-IV* criteria for subtypes.

DSM-IV, which superseded *DSM-III-R*, showed an increase in the emphasis on negative symptoms, specifically affective flattening, alogia, and avolition, which are now listed as characteristic symptoms of the disorder (14). Another change was the increase in duration of active symptoms to 1 month

TABLE 2.2. *Diagnostic criteria for schizophrenia subtypes*

Diagnostic Criteria for 295.30 Paranoid Type

A type of schizophrenia in which the following criteria are met:

A. Preoccupation with one or more delusions or frequent auditory hallucinations.
B. None of the following is prominent: disorganized speech, disorganized or catatonic behavior, or flat or inappropriate affect.

Diagnostic Criteria for 295.10 Disorganized Type

A type of schizophrenia in which the following critera are met:

A. All of the following are prominent:
   1. Disorganized speech
   2. Disorganized behavior
   3. Flat or inappropriate affect
B. The criteria are not met for catatonic type.

Diagnostic Criteria for 295.20 Catatonic Type

A type of schizophrenia in which the clinical picture is dominated by at least two of the following:

A. Motoric immobility as evidenced by catalepsy (including waxy flexibility) or stupor.
B. Excessive motor activity (that is apparently purposeless and not influenced by external stimuli).
C. Extreme negativism (an apparently motiveless resistance to all instructions or maintenance of a rigid posture against attempts to be moved) or mutism.
D. Peculiarities of voluntary movement as evidenced by posturing (voluntary assumption of inappropriate or bizarre postures, stereotyped movements, prominent mannerisms, or prominent grimacing).
E. Echolalia or echopraxia.

Diagnostic Criteria for 295.90 Undifferentiated Type

A type of schizophrenia in which symptoms that meet Criterion A are present, but the criteria are not met for the paranoid, disorganized, or catatonic type.

Diagnostic Criteria for 295.60 Residual Type

A type of schizophrenia in which the following criteria are met:

A. Absence of prominent delusions, hallucinations, disorganized speech, and grossly disorganized or catatonic behavior.
B. There is continuing evidence of the disturbance, as indicated by the presence of negative symptoms or two or more symptoms listed in Criterion A for schizophrenia, present in an attenuated form (e.g., odd beliefs, unusual perceptual experiences).

(less if successfully treated) (criteria A). Schizophreniform disorder is diagnosed if symptoms persist for more than 1 month but less than 6 months, whereas brief psychotic disorder is diagnosed if active symptoms persist for less than 1 month with a full return to premorbid level of functioning. See Chapter 6 for a more complete discussion of differential diagnosis.

Individuals with schizophrenia frequently have comorbid psychiatric and general medical disorders (18). The most common co-morbid disorder appears to be substance use disorder, especially abuse of alcohol and stimulants such as cocaine and amphetamines (19,20). Other commonly abused substances are nicotine, cannabis, phencyclidine (PCP), and LSD (18). These comorbidities lead to a worse prognosis and complicate treatment (21,22). Symptoms of other mental disorders, especially depression, and also obsessive-compulsive symptoms, somatic concerns, dissociative symptoms, and other mood or anxiety symptoms, are often seen with schizophrenia. Whether or not they reach the level of a diagnosable disorder, they can significantly worsen prognosis and require specific attention and incorporation into treatment planning (23). General medical disorders are often comorbid, especially those associated with poor self-care and lack of adequate medical care. (See Chapter 13 for discussion of treatment and management of dual diagnosis patients.)

Studies of Course and Outcome

In evaluating the results of long-term studies of the course and outcome of schizophrenia in order to generalize their results, it is important to note that there are serious problems in comparability of the data obtained in these studies. Criteria for diagnosis of schizophrenia varied from study to study, from cross-sectional Bleulerian criteria with or without the addition of Schneiderian criteria to those that used cross-sectional as well as longitudinal data in establishing the diagnosis. Hospital populations, from which samples of patients were drawn, varied considerably. For example, there were patients who resided in tertiary care private psychiatric hospitals, state hospitals for chronic patients, and hospitals with first admissions of acutely psychotic patients (18,24–31). Some investigators have postulated that the characteristics of the disorder may have changed over time, becoming more benign. It is extremely difficult to plot the course over many years, especially if patients are not evaluated prospectively at frequent intervals during the follow-up period.

What do we mean by outcome and how is it measured? Many studies have provided a global outcome measure, which, as Strauss and Carpenter have pointed out, is hardly sufficient to describe outcome (32,33). They demonstrated that there were semi-independent variables contained in the concept outcome, including schizophrenic symptomatology, work adjustment, social adjustment, and hospitalization. For example, an individual might have a reasonable social adjustment with some friends but be unable to work, whereas another individual could have moderate schizophrenic symptomatology and be able to hold a job. Many investigators now include quality of life as an important outcome variable. Another problem about measurement of outcome is that different studies used different methods and scales to measure it, some of which did not have good reliability.

It has become clear that the Kraepelinian notion of an inexorable biologically determined progression of the disorder leading to severe deterioration for most patients is not substantiated by long-term studies. The following are descriptions of some well-designed European studies, which used a cross-sectional approach to diagnosis and which demonstrated a variety of courses and outcomes. Manfred Bleuler reported on a study of 208 patients with schizophrenia that he had personally treated for at least 22 years or until their death (34). Additionally, he studied case reports of other individuals with schizophrenia who had been hospitalized. All patients had been diagnosed by several psychiatrists as schizophrenic. He found that after 5 years, the psychosis not only did not progress but tended to improve. After resolution of an acute episode, many patients remained underactive, lacking personal initiative, and had somewhat apathetic, colorless personalities—the so-called deficit symptoms of schizophrenia. The German psychiatrist Huber agrees with this observation, stating that the most common outcome after an acute episode is a nonpsychotic deficit state that occurs in at least 40% of patients (27). Bleuler found that most patients (50% to 75%) alternate for decades between acute psychotic phases and phases of improvement or recovery and that acute relapses become rarer with advanced age. Zubin and Spring postulate that individuals with schizophrenia have a biologically determined vulnerability to stress and that this vulnerability leads to relapse when the stress is severe enough (35).

Ciompi conducted a follow-up study at the Psychiatric University Hospital at Lausanne, Switzerland, for patients born between 1873 and 1897 and hospitalized from the early 1900s until 1972 (25). Many patients were lost to follow-up due to high mortality during the follow-up period and other factors, such as moving from the area. The 289 patients that constituted the follow-up sample were examined in their homes by experienced psychiatrists using a semistructured interview that lasted about 2 hours. Additional information was systematically collected from hospital files, family members, and other sources. The average duration between first admission and follow-up examination was 36.9 years, with 50% of cases having a follow-up of more than 40 years. Ciompi used four outcome measures: admission to the hospital, type of course, global outcome of schizophrenia, and social outcome (Fig. 2.2). Compared with Bleuler's reported 25%, only 10% of Ciompi's sample had only one psychotic episode and one hospitalization. Many of these patients probably would be diagnosed schizophreniform today. Global outcome of schizophrenia measured by symptomatology at the end state was favorable in 49% of cases (Fig. 2.3). Of these, 27% achieved

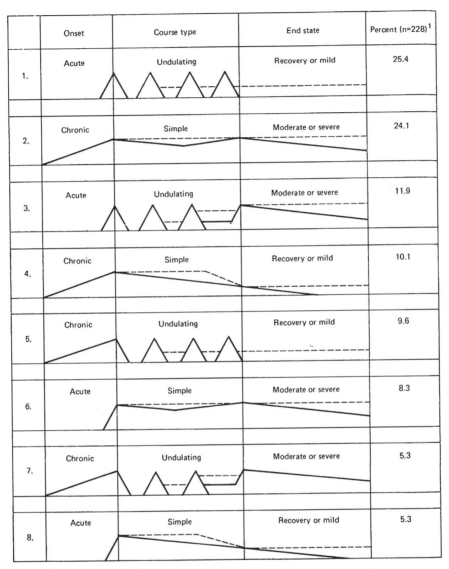

FIG. 2.2. Schematic representation of observed course types. In 61 cases (21.1% of 289), onset, course type, or end state could not be determined with certainty.

complete remission and 22% had minor residual schizophrenic symptomatology, 42% had unfavorable outcomes of intermediate or severe degree, and 9% had uncertain outcomes. Regarding social outcome, 40% of the patients lived with their families or by themselves, 20% were in community institutions, and the rest were in hospitals. Interestingly, although the mean age at

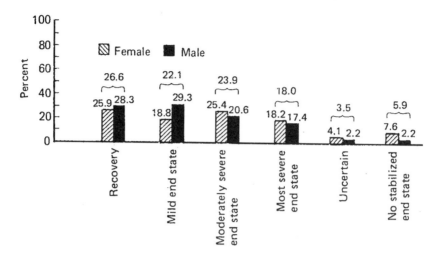

FIG. 2.3. "End states" according to criteria of M. Bleuler (1972).

follow-up was 74 years, more than half were still working either full or part time. On a global score of social adaptation only one-third were rated good or fair; the rest were rated as intermediate or bad social adaptation. Thus the main residual effect of the illness was not persistent schizophrenic psychopathology but impaired social functioning.

The German psychiatrist Huber (27) studied a sample of first hospital admissions of schizophrenic patients admitted to the University Psychiatric Clinic in Bonn between 1945 and 1959. Patients were systematically followed up between 1967 and 1973. Diagnosis was established through well-defined Bleulerian and Schneiderian criteria. Of the original group of patients to be studied, 142 were deceased, 48 refused an interview, and 34 could not be found. The follow-up sample consisted of 502 patients, whose last interview averaged 22.4 years after the initial hospitalization. Patients were usually interviewed in their homes. Eighty-five percent of them lived at home. He found 22% of the patients were in a state of complete remission, whereas 40% had no positive symptoms of schizophrenia but were considered to be in a residual deficit state. The remaining 35% demonstrated residual psychotic symptoms. Huber concluded that schizophrenia does not seem to be a disease of slow, progressive deterioration. Even in the second and third decades of illness, he found the potential for full or partial recovery. Approximately 56% of the sample were fully employed. Of these, one-third was employed below and two-thirds were employed at their previous occupational level. Patients seemed to maintain their clinical stability after the age of 50.

The basic conclusion from these and other long-term studies is that most patients alternate between acute psychotic episodes and stable phases with full or partial remission. The American Psychiatric Association Practice Guideline for the Treatment of Schizophrenia (36) describes three phases of the disorder for the purposes of integrating treatment:

1. *Acute phase.* This is the phase with florid psychotic symptoms such as delusions and/or hallucinations, involving severely disorganized thinking with greatly impaired functioning, so that individuals are usually unable to care for themselves. Negative symptoms become more severe during this phase as well.
2. *Stabilization phase.* During this phase acute psychotic symptoms gradually decrease in severity. This phase may last for an average of 6 months after the onset of an acute episode. During this phase the individual is most vulnerable to relapse.
3. *Stable phase.* Symptoms are relatively stable and almost always less severe than in the acute phase. Patients can be asymptomatic. Others can have nonpsychotic dysphoric symptoms, such as tension, anxiety, depression, or insomnia. Still others may have persisting negative and/or positive symptoms that are usually present in attenuated forms. When a patient in the stable phase starts to relapse, there is usually a prodromal phase, in which there is an increase in severity of nonpsychotic dysphoric symptoms, a possible emergence of low-level positive symptoms, and/or the appearance of particular idiosyncratic behaviors characteristic for that individual, during previous episodes (37). The prodromal period usually lasts for several days to a few weeks or even months.

The current state of knowledge makes it extremely difficult to predict the course and outcome for a particular patient. It is known that, generally, better prognosis is associated with being female, a family history of affective disorder, absence of family history of schizophrenia, good premorbid functioning, higher IQ, married marital status, acute onset with known precipitating stress, fewer and shorter prior episodes, complete remissions after acute episodes, advancing age, minimal comorbidity, paranoid subtype, and, during acute episodes, predominantly positive psychotic symptoms and not disorganized or negative symptomatology (36). Other patient variables that improve prognosis are positive response to antipsychotic medications, compliance with treatment, good coping skills in dealing with stress, and absence of severe character pathology. A supportive social environment can be protective against relapse. It is likely that with early intervention at the beginning of the first and subsequent episodes and optimal pharmacotherapy and psychosocial treatment throughout the course of the disorder, prognosis can be improved considerably, when compared with outcomes in the past.

EPIDEMIOLOGY

The National Institutes of Health–sponsored Epidemiologic Catchment Area Study (38) was a well-designed and well-implemented large-scale study of the epidemiology of mental illness in the United States. Teams of investigators at five sites interviewed a sample of almost 20,000 Americans, including those living at home and in hospitals, nursing homes, and prisons. Various adjustments of the data were made so that weighting of the results would provide a reasonably accurate estimate for the whole United States. For example, respondents were weighted so that their age, gender, and race reflected the same proportion as that found in the population of the United States as a whole in 1980. Diagnosis for schizophrenia was based on *DSM-III* (39).

Results of the ECA study showed that 1.3% of the population was identified as having a diagnosis of schizophrenia at some time in their lives. In any given year, approximately 1% of the population suffered from schizophrenia. Interestingly, despite changes in diagnostic criteria over many years, the overall lifetime prevalence of approximately 1% of the population is remarkably consonant with the earlier epidemiologic literature. There appears to be a uniform distribution of the disorder worldwide, although there may be some areas of high or low prevalence. Individuals are at more risk for developing the disorder if one or more first-degree family members are affected. Other risk factors include being single, coming from a low socioeconomic class, being the recipient of insults *in utero* (e.g., influenza during the second trimester, starvation, or Rh incompatibility), and having perinatal complications. Persons born in the winter months are also at higher risk (36).

REFERENCES

1. Fenton WS, Mosher LR, Matthews SM. Diagnosis of schizophrenia: a critical review of current diagnostic systems. *Schizophr Bull* 1981;7:452–476..
2. Kraepelin E. *Dementia praecox and paraphrenia.* Chicago: Chicago Medical Book, 1919. Barclay RM, translator.
3. Bleuler E. *Dementia praecox or the group of schizophrenias* (1911). New York: International Universities Press, 1950. Zinkin J, translator.
4. Schneider K. *Clinical psychopathology.* New York: Grune & Stratton, 1959.
5. Schneider K. Primary and secondary symptoms in schizophrenia. In: Hirsch SR, Shepherd M, eds. *Themes and variations in European psychiatry.* Bristol, England: John Wright, 1974:40–46.
6. Carpenter WT Jr, Strauss JS, Bartko JJ. Flexible system for the diagnosis of schizophrenia: report from the WHO International Pilot Study of Schizophrenia. *Science* 1973;182: 1275–1278.
7. Carpenter WT Jr, Strauss JS. Cross-cultural evaluation of Schneider's first-rank symptoms of schizophrenia: a report from the International Pilot Study of Schizophrenia. *Am J Psychiatry* 1974;131:682–687.
8. Andreasen NC, Flaum M. Schizophrenia: the characteristic symptoms [see comments]. *Schizophr Bull* 1991;17:27–49.

9. Silverstein ML, Harrow M. Schneiderian first-rank symptoms in schizophrenia. *Arch Gen Psychiatry* 1981;38:288–293.

10. Andreasen NC, Akiskal HS. The specificity of Bleulerian and Schneiderian symptoms: a critical reevaluation. *Psychiatr Clin North Am* 1983;6:41–54.

11. Kendall RE, Cooper JE, Gourlay AG. Diagnostic criteria of American and British psychiatrists. *Arch Gen Psychiatry* 1971;25:123–130.

12. Cooper JE, Kendall RE, Gurland BJ, et al. *Psychiatric diagnosis in New York and London.* London: Oxford University Press, 1972.

13. Carpenter WT Jr, Strauss JS, Bartko JJ. Flexible system for the diagnosis of schizophrenia: report from the WHO International Pilot Study of Schizophrenia. *Science* 1973;182: 1275–1278.

14. American Psychiatric Association. *Diagnostic and statistical manual of mental disorders,* 3rd ed. (*DSM-III*). Washington, DC: American Psychiatric Association, 1980.

15. Fenton WS, McGlashan TH. Testing systems for assessment of negative symptoms in schizophrenia [see comments]. *Arch Gen Psychiatry* 1992;49:179–184.

16. McGlashan TH, Fenton WS. The positive-negative distinction in schizophrenia. Review of natural history validators. *Arch Gen Psychiatry* 1992;49:63–72.

17. American Psychiatric Association. *Diagnostic and statistical manual of mental disorders,* 4th ed. (*DSM-IV*). Washington, DC: American Psychiatric Association, 1994.

18. Dixon L, Haas G, Weiden P, et al. Acute effects of drug abuse in schizophrenic patients: clinical observations and patients' self-reports. *Schizophr Bull* 1990;16:69–79.

19. Drake RE, Wallach MA. Substance abuse among the chronic mentally ill. *Hosp Commun Psychiatry* 1989;40:1041–1046.

20. Brady K, Anton R, Ballenger JC, et al. Cocaine abuse among schizophrenic patients. *Am J Psychiatry* 1990;147:1164–1167.

21. Test MA, Wallisch LS, Allness DJ, et al. Substance use in young adults with schizophrenic disorders. *Schizophr Bull* 1989;15:465–476.

22. Zisook S, Heaton R, Moranville J, et al. Past substance abuse and clinical course of schizophrenia. *Am J Psychiatry* 1992;149:552–553.

23. Fenton WS, McGlashan TH. The prognostic significance of obsessive-compulsive symptoms in schizophrenia. *Am J Psychiatry* 1986;143:437–441.

24. Bleuler ME. The long-term course of schizophrenic psychoses. In: Wynne L, Cromwell RL, Matthysse S, eds. *The nature of schizophrenia.* New York: Wiley, 1978:631–651.

25. Ciompi L. Catamnestic long-term study on the course of life and aging of schizophrenics. *Schizophr Bull* 1980;6:606–618.

26. Tsuang MT, Woolson RF, Fleming J. A. Long-term outcome of major psychoses. I. Schizophrenia and affective disorders compared with psychiatrically symptom-free surgical conditions. *Arch Gen Psychiatry* 1979;36:1295–1301.

27. Huber G, Gross G, Schuttler R, et al. Longitudinal studies of schizophrenic patients. *Schizophr Bull* 1980;6:592–605.

28. Vaillant GE. A 10-year followup of remitting schizophrenics. *Schizophr Bull* 1978;4: 78–85.

29. McGlashan TH. The Chestnut Lodge follow-up study. II. Long-term outcome of schizophrenia and the affective disorders. *Arch Gen Psychiatry* 1984;41:586–601.

30. Harding CM, Brooks GW, Ashikaga T, et al. The Vermont longitudinal study of persons with severe mental illness, II: Long-term outcome of subjects who retrospectively met DSM-III criteria for schizophrenia. *Am J Psychiatry* 1987;144:727–735.

31. Engelhardt DM, Rosen B, Feldman J, et al. A 15-year followup of 646 schizophrenic outpatients. *Schizophr Bull* 1982;8:493–503.

32. Strauss JS, Carpenter WT Jr. The prediction of outcome in schizophrenia. II. Relationships between predictor and outcome variables: a report from the WHO international pilot study of schizophrenia. *Arch Gen Psychiatry* 1974;31:37–42.

33. Strauss JS, Carpenter WT Jr. Prediction of outcome in schizophrenia. III. Five-year outcome and its predictors. *Arch Gen Psychiatry* 1977;34:159–163.

34. Bleuler MN. *The schizophrenic disorders: long term patient and family studies.* New Haven: Yale University Press, 1978.
35. Zubin J, Spring B. Vulnerability: a new view of schizophrenia. *J Abnorm Psychol* 1977; 86:103–126.
36. Practice guideline for the treatment of patients with schizophrenia. *Am J Psychiatry* 1997;154(Suppl).
37. Herz MI, Melville C. Relapse in schizophrenia. *Am J Psychiatry* 1980;80:801–805.
38. Robins LN, Regier DA. *Psychiatric disorders in America.* New York: The Free Press, 1991.
39. American Psychiatric Association. *Diagnostic and statistical manual of mental disorders,* 3rd ed. (*DSM-III*). Washington, DC: American Psychiatric Association, 1980.

3

General Principles of Treatment and Management*

Treatment and management of individuals with schizophrenia should be comprehensive and integrated because the disorder affects almost every aspect of a person's thinking, feeling, and behavior, and their manifestations vary over time. Comprehensive care consists of psychopharmacologic, psychotherapeutic, psychosocial, and rehabilitative treatment. It should include approaches that may be necessary to deal with cognitive deficits, impairment in functioning and judgment, and noncompliance with treatment. Since the affected individuals differ with respect to underlying personality, aspirations, motivations, clinical symptoms, and functional impairment, treatment planning should be individualized. It should be flexible with modifications made as the individual's clinical status and goals evolve over time. Continuity of care with no time limits for treatment is important since schizophrenia is generally a disorder that continues throughout a person's lifetime. Most treatment approaches, including pharmacotherapy, lose their efficacy when treatment is discontinued. Like many chronic medical disorders, the course of schizophrenia is usually phasic with acute episodes alternating between stable phases of full or partial remission. Accordingly, treatment strategies differ for each phase of the disorder. Active involvement with families should be offered routinely, emphasizing education about the illness, problem solving, and support. In view of the variety of interventions required to treat and manage individuals with schizophrenia, a team approach is often used. It is important that one member of the team have primary responsibility for coordinating treatment and management efforts (Table 3.1).

Goals of treatment for acute episodes are to reduce their frequency and symptom severity while limiting harmful behaviors that may occur. Goals for patients in the stable phase are to eliminate or, if this is impossible, minimize symptoms

---

*Except where specifically cited, references are omitted and will be found in other chapters of this book, where relevant.

TABLE 3.1. *Treatment stages in schizophrenia*

Stage	Clinical characteristics	Treatment goals
Acute 4–8 weeks	Acute psychotic symptoms, hallucinations, delusions, disorganized speech and behavior	Reduce psychotic symptoms with antipsychotic medications; protect patient from dangerous psychotic behavior
Stabilization (2–6 months)	Symptoms are improved but the patient remains vulnerable to relapse if drug dose is reduced or if there is environmental stress	Reduce the likelihood of symptom exacerbation; develop a plan for long-term treatment
Stable (indefinite)	Positive symptoms have been minimized or eliminated; negative symptoms may dominate the clinical presentation	Prevent psychotic relapse; reduce negative symptoms; facilitate social rehabilitation

while enhancing role functioning. In describing the various therapeutic and supportive roles of professionals who conduct treatment, the term *therapist* or *clinician* will be used, since roles in treatment and management vary among the mental health professions across the United States. Where it is the specific function of a particular mental health professional, that function will be designated as being carried out by that discipline (e.g., the psychiatrist establishing a diagnosis and managing medications). Following is a discussion of issues in treatment and management of individuals with schizophrenia. Subsequent chapters will deal with these issues in more detail.

EFFORTS TO ESTABLISH AND MAINTAIN
A THERAPEUTIC ALLIANCE

The therapeutic alliance is the cornerstone of treatment of individuals with schizophrenia. Treatment compliance is greatly enhanced when there is a respectful, trusting relationship between patient and therapist. The first step in developing a therapeutic alliance is for the therapist to attempt to "connect" with the person who has schizophrenia and not to think of the individual as "that schizophrenic." In other words, the therapist attempts to establish a relationship with the patient. There should be an attempt to establish a collaborative relationship; one in which the therapist and patient are working together to decrease or eliminate the negative effects of the disorder and help the patient to achieve reasonable goals and aspirations. The therapist should attempt to educate the patient about characteristics of schizophrenia as a disorder and encourage the patient to be free to comment on any aspect of the treatment process, including medications and their side effects. Continuity of care is important, since it takes time for the patient to develop a trusting relationship with the therapist, including the conviction that the therapist will be there, especially in times of crisis. The therapist can be more effective if he or she understands the patient as a person, with strengths, vulnerabilities, conflicts, coping mechanisms, goals, and aspirations. With this type of understanding, the psychiatrist can be most effective in delivering appropriate treatment for the patient.

Often there are impediments to the development of a trusting therapeutic alliance, both on the part of the patient and on that of the psychiatrist. Many patients, especially those with paranoid features, are not likely to trust anyone, especially a psychiatrist. Patients know that the psychiatrist has the power to hospitalize patients involuntarily. During acute episodes, when hospitalization may be necessary, patients can lose insight and reality testing and may blame the psychiatrist for hospitalization against the patient's will. Furthermore, a substantial number of individuals with schizophrenia deny their illness, and many do not comply with treatment, not only because they don't trust the psychiatrist, but also because they don't believe they have a disorder that needs treatment. When the patient is in the stable phase, it can be helpful for the psychiatrist to review the events, which may have precipitated relapse and the patient's prodromal symptoms and behaviors before the previous hospitalization. With this understanding, patients may develop more insight into the events leading up to relapse and recognize the development of early symptoms of future relapses. This approach can be beneficial in promoting better collaboration between psychiatrists and patients at the onset of future acute episodes.

Problems for the therapist in forming a positive relationship with the patient may be feelings of helplessness and resentment in the therapist, which can be elicited when patients are noncompliant and hostile. It is important for the therapist to be in touch with the possibility of having such negative feelings and to deal with them if present. Another problem is caused by a patient's negative symptoms—especially flatness of affect, poverty of speech, and amotivation—making it difficult for the psychiatrist to "connect" and empathize with the patient. It is important for the psychiatrist to recognize that although patients may exhibit little feeling, they often have a strong underlying need for the relationship. The inexperienced therapist may easily be led to believe that the relationship means very little to the patient, when in fact, the opposite may be true.

CONTINUITY OF CARE AND EARLY INTERVENTION

As stated earlier, it takes time for the patient to develop a trusting and meaningful relationship with the psychiatrist, and obviously, a component of a trusting relationship is the belief that that psychiatrist will remain with the patient over time. For the psychiatrist, usually it is only after treating the patient for a period of many months that symptoms of impending relapse can easily be recognized and differentiated from transient symptoms, which are of lesser consequence. With this information, the psychiatrist can intervene during the prodromal phase with increased medication and crisis supportive therapy to abort the development of an acute psychotic episode. This knowledge is gained with prolonged contact with an individual patient.

Stress Vulnerability

The psychiatrist needs to learn about the patient's specific vulnerabilities to stress and coping abilities to deal with stress. Individuals with schizophrenia have great vulnerability to biological, psychological, and social stressors that can lead to relapse (Fig. 3.1). The psychiatrist should attempt to learn whether any specific stressors have precipitated prior psychotic episodes. If treatment is to be successful, it is important to (a) avoid or decrease social stressors that may precipitate relapse and (b) utilize therapeutic interventions with the patient to increase coping skills and/or strengthen the support system so that patient's vulnerability to stress will be decreased. A combined approach of decreasing stress and strengthening the patient's ability to cope should decrease the likelihood of psychotic relapse.

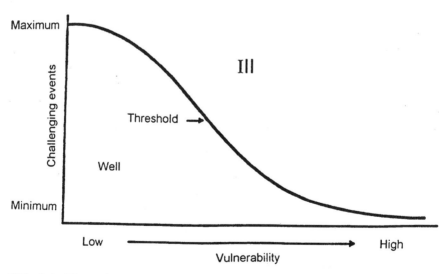

FIG. 3.1. The vulnerability–stress model. (Reprinted with permission from Zubin J, Spring B. Vulnerability—a new view of schizophrenia. Copyright © *Journal of Abnormal Psychology*, 1977;86:103–126.)

Various types of stress had been identified as being related to relapse, including that produced by overly ambitious therapists. Hogarty et al. found that symptomatic schizophrenia patients who were not on medication were more likely to relapse if they had social casework than were nonmedicated patients who had no psychosocial treatment (1). They postulated that the patient/therapist interaction was a stressful one because some therapists had overly ambitious expectations of their patient's performance and that patients were particularly vulnerable when not protected by antipsychotic medication. Similarly, a study by Linn et al. of day hospital programs demonstrated that patients had less favorable outcomes in day hospitals that had high patient turnover rates and a good deal of individual and group therapy than in those programs that had lower turnover rates and emphasized occupational and vocational therapies (2). Again, the inference was that the former programs were highly stimulating and stressful for patients. The therapist must be sensitive to the patient's strength and vulnerabilities and neither too demanding nor pessimistic in expectations for improved patient functioning. Both overstimulation and understimulation are harmful to schizophrenic patients.

Brown et al. found a marked increase in the frequency of occurrence of certain life events during the few weeks immediately before the onset of acute relapse in schizophrenic patients (3). The authors attempted to exclude events, which could have been the result rather than the cause of a recrudescence of symptoms, and this did not diminish the extent of the association. A study by Herz and Melville found that most patients questioned weeks and months after relapse were not able to identify a precipitating event (4). However, almost all patients interviewed during the prodromal phase of relapse could identify a specific precipitating event. Thus questioning closer to the time of the event and before relapse leads to better recall than later questioning, well after relapse has occurred.

Several studies indicate that a stressful family environment may help precipitate relapse in schizophrenic patients. Efforts to relieve family stress that involve support, problem solving, improving communication, and educating about characteristics of schizophrenia, its course, and outcome can be very helpful in reducing relapse. This topic is discussed in the section on family interventions.

Medication Management

Patients should be educated about the importance of taking antipsychotic medication, the functions of the medication, and common negative side effects. The psychiatrist should monitor the patient closely on a regular basis to evaluate antipsychotic medication effectiveness in decreasing or eliminating symptoms and any negative side effects that may appear. The approach should be collaborative, with open discussion about how the patient feels the medication is affecting him or her and whether the dosage should be adjusted. Patients need to understand that if they go off the medication on their own, they might temporarily feel the same or even better, but they are at much greater risk for relapse in the future. Discussions should also include perceptions of patients about their functioning and quality of life. It is useful to collaborate with the patient in setting short- and long-term goals. The concept of setting short-term goals is that the patient will feel some immediate gratification and improved motivation if the short-term goals are attained. It is especially important to set realistic short-term goals, so that there is a reasonable expectation they can be achieved.

Combating Demoralization

Demoralization is a serious problem in many individuals with schizophrenia. It is most frequent in younger, better-educated individuals who come to realize that their high aspirations that were held before onset of the disorder may have to be delayed or reduced. These individuals need to be supported in adjusting to the new reality of the effects of the disorder on their functioning. Therapy should emphasize the individual's strengths and help to formulate reasonable, realistic goals for the future. It is useful to collaborate in setting realistic short- and long-term goals. It is especially important to set realistic short-term goals where there is a reasonable expectation that they can be achieved in the near future to combat demoralization.

TREATMENT OF PHASES OF THE DISORDER

As stated earlier, schizophrenia is a long-term disorder with three phases: (a) acute, (b) stabilized, and (c) stable. In addition, before the onset of the acute phase, there is usually a prodromal phase consisting of severe dysphoric symptoms, occasionally mild psychotic symptoms, and specific prodromal behaviors that can be typical for a particular patient. An integrated system of care needs to be in place so that patients do not get lost between the cracks when transitioning from one phase to another. It is important to ensure that patients remain connected to the mental health system as they transition between programs (e.g., from hospital to day hospital to outpatient treatment or other treatment modalities). Unless these transitions are seamless, patients who are very much in need of treatment may become lost to the mental health system, with resulting relapse. Antipsychotic medication is indicated in all phases of schizophrenia with few exceptions. As a rule, a patient should be treated in the least restrictive environment that is likely to provide the optimal therapeutic outcome. Also, learning gained from treatment and rehabilitative programs is transferred most readily when these programs are carried out in settings closest to the environment where the learning will be applied.

General Principles and Goals of Treatment at Each Phase

Prodromal Phase of the Relapse Process

As stated previously, patients' family members and other significant others should be educated about prodromal symptoms of relapse and what steps to take when these symptoms appear. The program should be organized to provide rapid intervention when notified about the appearance of prodromal symptoms and behaviors. More frequent therapeutic contacts emphasizing support, reality testing, and an increase in antipsychotic medications can often reduce prodromal symptoms and prevent full relapse. Assertive outreach is especially important during this time since many patients lose insight and refuse treatment. Family members should be involved in the treatment whenever possible. To respond most effectively when immediate help is indicated, crisis intervention should be available 24 hours a day, 7 days a week. If logistically possible, it is preferable for family members to be in contact with the therapist during these times, since they may need support and since their knowledge of the patient's strengths, vulnerabilities, and typical symptomatic fluctuations can be useful. If feasible, it is preferable for the patient's regular therapist to provide crisis treatment, since a therapeutic relationship has already been established.

Acute Phase

During the acute phase, patients exhibit severe psychotic symptoms, both positive and negative. Their thinking is severely disorganized and judgment is greatly impaired. Goals of treatment are to reduce psychotic symptoms, to control disturbed behavior that might be harmful to the patients themselves or others, and to provide structure, protection, and support for the patient. Ordinarily, antipsychotic medication should be used immediately, since long delays in administration may lead to prolonged psychotic episodes and possibly negative effects on the long-term course of the disorder. Usually, severely psychotic patients are hospitalized; however, if the patient demonstrates some ability to cooperate in treatment and is not considered dangerous to himself or others, alternatives to hospitalization should be considered in discussions with the patient. Day hospital, crisis residence, intensive community treatment, and home care may be suitable, and provide a less restrictive environment than the hospital. In many situations, outcomes for patients in these programs are equal to or sometimes better than those in the hospital. Treatment in the hospital offers the advantage of a safe, secure, structured, and supervised environment while reducing stress on both patients and family members. In the hospital, the clinician can closely monitor the patient's level of symptoms and level of functioning as well as reaction to medications, including side effects.

When a patient is hospitalized for an acute episode, the goal is rapid stabilization of symptoms and not rehabilitation. Hospital personnel should provide a structured milieu to enhance the patient's orientation and functioning. Individual and/or group therapy, at this time, should be supportive and provide structure and reassurance. When feasible, contact with the family should be initiated immediately. This is a time when families are in crisis and most ready to collaborate in treatment. Often family members can provide information about the patient that is useful in treatment. Education of family members should begin at this time and support should be offered, since all members of the family are usually under stress. When the indications for hospitalization are no longer present, patients can be transferred to less intensive treatment programs. The decision to discharge is based not only on the patient's symptoms and functional status, but also on the availability of social supports and access to community treatment programs. Linkages to community programs should be made before the patient's discharge. Compliance can be improved if a member of the community treatment program meets with the patient in the hospital before discharge or the patient is offered the opportunity to visit the community program before discharge. It is important for the hospital or community program to follow up on the referral to ensure that the patient has not dropped out of treatment. If a patient does not follow through, every effort should be made to engage that patient in treatment, including telephone calls and home visits as indicated. Hospital discharge planning should also include arrangements for supportive housing, income maintenance, case management, and other services that may be helpful in enabling the patient to function optimally in the community.

Stabilization Phase

During the stabilization phase the patient is recovering from the acute episode and is highly vulnerable to relapse. Ordinarily, patients should be maintained on the same dosage of antipsychotic medication as they received at hospital discharge, with no reduction in dosage until the patient has completely stabilized in symptoms and functioning. This phase may last up to about 6 months after the onset of an acute episode. Since most patients are discharged from the hospital to community care when they have improved but have not yet reached symptom stability, it is extremely important that ambulatory care begin as soon as possible. As stated earlier, if patients do not follow through with treatment after hospital discharge, efforts should be made to contact them through outreach, including telephone calls, home visits, and involvement with family members. The aim of this phase is to facilitate resolution of symptoms, and therefore patients should be helped to adjust to life in the community by minimizing stress as much as possible and providing therapeutic support. Active collaboration with family members should be continued with emphasis on education about the disorder, its symptoms, course, and outcome; in addition, efforts should be made to minimize stress in the family environment. Therapists should not pressure patients by being unduly ambitious for them to perform at high levels vocationally and/or socially.

Stable Phase

After recovery from an acute psychotic episode, patients may be asymptomatic; manifest nonpsychotic dysphoric symptoms, such as tension, anxiety, or insomnia; frequently demonstrate deficit symptoms; or have positive symptoms that are of mild intensity. Goals of treatment in the stable phase are to minimize and if possible eliminate symptoms and help the patient to improve or at least maintain functioning and quality of life. Through education, close monitoring, and crisis intervention when prodromal symptoms appear, the possibility of relapse/rehospitalization can be reduced. There should be ongoing monitoring of side effects of the medication with dose adjustment reduced to a level that suppresses psychotic symptoms and is effective in preventing relapse. For many patients, treatment should not be limited to office visits. Active involvement with the patient in the community is indicated to improve functioning and assist the patient to adjust to life in the community. Crisis intervention should be available 24 hours a day, 7 days a week to intervene rapidly in times of crisis, especially during the onset of prodromal symptoms. Assertive outreach, which is a key feature of the Program for Assertive Community Treatment (PACT), should be used, especially in times of crisis or when patients are unwilling or unable to comply with treatment (5). This may involve telephone calls, home visits, and other meetings in the community with the patient and family members. Ongoing involvement with the family, either individually or in multifamily groups, is effective not only in preventing relapse but also in improving family functioning.

Treatment during the stable phase should be integrated and comprehensive, and should consist of pharmacotherapy, psychosocial and rehabilitative approaches, and community support programs. There is a great variation in the level of symptoms and functioning among individuals with schizophrenia in the stable state. The range of treatment and support services that would be helpful varies from patient to patient. For marginally adjusted patients, day treatment centers provide a supportive structure where socialization is facilitated and social skills and prevocational training are available. For patients who are noncompliant and/or poorly functioning, PACT, with its emphasis on active involvement with patient in the community and assertive outreach, has been shown to be very effective. Psychotherapeutic treatments can be conducted individually or in groups. Generally, supportive and cognitive behavioral therapy approaches are indicated rather than an insight-oriented approach. Studies suggest that cognitive behavioral therapy and training in improving coping skills are superior to a generic supportive approach. Training in social skills is useful for patients who have problems in social functioning. Remediation of cognitive deficits in schizophrenia may be attempted, although studies have shown little generalization and retention of learning over time using these approaches. Many patients can profit from involvement in vocational rehabilitation programs. It has been found that supportive employment programs are most useful in enabling patients not only to gain employment but also to retain the job. Implementing vocational rehabilitation in a sheltered workshop may be beneficial; however, often it is a dead-end situation rather than a step toward gainful employment. Continuing evaluation of a patient's performance in a sheltered workshop is necessary so that motivated patients can be advanced to higher levels of employment when they are considered ready to handle the increased responsibility. Case management services are used to ensure that patients can function adequately in the community, including housing with supervision if necessary, medical care, and financial support. Patients should be made aware of the existence of social clubs and self-help groups with the option of becoming involved if they so chose, and family members should be provided with information about the National Alliance for the Mentally Ill and other community resources.

ENSURING COMPREHENSIVE CARE THROUGH COLLABORATION BETWEEN MENTAL HEALTH AND OTHER SERVICE SYSTEMS OF CARE

Because many individuals with schizophrenia have functional deficits in a variety of spheres, comprehensive care should involve collaboration and coordination both of treatment programs within the mental health system and between that system and other community, medical, and governmental agencies. This collaboration usually includes housing and social service agencies, vocational rehabilitation programs, and medical care and governmental agencies involved in income maintenance and supplementation. Individuals with schizophrenia who have functional deficits that limit their ability to carry out independent lives and have trouble gaining access to needed services in the community are in need of a coordinated treatment approach. A member of the treatment team, usually the case manager, needs to link patients to necessary service programs and coordinate efforts with those programs. Usually it is important for the collaboration to be ongoing after the initial contacts have been made to ensure that comprehensive, integrated services continue to be delivered over time.

REFERENCES

1. Hogarty GE, Goldberg SC, Schooler NR, et al. Drug and sociotherapy in the aftercare of schizophrenic patients, II. Two-year relapse rates. *Arch Gen Psychiatry* 1974;31: 603–608.
2. Linn MW, Caffey EM, Klett CJ, et al. Day treatment and psychotropic drugs in the aftercare of schizophrenic patients. *Arch Gen Psychiatry* 1979;36:1055–1066.
3. Brown GW, Birley JL, Wing JK. Influence of family life on the course of schizophrenic disorders: a replication. *Br J Psychiatry* 1972;121:241–258.
4. Herz MI, Melville C. Relapse in schizophrenia. *Am J Psychiatry* 1980;80:801–805.
5. Stein LI, Test MA. Alternative to mental hospital treatment. I. Conceptual model, treatment program, and clinical evaluation. *Arch Gen Psychiatry* 1980;37:392–397.

4

Early-Intervention Prevention Programs

The term *early intervention* has been used to characterize treatment interventions at various stages in the development and course of schizophrenia. These include early intervention during the prodromal phase, which aims to prevent the onset of schizophrenia (primary prevention); treatment intervention during the early phases of a first schizophrenic episode (secondary prevention); and treatment intervention during the prodromal phase of relapse for patients with prior psychotic episodes (secondary and tertiary prevention). This chapter describes early-intervention programs designed to prevent the onset of schizophrenia and to prevent relapse in individuals already diagnosed with schizophrenia, their rationale, outcomes, and other related issues. Chapter 12 describes treatment strategies during the early phase of first-episode schizophrenia.

EARLY INTERVENTION TO PREVENT THE ONSET OF SCHIZOPHRENIA

Since schizophrenia is usually a long-term disorder associated with impairment in functioning and diminished quality of life and is treatable but not curable, it would be highly desirable to prevent it. Although this is an important goal, there are many problems, questions, and concerns about implementing this type of prevention program. The following are major issues regarding implementation: What are the criteria to determine whether psychiatric intervention should be instituted for a particular individual? What methods are available to identify high-risk individuals who will develop schizophrenia? Eighty-five percent of new cases of schizophrenia have no family history of this disorder. No biological marker exists that can invariably predict the development of schizophrenia. The current state of knowledge about prodromal symptoms, which occur before the onset of diagnosable schizophrenia, shows that they are often nonspecific and certainly do not lead invariably to schizophrenia even when there is no intervention (1–3).

Another problem is that the prodromal phase may last for weeks, months, or many years. It is unclear whether cognitive deficits, which could be used as a marker for high-risk individuals, are present in individuals well before the onset of prodromal symptoms, whether they occur during the prodromal phase or after the acute psychotic episode. Another problem is the type of treatment that should be offered when there appears to be a strong likelihood of developing schizophrenia and how long this treatment should last. Should it be psychosocial, psychopharmacologic, or both?

There are important ethical issues. If we educate patients and their family members about schizophrenia and tell them that the patient is at high risk of developing it, they will experience some degree of stigma and demoralization. Individuals who might never develop the disorder will be unnecessarily stigmatized.

A public health question is whether scarce treatment resources for individuals with diagnosed schizophrenia should be diverted to a case finding for high-risk individuals, many of whom will never become schizophrenic, even without treatment.

Despite these obstacles, this is an important area for investigation, since it is not uncommon for many individuals with schizophrenia to experience devastating effects of the disorder.

EXAMPLES OF PRIMARY PREVENTION STUDIES

Falloon et al. and Yung et al. carried out major studies of primary prevention (4,5). Falloon conducted a pilot study to determine whether early intervention could prevent the onset of schizophrenia in Buckingham County, England (4). The county had a population of 35,000 that was served primarily by a network of 16 family practitioners organized into four group practices. There were mental health teams consisting of a psychiatrist, nurse therapists, and other mental health professionals within each group practice. Identification of patients with prodromal symptoms was based on educating family practitioners to recognize these symptoms and refer such individuals to the mental health team, which provided assessment, early detection, and early intervention, if appropriate. Individuals considered in the prodromal phase were provided with an educational seminar about the early-intervention program within 24 hours. According to Falloon, patients and families were told that the patient might have early signs of schizophrenia and that treatment strategies that were highly effective in preventing major exacerbations in individuals with schizophrenia might ameliorate the current condition. It was made clear that the patient's current symptoms could be found in many different psychiatric disorders. The program offered home-based stress management and included the patient and key caregiver. Low-dose antipsychotic medications were given for periods of usually not longer than 2 weeks for targeted dysfunctional or dysphoric prodromal symptoms such as sleep disturbance, agitation, muddled thinking, or preoccupation with an odd idea. Treatment continued until the prodromal symptoms had remitted. This was followed by weekly meetings to improve problem-solving skills, education about prodromal symptoms, and information about what to do if symptoms returned.

More than 1,000 patients were referred by family practitioners over the 4 years of the pilot project. Of these, 16 cases demonstrated symptom patterns, which suggested prodromal states. One individual already had symptoms of an acute first episode of schizophrenia, which remitted within 4 weeks of treatment as an outpatient with low-dose neuroleptic medication and stress management. This patient was the only case of schizophrenia during the study, yielding an annual incidence rate of 0.75 per 100,000 over the study period. Falloon compared this rate with an epidemiologic study conducted 10 years earlier in the same county, using the same diagnostic criteria, which yielded an annual incidence rate in the total population of 7.4 per 100,000. This is a ground-breaking study that appears to have had positive results. However, it was not a controlled study. The county population was small (30,000), and there was a high rate of false positives (i.e., referrals to the mental health team). Falloon recognized that prodromal symptoms for schizophrenia are not specific.

Yung et al. in Australia inaugurated a service for early detection and prevention of schizophrenia called Personal Assistance and Crisis Evaluation (PACE) (5). The PACE Clinic was located at the Center for Adolescent Health, a generalist outpatient service and health promotion center. Patients did not risk the potentially stigmatizing effects of attending a psychiatric facility. The program targets help-seeking individuals who are symptomatic, usually referred from other psychiatric programs, primary care facilities, and networks of individuals who come in frequent contact with young people, including school counselors, teachers, and youth workers. Most of those referred had a long history of psychiatric symptoms. The average length of time since symptom onset was 86.6 weeks before referral and 41.4 weeks until treatment at the PACE facility. Thus symptoms were present for many for more than 2 years before treatment began at PACE. After a thorough initial evaluation, most who were accepted for the program displayed a number of high-risk factors, including both trait (e.g., family history of psychotic disorder) and state (e.g., the presence of low-grade psychopathology). This approach was used to reduce the risk of false positives. Patients who were accepted belonged to one of three groups and ranged in age from 16 to 30 years. Group 1 consisted of individuals with a combination of trait and state risk factors. For example, combining a family history of psychotic disorder, a schizotypal personality disorder, and the development of probable prodromal symptoms of schizophrenia as defined by two or more of the nine criteria for *DSM-III-R* (*Diagnostic and Statistical Manual of Mental Disorders,* 3rd ed.) schizophrenic prodrome (6). Group 2 consisted of individuals who had developed attenuated or subthreshold psychotic symptoms. They had one or more of the positive prodromal features from *DSM-III-R* schizophrenia, including markedly peculiar behavior; digressive, vague, overelaborate, or metaphorical speech; odd or bizarre ideation; magical thinking; or unusual perceptual experiences. Group 3 consisted of young people with a history of fleeting psychotic experiences that resolved spontaneously within 1 week.

Initially, the program offered primarily psychosocial treatment aimed at reducing stress and enhancing coping, which emphasized individualized case management and support, problem solving, and stress management. Family support was also provided. Generally, neuroleptic treatment was not used to avoid the negative side effects of these medications. The rates of onset of psychosis ranged from 21% to 40% of patients studied, depending on the exact criteria for selection and the length of the follow-up. Yung believes that in view of the high rate of onset of psychosis, it would be justified to use low-dose neuroleptic medication for this highly vulnerable population. To avoid prematurely stigmatizing or worrying patients and families, clinicians did not emphasize the risk of transition to psychosis or schizophrenia. The need for intervention was explained in relation to the patient's presenting problems. Preliminary results of this pilot project showed that in the first 20 months of operation, a total of 110 referrals occurred, of which 14% did not meet initial intake criteria, 22% didn't keep the clinic appointment, 65% were assessed, and 47% (52 patients) met the intake criteria. A subsample of 33 of the 52 patients was recruited into the research sample. In the first 20 months of operation, seven of the 33 patients (21%) in this sample progressed to psychosis.

The following are case examples of high-risk young individuals who were managed in the clinic.

Case 1. Resolution of an Apparent Incipient Psychosis

N.S.: A 17-year-old, single, unemployed male was referred because he was becoming suspicious (e.g., worried about cars following him and his friends turning against him). Symptoms had been present for about 4 to 5 days and had resulted in social withdrawal. He began to feel wary about going out with friends and leaving the house. Mental status examination showed that he exhibited persecutory ideas but without delusional intensity. He was able to see that he might be misinterpreting events. He was managed with supportive counseling and stress management. Psychological techniques included challenging his persecutory ideas and getting him to suggest alternative explanations for the apparently negative behavior of others toward him. Since he recognized that his persecutory ideas worsened with high anxiety levels, he was also instructed in relaxation techniques. His mental state improved and after 2 months of therapy he felt well. His persecutory ideas had resolved completely, and he had started a technical course at school. After 2 more months of follow-up, he was discharged from the clinic.

Case 2. Fluctuating Symptoms Possibly Related to Stress

C.C.: C.C. was a 17-year-old single female who had several months of perceptual abnormalities, unusual ideas, and increasing anxiety against a background of lifelong generalized anxiety. There was no family history of psychotic disorder. She described a sense that someone else was in the room with her whenever she was left alone. When she went to bed, she could hear noises, such as chairs moving and footsteps. These symptoms caused her marked anxiety and initial insomnia. She suspected that the devil had something to do with her experiences but was unsure, and she feared she would be thought crazy if she told people. She began to suspect that God and the devil knew about things. She believed that if she walked past a church, she needed to smile so God could see she was happy and protect her. If a graph at school was drawn in the shape of a cross, this reminded her of God and the devil. Evaluation revealed that she had attenuated psychotic symptoms. There was a hypnagogic component to her auditory phenomena and bizarre ideas, and they fluctuated in the course of a day and were not held with delusional intensity. C.C. was managed with supportive counseling and stress management techniques, similar to those described in case 1. Her family was also involved. After about 5 months, she gradually improved. Perceptual abnormalities and bizarre thoughts resolved, but she was still preoccupied with religious themes out of keeping with her background. This mental state remained until 12 months after initial presentation, when severity of symptoms increased after her mother was diagnosed with cancer. With treatment these symptoms decreased, but the patient was continued in treatment in the clinic. It was unclear how long follow-up treatment should continue.

Case 3. A Possible False Positive

J. S.: J.S. is a single, 22-year-old, unemployed man, with a family history of schizophrenia who presented with vague despair, a feeling he was different from others, and a personality change since leaving school 4 years ago. At that time, he drifted away from his friends, began to feel increasingly alienated, left his factory job, and became increasingly withdrawn. He used cannabis almost daily. On examination, there were no psychotic features, but there was marked euphoria and some circumstantiality of speech. He is still attending clinic after 15 months, receiving supportive therapy, with his mental status unchanged.

Case 4. Early Neuroleptics in "Attenuated Psychosis" with Resolution in Symptoms and Improvement in Functioning

T. P.: T.P. is a 19-year-old apprentice mechanic whose mother has a history of schizophrenia. He described 5 months of increasing social anxiety with a sense that others were talking about him, a feeling of being uncomfortable around others, and a fear he was becoming like his mother. He reported anxiety, sleeplessness, irritability, and increasing depression, and in the end contemplated suicide. On examination, there was no evidence of frank psychosis. In addition to receiving psychosocial treatment, he was started on a low dose of haloperidol 1.5 mg at night. There was marked improvement within 1 week of starting treatment and continued improvement over the following few months. Neuroleptic treatment was continued for 6 months, then stopped. After 5 more months there has been no return of symptoms and he no longer attends the clinic.

Case 5. The Transition from At-Risk Mental State to Frank Psychosis

J. J.: J. J. is a 19-year-old, single, unemployed male referred because of his poor motivation, sleep disturbance, and unusual countenance. There was no family history of psychotic disorder. At initial presentation, he described a long-standing lack of interest in things, poor motivation, anhedonia, and poor peer relationships. He had no friends, made no attempts to look for work, and was uninterested in doing anything. He ruminated about the nature of the world and was unsure of his place in it. Since age 15, he had intermittent hypnagogic auditory phenomena of an unrecognized voice calling his name, as well as vague persecutory ideas, such as believing that someone might be breaking into his house if his dog barked at night or that cars might be following him. He questioned whether he was just being paranoid. These ideas, which occurred once every 2 to 4 weeks, were fleeting and never lasted more than a few hours. The interviewer noted blunted affect, decrease of rapport, and occasional grimaces. He had previously been diagnosed with Tourette's syndrome. J. J. was followed up in clinic for 18 months and was treated with psychosocial interventions. He was reluctant to attend any groups. After 18 months of follow-up, he presented with increasing frequency and intensity of persecutory beliefs. When his paranoid ideas had been present for most of the day for 1 week and he was becoming increasingly convinced of them and distressed by them, he was considered psychotic. Haloperidol 3 mg daily was commenced, and after 1 week of treatment, he reported feeling much improved, much more relaxed, and less concerned by his symptoms. He continues in the treatment program.

Although the PACE Clinic pilot study results do not answer the question of whether the onset of schizophrenia can be prevented definitively, the program does appear to be useful. It targets individuals who appear to be at high risk of schizophrenia and who display sufficient psychopathology that psychiatric intervention is clearly indicated. These individuals are motivated for treatment, especially those who have a first-degree relative with schizophrenia who often fear developing the disorder. It appears that for many of these patients, psychosocial treatment alone is insufficient and low doses of antipsychotic medication are indicated. With the introduction of newer atypical antipsychotic medications, there is much less risk of neurologic side effects.

Even if this program does not prevent schizophrenia, it could be of great value in delaying its onset and could help decrease the likelihood of developing the psychosis by reducing stress in the environment, improving coping skills, and discouraging substance abuse, which can precipitate psychosis. In addition, the individual can gain a higher level of role functioning and status by advancing further in school, obtaining vocational training and work experience, and improving social skills.

If the risk of developing schizophrenia is handled sensitively to minimize fears, with emphasis on the effectiveness of treatment, patients and families will not be alarmed and demoralized needlessly. A combination of risk factors helps to identify individuals in need of treatment, whether or not they would go on to develop schizophrenia, and minimizes the risk of false positives. These patients should be monitored over periods of years and educated about early-warning signs for the development of schizophrenia. More research is necessary to clarify issues, such as which prodromal symptoms are key risk factors, the essential components of treatment, and the optimal length of treatment. Studies should be controlled to provide greater scientific validity of results.

EARLY INTERVENTION TO PREVENT RELAPSE

Long-term studies of the course and outcome of schizophrenia have shown that most patients alternate between acute psychotic phases and phases of improvement or recovery (2,7,8). It seems evident that attempts should be made to intervene clinically in the earliest phase of the relapse process to prevent full relapse and rehospitalization. If the clinician is to intervene early in the relapse process, obviously it is important to know what the earliest signs of relapse are. Docherty et al. reviewed the literature on the process of relapse in schizophrenia and concluded that despite its obvious importance, very little hard information was available on the decompensation process (9). Most studies had been carried out by gifted clinicians whose usual approach was a detailed case study in which information was gathered retrospectively from patients and family members. In 1975, Donlon and Blacker used a different approach, interviewing schizophrenic patients who were being withdrawn from medication and were beginning to relapse. However, their observations did not involve systematic ratings and their data were reported anecdotally.

Since the literature on the process of relapse was largely anecdotal, Herz and Melville decided to conduct a systematic study of a large sample of patients from two locations (1). Group A consisted of 99 outpatients and 80 family informants at two community mental health centers, and Group B, which was added later, consisted of 46 hospitalized patients who had recently experienced a psychotic episode. All patients were diagnosed as schizophrenic according to *DSM-II* criteria; none had a secondary diagnosis (10). Most patients had been hospitalized at least two or three times. At the time of the interviews, outpatients were considered to be symptomatically stable, and inpatients had recompensated sufficiently to cooperate with the research interviewer. A structured interview, "The Early Signs Questionnaire" (Fig. 4.1), was constructed based on items contained in the Psychiatric Status Schedule, Research Diagnostic Criteria, and clinical reports of the early decompensation process (11,12). "The Early Signs Questionnaire" contains items describing symptoms, feelings, and behaviors relevant to the prodro-

EARLY SIGNS QUESTIONNAIRE
(Patient Version)

To patient: I'm going to ask you some questions about how you have been feeling.

At baseline: Time frame is when patient <u>first</u> noticed symptoms prior to current hospitalization.

<u>Preface each questions with: "What are the first changes in your thoughts, feelings and behaviors you noticed when you were getting sick and had to come to the hospital? I will ask you some questions and I'd like you to let me know if you noticed any changes in these areas?"</u>

At episodes: Time frame is for current episode.

At subsequent follow-ups: Time frame is the past week.

<u>Preface each question with: "Have you noticed changes in the way you have been thinking or feeling? I will ask you some questions and I'd like you to let me know if you noticed any changes in theses areas."</u>

Note: Code "Don't Know" or no information as '9'.

Ask question one only at baseline or an episode, at other data collection points begin with question two.

_____ 1.   How many days was it from the time you first noticed changes in your thoughts, feelings and behaviors until you were hospitalized. _____ Days

_____ 2.   Moods shifted back and forth?
           1 = no   2 = slightly   3 = somewhat   4 = very much   5 = extremely

_____ 3.   Energy level high?
           1 = no   2 = slightly   3 = somewhat   4 = very much   5 = extremely

_____ 4.   Energy level low?
           1 = no   2 = slightly   3 = somewhat   4 = very much   5 = extremely

_____ 5.   Lost interest in doing things?
           1 = no   2 = slightly   3 = somewhat   4 = very much   5 = extremely

_____ 6.   Lost interest in the way you look or dress?
           1 = no   2 = slightly   3 = somewhat   4 = very much   5 = extremely

_____ 7.   Felt discouraged about the future?
           1 = no   2 = slightly   3 = somewhat   4 = very much   5 = extremely

FIG. 4.1. *Continued on next page*

_____ 8.   Trouble concentrating or thinking straight?
1 = no   2 = slightly   3 = somewhat   4 = very much   5 = extremely

_____ 9.   Thoughts so fast you can't keep up with them?
1 = no   2 = slightly   3 = somewhat   4 = very much   5 = extremely

_____ 10.   Afraid you are going crazy?
1 = no   2 = slightly   3 = somewhat   4 = very much   5 = extremely

_____ 11.   Puzzled or confused about what is going on around you?
1 = no   2 = slightly   3 = somewhat   4 = very much   5 = extremely

_____ 12.   Felt distant from friends and family?
1 = no   2 = slightly   3 = somewhat   4 = very much   5 = extremely

_____ 13.   Feeling that you don't fit in?
1 = no   2 = slightly   3 = somewhat   4 = very much   5 = extremely

_____ 14.   Religion became more meaningful to you than before?
1 = no   2 = slightly   3 = somewhat   4 = very much   5 = extremely

_____ 15.   Felt afraid that something bad was about to happen?
1 = no   2 = slightly   3 = somewhat   4 = very much   5 = extremely

_____ 16.   Felt others had difficulty understanding what you were saying?
1 = no   2 = slightly   3 = somewhat   4 = very much   5 = extremely

_____ 17.   Felt lonely?
1 = no   2 = slightly   3 = somewhat   4 = very much   5 = extremely

_____ 18.   Bothered by thoughts you can't get rid of?
1 = no   2 = slightly   3 = somewhat   4 = very much   5 = extremely

_____ 19.   Felt overwhelmed by demands or felt that too much is being asked of you?
1 = no   2 = slightly   3 = somewhat   4 = very much   5 = extremely

_____ 20.   Felt bored?
1 = no   2 = slightly   3 = somewhat   4 = very much   5 = extremely

_____ 21.   Trouble sleeping?
1 = no   2 = slightly   3 = somewhat   4 = very much   5 = extremely

_____ 22.   Feeling bad for no reason?
1 = no   2 = slightly   3 = somewhat   4 = very much   5 = extremely

FIG. 4.1. *Continued.*

_____ 23. Worrying that you had physical problems?
  1 = no   2 = slightly   3 = somewhat   4 = very much   5 = extremely

_____ 24. Felt tense and nervous?
  1 = no   2 = slightly   3 = somewhat   4 = very much   5 = extremely

_____ 25. Getting angry at little things?
  1 = no   2 = slightly   3 = somewhat   4 = very much   5 = extremely

_____ 26. Trouble sitting still and have to keep moving or pace up and down?
  1 = no   2 = slightly   3 = somewhat   4 = very much   5 = extremely

_____ 27. Felt depressed or worthless?
  1 = no   2 = slightly   3 = somewhat   4 = very much   5 = extremely

_____ 28. Trouble remembering things?
  1 = no   2 = slightly   3 = somewhat   4 = very much   5 = extremely

_____ 29. Eating less?
  1 = no   2 = slightly   3 = somewhat   4 = very much   5 = extremely

_____ 30. Heard voices or seen things that others don't hear or see?
  1 = no   2 = slightly   3 = somewhat   4 = very much   5 = extremely

_____ 31. Felt that people have been staring at you or talking about you?
  1 = no   2 = slightly   3 = somewhat   4 = very much   5 = extremely

Ask only at baseline and at an episode:

_____ 32. Were you aware you were getting ill again?
  1 = no   2 = slightly   3 = somewhat   4 = very much   5 = extremely

_____ 33. Did you develop any special behaviors around the time you were becoming ill
  that were not noted above? Code: 0 = No, 1 = Yes
  Please describe them:
  _____
  _____

_____ 34. Were there any special life events that occurred prior to the time you started
  feeling ill? Code: 0 = No, 1 = Yes
  Please describe them:
  _____
  _____

_____ 35. Were you cooperative with keeping appointments with your therapist?
  1 = no   2 = slightly   3 = somewhat   4 = very much   5 = extremely

FIG. 4.1. *Continued.*

_____ 36.   Did you take your medication as prescribed?

        1 = no   2 = slightly   3 = somewhat   4 = very much   5 = extremely

Interviewer reliability rating

_____ 37.   How reliable did you think this person's responses were?

            4 = Very reliable
            3 = Generally reliable
            2 = Generally unreliable
            1 = Very unreliable

For additional information please contact:

Marvin I. Herz, M.D.
Strong Ties
University of Rochester Medical Center
1650 Elmwood Ave.
Rochester, NY 14620
(716) 275-0300 x2338
Email. MARVLES@aol.com

FIG. 4.1. *Continued.*

mal phase of relapse. An interview normally lasted between 30 and 45 minutes. There is a patient version and a family version. Table 4.1 lists the most frequently reported symptoms by patients and families from the Herz/Melville project, and gives results from a later prospective study. Most patients and families reported that the relapse process is not sudden and abrupt and that, in fact, it usually lasts at least a week or more. Results from other retrospective and prospective studies have confirmed that dysphoric prodromal symptoms with occasional breakthroughs of mild psychotic symptoms usually occur early in the relapse process (2,13–18). Certain idiosyncratic behaviors may be present (e.g., a female patient beginning to wear excessive make-up or a patient withdrawing to his room, becoming increasingly preoccupied with religion, or wearing sunglasses during the night as well as during the day).

Based on these findings, Herz postulated that early intervention, consisting of close monitoring for prodromal symptoms and prompt clinical intervention when they appear, would be effective in preventing relapse in outpatients with schizophrenia (Fig. 4.2 and 4.3) (19). The first applications of this treatment strategy were studies to determine whether early intervention for patients taken off maintenance antipsychotic medication (intermittent or target medication) would be as effective as maintenance medication in preventing relapse and/or rehospitalization (20–24). Generally, results showed that maintaining a patient on antipsychotic medication was superior to intermittent medication in preventing relapse and rehospitalization.

TABLE 4.1. *Rank order of early symptoms of relapse most frequently reported by patients with schizophrenia*

Symptom	Prospective study (n = 66)	Retrospective study (n = 145)
Trouble sleeping	1	2
Trouble concentrating	2	4
Seeing friends less	3	9
Feeling overwhelmed	4	*
Hearing voices, seeing things	4	16
Mood shifts	6	*
Discouraged about the future	7	*
Doesn't fit in	7	*
Something bad will happen	9	*
Tense, nervous	9	1
Bored	9	1
Puzzled, confused	12	*
Laughed at, talked about	12	10
Depressed	19	3
Restless	14	5
Eating less	14	6
Enjoying things less	*	6
Lost interest in things	19	6
Can't remember things	27	11
Preoccupied with one or two things	16	11

*Not included on symptom list for this study.

Although these studies did not directly address the issue of whether early intervention during the prodromal phase had any clinical value, evidence suggests that it is effective in preventing relapse and/or rehospitalization for patients who are not on maintenance antipsychotic medication. Conventional drug placebo studies that did not monitor for prodromal symptoms or intervene when they appeared have reported relapse rates averaging 75% for placebo patients, whereas relapse rates for intermittent drug study patients were much lower, ranging from 30% to 50% (25). Thus it appears that if patients are off antipsychotic medication for any reason, early intervention during the prodromal phase is useful in preventing relapse. In a study of low-dose antipsychotic medication, Marder et al. found a significant advantage of supplementary oral fluphenazine over placebo when prodromal symptoms appeared, thus forestalling psychotic exacerbations (26). This was especially true during the second year of the study, when clinicians were better able to recognize prodromal symptoms in their patients. This study did not report on relapse and rehospitalization rates.

Since no empirical studies had been carried out that involved monitoring for prodromal symptoms and crisis intervention when they occurred for patients on standard doses of antipsychotic medication, Herz et al. conducted

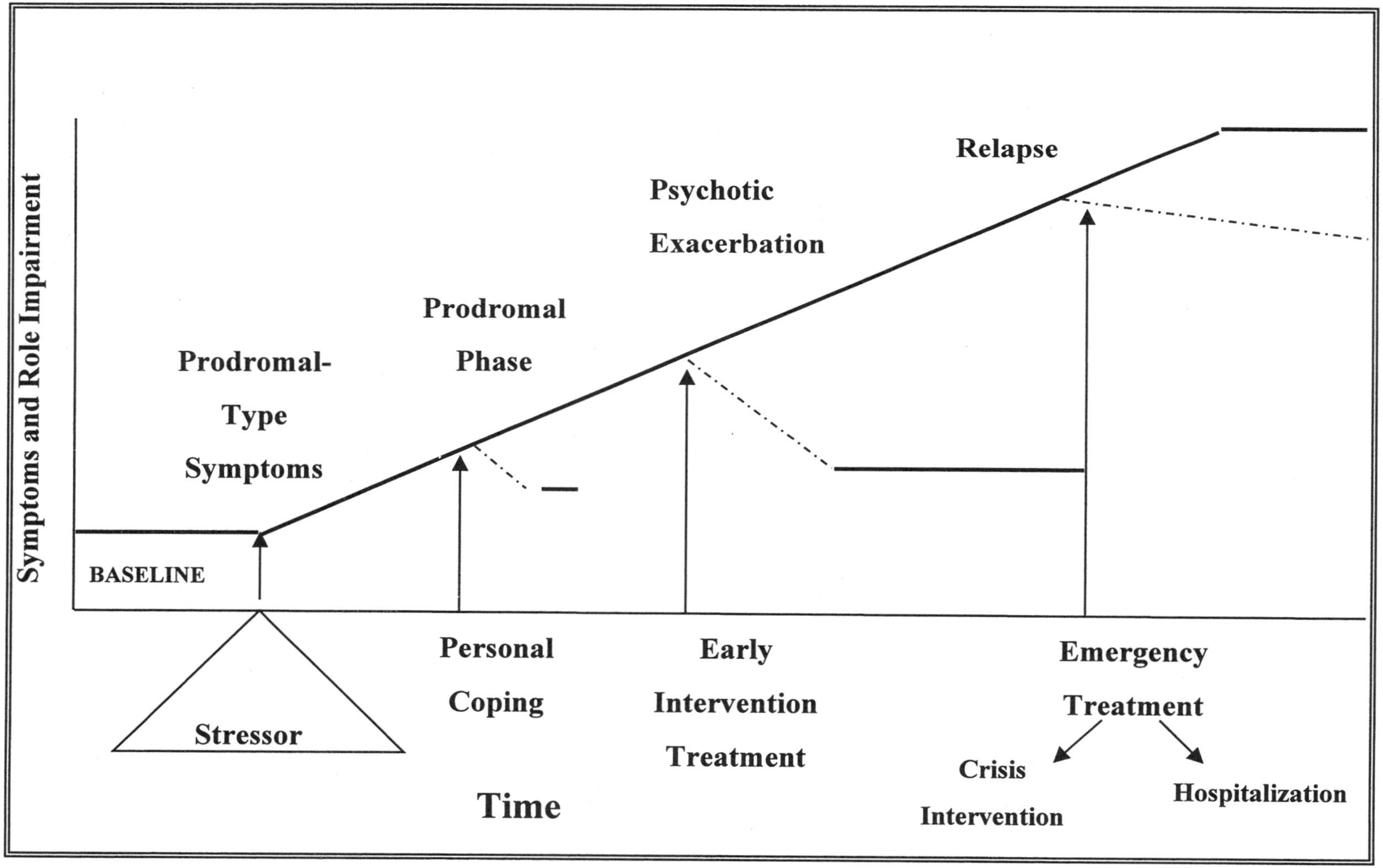
Symptoms and Role Impairment
BASELINE
Prodromal-
Type
Symptoms
Prodromal
Phase
Psychotic
Exacerbation
Relapse
Stressor
Personal
Coping
Early
Intervention
Treatment
Emergency
Treatment
Crisis
Intervention
Hospitalization
Time

FIG. 4.2.

Treatment of Decompensation

1. Stressor
   - Avoiding stress
   - Personal coping

2. Prodromal Symptoms
   - Reinforce coping strategies
   - Educate about symptom recognition
   - Supportive therapy
   - Increase medication

3. Early Psychotic Exacerbation
   - Continue #2

4. Relapse
   - Emergency Room

Crisis Intervention and
Alternatives to Hospitalization

Hospitalization

FIG. 4.3.

a randomized controlled study comparing an early-intervention approach with treatment as usual for patients maintained on standard doses of antipsychotic medication (27). The experimental treatment, called The Program for Relapse Prevention (PRP), incorporated the same psychosocial treatment that was used in an earlier study of intermittent medication by Herz et al. that resulted in the lowest relapse rate (30%) after 2 years for the placebo patients compared with all other intermittent drug studies (22). In addition to early treatment intervention in the prodromal phase, PRP includes weekly group therapy for patients, since it is an excellent treatment modality and provides a cost-effective vehicle for monitoring prodromal symptoms on a weekly basis. For many with schizophrenia, group therapy is at least as effective as individual therapy in preventing relapse and rehospitalization (28). Multifamily groups were conducted biweekly for the first 6 months and monthly thereafter for the 18-month study period. Multifamily groups are comparable in efficacy to individual family interventions in preventing relapse and rehospitalization, and are more cost-effective (29). Patients randomized into the treatment-as-usual control group were seen biweekly for medication management and brief support. Sessions lasted from 15 to 30 minutes.

RESULTS OF THE PRP EARLY-INTERVENTION PROGRAM

Forty-one patients were randomized into each group and followed for 18 months. Survival analysis showed that time to relapse and rehospitalization was statistically significantly less for the control group than for the experimental group. The only other variable, which was predictive of survival time, was compliance versus noncompliance. Noncompliant patients were significantly more likely to relapse and be hospitalized. Over the 18-month study period for all patients randomized, 34% of control patients relapsed, compared with 17% of experimental patients. This was a statistically significant difference. The difference was even greater in favor of the experimental group if patients who never complied with treatment were not included in the analysis. A key issue for the experimental group was whether prodromal symptoms could be detected early, triggering immediate clinical intervention. When the psychiatrist first detected episodes, 35% of control patients had already met the criteria for relapse (Global Assessment Scale scores of 30 or less and any positive Positive and Negative Syndrome Scale symptom equal or greater than 5), whereas only 4% of the experimental patient's episodes met relapse criteria. Control group treatment teams were usually surprised that the patients had already decompensated and were in the hospital. Before initiating this study, there were questions about whether experimental group treatment teams would declare that a patient was in the prodromal stage, too frequently resulting in many false positives. This did not turn out to be the case. No statistically significant differences existed in the number of episodes between the two groups. Experimental patients were on statistically significantly less antipsychotic medication by the end of the study, whereas control patients were taking approximately the same amount of medication. The experimental group had statistically significantly less hospital days than the control group but more ambulatory treatment sessions, which was predicted. The overall costs of treatment were equal for experimental and control groups. For compliant patients, the mean overall costs of treatment per patient were $2,500 less for the experimental group. However, this difference was not statistically significant.

CONCLUSION BASED ON THIS STUDY

The Program for Relapse Prevention reduced relapse and rehospitalization rates when compared with treatment as usual. The program was least effective for patients who were noncompliant with treatment. These patients refused to participate in all aspects of treatment, including taking antipsychotic medication. Six out of the nine noncompliant patients relapsed; the other three noncompliant patients were stable throughout the study. If patients, families, and treatment teams are educated about recognizing prodromal symptoms and close monitoring for their appearance with prompt clinical intervention when these symptoms occur, relapse and rehospitalization rates can be decreased considerably. Since prodromal symptoms are usually dysphoric affective symptoms, it is not easy for the psychiatrist and other team members to differentiate between minor symptomatic and behavioral fluctuations in a patient and those symptoms that signal the onset of the relapse process. As Marder et al. have pointed out, as a psychiatrist and other team members become more familiar with the patient, they can be more effective in differentiating minor fluctuations in symptoms from the beginning of a prodromal episode (26). Weekly therapeutic contact, including monitoring for prodromal symptoms, is recommended for at least 1 year; after that time, frequency of visits can be reevaluated if clinically indicated. It is important to involve family members in the treatment process. Clinical intervention for the family should include education about the disorder, especially with regard to prodromal symptoms, improvement of communication skills, and the ability to cope more effectively with behavioral manifestations of schizophrenia. In addition, family members are often more likely to recognize the onset of prodromal symptoms than are many patients, which makes them useful allies in the treatment process.

CASE VIGNETTES

To illustrate various clinical pictures that characterize prodromal episodes, the following case vignettes from the Herz et al. Intermittent Medication Study are presented (22).

Vignette 1. A Nonpsychotic Prodromal Episode in a Patient with No Baseline Psychotic Symptoms

John D., a 33-year-old white male diagnosed as a chronic paranoid schizophrenic, has been hospitalized twice. His baseline behavior was that of a quiet, pleasant, cooperative man who was compliant with medication and attendance at weekly group sessions. His affect was flat and he was socially isolated, with no meaningful relationships. His only social activities revolved around a supportive family that lived next door. At times he had been able to obtain gainful employment as an electrician.

John had one episode during the study. He presented for a scheduled individual session following his absence from a group meeting and reported sleep difficulties, only 3 to 4 hours of sleep a night over the course of four nights. He said he felt depressed and admitted to staying in bed for long periods, although he was not sleeping. He also reported increased irritability and diminished desire to engage in usual family social activities. He had recently quit a good job as an electrician because he felt unable to handle the pressure. The therapist thought that this was a minor episode that could be treated with lorazepam 1 mg at bedtime. However, about a week later, his mother called the therapist to report that John was increasingly withdrawn and irritable, remained in bed almost all day, and was unresponsive to her telephone calls. The therapist attempted to reach John by phone, but he refused to speak to her. Finally, 4 days later, he agreed to attend a session. He appeared somewhat unkempt and admitted to increased social isolation, tension and nervousness, increased irritability, poor appetite, and a marked decrease in his prior level of functioning. He was unable to attend to his usual household tasks and remained in bed almost all the time. Haloperidol 8 mg a day was initiated, twice his baseline dose. Two weeks later he began to stabilize and returned to baseline within 3 weeks.

Comment

This patient had gradual deterioration in functioning following the feeling of failure in a job. Introduction of a minor tranquilizer and supportive psychotherapy did not arrest the deterioration. Therefore antipsychotic medication was started, which had favorable results within a few weeks.

Vignette 2. A Patient with Baseline Psychotic Symptoms with Exacerbation of Schizophrenic Symptoms

Robert T. is a 30-year-old white male with a diagnosis of chronic undifferentiated schizophrenia. He had been hospitalized three times before entering the study. After hospital discharge, he was stabilized over a period of 6 months before entering the study, but he continued to have occasional nonthreatening auditory hallucinations. In treatment, he formed a positive relationship with the therapist, although he was somewhat dependent. As part of his treatment, he entered a vocational rehabilitation program and a sheltered workshop.

The episode occurred after 5 months in the study. The patient's mother reported increasingly withdrawn behavior over a period of 3 to 4 days, suspiciousness, and the patient's fear that the devil was controlling him. His baseline auditory hallucinations increased and became upsetting to him. ("I hear voices telling me that I am no good and they are laughing at me.") Active medication was initiated, trifluoroperazine 20 mg/day, twice his maintenance medication dose. Robert was seen every other day and required an increase in medication to 25 mg/day in the first week. As the symptoms improved and he stabilized, the medication was reduced to baseline over a 5-week period. It is possible that a life event contributed to this episode. The patient had an increase in his workload in the vocational rehabilitation program, and his supervisors started to pressure him to increase his speed and productivity.

Comment

In the case of a patient who has baseline delusions and hallucinations, it has been our experience that there is an immediate increase in these psychotic symptoms when a new episode starts to develop.

Vignette 3. Nonpsychotic Episodes Resolved Without Introduction of Antipsychotic Medication

Betty O. is a 27-year-old white female who was chronically anxious and received benzodiazepines in addition to her study medication for most of the 2 years in the study. Her diagnosis was schizoaffective depressed. When she entered the study, her baseline behavior was that of a quiet, soft-spoken woman who seemed helpless and dependent. She dressed rather seductively and was superficial in conversation. She denied hallucinations or delusions but was preoccupied somatically. Chronically anxious, with occasional anorexia and sleep difficulties, she had no friends and was extremely dependent on her family. Betty developed a very dependent relationship with her therapist and responded well to a supportive therapeutic approach.

A preprodromal episode (an episode not requiring introduction of antipsychotic medication according to the study protocol) was declared following the patient's termination from a vocational training program. She requested a therapy session and presented with complaints of increased anxiety and restlessness. She was unable to sit still. There was a decrease in sleep, from 8 to 5 hours per night, and a decrease in appetite. After supportive therapy sessions for 1 week, the symptoms disappeared. The patient had a similar experience when her mother went out of town for a week. She complained of continuous anxiety for 2 days with nausea and a decrease in appetite as well as sleep difficulties. Her hygiene was poor and she expressed fear that the therapist might abandon her.

During both episodes, she was given lorazepam 1 mg tid in addition to supportive counseling. These symptoms also lasted only 1 week.

Comment

Both of these episodes of symptom elevation resolved without the introduction of major tranquilizers in a schizophrenic patient. This underscores the importance of the therapist being able to relate to the patient, knowing the patient's typical reaction to stress, and understanding the patient's underlying personality. This was a chronically anxious, dependent, somewhat hysterical individual who was subject to mini-episodes that were not precursors of the relapse process.

Vignette 4. Patient with Early Symptoms of Hostility and Paranoia

Carol B. is a 53-year-old white female with a diagnosis of chronic paranoid schizophrenia. She had three hospitalizations before entering the study. Shortly after entering the study, the patient became anxious following a family argument about preparations for a bridal shower she was giving for one of her daughters. The daughter contacted the therapist and described Carol as increasingly hostile and argumentative, and talking to herself more than usual. The daughter could not convince the patient to see the therapist. When the therapist called Carol, she angrily hung up, accusing both the therapist and the doctor of not caring about her. Since she refused all contact with the study treatment staff, the family was encouraged to bring Carol to the emergency room.

Three weeks after entering the study, the patient was hospitalized. She reported receiving messages from the Virgin Mary and the ability to communicate directly with ET. She also admitted that she had stopped taking her study medications 2 weeks before.

The patient recompensated after 8 days in the hospital. Her study medications were switched to an equivalent dose of fluphenazine decanoate and she resumed study participation. Carol completed the remaining 2 years in the study without any further problems.

Comment

This case demonstrates the problem with compliance in a patient who becomes hostile, paranoid, and negative very early in a episode. Such patients typically have full-blown psychotic episodes, even when prodromal symptoms are recognized, because they refuse treatment.

Vignette 5. Prodromal Episode Followed by a Psychotic Episode Induced by Substance Abuse

Blanche R., diagnosed as chronic undifferentiated schizophrenic, is a 31-year-old black female with a history of two psychiatric hospitalizations. During this study, a prodromal episode began when the patient experienced dysphoric symptoms, such as feeling very tense and sad, loss of appetite, and insomnia. She was tearful in a therapy session and described mounting tension with her stepfather. ("He tells other people that I am crazy and that I have been sick.") She denied any psychotic symptoms. She continued to have counseling sessions and was put on lorazepam 1 mg bid. About a month later, she broke up with her boyfriend.

After a week, her therapist made a home visit and found the patient depressed, with decreased appetite and increased restlessness. The parents asked Blanche to move out of the house, stating that she was too difficult to live with. The patient agreed to look for an apartment within 2 weeks. She seemed to be improving and stated that she had resumed her relationship with her boyfriend. Her symptomatology had returned to baseline. However, about 1 week later, the patient presented for a scheduled session in an acute psychotic state, with gross thought disorganization and paranoid delusions that people wanted to hurt her. She said that she felt that she was a dog or a cat and that people were watching her on the street and would try to harm her. Inappropriately silly, she laughed frequently throughout the session. She was religiously preoccupied and stated that she was receiving biblical messages from the television and radio. She admitted to cocaine use for several days before this episode occurred. Antipsychotic medication was initiated and continued until the symptoms abated 3 weeks later. Cocaine and other illicit street drugs can rapidly precipitate florid acute psychotic symptomatology in vulnerable schizophrenic patients without the prior appearance of nonpsychotic dysphoric symptoms.

In our experience, patients who had the longest and most severe episodes and who were most likely to be rehospitalized tended to be markedly paranoid, with suspiciousness and delusions occurring early in the episode. As a result, these patients became uncooperative, refused medication, and refused to see the therapist, and their symptoms increased in severity without treatment. This was also true for patients who were uncooperative with treatment and refused maintenance antipsychotic medication (27). Heinrichs et al. reported that patients who lacked insight (i.e., failed to recognize they were becoming sicker) were more likely to have severe episodes and relapses (30). Similarly, outcomes are poor when patients and families wait too long before requesting therapeutic intervention or when the onset of psychotic symptomatology is rapid, often precipitated by illicit drugs and alcohol. Since family members generally recognize early prodromal symptoms more frequently than patients, it is important to have a collaborator, whether a family member, a case manager, or a manager of a single room occupancy hotel. Anyone who sees the patient at least weekly and is available to collaborate in the treatment process can be helpful.

Table 4.2 summarizes some of the techniques that can help to reduce the risk of relapse and rehospitalization. In treating individuals with schizophre-

TABLE 4.2. *Early intervention strategies that are useful in preventing relapse and rehospitalization*

Monitoring strategies	Obtain as accurate a history as possible concerning previous relapses, including • Types of prodromal symptoms and behaviors that occurred in previous relapse episodes. • Types of stressful events that led to previous relapse episodes.
Psychoeducation strategies	Educate patients, families, and others in close contact with the patient about • The nature of prodromal symptoms, including the types of symptoms the patient developed prior to previous episodes. • The relationship of stress to relapse. • The importance of seeking help at the beginning of a new episode (i.e., when prodromal symptoms first appear).
Pharmacologic strategies	Increase antipsychotic medication when prodromal symptoms appear.
Psychosocial strategies	Teach patients coping skills to deal with stress, thus reducing chances of relapse. Provide immediate crisis intervention for the patient when a new episode begins, including increased support, structure, reassurance, and assertive outreach (e.g., home visits, especially for uncooperative patients). Maintain continued, ongoing collaboration with family members and significant others and provide them with support, reassurance, and education.

nia, it is important to educate both patients and family members about prodromal symptoms. When such symptoms are reported, clinical intervention should occur as soon as possible. At the beginning of treatment, the psychiatrist should ask patients and family members about prodromal symptoms and behaviors that have occurred early in previous psychotic episodes. Similar prodromal symptoms and behaviors are likely to recur before future episodes. Therapeutic techniques include reassurance, support, reality testing, reinforcement of positive coping skills and defenses in the patient, and usually increased antipsychotic medication, according to the clinical needs of the patient. Patients should be seen frequently at least every few days. Home visits should be made if necessary, especially for patients who become uncooperative. Family members need to receive support, reassurance, and education about the situation, if possible, because this is a time of crisis for them as well as for the patient.

More research is needed to refine and improve our techniques for recognizing the early-warning signs of relapse and our treatment strategies for preventing full relapse. It would be extremely helpful if a biological marker for a prodromal episode could be identified. However, a great deal is already known, and the principles and practices described in this chapter should be routinely applied in the outpatient treatment of individuals with schizophrenia. If an early-intervention strategy is used, relapse and rehospitalization rates can be greatly reduced, thereby lessening the pain and suffering associated with psychotic episodes for both patients and families.

REFERENCES

1. Herz MI, Melville C. Relapse in schizophrenia. *Am J Psychiatry* 1980;80:801–805.
2. Huber G, Gross G, Schuttler R, et al. Longitudinal studies of schizophrenic patients. *Schizophr Bull* 1980;6:592–605.
3. American Psychiatric Association. *Diagnostic and statistical manual of mental disorders,* 4th ed. (*DSM-IV*). Washington, DC: American Psychiatric Association, 1994.
4. Falloon IR. Early intervention for first episodes of schizophrenia: a preliminary exploration. *Psychiatry* 1992;55:4–15.
5. Yung AR, McGorry PD, McFarlane CA, et al. Monitoring and care of young people at incipient risk of psychosis. *Schizophr Bull* 1996;22:283–303.
6. American Psychiatric Association. *Diagnostic and statistical manual of mental disorders,* 3rd ed., revised (*DSM-III-R*). Washington, DC: American Psychiatric Association, 1987.
7. Bleuler ME. The long-term course of schizophrenic psychoses. In: Wynne L, Cromwell RL, Matthysse S, eds. *The nature of schizophrenia.* New York: Wiley, 1978:631–651.
8. Ciompi L. The natural history of schizophrenia in the long term. *Br J Psychiatry* 1980; 136:413–420.
9. Docherty JP, Van Kammen DP, Siris SG, et al. Stages of onset of schizophrenic psychosis. *Am J Psychiatry* 1978;135:420–426.
10. American Psychiatric Association. *Diagnostic and statistical manual of mental disorders,* 2nd ed. (*DSM-II*). Washington, DC: American Psychiatric Associatio, 1968.
11. Spitzer RL, Endicott J, Cohen MS. Psychiatric status schedule. Evaluation Unit Biometrics Unit. New York: New York State Department of Mental Hygiene, 1968.
12. Spitzer RL, Endicott J, Robins E. Research diagnostic criteria. *Psychopharmacol Bull* 1975;11:22–25.
13. Heinrichs DU, Carpenter WT Jr. Prospective study of prodromal symptoms. *Am J Psychiatry* 1985;142:371–373.
14. Subotnik KL, Nuechterlein KH. Prodromal signs and symptoms of schizophrenic relapse. *J Abnorm Psychol* 1988;97:405–412.
15. Birchwood R, Smith J, MacMillan F, et al. Predicting relapse in schizophrenia: the development and implementation of an early signs monitoring system using patients and families as observers. *Psychol Med* 1989;19:649–656.
16. Kumar S, Thara R, Rajkumar S. Coping with symptoms of relapse in schizophrenia. *Eur Arch Psychiatry Clin Neurosci* 1989;239:213–215.
17. Tarrier N, Barrowclough C, Bamrah JS. Prodromal signs of relapse in schizophrenia. *Soc Psychiatry Psychiatr Epidemiol* 1991;26:157–161.
18. Henmi Y. Prodromal symptoms of relapse in schizophrenic outpatients: retrospective and prospective study. *Jpn J Psychiatry Neurol* 1993;47:753–775.
19. Herz MI. Prodromal symptoms and prevention of relapse in schizophrenia. *J Clin Psychiatry* 1985;46:22–25.
20. Carpenter WT Jr, Hanlon TE, Heinrichs DW, et al. Continuous versus targeted medication in schizophrenic outpatients: outcome results. *Am J Psychiatry* 1990;147: 1138–1148.
21. Jolley AG, Hirsch SR, Morrison G, et al. Trial of brief intermittent neuroleptic prophy-

laxis for selected schizophrenia outpatients: clinical and social outcome at two years. *Br Med J* 1990;301:847–852.

22. Herz MI, Glazer WM, Mostert MA, et al. Intermittent vs maintenance medication in schizophrenia: two-year results. *Arch Gen Psychiatry* 1991;48:333–339.

23. Pietzcker A, et al. Intermittent versus maintenance neuroleptic long-term treatment in schizophrenia: 2 year results of a German multicenter study. *J Psychiatr Res* 1993;27: 321–339.

24. Schooler NR, Keith SJ, Severe JB, et al. Relapse and rehospitalization during maintenance treatment of schizophrenia: the effects of dose reduction and family treatment. *Arch Gen Psychiatry* 1997;54:453–463.

25. Kane JM. Treatment programme and long-term outcome in chronic schizophrenia. *Acta Psychiatr Scand.Suppl* 1990;358:151–157.

26. Marder SR, Wirshing WC, Van Puten T, et al. Fluphenazine vs. placebo supplementation for prodromal signs of relapse in schizophrenia. *Arch Gen Psychiatry* 1994;51:280–287.

27. Herz MI., et al. A program for relapse prevention in schizophrenia: a controlled study. *Arch Gen Psychiatry* 2000;57:277–283.

28. Kanas N. *Group therapy for schizophrenic patients*. Washington, DC: American Psychiatric Press, 1996.

29. McFarlane WR. Multiple family groups and the treatment of schizophrenia. In: Herz MI, Keith SJ, Docherty JP, eds. *Psychosocial treatment of schizophrenia*. Amsterdam, The Netherlands: Elsevier, 1990:167–189.

30. Heinrichs DW, Cohen BP, Carpenter WT Jr. Early insight and the management of schizophrenic decompensation. *J Nerv Ment Dis* 1985;173:133–138.

5

Pharmacologic Treatment

OVERVIEW OF ANTIPSYCHOTIC MEDICATIONS

The discovery of chlorpromazine in Paris in the early 1950s led to a revolution in the treatment of schizophrenia and other psychiatric disorders. Chlorpromazine had specific effects in reducing psychiatric symptoms such as hallucinations and delusions. In contrast, earlier pharmacologic therapies tended to be nonspecific treatments that sedated patients and reduced agitation. The advantages of chlorpromazine became clear as it was widely adapted in Paris hospitals, where the atmosphere changed rapidly. A year after these agents were introduced the use of physical restraints was greatly reduced and observers noted that wards no longer had the odor of deteriorated patients. When the use of chlorpromazine spread elsewhere in Europe and North America, patients who were previously considered undischargeable were able to return to their communities.

The discovery of chlorpromazine's effectiveness led to a search for other agents with similar effects. This led to the introduction of a number of other drugs (including trifluoperazine, thioridazine, and perphenazine) that were also in the chemical class of phenothiazines. Subsequently, butyrophenone antipsychotics (e.g., haloperidol) and thioxanthenes (e.g., thiothixene) were developed and demonstrated to be effective. Table 5.1 lists representatives from each of the groups of the antipsychotics, including more recently introduced agents. It also uses a relatively recent form of subdividing antipsychotics. The older antipsychotics (i.e., the agents that were introduced into the United States before 1990) are referred to as either conventional antipsychotics or dopamine receptor antagonists (or DAs), since the therapeutic activity of these agents has been attributed to the blockade of central dopamine receptors, particularly D_2 receptors (see Chapter 1). In the past these agents have been referred to using a number of terms, including *major tranquilizer*, *neuroleptic*, and *antipsychotic*. The term *major tranquilizer* is inaccurate, since these agents—particularly the high-potency agents—can improve psychosis without sedating or making patients more tranquil. The term *neuroleptic* refers to the tendency of these drugs to cause neurologic side effects, particularly extrapyramidal effects. This term is reasonable for classifying

TABLE 5.1. *Daily dose range for commonly prescribed antipsychotics*

Types/Brand Name	Generic name	Dosage (average range, orally, per day)
Phenothiazines		
Aliphatics		
Thorazine	Chlorpromazine	100–1,000 mg
Sparine	Promazine	25–1,000 mg
Vesprin	Triflupromazine	20–150 mg
Piperidines		
Mellaril	Thioridazine	30–800 mg
Serentil	Mesoridazine	20–200 mg
Quide	Piperacetazine	20–160 mg
Piperzines		
Stelazine	Trifluoperazine	2–60 mg
Prolixin	Fluphenazine	5–40 mg
Trilafon	Perphenazine	2–60 mg
Tindal	Acetophenazine	40–80 mg
Compazine	Prochlorperazine	15–125 mg
Thioxanthenes		
Navane	Thiothixene	6–60 mg
Taractan	Chlorprothixene	10–600 mg
Dibenzoxiazepines		
Loxitane	Loxapine	20–150 mg
Butyrophenones		
Haldol	Haloperidol	3–50 mg
Dihydroindolones		
Moban	Molindone	15–225 mg
Dibenzodiazepines		
Clozaril	Clozapine	100–900 mg
Benzisoxazole		
Risperdal	Risperidone	2–10 mg
Thienobenzodiazepine		
Zyprexa	Olanzapine	5–20 mg
Dibenzothiazepine		
Seroquel	Quetiapine	75–750 mg
Benzothiazolylpiperazine		
Geodon	Ziprasidone	40–160 mg

Adapted from Janicak PG, Davis JM, Preskorn SH, Ayd Jr. FJ, *Principles and Practice of Psychopharmacotherapy,* 2nd ed. Baltimore: Williams & Wilkins, 1997.

the older DAs but should not be used for identifying newer drugs, since they are relatively free of extrapyramidal side effects (EPS). This text uses the term *antipsychotic* to describe all the drugs that are utilized for reducing psychosis. The newer agents are referred to as *second-generation antipsychotics* (SGAs) or *serotonin-dopamine antagonists*. The latter term is used since the activity of these agents has been associated with the blockade of 5-HT2A and D_2 receptors. Others have contrasted the two types of drugs as *atypical*, in comparison to typical agents, and as *newer*, as opposed to conventional drugs. This text does not use these terms, since the widespread use of *second-generation agents* makes the term *atypical* appear inaccurate. At this stage there is a consensus that the two types of drugs should be in separate classes, but the best terms to classify them remain controversial.

ANTIPSYCHOTIC MEDICATIONS AND ACUTE SCHIZOPHRENIA

The antipsychotics were the first psychoactive drugs that were clearly demonstrated to be effective for managing a serious mental illness. As a result, there was initial skepticism about their effectiveness. Their effectiveness challenged the views of some clinicians in the late 1950s and early 1960s who believed that psychosis was a psychological reaction related to early experiences and that only psychological treatment could have antipsychotic effects. Some believed that these agents were tranquilizers that represented a weaker form of treatment than psychotherapies, which were more likely to be curative. Although these early doubts about antipsychotics may have delayed their acceptance, they had a favorable effect, in that they placed a burden on psychopharmacologists to demonstrate the efficacy of these agents beyond any doubt. Early researchers on antipsychotics responded by focusing on the development of clinical research methods. This resulted in the development and refinement of the randomized clinical trial, a method for demonstrating the effectiveness of treatments that remains the standard to this day. In randomized clinical trials, patients are assigned to treatment conditions using randomization systems such as tables of random numbers. The outcome in each treatment group is measured using systems that reduce bias, such as double-blind medications where patients, clinicians, and raters do not know which drug (or placebo) the patient is receiving.

Nearly every double-blind, randomized, controlled study that compared an antipsychotic to a placebo in patients with schizophrenia found that the active drug was more effective. The National Institute of Mental Health and the Department of Veterans Affairs carried out the first important studies in the 1960s (1–3). Since then many research groups have replicated the positive findings in these studies. These studies also demonstrated that antipsychotics are effective for every subtype and subgroup of patients with schizophrenia. The Schizophrenia Patient Outcomes Research Team (PORT) reviewed this large body of work in 1998. The PORT (4) concluded that there is clear evidence that antipsychotics are effective for reducing positive symptoms of schizophrenia during acute psychotic episodes. Klein and Davis (5) reviewed studies that compared more than one antipsychotic and found that with the exception of meprazine and promazine, all these agents were equally effective. Although a number of studies, which will be reviewed later in this chapter, suggest that second-generation agents may be more effective than conventional drugs, the overall data have not yet established this advantage. The important exception is the advantage of clozapine for patients who have failed to respond to conventional drugs.

More than 40 years of experience with these agents has provided important information about their optimal use. Antipsychotics are effective for diminishing most symptoms of schizophrenia. They are most effective for managing the positive symptoms of schizophrenia (including hallucinations, delusions, suspiciousness) but are much less effective for the negative and neurocognitive symptoms. Even though negative and neurocognitive symptoms are less responsive than positive symptoms, double-blind studies indicate that these symptoms improve over the course of acute treatment (6,7). However, the response is complex, since rigidity or hypokinesia from EPS can appear to worsen negative symptoms and the anticholinergic side effects that are used to treat these same side effects can impair cognition. (There is evidence that newer antipsychotics, including clozapine, risperidone, olanzapine, and quetiapine, are more effective for cognitive and negative symptoms. This will be reviewed later in this chapter.)

All forms of schizophrenia improve with antipsychotics. However, the extent to which patients improve varies considerably. Whereas many patients improve to the point that they are nearly free of psychotic symptoms, others continue to manifest severe positive symptoms. Studies from the NIMH in the 1960s compared a number of conventional antipsychotics with a placebo. As noted, the differences between drug and placebo were clear. However, a substantial proportion of patients on drug did not fit the category of being much improved. The findings indicate that 60% of drug-treated patients improved to the extent that they achieved a complete remission or experienced only mild symptoms; the remaining 40% continued to experience psychotic symptoms. These studies also found that approximately 8% of patients are not improved with drug treatment. The 1995 PORT (4) found that conventional antipsychotics induced a remission of positive symptoms in about 70% of patients.

PHARMACOLOGIC MANAGEMENT OF ACUTE PSYCHOSIS

There are two important features of the antipsychotic drug response that can be used to develop a rational treatment plan. The first is that there is a delay between the point at which the patient obtains an adequate blood level of an antipsychotic and the beginning of clinical improvement. The second is that once patients receive an adequate amount of drug, increasing the dose does not lead to a more rapid or a better improvement. The remainder of this section presents the data supporting these principles.

As mentioned in Chapter 1, the antipsychotic activity of antipsychotics—with the possible exceptions of clozapine and quetiapine—is due to biological activities that occur when these drugs occupy D_2 dopamine receptors. Clozapine and quetiapine also have activity at these receptors, and their activity may depend on activity at D_2 as well as other receptors. Studies using positron emission tomography (PET) with selective D_2 receptor ligands such as raclopride make it possible to determine the proportion of D_2 receptors occupied by an antipsychotic in a particular individual at a particular time. These studies indicate that conventional antipsychotics are effective when approximately 80% of receptors are occupied (8). If the number of receptors that are occupied is increased by administering a higher dose, the patient may experience more severe extrapyramidal symptoms but is unlikely to experience a better antipsychotic response. Also, individuals who have less than 60% occupancy—with the exception of patients receiving clozapine and quetiapine—are unlikely to demonstrate an adequate drug response. Clozapine and quetiapine are effective when a smaller proportion of receptors are occupied. This approach of measuring D_2 occupancy has led to some interesting findings. For example, McEvoy and his co-workers (9) have suggested that a mean dose of haloperidol of 3.4 mg may result in antipsychotic effects with a therapeutic response and minimal EPS. Others (10) have found that 2 mg daily of haloperidol results in a D_2 occupancy of about 70%, suggesting that this dose is close to the dose that will provide optimal effects.

Evidence regarding the time course of antipsychotic response comes from studies of homovanillic acid (HVA) in plasma. HVA is a major metabolite of dopamine, and changes in its plasma concentration probably reflect changes in dopamine activity in brain. Studies in humans indicate that HVA levels rise after patients are started on an antipsychotic medication (11). The most likely explanation for this rise is that the blockade of dopamine receptors leads to a compensating increase in dopamine release from presynaptic terminals. This increase is reflected in an increase in HVA in plasma. Following this initial rise, there is a decrease in HVA below the pretreatment levels. There are studies suggesting that the reduction in HVA from pretreatment to the time of clinical response is related to the amount of improvement. This suggests that the antipsychotic response is associated with an initial increase in dopamine followed by decreased dopamine release and dopamine blockade.

These findings are consistent with what happens when acutely psychotic patients are administered an antipsychotic. Patients usually demonstrate most of their therapeutic gains during the first 6 weeks of drug treatment (7). However, many continue to improve during the next several months. Although some demonstrate relatively rapid improvement during the first few hours after starting on an antipsychotic, most require several days before a response can be detected. In some patients, the early effects are not truly antipsychotic; instead they are a manifestation of the antipsychotic's ability to slow the patient's motor and mental behavior. That is, patients will be quieter, less agitated, and demonstrate less motor agitation. However, the psychotic process that causes these patients to misinterpret reality will not improve until later. This suggests that the initial response is a manifestation of the global slowing in motor and cognitive activity rather than a true antipsychotic effect.

Because of this delay between the time an adequate drug level is reached and the onset of clinical response, clinicians cannot easily titrate an antipsychotic's dose against clinical effects. That is, if a patient has been receiving a reasonable dose of an antipsychotic (e.g., 4 mg of risperidone, 15 mg of olanzapine, or similar doses of other agents) and is not responding after 10 days, the clinician should not conclude that the dose is inadequate. The patient may require more time at his or her current dose, and a higher dose may only lead to more side effects. For this reason the goal of pharmacotherapy during the first days of treatment is to begin an adequate dose of antipsychotic, monitor the patient for side effects, ensure the patient's comfort and safety, and wait until he or she shows a response. There is a natural inclination to increase the dose of antipsychotic for patients who have failed to improve in the hope that this will result in a more rapid therapeutic response. However, empirical studies indicate that this practice seldom leads to better clinical results (12).

Selection of an Antipsychotic

Before the introduction of the SGAs, the decision as to which antipsychotic to choose was relatively simple. (See Table 5.2 for list of factors to consider in selecting an antipsychotic.) All the antipsychotics were more or less equally effective (with the possible exception of promazine and mepazine). The differences were in side effects and available routes of administration. The conventional antipsychotics can also be classified according to their antipsychotic potency rather than their chemical class. For example, low-potency antipsychotics such as chlorpromazine and thioridazine require more milligrams of drug. These agents are also associated with a greater likelihood of orthostatic hypotension (i.e., dizziness or fainting upon standing or sitting up), tachycardia (or rapid heartbeat), and anticholinergic effects (including dry mouth, blurry vision, constipation, and memory loss) (see Table 5.3). High-potency antipsychotics such as haloperidol or fluphenazine are less likely to cause hypotension, tachycardia, and anticholinergic effects but are more likely to cause EPS (including stiffness, tremor, and restlessness). Agents such as haloperidol or fluphenazine can be administered orally, as a short-acting intramuscular agent, or as a long-acting intramuscular agent. Selecting among these agents is

TABLE 5.2. *Factors to consider in selecting an antipsychotic*

Factor	Consider
Subjective response	A dysphoric subjective response to a particular drug predicts poor compliance with that drug
EPS sensitivity	A second-generation antipsychotic (SGA), esp. quetiapine or clozapine
Tardive dyskinesia	Clozapine or quetiapine (possibly an SGA)
Poor medication compliance or high risk of relapse	Long-acting antagonist (haloperidol or fluphenazine in the United States)
Weight	Ziprasidone
Sedation	Risperidone or ziprasidone
Prolactin elevation (decreased libido, irregular menses, galactorrhea)	Olanzapine, quetiapine, ziprasidone
Pregnancy	Probably haloperidol (most data supporting its safety)
Cognitive symptoms	Possibly an SGA
Negative symptoms	Possibly an SGA

EPS, extrapyramidal side effects.

usually based on the individual's tolerance or disability from certain classes of side effects and the preferred route of administration.

The newer agents have a different range of side effects. All the SGAs are characterized by a very low liability for causing EPS. Since, as described later in this chapter, EPS is usually the most serious and disabling of antipsychotic drug side effects, the SGAs represent a major improvement in antipsychotic drug therapy. Patients who experience EPS that cannot be managed with antiparkinson medications or a reduction in the dose of the antipsychotic should be changed to an SGA. However, the newer medications are associated with a range of side effects that can also be disabling in some patients. These include sedation, hypotension, and seizures with clozapine; EPS and prolactin elevation with risperidone; weight gain with olanzapine; and sedation with quetiapine (see Table 5.3). Concerns about all these side effects should guide the clinician in the selection of an SGA.

Evidence also suggests that the SGAs may be intrinsically more effective than DAs. This is certainly the case when patients are selected who are treatment refractory when managed with DAs. Studies with clozapine (13), risperidone (14,15), and olanzapine (16) have found substantial advantages for the newer agent when it is compared with an older agent in treatment-refractory individuals. As will be noted later, it is unclear if the newer drugs are more effective for patients who are not treatment refractory.

Other studies suggest advantages of the newer drugs, but they are not yet conclusive. Most of the studies comparing newer and older agents have been sponsored by drug companies, and most have used patients who are hospitalized and relatively poor responders to conventional drugs. This limitation is to be expected since individuals who are doing well on older agents are unlikely to be candidates for a study. An excellent scholarly review by Leucht and associates (17) used meta-analysis to compare outcomes between newer antipsychotic drugs and haloperidol. The results indicate that risperidone and olanzapine were slightly superior to haloperidol for positive and negative symptoms in schizophrenia and that quetiapine had similar effectiveness to haloperidol. The advantages of risperidone and olanzapine over haloperidol were very small. A review by Geddes and co-workers (18) found similar results. This latter review noted that newer drugs were more likely to have advantages over haloperidol when haloperidol was prescribed at excessive dosages. When lower doses were prescribed, haloperidol and newer drugs were similar.

On the other hand, both reviews acknowledge that there are large differences between older and newer drugs in their likelihood to cause EPS. This can be a critical advantage since many patients, if not most, will experience some degree of EPS, such as akathisia at the dose that is necessary to treat psychosis. Given the amount of discomfort even mild EPS can cause, this advantage can be a critical factor in drug selection for many patients. Moreover, there are findings (reviewed in Chapter 9) that indicate that SGAs are less likely to cause tardive dyskinesia.

First-episode patients are not selected on the basis of prior drug responses. Evidence suggests that newer agents are superior in this group. For example, a study comparing risperidone and haloperidol in first-episode patients found that risperidone resulted in a greater likelihood of improvement and less EPS (19). Other clinical reports suggest that first-episode patients treated with olanzapine (20) tend to do well and have fewer side effects than would be expected if they were treated with a DA. The case for prescribing a newer drug in first-episode patients is compelling. A patient's first experience with an antipsychotic may have an important impact on his or her attitude toward drug treatment. Although the differences in efficacy may be relatively small between older and newer drugs, EPS—particularly akathisia—can make patients feel miserable. As a result, patients on newer agents are likely to feel substantially better, and this is likely to result in substantially better adherence to drug treatment.

Other evidence suggesting advantages for the SGAs comes from studies that focused on dimensions of psychopathology other than positive symptoms. This possibility was first suggested by studies of clozapine. In a multicenter study comparing clozapine with chlorpromazine in severely ill treatment-refractory patients (13), clozapine resulted in greater improvement in nearly every dimension of psychopathology. Clozapine-treated patients were less depressed and less anxious. In addition, they demonstrated substantial improvements in items from the Brief Psychiatric Rating Scale (BPRS) that measured emotional withdrawal, motor retardation, and blunted affect. These items probably reflect the negative symptoms of schizophrenia and suggest that clozapine is more effective for negative symptoms than a conventional antipsychotic.

The advantages of clozapine and other newer antipsychotics for negative symptoms are still controversial. Clozapine has been the most carefully studied. Short-term trials such as the Kane et al. study (13) suggest an advantage for clozapine in negative symptoms. However, these advantages could be a result of improvements in so-called secondary negative symptoms. That is, negative symptoms will improve as patients improve in positive symptoms or as their mood improves. In addition, an advantage related to reduced EPS will appear as an advantage in negative symptoms. For these reasons, longer-term studies are probably a better indicator of the relative effects of an agent on negative symptoms. In these trials, clozapine has not been shown to have an advantage in negative symptoms (21,22). The issue is similar for studies of the other new antipsychotics: The short-term advantages of newer drugs for negative symptoms are less apparent during long-term treatment. It is interesting to note that studies have found advantages of clozapine (23) and olanzapine (24) for improving social adjustment during long-term treatment. This suggests that the measures of negative symptoms that are commonly used in these studies fail to measure the advantages of SGAs accurately. For example, the Rosenheck study found that patients who received clozapine were more likely to participate in psychosocial treatments. This suggests that the amotivation that is a critical component of negative symptoms demonstrates greater improvement on clozapine.

Other studies (reviewed by Keefe [25] and discussed later in this chapter) suggest that newer drugs also have advantages for neurocognitive functioning. Individuals with schizophrenia may have impairments in a number of neurocognitive domains, including memory, attention, and executive functioning. These impairments can have important effects on a patient's long-term social and vocational outcome. Therefore these advantages may be important in selecting an agent for patients with neurocognitive symptoms.

Another important consideration in selecting an antipsychotic is the available routes of administration. Antipsychotics can be administered as short-acting intramuscular agents for rapidly controlling agitated patients or as long-acting depot agents. Long-acting drugs (including fluphenazine decanoate and haloperidol decanoate in the United States and a variety of other agents elsewhere) are antipsychotics that are administered in a long-acting injectable form. An injection administered once every 2 to 4 weeks or longer provides a relatively stable drug level in the interval between injections. These long-acting drugs have important advantages for the stable phase of schizophrenia since the delivery of the drug does not depend on a patient tak-

TMAP

❖ *The Algorithms*

Antipsychotic Algorithm

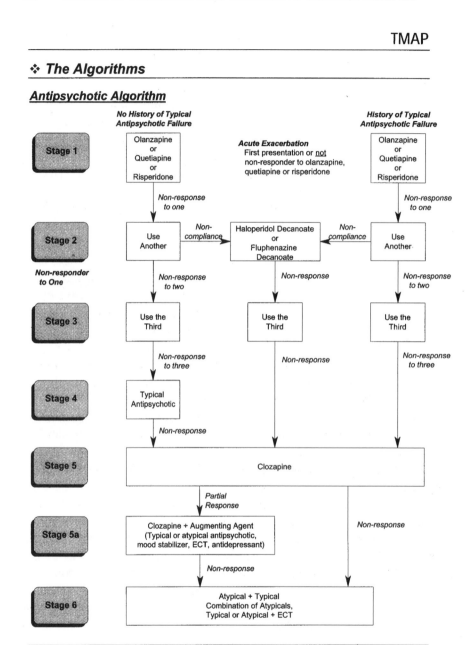

FIG. 5.1. Texas Medication Algorithm Project (TMAP).

ing his or her pills. As a result, they represent an effective means for treating patients who are known to be poor compliers. If the treatment plan includes the use of either a short-acting or a long-acting intramuscular form of the drug, patients should probably be treated with the oral form of the same drug.

A patient's personal preferences may also be helpful in selecting an agent. Patients who experience a poor subjective response to a drug because of uncomfortable side effects are likely to do poorly on that agent, usually because they are unlikely to take it reliably. Van Putten (26) found that a patient's response to a question such as, "Does this medication agree with you?" was a powerful predictor of that patient's treatment adherence.

Clozapine should not be administered as a first-line agent. The most important reason for limiting clozapine to a second-line agent is its tendency to cause agranulocytosis in some patients. This adverse effect occurs in less than 1% of clozapine-treated patients but is potentially fatal if it is not diagnosed at a relatively early stage. For this reason patients receiving clozapine are required to participate in a regular program of white blood cell monitoring. In addition, clozapine is associated with other side effects, such as sedation, postural hypotension, hypersalivation (or drooling), and seizures.

Thioridazine (Mellaril) and mesoridazine (Serentil) are also second-line agents. Although these drugs had been widely prescribed before the introduction of the SGAs, recent studies found they were associated with prolongation of the QT interval of the electrocardiogram. As a result, these agents have the potential for causing fatal ventricular arrhythmias.

A number of treatment algorithms have been developed to assist clinicians in selecting a drug. The most influential and the most useful is the Texas Medication Treatment Algorithm project, or TMAP (Fig. 5.1). Although for most patients the basis for deciding among antipsychotics is not based on empirical studies, the algorithm was developed with expert consultation and provides reasonable guidance to clinicians. It advocates the use of second-generation antipsychotics before older agents and suggests that clozapine be prescribed after all the newer agents have been tried. In our opinion, this is reasonable in most cases, although we believe that clozapine should be prescribed sooner in patients who fail one or two agents when psychosis remains severe.

Dopamine Receptor Antagonists

The dopamine receptor antagonists (or DAs) include all the conventional antipsychotic drugs. These agents are usually categorized as having low, medium, or high potency, depending on the drug dose that is effective for managing psychosis. For example, haloperidol is high potency, since as little as 2 to 20 mg daily is effective for treating psychosis, whereas chlorpromazine, a low-potency agent, requires 300 to 1,000 mg daily to be effective. The potency of the drug is also associated with its ability to block D_2 dopamine receptors. That is, DAs are effective when they occupy about 80% of dopamine receptors. A much lower dose of haloperidol will result in this level of receptor occupancy than with chlorpromazine. As a result, high-potency agents are more likely to cause EPS and low-potency agents are more likely to cause sedation, anticholinergic side effects (including dry mouth, constipation, and blurred vision), and postural hypotension (or dizziness when rising).

The DAs can also be categorized according to their chemical group. The first antipsychotics were the phenothiazines, which included chlorpromazine, thioridazine, perphenazine, and fluphenazine. This group was followed by the butyrophenones (e.g., haloperidol) and the thioxanthenes (e.g., thiothixene). As noted in Table 5.1, the side profiles of these agents are associated with their potency rather than the chemical class.

There are factors that can be useful in choosing among these agents. As mentioned earlier, fluphenazine and haloperidol are available in long-acting, injectable forms. Thioridazine is associated with retinal pigmentation at higher doses. As a result, patients should not be treated with more than 800 mg daily. Thioridazine should be considered a second-line agent since it is associated with substantial prolonging of the QT interval (or the adjusted Qtc) of the electrocardiogram. For this reason thioridazine should not be combined with other drugs that prolong the QT or with drugs such as paroxetine that can inhibit its metabolism. Haloperidol is recommended for pregnant patients because more data support its safety and not because it has proven to be safer than other drugs.

Side Effects of Dopamine Receptor Antagonists

Acute Extrapyramidal Syndromes

The most common and probably the most distressing side effects of dopamine receptor antagonists are acute extrapyramidal side effects or EPSs. These syndromes consist of (a) acute dystonias that are intermittent and sustained spasms of the muscles of the head and the neck, leading to involuntary movements; (b) akathisias, which consist of a subjective experience of restlessness with or without restless motor movements; and (c) drug-induced parkinsonism, which includes all the common motor symptoms of idiopathic parkinsonism, including rigidity, bradykinesia, shuffling gait, and tremor.

Although dystonias are the least common manifestation of EPS, they can be the most frightening. Patients may experience the sudden onset of uncomfortable paralysis that may affect the neck, the tongue, the eye muscles, or other muscle groups. Dystonias often occur during the first hours or days of drug treatment and are more common in younger patients, particularly young men. An antiparkinson medication such as benztropine frequently prevents dystonias. When dystonias occur they nearly always respond rapidly to anticholinergic antiparkinson medication. For example, 2 mg of benztropine administered intramuscularly or intravenously is usually sufficient to treat a dystonia.

Akathisias represent the most common type of EPS. When patients are administered conventional doses of a high-potency conventional dopamine antagonist, most experience some restlessness. Some patients who experience akathisia report difficulty sitting still. Others may be more anxious or irritable. A clinician who fails to inquire about the patient's feeling restless may miss the diagnosis of akathisia.

Patients with akathisia may demonstrate abnormal movements such as shifting the weight from foot to foot, walking on the spot, being unable to keep the legs still, and shifting position in a chair. Akathisias may appear during the first days of drug treatment, but more often they appear after 5 days. This side effect may be difficult to differentiate from psychotic agitation, because patients who experience severe akathisias may be angry and irritable. The problem can be compounded when the clinician, believing that the patient is experiencing psychotic agitation, increases the antipsychotic dose in individuals who are already restless.

Akathisias can be managed by reducing the antipsychotic dose, by prescribing adjunctive anticholinergic antiparkinson medications (e.g., 1 or 2 mg twice daily of benztropine), or by adding beta blockers such as propranolol (at doses of 10 to 40 mg twice daily). Studies comparing anticholinergics and beta blockers, as well as our experience, suggest that beta blockers are more effective.

Drug-induced parkinsonism affects about one-third of patients treated with a dopamine receptor antagonist. It is more common in the elderly but can affect all age groups. This side effect usually appears during the first days of drug treatment and may persist until the drug dose is reduced or an antiparkinson medication is prescribed. Drug-induced parkinsonism can be diagnosed in its milder stages by noting a decrease in the arm swing while the patient is walking. In its milder forms, drug-induced parkinsonism may also appear as a decrease in spontaneous gestures, a masked facial expression, apathy, unspontaneous speech, and difficulty in initiating usual activities. Drug-induced parkinsonism almost always responds to an anticholinergic antiparkinson medication or to amantadine. Other patients may respond to a reduction in their antipsychotic dose.

The monitoring of patients on antipsychotic medications should include regular evaluation for EPS and tardive dyskinesia. If a patient is receiving a conventional antipsychotic, each visit should include screening for parkinsonism and akathisia. The Extrapyramidal Rating Scale is a useful instrument for monitoring EPS (Fig. 5.2) (27). Patients should be administered the Abnormal Involuntary Rating Scale (AIMS) or a similar instrument for measuring tardive dyskinesia at least yearly (Fig. 5.3) (28).

SIMPSON-ANGUS SCALE (SAS)

Enter appropriate code in boxes below.

1. GAIT

SCORE
0 = Normal
1 = Mild dimunition in swing while the patient is walking
2 = Obvious dimunition in swing suggesting shoulder rigidity
3 = Stiff gait with little or no arm swinging noticeable
4 = Rigid gait with arms slightly pronated; or stooped-shuffling gait with propulsion and retropulsion
9 = Not ratable

2. ARM DROPPING

SCORE
0 = Normal, free with loud slap and rebound
1 = Fall slowed slightly with less audible contact and little rebound
2 = Fall slowed, no rebound
3 = Marked slowing, no slap at all
4 = Arms fall though against resistance; as though through glue
9 = Not ratable

3. SHOULDER SHAKING

SCORE
0 = Normal
1 = Slight stiffness and resistance
2 = Moderate stiffness and resistance
3 = Marked rigidity with difficulty in passive movement
4 = Extreme stiffness and rigidity with almost a frozen joint
9 = Not ratable

4. ELBOW RIGIDITY

SCORE
0 = Normal
1 = Slight stiffness and resistance
2 = Moderate stiffness and resistance
3 = Marked rigidity with difficulty in passive movement
4 = Extreme stiffness and rigidity with almost a frozen joint
9 = Not ratable

5. WRIST RIGIDITY

SCORE
0 = Normal
1 = Slight stiffness and resistance
2 = Moderate stiffness and resistance
3 = Marked rigidity with difficulty in passive movement
4 = Extreme stiffness and rigidity with almost a frozen joint
9 = Not ratable

6. LEG PENDULOUSNESS

SCORE
0 = The legs swing freely
1 = Slight dimunition in the swing of the legs
2 = Moderate resistance to swing
3 = Marked resistance and damping of swing
4 = Complete absence of swing
9 = Not ratable

7. HEAD DROPPING

SCORE
0 = The head falls completely with a good thump as it hits the table
1 = Slight slowing in fall, mainly noted by lack of slap as head meets the table
2 = Moderate slowing in the fall quite noticeable to the eye
3 = Head falls stiffly and slowly
4 = Head does not reach examining table
9 = Not ratable

8. GLABELLAR TAP

SCORE
0 = 0-5 blinks
1 = 6-10 blinks
2 = 11-15 blinks
3 = 16-20 blinks
4 = 21 or more blinks
9 = Not ratable

9. TREMOR

SCORE
0 = Normal
1 = Mild finger tremore, obvious to sight and touch
2 = Tremor of hand or arm occurring spasmodically
3 = Persistent tremor of one or more limbs
4 = Whole body tremor
9 = Not ratable

10. SALIVATION

SCORE
0 = Normal
1 = Excess salivation so that pooling takes place if mouth is open and tongue is raised
2 = Excess salivation is present and might occasionally result in difficulty speaking
3 = Speaking with difficulty because of excess salivation
4 = Frank drooling
9 = Not ratable

FIG. 5.2.

Abnormal Involuntary Movement Scale (AIMS)

Examination Procedure

Either before or after completing the examination procedure, observe the patient unobtrusively at rest (e.g., in the waiting room).

The chair to be used in this examination should be a hard, firm one without arms.

1. Ask the patient whether there is anything in his or her mouth (such as gum or candy) and, if so, to remove it.

2. Ask about the *current* condition of the patient's teeth. Ask if he or she wears dentures. Ask whether teeth or dentures bother the patient *now*.

3. Ask whether the patient notices any movements in his or her mouth, face, hands, or feet. If yes, ask the patient to describe them and to indicate to what extent they *currently* bother the patient or interfere with activities.

4. Have the patient sit in chair with hands on knees, legs slightly apart, and feet flat on floor. (Look at the entire body for movements while the patient is in this position.)

5. Ask the patient to sit with hands hanging unsupported—if male, between his legs, if female and wearing a dress, hanging over her knees. (Observe hands and other body areas).

6. Ask the patient to open his or her mouth. (Observe the tongue at rest within the mouth.) Do this twice.

7. Ask the patient to protrude his or her tongue. (Observe abnormalities of tongue movement.) Do this twice.

8. Ask the patient to tap his or her thumb with each finger as rapidly as possible for 10 to 15 seconds, first with right hand, then with left hand. (Observe facial and leg movements.) [±activated]

9. Flex and extend the patient's left and right arms, one at a time.

10. Ask the patient to stand up. (Observe the patient in profile. Observe all body areas again, hips included.)

11. Ask the patient to extend both arms out in front, palms down. (Observe trunk, legs, and mouth.) [activated]

12. Have the patient walk a few paces, turn, and walk back to the chair. (Observe hands and gait.) Do this twice. [activated]

FIG. 5.3.

(Continued on next page)

Scoring Procedure

Complete the examination procedure before making ratings.

For the movement ratings (the first three categories below), rate the highest severity observed. 0=none, 1=minimal (may be extreme normal), 2=mild, 3=moderate, and 4=severe. According to the original AIMS instructions, one point is subtracted if movements are seen only on activation, but not all investigators follow that convetion.

Facial and Oral Movements

1. Muscles of facial expression,
   e.g., movements of forehead, eyebrows, periorbital area, cheeks. Include frowning, blinking, grimacing of upper face.

   0 1 2 3 4

2. Lips and perioral area,
   e.g., puckering, pouting, smacking.

   0 1 2 3 4

3. Jaw,
   e.g., biting, clenching, chewing, mouth opening, lateral movement.

   0 1 2 3 4

4. Tongue,
   Rate only increase in movement both in and out of mouth, not inability to sustain movement.

   0 1 2 3 4

Extremity Movements

5. Upper (arms, wrists, hands, fingers),
   Include movements that are chronic (rapid, objectively purposeless, irregular, spontaneous) or athetoid (slow, irregular, complex, serpentine). Do not include tremor (repetitive, regular, rhythmic movements).

   0 1 2 3 4

6. Lower (legs, knees, ankles, toes),
   e.g., lateral knee movement, foot tapping, heel dropping, foot squirming, inversion and eversion of foot.

   0 1 2 3 4

FIG. 5.3. *Continued.*

Trunk Movements

7. Neck, shoulders, hips,
   e.g., rocking, twisting, squirming, pelvic gyrations. Include diaphragmatic movements.

   0 1 2 3 **4**

Global Judgements

8. Severity of abnormal movements.

   0 1 2 3 4
   based on the highest single score on the above items.

9. Incapacitation due to abnormal movements.

   0 = none, normal
   1 = minimal
   2 = mild
   3 = moderate
   4 = severe

10. Patient's awareness of abnormal movements.

    0 = no awareness
    1 = aware, no distress
    2 = aware, mild distress
    3 = aware, moderate distress
    4 = aware, severe distress

Dental Status

11. Current problems with teeth and/or dentures.

    0 = no
    1 = yes

12. Does patient usually wear dentures?

    0 = no
    1 = yes

FIG. 5.3. *Continued.*

Endocrine Effects

Conventional antipsychotics (and risperidone) influence the secretion of hormones in the pituitary and elsewhere, mainly due to their blockade of dopamine receptors. All conventional antipsychotics increase serum prolactin concentration in the usual clinical dose range (29). This occurs because prolactin secretion by the anterior pituitary is tonically inhibited by dopamine. Therefore blockade of dopamine receptors in the tuberoinfundibular pathway results in prolactin elevation. This sometimes produces gynecomastia (the development of breast tissue in men) and galactorrhea (the secretion of fluid from a woman's breast). Antipsychotics also suppress levels of luteinizing hormone (LH) and follicle stimulating hormone (FSH) (30).

The hormonal effects of these agents can be clinically important. Women may develop amenorrhea and inhibition of orgasms. Chronic elevations in prolactin may also decrease libido and lead to osteoporosis, although this remains unsubstantiated. Nevertheless, when the only available antipsychotics elevated prolactin, these side effects were usually viewed as acceptable. However, in the presence of these side effects and an elevated prolactin, clinicians should consider a change to olanzapine, ziprasidone, quetiapine, or clozapine.

Second-Generation Antipsychotics or Serotonin Dopamine Antagonists

The second-generation antipsychotics (SGAs) or the serotonin dopamine antagonists (SDAs) are associated with a much lower potential for causing EPS when compared with DAs. Since EPS is usually the most disturbing antipsychotic side effect, the availability of these newer agents is an important breakthrough. Although most patients who are changed to an SDA will report a substantial improvement in the way they feel, these drugs are also associated with other side effects. As noted in Tables 5.3 and 5.4, there are substantial differences in the receptor profiles and the side effects of the different SGAs. For this reason these agents will be discussed separately.

Clozapine

Clozapine's history is interesting in that it reveals how a highly effective drug was almost lost to psychiatry. From early trials that were completed during the 1970s it was clear that clozapine was a very effective antipsychotic with negligible EPS. The enthusiasm generated by clozapine turned to despair when patients died from agranulocytosis. This led to a near halt in research on clozapine and attempts to change patients to other agents. However, some deteriorated substantially when they were switched. These

TABLE 5.3. Side effects of selected antipsychotics

	Conventional antipsychotic	Clozapine	Risperidone	Olanzapine	Quetiapine	Ziprasidone
Agranulocytosis	±	++	±	±	±	±
Anticholinergic	± to +++	+++	±	+ to ++	±	±
EPS	+ to +++	0 to ±	± to +	± to +	0 to +	± to +
Orthostatic hypotension	+ to +++	+++	++	+	++	+
Seizures	± to +	++ to +++	±	±	±	±
Prolactin elevation	++ to +++	0	++	±	±	±
Sedation	+ to +++	+++	+	++	++	+
Tardive dyskensia	+++	0	±	±	±	±
Weight gain	+ to +++	+++	++	+++	++	+

Key: 0, none; ±, slight; +, low; ++, moderate; +++, high–moderate. EPS, extrapyramidal side effects.

TABLE 5.4. *Receptor affinities for selected antipsychotics*

	Dopamine D$_2$	Serotonin 5-HT$_{2A}$	Adrenergic α_1	Histamine H$_1$	Muscarinic M$_1$
Clozapine	++	+++	+++	++++	++++
Risperidone	++++	++++	++	++	0
Olanzapine	+++	+++	+++	++++	++++
Quetiapine	++	+	++++	++++	+
Ziprasidone	++++	++++	++	+	0
Haloperidol	++++	0	+	0	0

Key: 0, none; ±, slight; +, low; ++, moderate; +++, high–moderate; ++++, high.
Adapted from Pickar D. Prospects for pharmacotherapy of schizoprenia. *Lancet* 1995; 345:557–562.

patients were changed back to clozapine and carefully monitored with regular white blood cell counts. It was subsequently confirmed that clozapine-induced agranulocytosis was reversible. If clozapine was discontinued before patients developed infections, the drug could be administered safely (31). Moreover, studies revealed that clozapine was particularly effective for patients who were severely ill and for those who failed to respond to conventional DAs.

These observations led to attempts to gain approval for clozapine in the United States for patients who failed to respond to other antipsychotics. This resulted in a multicenter study (13) in which severely ill inpatients with a history of poor responsiveness to at least three antipsychotics were assigned to a 6-week comparison of either clozapine or chlorpromazine with benztropine. Clozapine was significantly more effective on a broad range of psychopathology that included both positive and negative symptoms. It is interesting to note that clozapine patients improved more than those on chlorpromazine in nearly everything that was measured in the study. Clozapine-treated individuals were less anxious, less depressed, and less agitated. This breadth of improvement suggested that clozapine was not only more effective than the older agent, but qualitatively different. These advantages of clozapine were confirmed after the drug was available in the United States in 1990.

In the multicenter trial of Kane and co-workers (13) 30% of clozapine-treated patients met stringent improvement criteria. However, this study lasted only 6 weeks. Other studies suggest that this percentage would have been substantially higher if the study had continued for a longer time. For example, a 16-week trial by Pickar et al. (32) found a 38% improvement rate. A more recent report (33) found that 60% of treatment-refractory patients improved after a 29-week trial with clozapine.

Other studies suggest other advantages of clozapine. A study of patients in Connecticut State Hospitals (34) found that patients who were discharged from the hospital on clozapine were more likely to remain out of the hospital. A VA Cooperative Study (35) found that clozapine was also associated with a decreased need for hospitalization. In addition, clozapine-treated patients experienced improvement in their quality of life.

Clozapine Side Effects

The most serious side effect of clozapine is agranulocytosis, which is potentially fatal. Agranulocytosis, by definition, occurs when the absolute neutrophil count is below 500/mm^3. Recent data indicated that only 0.38% of clozapine-treated patients developed agranulocytosis and 2.95% developed leukopenia (or a low white blood cell count). The death rate from clozapine-induced agranulocytosis was only 0.012%, indicating that with the monitoring system, clozapine is a safe compound. Most cases of agranulocytosis appear during the first 3 months of treatment. After 6 months the risk for agranulocytosis decreases substantially.

In the United States clozapine patients are monitored with a weekly blood count for the first 6 months, followed by monitoring every other week. Guidelines for monitoring patients on clozapine are as follows: If the white blood count (WBC) is 3,000 to 3,500 and the neutrophil count is less than 1,500, the WBC should be monitored twice weekly until the count is greater than 3,500. If the WBC is 2,000 to 3,000 or the neutrophil count is 1,000 to 1,500, clozapine should be discontinued and the WBC should be checked daily. If the WBC is less than 2,000 or the neutrophil count is below 1,000, patients should be considered to have agranulocytosis; clozapine should be discontinued and the WBC count should be followed daily. At this time, patients should be monitored for evidence of infection and protective isolation, and bone marrow aspiration should be considered.

When agranulocytosis is diagnosed, the patient should be followed by a hematologist and the addition of granulocyte colony stimulating factor (GCSF) should be considered. Most patients recover within 2 to 3 weeks. Those who have developed agranulocytosis should not be rechallenged with clozapine, since they are at greater risk of developing agranulocytosis.

The most common side effect of clozapine is sedation, which is experienced by most clozapine patients. This is also the side effect that most commonly limits the dose of clozapine. Other common side effects include hypersalivation, tachycardia, orthostatic hypotension, constipation, and weight gain. Clozapine can induce seizures in a substantial proportion of patients. Patients who experience seizures are often doing well on clozapine and can usually be managed by reducing the dose or by adding an anticonvulsant such as valproic acid. The tachycardia can usually be adequately managed by adding a beta-blocker such as atenolol. The hypersalivation from clozapine is usually most prominent when the patient is asleep. Patients complain of waking in the night with the experience that they are choking on their saliva. Some complain of sufficient amounts of saliva to soak their pillow. The hypersalivation is probably related to decreased swallowing of saliva rather than to increased production. For this reason anticholinergic agents are seldom helpful. Although a number of treatments have been tried, none are effective, and management is usually confined to adjusting the clozapine dose or placing a towel on the patient's pillow.

Weight gain with clozapine can be a particularly difficult side effect. A meta-analysis by Allison and co-workers (36) found that clozapine was associated with an average weight gain of 4.45 kg over 10 weeks. Clinicians have found occasional patients who respond to clozapine but at the cost of 50 or more pounds of weight gain. Recent attention has also focused on patients who develop diabetes during clozapine treatment. One study found that nearly 37% of clozapine-treated patients developed diabetes (37). Although the mechanism is unclear, the weight gain with clozapine may contribute, as may a resistance to insulin (38). Approaches to weight gain and the onset of diabetes are discussed in Chapter 9.

Prescribing Clozapine

Patients who are treated with clozapine should be enrolled in a program that ensures that weekly blood monitoring occurs for the first 6 months and that every-other-week monitoring takes place thereafter. Patients are usually started on 12.5 mg and the dose is gradually increased by 25-mg increments until patients reach the therapeutic range. This range is commonly between 300 and 500 mg daily. Sedation and orthostatic hypotension usually limit the rate at which clozapine's dose can be increased. Once patients reach the therapeutic range, it may take 3 to 6 months for patients to demonstrate a therapeutic response. For this reason most patients who are treated with clozapine should have a trial that lasts at least 3 months. If patients show no improvement at all for 3 months, it is unlikely that they will respond to clozapine. If, on the other hand, they demonstrate modest or minimal improvement, it may be useful to observe them for a longer period of time to determine the extent to which they will eventually improve.

Monitoring clozapine plasma levels can be useful under some circumstances. A number of studies (39–41) have found that clozapine levels that fall below a certain level—usually below 350 ng/mL—are usually associated with an inadequate response. This suggests two circumstances when ordering a clozapine level may be helpful. First, when patients are demonstrating an inadequate therapeutic response and the plasma level is low, a dosage increase may be helpful. In addition, when patients are experiencing side effects such as sedation or hypotension and the clozapine level is high, a dosage reduction may be useful.

Selecting Patients for Clozapine

When newer antipsychotics were introduced after clozapine it was hoped that these agents would have clozapine's pattern of effectiveness and a much better side effect profile. Although all the newer agents are much easier to administer than clozapine, it is unclear if any can reproduce clozapine's effects in severely ill patients who are refractory to conventional dopamine antagonists. Although some later studies suggest that newer agents are as effective as clozapine in populations of treatment-refractory patients (14), these agents have rarely been studied in the severely ill individuals represented in the multicenter clozapine study (13). Given the difficulties in prescribing clozapine, such as the need for blood monitoring and the range of side effects, it is reasonable to give refractory patients a trial on one of the newer second-generation drugs before they receive clozapine. If the patient fails to recover on one or more new drugs, a trial of clozapine should be considered. Clinicians should also consider the cost of delaying a clozapine trial in patients who may respond. The time spent on less effective drugs may mean weeks or months of delayed recovery and time lost.

Risperidone

Risperidone was first introduced in the United States in 1994 or about 4 years after the approval of clozapine. It was the first of a group of newer second-generation antipsychotics (SGAs) characterized by substantial 5-HT$_{2A}$ as well as D$_2$ activity. Risperidone shares with the other SDAs the property of causing minimal EPS at clinically effective doses. There is also evidence that risperidone shares clozapine's property of being more effective than conventional agents at treating negative and cognitive symptoms of schizophrenia. Unlike clozapine, risperidone has a relatively benign side effect profile. As a result, it can be prescribed as a first-line antipsychotic.

Effectiveness of Risperidone

A number of double-blind and uncontrolled studies support risperidone's effectiveness (reviewed in ref. 12). The largest risperidone study (42) was a multinational study that was carried out in several European, South American, and Asian countries as well as in South Africa. In this trial, patients with schizophrenia were randomly assigned to a double-blind comparison of 10 mg daily of haloperidol or 1, 4, 8, 12, or 16 mg of risperidone. The 1-mg risperidone dose was used as the comparator, since it was considered to be a relatively ineffective dose. This proved to be the case since all the other risperidone doses as well as the haloperidol group demonstrated greater improvement on the total Positive and Negative Syndrome Scale (PANSS) than the 1-mg risperidone group. Nevertheless, it is interesting to note that more than 50% of the 1-mg risperidone patients met criteria for improvement. This suggests that doses as low as 1 mg may be effective for some patients. In this study, the 4- and 8-mg risperidone doses were the most effective. This finding is important since another study (the North American trial, discussed later) found 6 mg to be the most effective dose.

The most important placebo-controlled trial was carried out in Canada (43) and the United States (44). Acutely ill patients with schizophrenia were randomly assigned to groups that received 2, 6, 12, or 16 mg of risperidone; 20 mg of haloperidol; or placebo. Clinical outcome was evaluated with the PANSS. EPS was measured using the Extrapyramidal Symptom Rating Scale and by monitoring the prescribing of antiparkinson medications.

The results from the United States and Canadian studies were nearly identical. In the larger U.S. trial, risperidone at doses above 2 mg and haloperidol 20 mg were consistently more effective for total PANSS and positive symptoms than placebo. The most effective dose of risperidone was 6 mg, which was significantly more effective than haloperidol. Risperidone 6 and 16 mg, but not haloperidol, resulted in significant improvements in negative symptoms as measured by the PANSS. There were similar results when the proportion of patients meeting criteria for improvement (20% or greater improvement in total PANSS or BPRS) was considered (Fig. 5.1).

More recently, the findings from the Canadian and U.S. trial have been combined and reanalyzed (45). The original study analyzed data using three psychopathologic dimensions: positive, negative, and general psychopathology. The reanalysis used factor analysis to identify the dimensions of psychopathology. Five factors were identified that corresponded to positive symptoms, negative symptoms, disorganized symptoms, anxiety/depression, and excitement agitation. When the risperidone doses that were effective (i.e., 6 to 16 mg) were combined, risperidone was more effective for all five factors than placebo. In addition, the largest differences between risperidone and haloperidol were in items that were related to negative symptoms and anxiety/depression. Careful analysis of the data indicated that these advantages of risperidone were not related to its lower likelihood of causing EPS. These results are consistent with the findings with clozapine, which suggest that newer antipsychotics are qualitatively different from older drugs and the differences are likely to be found in advantages for negative symptoms as well as depression and anxiety. A limitation of this study was that haloperidol was prescribed at 20 mg, a dose that many consider too high.

Other studies have focused on the effects of risperidone on the neurocognitive symptoms in schizophrenia. Individuals with schizophrenia often demonstrate impairments in attention, memory, and concentration. Students who have recently developed this illness may complain of an inability to read with comprehension or to study. Research indicates that the severity of these neurocognitive symptoms is related to the severity of educational and vocational disability in schizophrenia. A recent study by Michael Green (46) indicates that risperidone may be more effective than older drugs for verbal working memory. Verbal working memory is the type of memory that one uses to memorize a telephone number for a brief period of time. Rather than storing the number in long-term memory, one is likely to forget the number after it is dialed. Being able to maintain information in working memory is probably important for most information processing. A student with impaired working memory might have difficulty reading with adequate comprehension. Many patients with schizophrenia have impairments in working memory, which affects their ability to work or succeed in school. If further studies with risperidone or other new antipsychotics indicate that these agents are effective for working memory, this would be an important innovation in the management of schizophrenia. Other studies with risperidone indicate that it also has advantages for secondary or long-term memory (47).

Side Effects of Risperidone

The most characteristic feature of risperidone and all the newer antipsychotics is their relatively weak tendency to cause EPS, including stiffness and restlessness, at their effective doses. This does not mean that risperidone does not cause EPS. Risperidone is associated with EPS, particularly at higher doses. However, in contrast to such drugs as haloperidol, most patients can be treated with a dose of risperidone that does not cause discomforting EPS. For example, in the U.S. and Canadian trial that was discussed previously (43,44), the most effective dose of risperidone, 6 mg daily, was associated with similar rates of using such anti-EPS drugs as benztropine (Cogentin) or trihexyphenidyl (Artane) as placebo. Since the average dose of risperidone is probably close to 4 mg daily, it is apparent that finding an effective dose that does not cause EPS is usually possible.

Other side effects of risperidone include mild sedation, weight gain, and postural hypotension, which is a tendency for blood pressure to fall when a person stands or sits up. Risperidone can also cause sexual problems in men. These problems with erections and ejaculation may be experienced as a loss of sexual potency and may cause men to stop taking their medication. It is important that patients verbalize these concerns to their clinicians since they can usually be reassured that this is a side effect that often can be managed.

Risperidone, along with all the older antipsychotics, also elevates prolactin, a hormone that is secreted by the pituitary gland. Elevations in prolactin can lead to irregular menstrual periods in women as well as secretions
from the breast. Chronic elevations in prolactin may also decrease libido in
both men and women.

Dosing of Risperidone

When risperidone was first marketed in the United States its manufacturer,
Janssen Pharmaceuticals, recommended that most patients receive 6 mg a
day. It was further recommended that patients be started on 2 mg the first day
(to minimize hypotension), increased to 4 mg the second day, and stabilized
on 6 mg. However, experience with risperidone indicated that many patients
did well on lower doses. There is an emerging consensus in both Europe and
the United States that the average dose of risperidone for treating schizophrenia is about 4 mg daily. Others require doses up to 16 mg for an optimal
response. Elderly patients frequently start on 0.5 mg daily and stabilize on
0.5 to 2 mg daily.

A reasonable dosing strategy for risperidone is to start patients with schizophrenia on 2 mg daily. If patients have a history of increased sensitivity to
EPS, they should be maintained on that dose for 2 to 6 weeks. Otherwise, if
the dose of 2 mg daily is well tolerated for 1 or 2 days, the dose can be increased to 4 mg daily. Patients who fail to improve on this dose can be increased to 5 or 6 mg if they fail to improve after a 4- to 6-week trial.

Olanzapine

Olanzapine was introduced in the United States, Canada, and most of Europe in 1996. It resembles clozapine in that it affects a number of neurore-
ceptors in addition to 5-HT2A and D_2. These include 5-HT_{2c}, 5-HT_3, 5-HT_6,
α_1, D_1, D_4, M_1, and H_1 receptors. But in contrast to clozapine, it has a remarkably benign side effect profile and is relatively easy for clinicians to
prescribe and for patients to take. When olanzapine is administered orally it
has a half-life of about 31 hours, which indicates that patients can be treated
with a single daily dose. Since it has relatively weak affinity for hepatic P450
cytochromes, it is unlikely to be associated with significant drug/drug interactions.

Effectiveness of Olanzapine

The largest study of olanzapine was an international trial in which patients
received 5 to 20 mg of either haloperidol or olanzapine (48). Clinicians
titrated olanzapine patients to a mean dose of 13.2 mg daily, and haloperidol

patients were titrated to 11.8 mg. Since this study included 1,996 patients, it provides useful information regarding the relative efficacy of the two agents. Olanzapine was significantly more effective than haloperidol in improving total scores on the BPRS. In addition, negative symptoms on the PANSS demonstrated greater improvement on olanzapine. Depressive symptoms as measured by the Montgomery-Asberg Depression Rating Scale (MADRS) also demonstrated significantly greater improvement with olanzapine. There was no significant difference in positive symptoms.

Olanzapine's effectiveness was also evaluated in a double-blind comparison of three dose ranges of olanzapine (2.5 to 7.5, 7.5 to 12.5, 12.5 to 17.5 mg/day), haloperidol (10 to 20 mg/day), or placebo in 335 patients with schizophrenia (49). The middle and highest doses of olanzapine and haloperidol (i.e., 7.5 to 17.5 mg/day) were more effective than placebo on total BPRS as well as positive symptoms. Both the low-dose and the high-dose ranges of olanzapine (but not the middle range or haloperidol) were more effective than placebo on the Scale for the Assessment of Negative Symptoms (SANS). This study indicates that the higher dose range of 12.5 to 17.5 mg/day is probably the most appropriate for treating acute psychosis in schizophrenia. This is also consistent with the experiences of clinicians who have prescribed olanzapine since its introduction. In the United States, the average dose of olanzapine for acute schizophrenia is in the range of 15 to 20 mg daily.

There is also evidence that olanzapine can be effective in improving the cognitive disturbances associated with schizophrenia. One study (50) found that treatment with olanzapine led to improvements in a number of cognitive areas, including memory, attention, motor skills, and executive functioning.

Side Effects of Olanzapine

Short-term treatment with olanzapine is characterized by a remarkably benign side effect profile. An idea of its side effects can be gained from a study in which an overview of a drug's side effect profile can be gained from comparing the agent to a placebo. In the study by Beasley and co-workers (49), the most common side effects of olanzapine were somnolence (39% versus 16% on placebo), dizziness (17% versus 3% on placebo), and constipation (15% versus 0 on placebo). Only 5.8% of the patients who received the higher dose range (12.5 to 17.5 mg daily) were discontinued because of adverse effects (compared with 10.3% on placebo). This indicates that olanzapine is very well tolerated in acute treatment.

The large study ($N = 1,996$) comparing 5 to 20 mg of olanzapine and haloperidol provides an opportunity to compare olanzapine with a conventional antipsychotic (48). Patients who received haloperidol were more likely to experience EPS, psychomotor activation, vomiting, and weight loss, whereas those who received olanzapine were more likely to experience dry mouth, weight gain, and increased appetite (49). Those who received haloperidol were more likely to have their medication discontinued for adverse effects (7.3%) than those who received olanzapine (4.5%).

Measures of EPS support olanzapine's low liability. In the previously mentioned double-blind studies (48,49) rates of EPS as measured by the Simpson-Angus Scale were substantially and significantly higher on haloperidol. In the Beasley et al. study, EPS ratings were no greater on olanzapine than on placebo. Another method of comparing EPS on two agents is to compare the use of anticholinergic medications for EPS. The proportion of patients receiving anticholinergics on olanzapine and placebo was similar. In addition, rates of akathisia as measured by the Barnes Akathisia Scale were similar on olanzapine and placebo (Fig. 5.4). These findings and clinical experience indicate that olanzapine is associated with very little EPS in doses to 17.5 mg. No data are available regarding EPS at doses of 20 mg or more daily.

As mentioned earlier, olanzapine is associated with a risk of weight gain. In acute studies weight gain was in the range of 2 to 3 kg (49). When the results of several studies were combined, 40.5% of olanzapine patients gained 7% or more of their weight compared with 12.4 % of patients who received haloperidol. This is consistent with the observations of clinicians who have confirmed that weight gain is one of the most common adverse effects associated with olanzapine treatment. There is also evidence that olanzapine can be associated with hyperglycemia and the emergence of diabetes. This possible side effect is discussed in greater detail in Chapter 9.

Olanzapine appears to be less likely to elevate prolactin above normal levels than conventional dopamine receptor antagonists. Although it is associated with transient prolactin elevation, patients treated with olanzapine had levels that returned to the normal range (49). This is an important advantage of olanzapine since women on conventional agents or risperidone may develop irregular menstrual periods or galactorrhea.

Starting Patients on Olanzapine

Olanzapine can be prescribed at an initial dose of 5 or 10 mg daily, depending on the patient's sensitivity to medications. Elderly patients may be started to 2.5 to 5 mg daily. Most adult, nonelderly patients with schizophrenia respond to doses in the range of 10 to 20 mg daily, but some require 25 mg. Case reports suggest that some patients respond to higher doses. Elderly patients should be treated with 2.5 to 7.5 mg/day. As mentioned earlier, olanzapine can be administered in a single daily dose.

BARNES AKATHISIA RATING SCALE (BAS, BARS)

INSTRUCTIONS

Patient should be observed while seated, and then standing while engaged in neutral conversation (for a minimum of 2 minutes in each position). Symptoms observed in other situations, for example, while engaged in activity on the ward, may also be treated. Subsequently, the **subjective** phenomena should be elicited by direct questioning. Put appropriate code in box below.

OBJECTIVE

0 = Normal, occasional fidgety movements of the limbs

1 = Presence of characteristic restless movements: shuffling or tramping movements of the legs and feet or swinging of one leg, while sitting, *and/or* rocking from foot to foot or "walking on the spot" when standing, *but* movements present for less than half the time observed

2 = Observed phenomena, as described in (1) above, which are present for at least half the observation period

3 = Patient is constantly engaged in characteristic restless movements, *and/or* has the inability to remain seated or standing without walking or pacing, during the time observed

SUBJECTIVE
AWARENESS OF RESTLESSNESS

0 = Absence of inner restlessness

1 = Nonspecific sense of inner restlessness

2 = Patient is aware of an inability to keep the legs still, or a desire to move the legs, *and/or* complains of inner restlessness aggravated specifically by being required to stand still

3 = Awareness of an intense compulsion to move most of the time *and/or* reports a strong desire to walk or pace most of the time

DISTRESS RELATED TO RESTLESSNESS

0 = No distress

1 = Mild

2 = Moderate

3 = Severe

GLOBAL CLINICAL ASSESSMENT OF AKATHISIA

0 = *Absent* – no evidence of awareness of restlessness. Observation of characteristic movements of akathisia in the absence of a subjective report of inner restlessness or compulsive desire to move the legs should be classified as pseudoakathisia

1 = *Questionable* – nonspecific inner tension and fidgety movements

2 = *Mild Akathisia* – awareness of restlessness in the legs *and/or* restlessness worse when required to stand still. Fidgety movements present, but characteristic restless movements of akathisia not necessarily observed. Condition causes little or no distress.

3 = *Moderate Akathisia* – awareness of restfulness as described for mild akathisia above, combined with characteristic restless movements such as rocking from foot to foot when standing. Patient finds the condition distressing.

4 = *Marked Akathisia* – subjective experience of restlessness includes a compulsive desire to walk or pace. However, the patient is able to remain seated for at least 5 minutes. The condition is obviously distressing.

5 = *Severe Akathisia* – the patient reports a strong compulsion to pace up and down most of the time. Unable to site or lie down for more than a few minutes. Constant restlessness which is associated with intense distress and insomnia.

FIG. 5.4.

Quetiapine

Quetiapine is a dibenzothiazepine derivative with low to moderate affinity for 5-HT_{1A} and 5-HT_{2A}, moderate to high activity for α_1, and α_2, and H_1 receptors, but weaker activity at D_1 and D_2 receptors. In contrast to risperidone and olanzapine, quetiapine has a low affinity for D_2 receptors. This may explain why quetiapine has very low liability for causing EPS. An interesting characteristic of quetiapine is that it appears to have lower D_2 occupancy 12 hours after dosing than any other effective antipsychotic, including clozapine (51). However, there is a transient increase in occupancy to about 60% for 2 to 3 hours after dosing. This suggests that even transitory increases in D_2 occupancy may be sufficient for eliciting an antipsychotic response.

One limitation of quetiapine is that it has a relatively short half-life of about 7 hours. With most agents this half-life would indicate that a drug should be administered at least three times daily. However, receptors remain occupied after quetiapine blood levels have fallen, suggesting that twice-daily dosing should be sufficient. The effectiveness of twice-daily dosing is also supported by a clinical trial that compared the administration of quetiapine two or three times daily (52).

Efficacy of Quetiapine

A number of studies demonstrate that quetiapine is an effective antipsychotic. One study (53) compared a low dose of quetiapine (up to 250 mg daily), a higher dose (up to 750 mg), and a placebo. The higher dose of quetiapine was more effective than placebo for BPRS total scores. An interesting feature of this study was that the higher dose was also significantly more effective in reducing summary scores on the Scale for the Assessment of Negative Symptoms (SANS), indicating that quetiapine appears to be effective for negative symptoms. In another trial (54), 5 doses of quetiapine (75, 150, 300, 600, and 750 mg daily), 12 mg of haloperidol, and placebo were compared in 361 patients. The findings indicate that quetiapine in the range of 150 to 800 mg daily is more effective than a placebo. In this study, the most effective dose of quetiapine was 300 mg. However, clinical experience suggests that the most effective doses of quetiapine are much higher. The clinical experiences of many psychiatrists indicate that most patients tend to do well on doses greater than 500 mg daily.

Side Effects of Quetiapine

The most common side effects of quetiapine are drowsiness and postural hypotension. These effects can usually be minimized by starting patients on a low dose of quetiapine (e.g., 25 mg twice daily) and gradually titrating the dosage upward. Less common side effects include headache, constipation, dry mouth, and tachycardia (or rapid heartbeat). Although the EPS liability of quetiapine has not been directly compared with other new drugs, it appears to have very low levels, similar to clozapine. For example, in the large international study mentioned earlier (54), levels of EPS were similar to placebo. This lack of EPS has been supported in all the carefully done studies with quetiapine, suggesting that this drug is more similar to clozapine based on its EPS profile and its low affinity for D_2 receptors. Quetiapine does not appear to elevate serum prolactin levels above the normal range (55), indicating that it is less likely to cause galactorrhea or menstrual disturbances in women. Weight gain, a side effect of nearly all the newer agents, appears to be somewhat less than that with such agents as olanzapine or clozapine.

Quetiapine has been associated with the development of lens opacities in dogs chronically treated with the drug. Although there is no indication that humans who are treated with quetiapine are more likely to develop cataracts than patients treated with other antipsychotics (or that quetiapine even raises the vulnerability to cataracts), it is recommended that patients who are treated with quetiapine receive regular eye examinations. Since cataracts develop very slowly, patients can be started on quetiapine without an eye examination. Once it is determined that quetiapine is effective for an individual, eye examinations using a slit lamp or other methods should take place every 6 months.

Starting Patients on Quetiapine

Patients who are started on quetiapine usually tolerate 25 mg bid or tid without serious adverse effects or discomfort. The dose can then be gradually increased by 25 or 50 mg daily with monitoring for drowsiness and postural hypotension until the patient is receiving a therapeutic dose. Double-blind studies and clinical experience indicate that most patients will have an optimal response at approximately 300 mg. However, clinicians are observing that 300 mg is frequently insufficient. As a result, they are reporting that quetiapine is most effective in the range of 500 to 750 mg daily. Quetiapine is usually well tolerated up to 800 mg. As with other agents, elderly patients and children should be treated with lower doses.

Ziprasidone

Ziprasidone is a benzothiazolylpiperazine compound with a high affinity for 5-HT$_{2A}$ receptors as well as D_2 receptors. It stands out from the other second-generation antipsychotics by having a higher ratio of 5-HT$_{2A}$ to D$_2$ receptors than any of the other newer antipsychotics (56). Ziprasidone also has high affinity for 5-HT$_{1A}$, 5-HT$_{1D}$, and 5-HT$_{2C}$ receptors. In PET studies its activity resembles that of risperidone and olanzapine by occupying 77% of D$_2$ and 98% of 5-HT$_{2A}$ at effective clinical doses (57,58).

Efficacy of Ziprasidone

A number of studies in acute schizophrenia have documented that ziprasidone is an effective antipsychotic. These studies, when combined, also provide valuable information about ziprasidone's effective dose range. A study (59) comparing 4, 10, 40, and 160 mg/day of ziprasidone with 15 mg/day of haloperidol found that 160 mg appeared to be the most effective dose. Moreover, this dose of ziprasidone was associated with less EPS than haloperidol. A later study (60) clarified the dosing of ziprasidone by comparing 40 and 120 mg/day with placebo. The results indicated that the 120-mg dose was effective, whereas the 40-mg dose was similar to placebo in some measures. Daniel and co-workers (61) compared 80 and 160 mg/day of ziprasidone and placebo in a large multicenter study of acutely psychotic individuals with schizophrenia. Both of the ziprasidone doses were superior to placebo. Taken together, these studies suggest that the effective dose range is between 80 and 160 mg daily. Moreover, ziprasidone resembles the other second-generation agents in its effectiveness for positive, negative, and mood symptoms. At the time of this writing, there were no trials that focused on ziprasidone's effects on neurocognitive symptoms.

Ziprasidone was also evaluated in a long-term maintenance trial in Europe (62). The study randomized stabilized patients to 40, 80, or 160 mg/day of ziprasidone or placebo. During the following year, all three doses of ziprasidone led to a statistically significant reduction in relapse risk when compared with placebo. Patients who received ziprasidone also had reductions in negative symptoms as well as mood symptoms that were sustained through the 1-year study.

Side Effects of Ziprasidone

Ziprasidone appears to have a relatively benign side effect profile. Its high affinity for sertonergic receptors indicated that it might have a high incidence of headache and GI discomfort. However, neither appears to be a serious liability with ziprasidone (63). Acute studies have found that the most common side effects of ziprasidone are mild dyspepsia, nausea, dizziness, and mild drowsiness. In most studies, EPS—including parkinsonism and akathisia—were similar to those of placebos. Prolactin elevation with ziprasidone was transitory, with patients demonstrating small increases after the initiation of treatment followed by a return to normal levels.

One of the strong advantages of ziprasidone is its tendency to cause less weight gain than newer antipsychotics. In the review by Allison (64) weight gain on ziprasidone was negligible (0.04 kg) after 10 weeks when compared with 2.1 kg on risperidone, 4.15 kg on olanzapine, and 4.45 kg on clozapine. This is an important advantage for ziprasidone when compared with the other second-generation agents. Obesity is a serious comorbidity that is very common with schizophrenia. As mentioned earlier, there is evidence that weight gain can be severe in some patients and result in diabetes.

Ziprasidone is associated with prolongation of the QT interval of the electrocardiogram. This was a serious concern when the application for ziprasidone was first submitted to the U.S. Food and Drug Administration and led to a delay in its approval. QT prolongation is a serious concern, since it can lead to a potentially fatal ventricular arrhythmia known as "torsades de pointes." The FDA and Pfizer, the drug's developer, agreed on a study that compared the QT_c (which is the QT interval adjusted for the heart rate) of a number of newer and older antipsychotics. The study found that there was a prolongation of the QT_c with ziprasidone, but the duration was relatively brief and did not lead to patients reaching durations such as 500 msec, which have been associated with an increased risk of arrhythmias. It is interesting to note that this study confirmed that thioridazine (Mellaril) led to a much more substantial prolongation than any of the other agents. This led the FDA to recommend that thioridazine be limited to patients who could not be managed on other antipsychotics.

The issue with ziprasidone is more complex. On the one hand, there is no evidence to this date that any patients on ziprasidone have developed torsade de pointes. A small increase in the risk of arrhythmia is likely with ziprasidone, but the amount is difficult to quantify until after ziprasidone has been administered to a large number of patients.

Starting Patients on Ziprasidone

The package insert for ziprasidone states that this drug's tendency to prolong the QT interval would lead in many cases to the conclusion that "other agents should be tried first." It also states that it is unknown if ziprasidone will increase the risk of sudden death. Ziprasidone should probably not be prescribed for patients with prolonged QT intervals or those who have a history of arrhythmias. Although there is no requirement for monitoring patients on ziprasidone, these restrictions suggest that it is probably good practice for physicians to order an EKG before prescribing ziprasidone. After patients have been stabilized, it is also advisable to order a cardiogram to ensure that the QT interval is less than 500 msec. Ziprasidone should also not be prescribed for patients receiving other agents that prolong the QT interval. Once patients are treated with ziprasidone, they should be told to report episodes of dizziness, syncope, or palpitations.

In deciding whether to select ziprasidone, it is also important to consider that it is the only second-generation drug that does not lead to weight gain. It is conceivable that the health risks associated with weight gain are greater than the risks associated with arrhythmias on ziprasidone.

Nonelderly patients should be started on 20 mg of ziprasidone bid and increased, if necessary, to as much as 80 mg bid. It is further recommended that ziprasidone be taken with food. There is relatively little experience with ziprasidone at doses above 80 mg bid. Moreover, very little is known about the cardiac effects of higher doses. Until more information is available, clinicians should not prescribe higher doses.

Aripiprazole

Aripiprazole is a quinolinone derivative that may become available in 2002. Aripiprazole has substantial $5\text{-}HT_{2A}$ and D_2 activity that is similar to other second-generation drugs. It differs in having some partial agonist activity at D_2 receptor. As a partial agonist/antagonist, aripiprazole may act as an antagonist when there is high dopamine activity and as an agonist when dopamine activity is low. In theory this agent would serve to normalize dopamine receptors. Aripiprazole has minimal anticholinergic activity.

At the time of publication there are no published data regarding the clinical effectiveness of aripiprazole. Preliminary reports indicate that both 15 and 30 mg of aripiprazole are clinically effective doses. Moreover, these doses are associated with relatively mild side effects, including minimal weight gain and EPS. Aripiprazole appears to result in a decrease in serum prolactin, which may result from its agonist activity.

Iloperidone

Iloperidone is a piperidinyl-benzisoxasole compound that may become available to clinicians in 2002. It has high affinity for $5\text{-}HT_{2A}$, $5\text{-}HT_6$, D_2, D_3, and α_1 adrenergic receptors. Its high affinity for norepinephrine receptors resembles that of clozapine. Although published reports are unavailable, data from Phase II trials demonstrated efficacy in patients at doses of 8 mg/day, and tolerability was good up to 32 mg/day. Early unpublished reports suggest that iloperidone will resemble other second-generation drugs in having minimal EPS.

Other Medications for Individuals with Schizophrenia

Antiparkinson Medications

Antiparkinson medications are frequently prescribed for the management of acute extrapyramidal symptoms. The most commonly prescribed antiparkinson medications are anticholinergic and include benztropine (Cogentin), trihexyphenidyl (Artane), and biperiden (Akineton). These agents are effective for all the manifestations of EPS, including parkinsonism and dystonia. Akathisia responds to beta blockers, including propranolol (Inderal), and anticholinergics. Amantadine (Symmetrel) is a dopamine agonist that is occasionally effective for treating parkinsonism. More potent dopamine agonists (e.g., bromocriptine) and indirect dopamine agonists (e.g., levodopa) are usually not selected since they may aggravate psychotic symptoms.

One of the most dramatic treatment responses in psychiatry occurs when an acute dystonia is treated with IM or IV diphenhydramine (Benadryl) (50 mg in adults, 25 mg in children) or IM or IV benztropine (Cogentin) (2 mg in adults). The response is almost immediate, although complete resolution of the dystonia may take 20 to 30 minutes. Once patients demonstrate a response, an oral antiparkinson medication should be prescribed to prevent a recurrence of the dystonia.

Antipsychotic-induced parkinsonism usually responds to oral anticholinergic agents. When symptoms such as tremor or rigidity emerge, patients should have their antipsychotic dose reduced whenever possible. If this is ineffective, the patient should be started on an oral anticholinergic, such as benztropine 1 to 2 mg bid or trihexyphenidyl 2 mg tid. If anticholinergic side effects do not allow an adequate dose or if the agent is not completely effective, amantadine 100 mg bid or tid can be added to the anticholinergic. If these treatments are unsuccessful, changing the patient to a newer antipsychotic should be considered.

Although anticholinergics are often prescribed for akathisia, they are often less effective than they are for parkinsonism. Central-acting beta blockers such as propranolol have been found by some to be more effective than anticholinergics for managing akathisia (65). Most akathisia patients respond to 10 to 80 mg daily of propranolol. When patients are treated with a beta blocker, pulse and blood pressure should be monitored.

Side Effects of Antiparkinson Medications

The side effects of antiparkinson medications can be predicted from their primary therapeutic action. That is, the anticholinergic agents can cause dry mouth, decreased sweating, blurred vision, urinary retention, and constipation. These side effects can be serious in some individuals and uncomfortable in others. These agents can also impair memory, a side effect that may be most apparent in elderly patients. However, anticholinergics may also have memory effects in young adults (66). That is, subtle memory impairments from these agents can add to the problems that patients may have in school or the workplace.

Beta blockers can cause bronchospasm and should be avoided in patients with illnesses of the lung or bronchial asthma. These agents can cause bradycardia (or slowing of the heart). This is usually a benign effect, but it can contribute to heart failure in some individuals with cardiac disease, and it can impair exercise performance in others (67).

Amantadine has side effects that can be expected for an agent that functions as a mild stimulant. It can cause nausea, dizziness, insomnia, poor concentration, and irritability. These side effects are seldom severe and are usually preferred by patients to the effects of anticholinergics.

Benzodiazepines

Benzodiazepines are commonly added to antipsychotics for a number of indications, including anxiety, akathisia, and agitation. These agents have been tried as a substitute for antipsychotics and have been found on occasion to be more effective than placebo (reviewed in ref. 68). Although there is relatively little information about the effectiveness of benzodiazepines compared with antipsychotics, benzodiazepines are considerably less effective. As a result, most attention has focused on these agents as adjunctive agents for patients who have been stabilized on an antipsychotic.

The strongest evidence supports benzodiazepines as treatments for agitation in schizophrenia (68). This is consistent with the observations from clinicians (69) who have found that the addition of a benzodiazepine to an antipsychotic can be effective for disruptive behaviors in inpatient and outpatient settings. Although there is little empirical evidence that any particular agent from this group is more effective than any other, lorazepam has the advantage of reliable absorption when it is administered either orally or parenterally (7). Moreover, combining a drug such as lorazepam with a high-potency antipsychotic is probably safer and as effective as large doses of antipsychotics in controlling excitement and motor agitation (69). Oral clonazepam has also been found to be helpful in similar circumstances (70).

Research studies are more ambiguous about the effectiveness of benzodiazepines for anxiety in schizophrenia. When studies found that benzodiazepines were effective, these effects were sometimes not sustained (70). Nevertheless, these are probably the safest agents for reducing severe anxiety. Other studies found that benzodiazepines were effective for negative symptoms. However, this finding has not been confirmed in every study (71).

Common side effects of benzodiazepines include sedation, ataxia, cognitive impairment, and a tendency to cause behavioral disinhibition in some patients. This latter side effect can be a serious problem in those being treated for agitation. Withdrawal reactions from benzodiazepines can include psychosis and seizures. In addition, patients with schizophrenia are vulnerable to both abuse and addiction to these agents. These observations support the practice of limiting benzodiazepine use as a chronic treatment and preserving them for periods of acute agitation.

Lithium

Lithium is frequently prescribed as an adjunctive treatment for patients with schizophrenia or schizoaffective illness who demonstrate unstable moods. It has also been prescribed for patients who are relatively poor responders to an antipsychotic. A number of studies evaluated the effectiveness of lithium prescribed alone for schizophrenia (72,73). These studies suggested that lithium effects were inconsistent and clearly inferior to antipsychotics. Nearly all the studies focused on adding lithium to an antipsychotic.

The most consistent effect for lithium is in patients with mood symptoms. Lerner et al. (74) found that lithium was useful for decreasing both depression and thought disturbance in individuals who were depressed. Lithium was ineffective for individuals who were not depressed. Other studies have provided evidence that lithium is effective when added to an antipsychotic for individuals with schizoaffective disorder. For these patients, lithium is effective for reducing both excitement and depression (75).

The effects of lithium are less clear for patients who have an inadequate response to antipsychotics. Although there are indications that lithium may benefit some poor antipsychotic responders (reviewed in ref. 76), these improvements are somewhat inconsistent. Moreover, the availability of clozapine and other new antipsychotics has decreased the use of lithium for this group of patients.

Patients who are treated with lithium as an adjunctive medication are treated similarly to bipolar patients. When feasible, the patient should be stabilized on the antipsychotic before lithium is introduced. The dose should be sufficient to maintain a lithium level of 0.8 to 1.2 meq/L, and the lithium level should be monitored. Since lithium can worsen EPS and contribute to neuroleptic malignant syndrome, the severity of extrapyramidal symptoms should be assessed carefully as the lithium level rises.

Lithium can cause a variety of side effects, including tremor, sedation, cognitive and other memory disturbances, weight gain, polyuria (excessive urination), polydipsia (excessive fluid intake), gastrointestinal disturbances (e.g., diarrhea), hair loss, and acne. When serum levels of lithium are elevated, patients can develop serious toxic reactions with confusion, impaired consciousness, and ataxia (poor coordination).

Other Anticonvulsants

Although there is relatively little evidence from controlled trials, carbamazepine and valproate are commonly prescribed as adjunctive medications for the same indications as lithium. As with lithium, there is relatively little support for valproate as monotherapy for schizophrenia (77). Studies suggest that carbamazepine is effective as an adjunctive medication for aggressive or violent patients (78). However, the common indication of valproate or carbamazepine in schizophrenia and schizoaffective illness is for unstable moods. Recent evidence (79) indicates that valproate is being prescribed more frequently and that the use of lithium and carbamazepine may be declining. This change in practice is probably a result of the side effect profile of valproate, which is considerably milder than the other two agents.

As with lithium, valproate and carbamazepine are prescribed in the same manner as they are in bipolar disorder. An important consideration with carbamazepine is its tendency to decrease plasma levels by enhancing metabolism of the antipsychotic. For example, reports indicate that haloperidol levels can be halved when carbamazepine is added (80). In addition, carbamazepine should not be prescribed with clozapine, since it can lower the white blood count. As a result, there will be less of a safety margin if patients develop agranulocytosis.

Antidepressant Medications in Schizophrenia

Patients with schizophrenia commonly complain of depression. Episodes of depressed mood can occur at different phases of schizophrenia, and these episodes can have different causes. The causes of depression can include the following:

1. Depression as a component of psychosis.
2. Depression secondary to antipsychotic-induced parkinsonian side effects or akinetic depression.
3. Postpsychotic depression or depression associated with the demoralization that occurs in some patients.
4. Depression that can be comorbid with schizophrenia.

Another dilemma in evaluating depression in schizophrenia can occur when negative symptoms such as amotivation and anhedonia are difficult to discriminate from schizophrenia.

Individuals who are experiencing depression as a component of an acute psychotic episode usually improve as they recover from psychosis. The best course for these patients is to use antipsychotics and to introduce antidepressants if depression continues after the psychotic symptoms have remitted. If depression is secondary to EPS it usually responds to decreasing the antipsychotic dose, adding antiparkinson medications, or changing the drug to a second-generation agent with a lower potential for inducing EPS. Depression that is secondary to demoralization may be the most difficult to treat. This form may respond to either antidepressant medications or psychotherapy.

Evidence suggests that adding antidepressants to antipsychotics can be effective in reducing depression in patients with schizophrenia who also have full depressive syndromes. These individuals have the full depressive syndrome as defined in the criteria for major depressive disorder. Studies by Siris and co-workers (81) indicate that antidepressants are effective in reducing depression, although these agents are ineffective for psychotic symptoms. Although these studies focused on tricyclic antidepressants, the effects of Selective Serotonin Reuptake Inhibitors (SSRIs) are likely to be similar.

Clinicians who have decided to add an antidepressant to an antipsychotic should prescribe drug doses that are similar to those prescribed for depression. After patients have recovered from depression, antidepressants can usually be discontinued without causing a relapse of depression. Drug/drug interaction should also be considered. For example, antidepressants such as fluoxetine and paroxetine are potent inhibitors of CYP2D6, the cytochrome P450 enzyme that metabolizes haloperidol, perphenazine, thioridazine, and others. When either of these antidepressants is combined with one of the antipsychotics, the antipsychotic plasma level may increase, resulting in more side effects.

PHARMACOLOGIC MANAGEMENT OF SCHIZOAFFECTIVE DISORDER

Clinicians differ in their tendency to discriminate schizoaffective disorder and schizophrenia. This is in part because patients present differently at different times in their illness, but also because practitioners may differ in how they interpret the criteria. The criteria for schizoaffective disorder include the co-occurrence of mood and psychotic symptoms as well as the persistence of psychotic symptoms for 2 weeks after the remission of mood symptoms. However, this can be difficult to separate from bipolar illness with psychosis, on the one hand, or depressed episodes that are common in individuals with schizophrenia, on the other. Moreover, few studies have focused directly on the management of schizoaffective illness. Studies that have been done suggest that the pharmacotherapy of schizoaffective illness does not differ from the management of schizophrenia with depression or excitement as comorbidities.

Lithium has been studied as an adjunct to antipsychotics in patients with schizoaffective disorder, manic type. However, these studies have included a relatively small number of patients, and the results are ambiguous (75). Although it is a common practice to add an antidepressant to an antipsychotic in patients with schizoaffective disorder, depressed type, there is inadequate empirical support for this practice. Other studies suggest that second-generation antipsychotics may have advantages for schizoaffective patients. However, it is unclear if changing a patient to a newer antipsychotic is preferable to combining an older drug with an antidepressant. Alternatively, it may be reasonable to combine a newer drug with an antidepressant, although this strategy has not been studied adequately with controlled trials. A review by Levinson and co-workers (82) found that distinguishing between schizophrenia and schizoaffective disorder was not useful in planning treatments. Rather, treatments with mood-stabilizing agents or antidepressants as adjuncts to (45) antipsychotics should be prescribed based on a patient's mood symptoms.

To summarize this confusing area, controlled studies give little guidance to the clinician who is planning the treatment of patients with schizoaffective disorder. Rather, treatment principles should be borrowed from studies of patients with schizophrenia and either depression or excitement. We recommend adding antidepressants when stabilized patients with schizoaffective disorder are depressed. When there is evidence of excitement, a mood-stabilizing agent such as lithium, carbamazepine, or valproate should be considered. Second-generation antipsychotics probably have advantages over older agents for these patients, since they tend to reduce depressive symptoms in many patients (45,48).

REFERENCES

1. Laskey JJ, Kett CJ, Caffey EM, et al. Drug treatment of schizophrenic patients. *Dis Nerv Syst* 1962;23:698.
2. National Institute of Mental Health-Psychopharmacology Service Center Collaborative Study Group. Phenothiazine treatment in acute schizophrenia. *Arch Gen Psychiatry* 1964;10:246.
3. May PR. *Treatment of schizophrenia: a comparative study of five treatment methods.* New York: Science House, 1968.
4. Lehman AF, Steinwachs DM. Translating research into practice: the Schizophrenia Patient Outcomes Research Team (PORT) treatment recommendations. *Schizophr Bull* 1998;24:1–10.

5. Klein DF, Davis JM. *Diagnosis and drug treatment of psychiatric disorders* Baltimore: Williams & Wilkins, 1969.
6. Spohn HE, Lacousiere R, Thompson K, et al. Phenothiazine effects of psychological and psychophysiological dysfunction in chronic schizophrenics. *Arch Gen Psychiatry* 1964; 34:1281–1285.
7. Janicak PG, Davis JM, Preskorn SH, et al. *Principles and practice of psychopharmacology.* Baltimore: Williams & Wilkins, 1993.
8. Farde L, Nordstrom AL, Wiesel FA, et al. Positron emission tomographic analysis of central D_1 and D_2 dopamine receptor occupancy in patients treated with classical neuroleptics and clozapine. Relation to extrapyramidal side effects. *Arch Gen Psychiatry* 1992; 49:538–544.
9. McEvoy JP, Schooler NR, Wilson WH. Predictors of therapeutic response to haloperidol in acute schizophrenia. *Psychopharmacol Bull* 1991;27:97–101.
10. Kapur S, Zipursky R, Jones C, et al. A positron emission tomography study of quetiapine in schizophrenia: a preliminary finding of an antipsychotic effect with only transiently high dopamine D_2 receptor occupancy. *Arch Gen Psychiatry* 2000;57:553–559.
11. Swigar ME, Jatlow PI, Goicoechea N, et al. Ratio of serum prolactin to haloperidol and early clinical outcome in acute psychosis. *Am J Psychiatry* 1984;141:1281–1283.
12. Marder SR. Clinical experience with risperidone. *J Clin Psychiatry* 1996;57[Suppl 9]: 57–61.
13. Kane JM, Honigfeld G, Singer J, et al. Clozapine for the treatment-resistant schizophrenic: a double-blind comparison versus chlorpromazine/benztropine. *Arch Gen Psychiatry* 1988;45:789–796.
14. Bondolfi G, Dufour H, Patris M, et al. Risperidone versus clozapine in treatment-resistant chronic schizophrenia: a randomized double-blind study. The Risperidone Study Group [see comments]. *Am J Psychiatry* 1998;155:499–504.
15. Wirshing DA, Marshall BD Jr. Green MF, et al. Risperidone in treatment-refractory schizophrenia. *Am J Psychiatry* 1999;156:1374–1379.
16. Breier A, Hamilton SH. Comparative efficacy of olanzapine and haloperidol for patients with treatment-resistant schizophrenia [see comments]. *Biol Psychiatry* 1999;45: 403–411.
17. Leucht S, Pitschel-Walz G, Abraham D, et al. Efficacy and extrapyramidal side-effects of the new antipsychotics olanzapine, quetiapine, risperidone, and sertindole compared to conventional antipsychotics and placebo: a meta-analysis of randomized controlled trials. *Schizophr Res* 1999;35:51–68.
18. Geddes J, Freemantle N, Harrison P, et al. Atypical antipsychotics in the treatment of schizophrenia: systematic overview and meta-regression analysis. *BMJ* 2000;321:1371–1376.
19. Emsley RA. Risperidone in the treatment of first-episode psychotic patients: a double-blind multicenter study. *Schizophr Bull* 1999;25:721–729.
20. Sanger TM, Lieberman JA, Tohen M, et al. Olanzapine versus haloperidol treatment in first-episode psychosis. *Am J Psychiatry* 1999;156:79–87.
21. Buchanan RW, Breier A, Kirkpatrick B, et al. Positive and negative symptom response to clozapine in schizophrenic patients with and without the deficit syndrome. *Am J Psychiatry* 1998;155:751–760.
22. Rosenheck R, Dunn L, Peszke M, et al. Impact of clozapine on negative symptoms and on the deficit syndrome in refractory schizophrenia. *Am J Psychiatry* 1999;156:88–93.
23. Rosenheck R, Tekell J, Peters J, et al. Does participation in psychosocial treatment augment the benefit of clozapine? *Arch Gen Psychiatry* 1998;55:618–625.
24. Hamilton SH, Revicki DA, Genduso LA, et al. Olanzapine versus placebo and haloperidol: quality of life and efficacy results of the North American double-blind trial. *Neuropsychopharmacology* 1998;18:41–49.
25. Keefe RS, Silva SG, Perkins DO, et al. The effects of atypical antipsychotic drugs on neurocognitive impairment in schizophrenia: a review and meta-analysis. *Schizophr Bull* 1999;25:201–222.

26. Van Putten T, May PR, Marder SR. Response to antipsychotic medication: the doctor's and the consumer's view. *Am J Psychiatry* 1984;141:16–19.

27. Simpson G, Angus JSW. A rating scale for extrapyramidal side effects. *Acta Psychiatr Scand Suppl* 1970;212:9–11.

28. Guy W. ECDEU Assessment manual for pscyhopharmacology. US Dept. Health, Education, and Welfare Publication (ADM) 76-338. Rockville, MD: National Institute of Mental Health, 1976.

29. Meltzer HY, Long-term effects of neuroleptic drugs on the neuroendocrine system. *Biochem Psychopharmacol* 1985;40:59–68.

30. Reichlin S. Neuroendocrinology. In: Williams RH, ed. *Textbook of endocrinology,* 8th ed. Philadelphia: WB Saunders, 1992:135–219.

31. Honigfeld G, Arellano F, Sethi J, et al. Reducing clozapine-related morbidity and mortality: 5 years of experience with the Clozaril National Registry. *J Clin Psychiatry* 1998; 59[Suppl 3]:3–7.

32. Pickar D, Owen RR, Litman RE, et al. Clinical and biologic response to clozapine in patients with schizophrenia: crossover comparison with fluphenazine [see comments]. *Arch Gen Psychiatry* 1992;49:345–353.

33. Kane JM, Marder SR, Schooler N, et al. Clozapine and haloperidol in moderately refractory schizophrenia: a six-month double-blind comparison. *Arch Gen Psychiatry,* in press.

34. Essock SM, Frisman LK, Covell NH, et al. Cost-effectiveness of clozapine compared with conventional antipsychotic medication for patients in state hospitals [In Process Citation]. *Arch Gen Psychiatry* 2000;57:987–994.

35. Rosenheck R, Cramer J, Xu W, et al. A comparison of clozapine and haloperidol in hospitalized patients with refractory schizophrenia. Department of Veterans Affairs Cooperative Study Group on Clozapine in Refractory Schizophrenia [see comments]. *N Engl J Med* 1997;337:809–815.

36. Allison DB, Mentore JL, Heo M, et al. Antipsychotic-induced weight gain: a comprehensive research synthesis. *Am J Psychiatry* 1999;156:1686–1696.

37. Henderson DC, Cagliero E, Gray C, et al. Clozapine, diabetes mellitus, weight gain, and lipid abnormalities: a five-year naturalistic study. *Am J Psychiatry* 2000;157:975–981.

38. Wirshing DA, Spellberg BJ, Erhart SM, et al. Novel antipsychotics and new onset diabetes. *Biol Psychiatry* 1998;44:778–783.

39. Potkin SG, Buchsbaum MS, Jin Y, et al. Clozapine effects on glucose metabolic rate in striatum and frontal cortex. *J Clin Psychiatry* 1994;55[Suppl B]:63–66.

40. Miller DD, Fleming F, Holman TL, et al. Plasma clozapine concentrations as a predictor of clinical response: a follow-up study. *J Clin Psychiatry* 1994;55[Suppl B]:117–121.

41. Vander Zwaag C, McGee M, McEvoy JP, et al. Response of patients with treatment-refractory schizophrenia to clozapine within three serum level ranges. *Am J Psychiatry* 1996;153:1579–1584.

42. Peuskens J. Risperidone in the treatment of patients with chronic schizophrenia: a multinational, multi-centre, double-blind, parallel-group study versus haloperidol. *Br J Psychiatry* 1995;166:712–26; discussion 727–723.

43. Chouinard G, Annable L, Turnier L, et al. A double-blind randomized clinical trial of rapid tranquilization with IM clonazepam and IM haloperidol in agitated psychotic patients with manic symptoms [see comments]. *Can J Psychiatry* 1993;38[Suppl 4]: S114–S121.

44. Marder, SR, Meibach RC. Risperidone in the treatment of schizophrenia. *Am J Psychiatry* 1994;151:825–835.

45. Marder SR, Davis JM, Chouinard G. The effects of risperidone on the five dimensions of schizophrenia derived by factor analysis: combined results of the North American trials. *J Clin Psychiatry* 1997;58:538–546.

46. Green MF, Marshall BD Jr, Wirshing WC, et al. Does risperidone improve verbal working memory in treatment-resistant schizophrenia? *Am J Psychiatry* 1997;154:799–804.

47. Kern RS, Green MF, Marshall BD Jr, et al. Risperidone vs. haloperidol on reaction time,

manual dexterity, and motor learning in treatment-resistant schizophrenia patients. *Biol Psychiatry* 1998;44:726–732.

48. Tollefson GD, Beasley CM Jr, Tran PV, et al. Olanzapine versus haloperidol in the treatment of schizophrenia and schizoaffective and schizophreniform disorders: results of an international collaborative trial [see comments]. *Am J Psychiatry* 1997;154:457–465.

49. Beasley CM Jr, Tollefson G, Tran P, et al. Olanzapine versus placebo and haloperidol: acute phase results of the North American double-blind olanzapine trial [see comments]. *Neuropsychopharmacology* 1996;14:111–123.

50. Purdon SE, Jones BD, Stip E, et al. Neuropsychological change in early phase schizophrenia during 12 months of treatment with olanzapine, risperidone, or haloperidol. *Arch Gen Psychiatry* 2000;57:249–258.

51. Kapur S, Zipursky R, Jones C, et al. A positron emission tomography study of quetiapine in schizophrenia: a preliminary finding of an antipsychotic effect with only transiently high dopamine D_2 receptor occupancy. *Arch Gen Psychiatry* 2000;57:553–559.

52. King DJ, Link CG, Kowalcyk, B. A comparison of bid and tid dose regimens of quetiapine (Seroquel) in the treatment of schizophrenia. *Psychopharmacology (Berl)* 1998;137:139–146.

53. Small JG, Hirsch SR, Arvanitis LA, et al. Quetiapine in patients with schizophrenia: a high- and low-dose double-blind comparison with placebo. *Arch Gen Psychiatry* 1997;54:549–557.

54. Arvanitis LA, Miller BG. Multiple fixed doses of "Seroquel" (quetiapine) in patients with acute exacerbation of schizophrenia: a comparison with haloperidol and placebo. *Biol Psychiatry* 1997;42:233–246.

55. Peuskens J, Link CG. A comparison of quetiapine and chlorpromazine in the treatment of schizophrenia. *Acta Psychiatr Scand* 1997;96:265–273.

56. Seeger TF, Seymour PA, Schmidt AW, et al. Ziprasidone (CP-88,059): a new antipsychotic with combined dopamine and serotonin receptor antagonist activity. *J Pharmacol Exp Ther* 1995;275:101–113.

57. Bench CJ, Lammertsma AA, Grasby PM. The time course of binding to striatal dopamine D_2 receptors by the neuroleptic ziprasidone (CP-88,059–01) determined by positron emission tomography. *Psychopharmacology (Berl)* 1996;124:141–147.

58. Fischman AJ, Bonab AA, Babich JW, et al. Positron emission tomographic analysis of central 5-hydroxytryptamine2 receptor occupancy in healthy volunteers treated with the novel antipsychotic agent, ziprasidone. *J Pharmacol Exp Ther* 1996;279:939–947.

59. Goff DC, Posever T, Herz L, et al. An exploratory haloperidol-controlled dose-finding study of ziprasidone in hospitalized patients with schizophrenia or schizoaffective disorder. *J Clin Psychopharmacol* 1998;18:296–304.

60. Keck PE, Buffenstein, et al. Ziprasidone 40 and 120 mg/da in the acute exacerbation of schizophrenia and schizoaffective disorder: a 4-week placebo-controlled trial. *Psychopharmacology* 1998;140:173–184.

61. Daniel DG, Zimbroff DL, Potkin SG, et al. Ziprasidone 80 mg/day and 160 mg/day in the acute exacerbation of schizophrenia and schizoaffective disorder: a 6-week placebo-controlled trial. *Neuropsychopharmacology* 1999;20:491–505.

62. Arato MR, O'Connor, et al. Ziprasidone in the long-term treatment of negative symptoms and prevention of exacerbation of schizophrenia. *Eur Psychiatry* 1998;13:303s.

63. Potkin SG, Cooper S. Ziprasidone and zotepine: clinical use and experience. In: Buckley PF, Waddington JL, eds. *Schizophrenia and mood disorders: the new drug therapies in clinical practice.* Oxford, U.K.: Butterworth-Heinemann 2000;1:49–58.

64. Allison DB, Mentore JL, Heo M, et al. Antipsychotic-induced weight gain: a comprehensive research synthesis. *Am J Psychiatry* 1999;156:1686–1696.

65. Fleischhacker WW, Roth SD, Kane JM. The pharmacologic treatment of neuroleptic-induced akathisia [see comments]. *J Clin Psychopharmacol* 1990;10:12–21.

66. Gelenberg AJ, Van Putten T, Lavori PW, et al. Anticholinergic effects on memory: benztropine versus amantadine. *J Clin Psychopharmacol* 1989;9:180–185.

67. Stanilla JK, Simpson GM. *Treatment of extrapyramidal side effects. The American Psychiatric Press textbook of psychopharmacology.* Washington, DC: American Psychiatric Press, 1998:349–375.
68. Wolkowitz OM, Pickar D. Benzodiazepines in the treatment of schizophrenia: a review and reappraisal [see comments]. *Am J Psychiatry* 1991;148:714–726.
69. Salzman C, Green AI, Rodriguez-Villa F, et al. Benzodiazepines combined with neuroleptics for management of severe disruptive behavior. *Psychosomatics* 1986;27[1 Suppl]:17–22.
70. Altamura AC, Mauri MC, Mantero M, et al. Clonazepam/haloperidol combination therapy in schizophrenia: a double blind study. *Acta Psychiatr Scand* 1987;76:702–706.
71. Csernansky JG, Riney SJ, Lombrozo L, et al. Double-blind comparison of alprazolam, diazepam, and placebo for the treatment of negative schizophrenic symptoms. *Arch Gen Psychiatry* 1988;45:655–659.
72. Alexander PE, Van Kammen DP, Bunney WE Jr. Antipsychotic effects of lithium in schizophrenia. *Am J Psychiatry* 1979;136:283–287.
73. Shopsin B, Kim SS, Gershon JS. A controlled study of lithium vs. chlorpromazine in acute schizophrenics. *Br J Psychiatry* 1971;119:435–440.
74. Lerner Y, Mintzer Y, Schestatzky M. Lithium combined with haloperidol in schizophrenic patients. *Br J Psychiatry* 1988;153:359–362.
75. Biederman J, Lerner Y, Belmaker RH. Combination of lithium carbonate and haloperidol in schizo-affective disorder: a controlled study. *Arch Gen Psychiatry* 1979;36:327–333.
76. Wolkowitz OM. Rational polypharmacy in schizophrenia. *Ann Clin Psychiatry* 1993;5: 79–90.
77. McElroy SL, Keck PE Jr, Pope HG Jr. Sodium valproate: its use in primary psychiatric disorders. *J Clin Psychopharmacol* 1987;7:16–24.
78. Okuma T, Yamashita I, Takahashi R, et al. A double-blind study of adjunctive carbamazepine versus placebo on excited states of schizophrenic and schizoaffective disorders. *Acta Psychiatr Scand* 1989;80:250–259.
79. Fenn HH, Robinson D, Luby V, et al. Trends in pharmacotherapy of schizoaffective and bipolar affective disorders: a 5-year naturalistic study. *Am J Psychiatry* 1996;153: 711–713.
80. Jann MW, Ereshefsky L, Saklad SR, et al. Effects of carbamazepine on plasma haloperidol levels. *J Clin Psychopharmacol* 1985;5:106–109.
81. Bermanzohn PC, Siris SG. Battle against therapeutic nihilism in caring for patients who exhibit the negative symptoms of schizophrenia (NSS). *Compr Psychiatry* 1994;35:478.
82. Levinson DF, Umapathy C, Musthaq M. Treatment of schizoaffective disorder and schizophrenia with mood symptoms. *Am J Psychiatry* 1999;156:1138–1148.

Treating and Managing the Phases of Schizophrenia

6

Evaluation of the Acutely Psychotic Patient

Psychosis is a clinical state rather than a particular disorder. It can be a manifestation of schizophrenia or of a number of other medical and psychiatric illnesses. For this reason the medical axiom of first establishing a diagnosis and then instituting treatment remains an important principle for managing psychosis. But other issues are very important in evaluating psychosis, including the safety of the patient and others and the factors that may have led to the current state. These factors may include the environment in which the patient lives, poor compliance with medication, or use of alcohol or street drugs. Often these evaluations will take place in the pressured setting of an emergency room or a psychiatric hospital, which can be highly stressful for the patient, family members, and others.

The initial evaluation of a psychotic patient focuses on a number of issues that need to be addressed according to their priority. These issues include the safety of the patient and others (including the evaluator); the ability of the patient to participate in decisions regarding the evaluation and treatment process; the appropriate setting for managing the patient's psychosis; the role of the family and others in decision making about management; medical issues that need to addressed; and diagnosis.

ASSESSING PATIENT SAFETY

As noted later, psychosis can result from a number of medical conditions. For this reason it is important for the clinician to rule out urgent medical problems that may present with psychotic symptoms. At an early stage, the clinician should evaluate the patient's state of consciousness. This includes an evaluation of the patient's alertness, level of distress, orientation, and evidence of recent trauma. Monitoring a patient's vital signs is also an essential component of a safety evaluation. Changes in body temperature, pulse, and blood pressure are often evidence of medical problems that require immediate attention. The patient or another informant such as a relative may also provide information about medications or other substances that the patient has recently taken.

It is sometimes unwise or impossible to obtain the thorough psychiatric history that is necessary for the evaluation of a psychotic patient. Under these circumstances clinicians should concentrate on information from the patient, medical records, and other informants that is essential to ensure that the patient and those around him or her are safe. This information includes a history of dangerous behavior while psychotic, which may include assaults, suicide attempts, and self-injuries. Patients who are psychotic may also have neglected their own care. As a result, it is important to inquire about whether patients have been eating properly, sleeping, and taking medication.

The content of delusions or hallucinations may also provide important information about the patient's safety. Thus suspicious ideas about individuals in the patient's life can indicate if others are in danger. Patients who can find evidence supporting their delusions and who are distressed as a result of delusions are more likely to engage in dangerous behavior (1). Delusions that are likely to be associated with dangerous behavior include those associated with immediate threats to the patient or others, particularly when the patient lacks insight regarding these beliefs. The evaluation of an acutely psychotic patient should always include an assessment of the content of hallucinations. Those of most concern to clinicians may be command hallucinations to kill or harm the patient or others. For these patients the most important factor may be the individual's perceived ability to resist the hallucinations. For example, one individual may experience auditory hallucinations commanding him to hurt himself but may be comfortable with his ability to not act in response to the voices. Another may experience hallucinations that are intense and unrelenting, but the content may be benign. However, the latter patients may become dangerous if the content of the hallucinations shifts to voices that exhort the patient to commit violent acts. For each of these circumstances the best information regarding the safety of the patient is likely to come from an accurate history.

It is important for clinicians to inquire directly whether an acutely psychotic patient is having violent thoughts about any individuals. Patients with compelling psychotic experiences may be more dangerous than they appear. A patient who is experiencing command hallucinations to harm a particular individual may be at a high risk for committing a homicide, even though consciously that individual harbors no ill feeling toward the possible victim. Data from the Epidemiologic Catchment Area survey indicated that 8% to 10% of those with schizophrenia reported that they had engaged in some form violent behavior during the prior year (2). Although this is a very high risk, it represents only about 3% of community violence. Moreover, violence by these individuals is often preventable if they are placed in a safe environment and treated.

It is important to emphasize that patients with schizophrenia may be at a severe risk for suicide. Studies have shown that at least 10% of patients with schizophrenia commit suicide, which is the most common cause of death in those with schizophrenia during the young adult and middle years. During the acute phase, patients with severe depressive and/or paranoid symptomatology often accompanied by command hallucinations are most likely to attempt suicide. Other important predictors of completed suicide are prior attempts, impulsivity, history of violence, feeling of hopelessness, and severe akathesia. Patients with a predominance of negative symptoms are not likely to commit suicide.

ESTABLISHING A SAFE ENVIRONMENT

The evaluation of the psychotic patient should take place in an environment that feels as safe as possible for both the patient and the evaluator. The evaluator should be alert to a number of conditions that can lead to the patient's feeling unsafe, including frightening delusions and hallucinations, thought disorganization, intense suspiciousness, agitation, irritability, or self-destructive impulses or ideas. If the clinician feels that it will be unsafe to be alone with the patient, others should be brought into the interview. It is important to emphasize that the need for safety is likely to override the usual practice of protecting the privacy of communications between a patient and a clinician. Other possible environmental manipulations include leaving the door of the interview room open, sitting between the door and the patient so that the patient cannot block the interviewer from exiting, performing the interview in a public space such as the day room of a hospital, increasing the distance between the patient and the interviewer, and in extreme cases using forms of physical restraint. Some patients may be impossible to evaluate until they receive calming medication such as an antipsychotic or a benzodiazepine. Patients who are concerned about their ability to control their own behavior may appreciate physical measures that can ensure the safety of others.

If the clinician senses that the patient is uncomfortable, it is usually appropriate to inquire about the source of the discomfort. If these involve suspicions about the interviewer or about others in the room, it is usually helpful to address these concerns directly.

Some may find that a restatement regarding the purpose of the interview and the role of the clinician is reassuring. The goal of these interactions is to have the patient view the clinician as an ally who can be trusted. Patients who are experiencing command hallucinations may find it helpful to report the contents of the hallucinations to the clinician.

Interviewing hostile and psychotic patients can be a disturbing experience for both the patient and the clinician, particularly when there is no rational source for the patient's anger. Although some patients may respond well when the interviewer provides assurance that the patient's anger at the interviewer is based on misperceptions, others will be unable to accept these reassurances. Arguing with a delusional patient is seldom helpful and may actually increase the patient's hostility. Rather, it is usually more effective to openly acknowledge that the patient and the interviewer have different perceptions about the current interaction but that the importance of the interview makes it necessary to proceed.

Clinicians may find it difficult to avoid becoming angry when patients are hostile and provocative. However, displays of anger or even evidence of irritation can reinforce the patient's view that the world is hostile toward him. Confronting an angry, psychotic patient can lead to an escalation of anger when the important goal is to have the patient view the treatment providers as supportive and helpful. A frightened interviewer can make the patient anxious. Therefore providing staff presence and support to contain any potential violence by the patient can be reassuring to both the patient and the interviewer. A calm tone of voice and a nonthreatening manner are often helpful, particularly when patients are experiencing substantial disorganization in their thinking. One of the most difficult tests of a clinician's professionalism may be the challenge of remaining objective and calm when dealing with a hostile patient.

PARTICIPATION IN DECISION MAKING REGARDING EVALUATION

Acutely psychotic patients may be disinterested in talking with the interviewer and refuse to provide useful information, especially if they deny their illness. Under these circumstances the clinician is forced to make a decision regarding further evaluation. Consulting with family or other acquaintances may be the most useful strategy for determining whether an evaluation should continue. Understanding the origins of the refusal to cooperate can be helpful in developing a strategy to elicit the patient's cooperation. If the refusal is related to suspiciousness, allowing the patient to verbalize feelings of mistrust may be helpful and may provide opportunities for the clinician to explain the goal of the evaluation. If, on the other hand, a patient's lack of cooperation is related to a disagreement with family members or another acquaintance, often about the need for emergency care and/or hospitalization, the clinician may be viewed as an agent of the other party. In these cases, clearly stating that the evaluation is taking place for the welfare of the patient may reassure the patient that information provided is confidential and will not be shared with family members unless the patient agrees.

It may be more difficult to engage a severely psychotic patient who is negativistic. These patients commonly refuse to do anything that the interviewer requests. They may be completely mute or evasive when interviewed. Eugen

Bleuler has suggested that negativism in schizophrenia can be related to severe thought disorganization with associated ambivalence. Under these conditions patients may see cooperating as making a decision. Individuals who are tormented by ambivalence may choose to do nothing rather than cooperate. These patients may experience relief if the clinician verbalizes clear and direct recommendations.

It is not unusual for patients to refuse to participate in an interview because they firmly believe that the interview is unnecessary. Patients may not perceive themselves as being ill, or they may have had experiences with the mental health system that cause them to refuse to cooperate. Some who are brought in involuntarily by the police or others may have no interest in cooperating with individuals who are viewed as extensions of the legal system.

Case 6.1

A 42-year-old man came to the psychiatric emergency room of a veteran's hospital complaining of auditory hallucinations telling him to kill himself, as well as two voices that spoke of a plot to kill him. On the day before admission he was in a fistfight for reasons that he could not explain. He reported that he had not taken his olanzapine for about 3 months because he was "trying to live without medication." He gave a history of multiple hospitalizations for schizophrenia, including a 3-year hospitalization at a facility for the criminally insane. The forensic hospitalization followed his being found not guilty by reason of insanity for an armed robbery.

A physical examination was normal. The patient explained that he did not believe that he was suicidal or homicidal at the time of admission. He denied recent drug or alcohol use, although he acknowledged that these had been problems in the past. A urine toxic screen was positive for recent cocaine use.

This patient was admitted to the hospital voluntarily and closely observed for homicidal and suicidal behavior. A number of signs indicated that he was at substantial risk for dangerous behavior. These included command hallucinations telling him to kill himself; hallucinations that were threatening to the patient; a history of criminal behavior; and recent use of cocaine. The issue of whether the patient suffered from a cocaine psychosis or schizophrenia was of less immediate importance than the need to hospitalize this patient and to ensure his safety and that of those around him.

INTERVIEWING THOUGHT-DISORDERED PATIENTS

Patients who are severely thought disordered may respond poorly to vague questions that require them to organize complex thoughts. This conflicts with the usual practice for nonpsychotic patients of beginning an interview with open-ended questions that permit patients to describe experiences in their own words. A reasonable approach is to begin with a general question such as, "Why did you come to the hospital (or clinic)?" The interviewer can observe the patient's response to this question and then move to more specific inquiries if necessary. For example, if the patient finds it difficult to formulate an answer to the previously mentioned question, the interviewer can inquire about the circumstances that led up to the current visit. It may be helpful for the interviewer to observe how the patient responds to questions with different levels of complexity and to adjust the amount of structure accordingly. In general, for severely thought-disordered patients, it is best to ask simple, concise, direct questions.

INTERVIEWING OTHER INFORMANTS

Family members and other close acquaintances may play a vital role in understanding the events that preceded a psychotic episode. When patients are too disorganized or uncooperative to give an accurate history, these informants may be an essential part of the psychiatric evaluation. Even when patients are cooperative, there are a number of reasons for involving family members and others in the initial evaluation. Psychosis may have led patients to misinterpret events that took place before relapse. The views of another individual who is close to the patient may assist the clinician in obtaining a more accurate understanding of the onset of the episode. Family members may also be aware of such behavior as substance abuse or failure to take medication that the patient may be reluctant to disclose. Obtaining a recent history may also assist the clinician in understanding clinical phenomena that may have characterized a prepsychotic state. The work of Herz and others indicates that psychotic states are frequently preceded by nonpsychotic, prodromal periods that may last up to a month or more (3). Characterizing these prodromal periods at an early stage may be a useful component in a long-term program of relapse prevention. (See Chapter 4 for a discussion of early-intervention strategies.)

Involving the family and other close acquaintances in the initial assessment of an episode may have other benefits. Family members and others are most likely to be concerned about the patient's illnesses at this time. Engaging them in a treatment alliance in which they are viewed as important participants in a treatment plan may be useful in a long-term management plan. The onset of an illness episode may also be a useful time for educating family members about schizophrenia and its treatment. As noted in a later section, substantial evidence indicates that family education is an effective intervention in schizophrenia.

It is also important for treatment teams to respect a patient's right of privacy. Unless the situation is urgent, family members should be contacted only with the patient's consent. If patients are suspicious of family members or angry with them, the purpose of the contact should be defined. The clinician should make every attempt to avoid the appearance that the treatment team is allied with the family's goals rather than the patient's, which could contribute to the feelings of distrust, resentment, loneliness, and isolation that are common in suspicious individuals.

FACTORS THAT MAY CONTRIBUTE TO RELAPSE

Whenever feasible the psychiatric history should include a review of factors that may have contributed to the patient's relapse. These may include stressors in the patient's environment, changes in pharmacotherapy, substance abuse, and medical illnesses. The interviewer should ask specific questions about the patient's recent medications. Although patients may report that they have been taking their medication, a more careful inquiry may reveal that adherence to a medication schedule has become irregular, with frequent missed doses. Interviewers may find it helpful to ask about compliance in a manner that is not likely to lead to defensiveness. For example, the interviewer can ask the patient about any difficulties remembering to take medication several times a day. Questions about side effects of medication may reveal that the patient has adjusted the dose as a response to discomfort. It is also important to ask about other medications that may interfere with the patient's antipsychotic level (see Chapter 5) or factors such as changes in smoking habits or diet that can influence drug levels.

Patients should also be asked about prior responses to antipsychotics and particularly their own preferences among antipsychotic medications. Preferences among drugs are usually due to the patient's subjective response, which is usually related to side effects. Moreover, Van Putten and co-workers found that a patient's early subjective response to an antipsychotic was an excellent predictor of how the patient would respond to that agent (4). This relationship probably resulted because patients who did not experience discomforting side effects on a drug were more likely to continue taking it.

The use of alcohol or street drugs is a common precipitant of psychotic relapse. Moreover, it may be impossible to differentiate a relapse that is directly related to substance use from one that is not. This problem is often complicated by the unreliability of the patient's report about his or her substance use. As a result, it is helpful to inquire whether family members or other acquaintances have observed evidence of alcohol or drug abuse. Further information about substance abuse can be obtained from laboratory tests, including urine and blood screening for substances of abuse and liver function tests. When patients report that drinking or marihuana use are trivial, careful questioning about the amount and frequency of use may reveal that the patient is underreporting the amount of use.

PHYSICAL AND LABORATORY EVALUATION

A physical examination is essential for the evaluation of every acutely psychotic patient. The examining psychiatrist, another physician, or a physician extender such as a nurse practitioner may perform the examination. The thoroughness of the examination will depend upon the cooperativeness of the patient. If a patient is uncooperative with a complete examination, the individual may permit the monitoring of vital signs. Additional, important information (e.g., level of consciousness, nutritional state, evidence of recent trauma, level of hydration, alcohol on the patient's breath, unusual pupillary size, skin color, abnormal movements, coordination, gait, posture) can be documented for patients who refuse to be examined.

The medical evaluation of an acutely psychotic patient meets a number of important needs. First, a physical and laboratory examination is essential for diagnosing the cause of the current episode. For example, by ruling out medical and neurologic causes of the current episode, the clinician can establish a psychiatric diagnosis before beginning treatment. In the case of individuals with a well-known psychiatric illness, a medical evaluation can detect medical causes (e.g., electrolyte disturbances or street drug abuse) that may have destabilized the patient. Finally, a physical examination and basic laboratory studies should be completed, when possible, before pharmacotherapy.

A number of concerns should guide the physical examination. In addition to ruling out neurologic illnesses, the evaluation of neurologic signs and symptoms is important for assessing movement disorders such as parkinsonism or tardive dyskinesia that may influence drug selection. Other concerns during the physical examination are the presence of cataracts, abnormal blood pressure, and heart rate.

The laboratory evaluation should include blood and urine screens for drugs of abuse, a complete blood count (CBC), and blood tests for electrolytes, glucose, and liver, renal, and thyroid function. Other evaluations that should be considered are pregnancy tests, electrocardiograms when cardiac disease or age is a factor, and human immunodeficiency virus and syphilis tests when relevant. In general, it is best to conduct neuropsychological testing for cognitive functioning after a patient has recovered from an acute episode. Testing at this time will yield a more accurate assessment of cognitive deficits, since severe positive and negative symptoms during acute episodes can affect test results.

PATIENT INTERVIEW

Whenever possible, the interviewer should describe the aims of the interview to the patient. For patients who are acutely psychotic, the primary goal is to ensure safety of the patient as well as those with whom the patient comes into contact. A second priority is to assess and treat, whenever possible, any discomfort or personal suffering the patient may be experiencing. In acute psychosis the goal usually includes establishing a provisional diagnosis as well as identifying other diagnoses that should be considered (5). The interview should also identify medical conditions that may influence management decisions. In addition, the interview should provide information about environmental factors that may affect the patient's condition as well as the patient's ability to cooperate with the evaluation.

The psychiatric interview usually focuses on the most recent factors that preceded the evaluation. These include the patient's view of events and personal experiences. These experiences may include mood and anxiety as well as psychotic experiences such as hallucinations, delusions, or suspiciousness. The information should include the time course of recent events, with the most recent being most important. It may also be valuable to focus on experiences that may have been misinterpreted and how these misinterpretations may have affected the patient's behavior. If the patient does not volunteer information about psychotic experiences, the interviewer should inquire about common psychotic symptoms, such as auditory and visual hallucinations, delusions, suspiciousness, ideas of reference, and experiences of being controlled. Table 6.1 includes well-tested questions from the Structured Clinical Interview for DSM-IV (SCID).

TABLE 6.1. *Examples of critical psychosis questions from the SCID*

- Has it ever seemed like people were talking about you or taking special notice of you?
- What about anyone going out of their way to give you a hard time, or trying to hurt you?
- Did you ever feel that someone or something outside yourself was controlling your thoughts or actions against your will?
- What about receiving special messages from the TV, radio, or newspaper, or from the way things were arranged around you?
- Did you ever hear things that other people couldn't hear, such as noises, or the voices of people whispering or talking?
- What did you hear? How often did you hear it? Have the voices been telling you to hurt yourself or other people?
- How many voices did you hear? Were they talking to each other?

SCID, Structured Clinical Interview for DSM-IV.

In addition to documenting the presence or absence of psychotic symptoms, the interview should attempt to characterize the severity of each symptom. For example, mild suspiciousness should be differentiated from severe suspicious delusions that may cause the patient to become aggressive. Patients with more severe delusions may have an unwavering belief that the delusion is real and may be more preoccupied and troubled by the delusion. Patients with more severe hallucinations will also fail to comprehend that the hallucination is a symptom of their illness and will find that the experience is more compelling and disturbing. For example, patients may experience auditory hallucinations of voices that are loud and angry, and from which the patient cannot be distracted. Among the most serious forms of hallucinations are command hallucinations, which the patient finds difficult to resist.

It is usually not advisable for the interviewer to challenge the patient's abnormal perceptions and beliefs. This may put the clinician in the difficult position of needing to respond when the patient asks whether he or she is believed. One approach is to state that you believe that these perceptions or beliefs are real to the patient. It is not useful to engage the patient in a discussion of the clinician's opinions, but to emphasize that the goal of the interview is to understand the patient's beliefs and experiences.

It is important for the clinician to document the patient's psychopathology during the initial interview. This information is likely to be valuable in establishing therapeutic targets and in monitoring improvement during subsequent weeks. Scales such as the Brief Psychiatric Rating Scale (BPRS) provide a template for documenting the severity of important symptoms (Fig. 6.1) (6).

BPRS (BRIEF PSYCHIATRIC RATING SCALE)

DIRECTIONS: There are 19 items to be rated. The starred items (3, 4, 6, 7, 13, 14, 16, 17, 18 and 19) should be rated on the basis of observations made during the interview. For these items 1=Not observed. The remaining items should be rated on the basis of reported (i.e., subjective) information pertaining to the past week. For these items, 1=Not reported.

_____ 1. **SOMATIC CONCERN:** DURING THE PAST WEEK, HOW HAS YOUR PHYSICAL HEALTH BEEN? DO YOU FEEL YOU ARE PHYSCIALLY ILL IN ANY WAY? (WHAT DO YOU THINK IS WRONG?) (HOW SERIOUS IS IT?) HAVE YOU WORRIED ABOUT YOUR HEALTH RECENTLY?
Degree of concern over present bodily health. Rate the degree to which physical health is perceived as a problem by the patient, whether complaints have a realistic basis or not. Do not rate mere reporting of somatic symptoms. Rate only concern for (or worrying about) physical problems (real or imagined). Rate on the basis of reported (i.e., subjective) information pertaining to the past week.
1 = Not Reported
2 = Very Mild: occasionally is somewhat concerned about body, symptoms or physical illness
3 = Moderate: occasionally is moderately concerned, or often is somewhat concerned
4 = Moderate: occasionally is very concerned, or often is moderately concerned
5 = Moderately severe: often is very concerned
6 = Severe: is very concerned most of the time
7 = Very Severe: is very concerned nearly all of the time
8 = Cannot be assessed adequately because of severe formal thought disorder, uncooperativeness, or marked evasiveness/guardedness, or: Not assessed.

_____ 2. **ANXIETY:** DURING THE PAST WEEK HAVE YOU FELT VERY FRIGHTENED OR ANXIOUS? HAVE YOU WORRIED A LOT? (WHAT DO YOU WORRY ABOUT?) HAVE YOU HAD THE FEELING THAT SOMETHING TERRIBLE MIGHT HAPPEN?
Worry, fear, or overconcern for present or future. Rate solely on the basis of verbal report of patient's own subjective experiences. Do not infer anxiety from physical signs or from neurotic defense mechanisms. Do not rate if restricted to somatic concern. (enter 99)
1 = Not reported
2 = Very Mild: occasionally feels somewhat anxious
3 = Mild: occasionally feels moderately anxious, or often feels somewhat anxious
4 = Moderate: occasionally feels very anxious, or often feels moderately anxious
5 = Moderately severe: often feels very anxious
6 = Severe: feels very anxious most of the time
7 = Very Severe: feels very anxious nearly all the time
9 = Cannot be assessed adequately because of severe formal thought disorder, uncooperativeness or marked evasiveness/guardedness, or: Not assessed.
99 = Not rated

FIG. 6.1.

(Continued on next page)

_____ 3. **EMOTIONAL WITHDRAWAL:** Deficiency in relating to the interviewer and to the interview situation. Overt manifestations of this deficiency include poor/absence of eye contact, failure to orient oneself physically toward the interviewer, and a general lack of involvement or engagement in the interview. Distinguish from BLUNTED AFFECT, in which deficits in facial expression, body gesture, and voice pattern are scored.
1 = Not observed
2 = Very Mild: e.g., occasionally exhibits poor eye contact
3 = Mild: e.g., as above, but more frequent
4 = Moderate: e.g., exhibits little eye contact, but still seems engaged in the interview and is appropriately responsive to all questions
5 = Moderately Severe: e.g., stares at floor or orients self away from interviewer, but still seems moderately engaged
6 = Severe: e.g., as above, but more persistent or pervasive
7 = Very Severe: e.g., appears "spacey" or "out of it" (total absence of emotional relatedness), and is disproportionately uninvolved or unengaged in the interview
9 = Cannot be assessed (e.g., scored from audiotape)

_____ *4. **CONCEPTUAL DISORGANIZATION:** Degree of speech incomprehensibility. Include any type of formal thought disorder (e.g., loose associations, incoherence, flight of ideas, neologisms). DO NOT include mere circumstantiality or pressured speech, even if marked. DO NOT rate on the basis of the patient's subjective impressions (e.g., "my thoughts are racing. I can't hold a thought." "my thinking gets all mixed up"). Rate *ONLY* on the basis of observations made during the interview.
1 = Not observed
2 = Very mild: e.g., somewhat vague, but of doubtful clinical significance
3 = Mild: e.g., frequently vague, but the interview is able to progress smoothly
4 = Moderate: e.g., occasional irrelevant statements, infrequent use of neologisms, or moderate loosening of associations
5 = Moderately Severe: as above, but more frequent
6 = Severe: formal thought disorder is present for most of the interview, and the interview is severely strained
7 = Very Severe: very little coherent information can be obtained
9 = Not assessed

_____ 5. **GUILT FEELINGS:** DURING THE PAST WEEK HAVE YOU BEEN BLAMING YOURSELF FOR ANYTHING? HAVE YOU BEEN FEELING GUILTY? (DO YOU FEEL THAT YOU DESERVE PUNISHMENT?) (HAVE YOU BEEN THINKING ABOUT THIS A LOT?)
Overconcern or remorse for past behavior. Rate on the basis of the patient's subjective experiences of guilt as evidenced by verbal report. Do not infer guilt feelings from depression, anxiety or neurotic defenses.
1 = Not reported
2 = Very Mild: occasionally feels somewhat guilty
3 = Mild: occasionally feels moderately guilty, or often feels somewhat guilty
4 = Moderate: occasionally feels very guilty, or often feels moderately guilty
5 = Moderately Severe: often feels very guilty

FIG. 6.1. *Continued.*

6 = Severe: feels very guilty most of the time, or encapsulated delusion of guilt
7 = Very Severe: agonizing constant feelings of guilt, or pervasive delusion(s) of guilt
9 = Cannot be assessed adequately because of severe formal thought disorder, uncooperativeness, or marked evasiveness, guardedness, or Not assessed.

_____ 6. **TENSION:** Rate motor restlessness (agitation) observed during the interview. DO NOT rate on the basis of subjective experiences reported by the patient. Disregard suspected pathogenesis (e.g., tardive dyskinesia).
1 = Not observed.
2 = Very Mild: e.g., occasionally fidgets
3 = Mild: e.g., frequently fidgets
4 = Moderate: e.g., constantly fidgets, or frequently fidgets, wring hands and pulls clothing
5 = Moderately Severe: e.g., constantly fidgets, wring hands and pulls clothing
6 = Severe: e.g., cannot remain seated (i.e., must pace)
7 = Very Severe: e.g., paces in a frantic manner
8 = Cannot be assessed (e.g., scored from audiotape)

_____ *7. **MANNERISMS AND POSTURING:** Unusual and unnatural motor behavior. Rate only abnormality of movements; do not rate simple heightened motor activity here. Consider frequency, duration, and degree of bizarreness. Disregard suspected pathogenesis.
1 = Not observed.
2 = Very Mild: odd behavior but of doubtful clinical significance, e.g., occasional unprompted smiling, infrequent lip fashion, intermittent abnormal finger movements
3 = Mild: strange behavior but not obviously bizarre, e.g., infrequent head-tilting (side to side) in a rhythmic fashion, intermittent abnormal finger movements
4 = Moderate: e.g., assumes yoga position for a brief period of time, infrequent tongue protrusions, rocking
5 = Moderately Severe: e.g., assumes and maintains yoga positions throughout interview, unusual movements in several body areas
6 = Severe: as above, but more frequent, intense, or pervasive
7 = Very Severe: e.g., bizarre posturing throughout most of the interview, continuous abnormal movements in several body areas
9 = Cannot be assessed (e.g., scored from audiotape)

_____ 8. **GRANDIOSITY:** DURING THE PAST WEEK HAVE YOU FELT MORE SELF-CONFIDENT THAN USUAL? DO YOU HAVE ANY SPECIAL ABILITIES OR TALENTS? DO YOU FEEL THERE IS A SPECIAL PURPOSE OR MISSION TO YOUR LIFE? (HAVE YOU THOUGHT YOU MIGHT BE SOMEBODY RICH OR FAMOUS?)
Inflated self-esteem (self-confidence), or inflated appraisal of one's talents, powers, abilities, accomplishments, knowledge, importance, or identity. Do not score mere grandiose quality of claims (e.g., "I'm the worst sinner in the world." "The entire country is trying to kill me") unless the guilt/persecution is related to some special, exaggerated attributes of the individual. Also, the patient must claim exaggerated attributes: e.g., if

FIG. 6.1. *Continued.*

patient denies talents, powers, etc., even if he or she states that <u>others</u> indicate that he/she has these attributes, this item should not be scored (enter 99)

1 = Not reported

2 = Very Mild: e.g., is more confident than most people, but of only possible clinical significance

3 = Mild: e.g., definitely inflated self-esteem or exaggerates talents somewhat out of proportion to the circumstances

4 = Moderate: e.g., inflated self-esteem clearly out of proportion to the circumstances, or suspected grandiose delusion(s)

5 = Moderately Severe: e.g., a single (definite) encapsulated grandiose delusion, or multiple (definite) fragmentary grandiose delusions

6 = Severe: e.g., a single (definite) grandiose delusion/delusional system, or multiple (definite) delusions that the patient seems preoccupied with

7 = Very Severe: e.g., as above, but nearly all conversations is directed toward the patient's grandiose delusion(s)

9 = Cannot be assessed adequately because of severe formal thought disorder, uncooperativeness, or marked evasiveness/guardedness, or Not assessed

99 = Not scored

_____ 9. **DEPRESSIVE MOOD:** IN THE PAST WEEK HAVE YOU HAD LESS INTEREST IN YOUR USUAL ACTIVITIES? HAVE YOU FELT SAD OR DEPRESSED? (HAVE YOU CRIED AT ALL?) (HOW BAD IS THE FEELING?) (HOW LONG DOES IT LAST?)

Subjective report of feeling depressed, blue, "down in the dumps," etc. Rate only degree of reported depression. Do not rate on the basis of inferences concerning depression based upon general retardation and somatic complaints.

1 = Not reported

2 = Very Mild: occasionally feels somewhat depressed

3 = Mild: occasionally feels moderately depressed, or often feels somewhat depressed

4 = Moderate: occasionally feels very depressed, or often feels moderately depressed

5 = Moderately Severe: often feels very depressed

6 = Severe: feels very depressed most of the time

7 = Very Severe: feels very depressed nearly all of the time

9 = Cannot be assessed adequately because of severe formal thought disorder, uncooperativeness, or marked evasiveness/guardedness, or Not assessed

_____ 10. **HOSTILITY:** DURING THE PAST WEEK HAVE YOU BEEN FEELING IRRITABLE? HOW HAVE YOU BEEN GETTING ALONG WITH OTHER PEOPLE? (HAVE YOU GOTTEN IN ANY ARGUMENTS OR FIGHTS?) HAVE YOU BEEN EASILY ANNOYED OR ANGERED? (HOW STRONGLY HAVE YOU FELT THIS WAY?) (HOW MUCH OF THE TIME?)

Animosity, contempt, belligerence, disdain for other people outside the interview situation. Rate solely on the basis of the verbal report of feelings and actions of the patient toward others during the week. Do not infer hostility from neurotic defenses, anxiety or somatic complaints.

1 = Not reported

FIG. 6.1. *Continued.*

2 = Very Mild: occasionally feels somewhat angry

3 = Mild: often feels somewhat angry, or occasionally feels moderately angry

4 = Moderate: occasionally feels very angry, or often feels moderately angry or occasionally yells at others

5 = Moderately Severe: often feels very angry; often yells at others or occasionally threatens to harm others

6 = Severe: has acted on his anger by becoming physically abusive on one or two occasions or makes frequent threats to harm others

7 = Very Severe: has been physically aggressive and/or required intervention to prevent assaultiveness on several occasions; or any serious assaultive act

9 = Cannot be assessed adequately because of severe formal thought disorder; uncooperativeness, or marked evasiveness/guardedness, or Not assessed

____ 11. **SUSPICIOUSNESS:** HOW DID YOU GET ALONG WITH PEOPLE IN GENERAL DURING THE PAST WEEK? DO YOU FEEL THAT YOU HAV BE ON GUARD WITH PEOPLE? HAS ANYONE BEEN GIVING YOU A HARD TIME, OR ACCUSING YOU OF THINGS? HAS ANYONE DELIBERATELY TRIED TO ANNOY YOU? TRIED TO HARM YOU?

Belief (delusional or otherwise) that others have now, or have had in the past, malicious or discriminatory intent toward the patient. On the basis of verbal report, rate only those suspicions which are currently held whether they concern past or present circumstances.

1 = Not reported

2 = Very Mild: rare instances of distrustfulness which may or may not be warranted by the situation

3 = Mild: occasional instances of suspiciousness that are definitely not warranted by the situation

4 = Moderate: more frequent suspiciousness, or transient ideas of reference

5 = Moderately Severe: pervasive suspiciousness, or frequent ideas of reference

6 = Severe: definite delusion(s) of reference or persecution that is (are) not wholly pervasive (e.g., an encapsulated delusion)

7 = Very Severe: as above, but more widespread, frequent, or intense

9 = Cannot be assessed adequately because of severe formal thought disorder, uncooperativess, or marked evasiveness/guardedness, or Not assessed

____ 12. **HALLUCINATORY BEHAVIOR:** HAVE YOU HAD ANY UNUSUAL EXPERIENCES DURING THE PAST WEEK? DO YOU SEEM TO HEAR VOICES WHEN THERE'S NO ONE AROUND, AND NOTHING ELSE TO EXPLAIN IT? HAVE YOU HAD VISIONS, OR SEEN THINGS THAT OTHERS COULDN'T SEE? IS THERE ANYTHING UNUSUAL ABOUT THE WAY THINGS FEEL OR TASTE, OR SMELL? (HOW OFTEN DO YOU [HEAR VOICES]?) DO YOUR VOICES MAKE IT HARD TO CONCENTRATE?) (DO THEY TELL YOU TO DO THINGS?)

Perceptions (in any sensory modality) in the absence of an identifiable external stimulus. Rate only those experiences that have occurred during the last week. DO NOT rate "voices in my head," or "visions in my mind" unless the patient can differentiate between these experiences and his or her thoughts.

1 = Not reported

FIG. 6.1. *Continued.*

2 = Very Mild: suspected hallucinations only
3 = Mild: definite hallucinations, but insignificant, infrequent, or transient (e.g., occasional formless visual hallucinations, a voice calling the patient's name)
4 = Moderate: as above, but more frequent or extensive (e.g., frequently sees the devil's face, two voices carry on lengthy conversations)
5 = Moderately Severe: hallucinations are experienced nearly every day, or are a source of extreme distress
6 = Severe: as above, and has had a moderate impact on the patient's behavior (e.g., concentration difficulties leading to impaired work functioning)
7 = Very Severe: as above, and has had a severe impact (e.g., attempts suicide in response to command hallucinations)
9 = Cannot be assessed adequately because of severe formal thought disorder, uncooperativeness, or marked evasiveness/guardedness, or Not assessed

_____ *13. **MOTOR RETARDATION:** Reduction in energy level evidenced in slowed movements. Rate on the basis of observed behavior of the patient only; do not rate on the basis of patient's subjective impression of his or her own energy level.
1 = Not observed
2 = Very Mild and of doubtful clinical significance
3 = Mild: e.g., conversation is somewhat retarded, movements somewhat slowed
4 = Moderate: e.g., conversation is noticeably retarded but not strained
5 = Moderately Severe: e.g., conversation is strained, moves very slowly
6 = Severe: e.g., conversation is difficult to maintain, hardly moves at all
7 = Very Severe: e.g., conversation is almost impossible, does not move at all throughout the interview
9 = Cannot be assessed (e.g., scored from audiotape)

_____ *14. **UNCOOPERATIVENESS:** Evidence of resistance, unfriendliness, resentment, and lack of readiness to cooperate with the interviewer. Rate only on the basis of the patient's attitude and responses to the interviewer and the interview situation; do not rate on the basis of reported resentment or uncooperativeness outside the interview situation.
1 = Not observed
2 = Very Mild: e.g., does not seem motivated
3 = Mild: e.g., seems evasive in certain areas
4 = Moderate: e.g., monosyllable, fails to elaborate spontaneously
5 = Moderately Severe: e.g., expresses resentment and is unfriendly throughout the interview
6 = Severe: e.g., refuses to answer a number of questions
7 = Very Severe: e.g., refuses to answer most questions
9 = Cannot be assessed

_____ 15. **UNUSUAL THOUGHT CONTENT:** HAVE YOU HAD ANY DIFFICULTY WITH YOUR THINKING IN THE PAST WEEK? DO CERTAIN THINGS HAVE SPECIAL MEANING FOR YOU? (GIVE ME AN EXAMPLE.) IS THERE ANY INTERFERENCE WITH YOUR THOUGHTS? IS THERE ANYTHING

FIG. 6.1. *Continued.*

CONTROLLING YOUR THOUGHTS OR MOVEMENTS? DO YOU SEE
REFERENCES OT YOURSELF IN SURPRISING PLACES, LIKE ON TV?
Severity of delusions of any type—consider conviction, and effect on actions. Assume
full conviction if patient has acted on his or her beliefs. Rate on the basis of reported (i.e.,
subjective) information pertaining to the past week.
1 = Not reported
2 = Very Mild: delusion(s) suspected or likely
3 = Mild: at times, patient questions his or her belief(s) (partial delusion)
4 = Moderate: full delusional conviction, but delusion(s) has little or no influence on
behavior
5 = Moderately Severe: full delusional conviction, but delusion(s) has only occasional
impact on behavior
6 = Severe: delusion(s) has significant effect, e.g., neglects responsibilities because of
preoccupations with belief that he/she is God
7 = Very Severe: delusion(s) has major impact, e.g., stops eating because believes food is
poisoned
9 = Cannot be assessed adequately because of severe formal thought disorder,
uncooperativess, or marked evasiveness/guardedness, nor Not assessed

_____ *16. **BLUNTED AFFECT:** Diminished affective responsivity, as characterized by
deficits in facial expression, body gesture, and voice pattern. Distinguish from
EMOTIONAL WITHDRAWAL, in which the focus is on interpersonal impairment
rather than affect. Consider degree and consistency of impairment.
1 = Not observed
2 = Very Mild: e.g., occasionally seems indifferent to material that is usually
accompanied by some show of emotions
3 = Mild: e.g., somewhat diminished facial expression, or somewhat monotonous voice
or somewhat restricted gestures
4 = Moderate: e.g., as above, but more intense, prolonged or frequent
5 = Moderately Severe: e.g., flattening of affect, including at least two of the three
features: severe lack of facial expression, monotonous voices, or restricted body gestures
6 = Severe: e.g., profound flattening of affect
7 = Very Severe: e.g., totally monotonous voice, and total lack of expressive gestures
throughout the evaluation
9 = Cannot be assessed (e.g., scored from audiotape)

_____ *17. **EXCITEMENT:** Heightened emotional tone, including irritability and
expansiveness (hypomanic affect). Do not infer affect from statement of grandiose
delusions.
1 = Not observed
2 = Very Mild and of doubtful clinical significance
3 = Mild: e.g., irritable or expansive at times
4 = Moderate: e.g., frequently irritable or expansive
5 = Moderately Severe: e.g., constantly irritable or expansive; or, at times, enraged or
euphoric
6 = Severe: e.g., enraged or euphoric throughout most of the interview

FIG. 6.1. *Continued.*

7 = Very Severe: e.g., as above, but to such a degree that the interview must be terminated prematurely
9 = Cannot be assessed

_____ *18. **DISORIENTATION:** NOW I WANT TO ASK YOU SOME STANDARD QUESTIONS THAT WE USUALLY ASK AT THIS POINT. WHAT IS TODAY'S DATE? (WHAT DAY OF THE WEEK IS IT? WHAT MONTH? WHAT DAY OF THE MONTH? WHAT YEAR?) WHERE ARE WE NOW?
Confusion or lack of proper association for person, place, or time.
1 = Not observed
2 = Very Mild: e.g., seems somewhat confused
3 = Mild: e.g., indicates 1982 when, in fact, it is 1983
4 = Moderate: e.g., indicates 1978
5 = Moderately Severe: e.g., is unsure where he/she is
6 = Severe: e.g., has no idea where he/she is
7 = Very Severe: e.g., does not know who he/she is
9 = Cannot be assessed adequately because of severe formal thought disorder, uncooperativeness, or marked evasiveness/guardedness, or Not assessed

_____ *19. **INAPPROPRIATE AFFECT:**
Affect expressed is inappropriate or incongruous with the context of the situation. Most typically, this manifestation of affective disturbance takes the form of smiling or assuming a silly facial expression while talking about a serious or sad subject.
1 = Not observed
2 = Very Mild: questionable
3 = Mild: at least one clear instance of inappropriate smiling or other inappropriate affect
4 = Moderate: at least two clear instances of inappropriate affect
5 = Moderately Severe: occasional to frequent instances of inappropriate affect
6 = Severe: frequent instances of inappropriate affect
7 = Very Severe: affect is inappropriate most of the time
9 = Cannot be assessed adequately because of severe formal thought disorder, uncooperativeness, or marked evasiveness/guardedness, or Not assessed

FIG. 6.1. *Continued.*

DIFFERENTIAL DIAGNOSIS

Case Example

Mr. D. is a 32-year-old man who came to the emergency room complaining of auditory hallucinations and self-destructive thoughts. Although he had been treated with haloperidol in the past, he had been compliant with medication for the 6 months before admission. He also complained of decreased appetite, decreased sleep, and memory impairment. On evaluation, his speech was mildly pressured and he appeared anxious. He complained of auditory hallucinations that told him to harm himself. Despite the hallucinations, he denied that he would harm himself and reported that the hallucinations did not compel him to harm himself. A telephone call to his mother revealed that he had a 10-year history of schizophrenia and that he improved on antipsychotic medication. The patient's physical examination was unremarkable. His laboratory examination revealed hypertriglyceridemia and hypercholesterolemia.

On admission to a psychiatric unit, the nursing staff noted that Mr. D had a number of obsessions as well as compulsions to wash his hands. In addition, his mood was moderately depressed and he expressed hopelessness about his current life situation.

The patient reported that he would not take haloperidol because it caused visual impairment. The visual problem was considered likely to have resulted from blurred vision from benztropine that was prescribed with his antipsychotics. He agreed to a trial of risperidone and was treated with 4 mg daily. After 2 weeks of treatment his auditory hallucinations and depression remitted. He continued to have hand-washing compulsions, although their frequency diminished.

This case emphasizes that patients who are acutely psychotic may also have severe symptoms that are not actually psychotic. In this case, the patient experienced both depression and obsessive-compulsive symptoms. Although the history suggested that the patient suffered from schizophrenia, it was impossible to rule out a schizoaffective disorder at the time of admission. The clinician appropriately treated the patient with only an antipsychotic, which led to clinical improvement of the psychosis, depression, and obsessive-compulsive symptoms. Clinical observation and additional documentation of the psychiatric history will be helpful in clarifying the diagnosis. Following an initial evaluation, the clinician appropriately assigned a provisional diagnosis of schizophrenia, rule out schizoaffective disorder and began treating the patient's psychosis.

As mentioned earlier, an acute psychosis is a clinical syndrome that can result from a number of different disorders. The process of establishing a diagnosis includes gathering historical information, the current mental state, and physical and laboratory findings. This information is used as the basis for ruling out or ruling in various diagnostic possibilities. Since no single diagnostic feature or laboratory finding is unique to schizophrenia, the diagnosis is made after other illnesses are excluded. Figure 6.2 outlines the diagnostic process for a psychotic episode. The first consideration is to rule out psychoses that are secondary to medical or neurologic disorders. These can

1. Assure the patient's immediate safety and those around him/her.

2. Rule out acute medical conditions that can cause delirium or psychosis.

3. Rule out psychosis secondary to medical or toxic causes.

4. Rule out psychosis that is secondary to mood disorders, schizophreniform disorders, delusional disorders, brief psychotic episodes, and psychoses not otherwise specified.

FIG. 6.2. Diagnostic process in schizophrenia.

be roughly categorized into neurodegenerative diseases (e.g., Huntington's disease), infections (e.g., HIV), focal lesions (e.g., tumors), metabolic encephalopathies (e.g., hepatic encephalopathy), endocrine abnormalities (e.g., hyperthyroidism), and toxic encephalopathies (e.g., phencyclidine intoxication). Although a careful evaluation usually is sufficient for ruling out these other disorders, there are circumstances when the diagnosis is complicated. For example, patients with schizophrenia may also have medical and neurologic disorders.

It is uncommon for neurodegenerative diseases to appear initially as psychoses. Among the degenerative disorders, Alzheimer's disease is probably the most common cause of acute psychotic symptoms. However, other evidence of dementia, particularly memory loss, usually precedes psychosis. About 30% to 40% of Alzheimer's patients will experience delusions at some time during their illness. Delusions are often paranoid and seldom systematized (7).

Other neurodegenerative diseases that may present as psychosis include Huntington's disease, Wilson's disease, multiple sclerosis, and metachromatic leukodystrophy.

Although psychotic symptoms are relatively uncommon in HIV encephalopathy, this diagnosis should be considered in patients who have HIV risk factors. One study found that patients with HIV encephalopathy were more likely to have a history of substance abuse and more likely to have neuropsychological impairment than HIV patients without psychosis (8).

Psychosis can occur in temporal lobe epilepsy and in other forms of seizure disorders. Psychotic symptoms can occur during seizures (ictal), following seizures (postictal), and between seizures (interictal) (9). Interictal psychoses are probably the most difficult to distinguish from schizophrenia. Aside from a history of a seizure disorder, other features that suggest interictal seizures are a predominance of visual over auditory hallucinations, a lack of negative symptoms, and unsystematized delusions.

Psychotic symptoms such as delusions and hallucinations can be presenting symptoms in a number of metabolic encephalopathies (e.g., renal failure, hepatic failure); endocrine disorders affecting the thyroid, parathyroid, or adrenal glands; and collagen diseases (e.g., systemic lupus erythematosis). Such drugs as l-dopa, anticholinergics, and certain groups of antihypertensives can also cause symptoms that can be confused with schizophrenia. Alcohol withdrawal can result in intense delusions and hallucinations. Moreover, chronic alcoholism can result in hallucinations that fail to remit for years after the cessation of drinking.

Perhaps the most common secondary psychotic reactions that can be confused with schizophrenia are those caused by substances of abuse. More than half of patients with nonaffective psychoses met criteria for a substance abuse disorder at some time during their life (10). Substances that can cause psychotic symptoms that resemble those in schizophrenia include lysergic acid diethylamide (LSD), phencyclidine hydrochloride (PCP), cocaine, amphetamines, and mescaline. The difficult dilemma for clinicians stems from the fact that these agents can also worsen psychotic symptoms in individuals with schizophrenia or exacerbate symptoms in patients who have been stabilized. Consequently, positive urine or blood toxicologies do not mean that the current psychotic state results from drug intoxications. Distinguishing a drug-induced psychosis from a psychotic exacerbation caused by drugs often requires a careful psychiatric history and a period of drug-free observation. Since such drugs as amphetamines may have long half-lives, an observation period of weeks rather than days may be necessary for a diagnosis (11). Other conditions (e.g., alcoholic hallucinosis) can persist for years after alcohol use has ceased.

A number of signs or symptoms should raise a clinician's suspicion that a patient may have a psychosis that is secondary to a medical disorder or substance use. These include clouded consciousness and confusion. Unstable vital signs such as tachycardia or increased blood pressure can suggest amphetamine intoxication, alcohol withdrawal states, or endocrine abnormalities. Hallucinations, whether auditory, olfactory, tactile, or visual, that are particularly vivid should suggest that the patient may be experiencing a secondary psychosis. Moreover, although visual and olfactory hallucinations can occur in schizophrenia, their presence should lead the clinician to search for other disorders than schizophrenia.

After medical conditions and substance abuse have been ruled out as the cause of a psychotic condition, the clinician should rule out psychiatric conditions other than schizophrenia. Although reaching an accurate diagnosis is clearly important, there is less urgency than with medical and substance-induced conditions that may be life-threatening, on the one hand, or correctable, on the other. Moreover, the initial treatment of a psychotic condition may be similar if the underlying condition is due to an affective or a

TABLE 6.2. *Differential diagnosis of schizophrenia*

Psychotic disorders due to general medical conditions, delirium
Psychotic disorders due to general medical conditions, dementia
Substance-induced psychotic disorder
Substance-induced delirium
Substance-induced persisting dementia
Mood disorder with psychotic features
Schizoaffective disorder
Schizophreniform disorder
Brief psychotic disorder
Delusional disorder
Psychotic disorder not otherwise specified

schizophrenic illness. In acute settings, it may be most useful for the clinician to treat an illness that cannot be diagnosed definitively and to postpone a final diagnosis until adequate information is assembled.

Table 6.2 lists psychiatric conditions that should be ruled out. The most common discrimination that is likely to occur is among mood disorders with psychotic features, schizoaffective disorders, and schizophrenia. In mood disorders, psychosis can occur in either bipolar disorder or major depressive disorder. The differentiation among these disorders cannot be made in a single point in time, since severe mood symptoms can occur in schizophrenia and hallucinations and delusions can occur in mood disorders. The differentiation involves investigating the time course of symptoms and noting the predominance of certain features over the course of the illness (reviewed in *DSM-IV*). If the psychotic symptoms only occur when the patient has a mood disorder, then the diagnosis is most likely a mood disorder. Patients with schizoaffective disorders usually have mood symptoms that occur for a substantial portion of the duration of psychotic symptoms. Delusions or hallucinations must be present for at least 2 weeks in the absence of mood symptoms. This can be difficult to differentiate from mood symptoms in schizophrenia, which usually occur for a relatively brief duration compared with psychotic symptoms.

Other disorders in Table 6.2 are easier to rule out. Schizophreniform disorder is ruled by its shorter duration; brief psychotic disorders are defined as lasting only a day to 1 month; and delusional disorder is characterized by nonbizarre delusions and the absence of other deficits that are characteristic of schizophrenia.

REFERENCES

1. Buchanan A. The investigation of acting on delusions as a tool for risk assessment in the mentally disordered. *Br J Psychiatry Suppl* 1997;32:12–16.

2. Swanson JW, Holzer CE III, Ganju VK, et al. Violence and psychiatric disorder in the community: evidence from the Epidemiologic Catchment Area surveys [published erratum appears in *Hosp Community Psychiatry* 1991;42:954–955]. *Hosp Community Psychiatry* 1990;41:761–770.
3. Herz MI., Melville C. Relapse in schizophrenia. *Am J Psychiatry* 1980;80:801–805.
4. Van Putten T, May PR, Marder SR. Akathisia with haloperidol and thiothixene. *Arch Gen Psychiatry* 1984;41:1036–1039.
5. American Psychiatric Association. Practice Guideline for psychiatric evaluation of adults. *Am J Psychiatry* 1995;152:67–80.
6. Overall JE, Gorham DE. The Brief Psychiatric Rating Scale. *Psychol Rep* 1961;10: 799–812.
7. Jeste DV, Heaton SC, Paulsen JS, et al. Clinical and neuropsychological comparison of psychotic depression with nonpsychotic depression and schizophrenia. *Am J Psychiatry* 1996;96:490–496.
8. Sewell DD, Jeste DV, Atkinson JH, et al. HIV-associated psychosis: a study of 20 cases. San Diego HIV Neurobehavioral Research Center Group. *Am J Psychiatry* 1994;151: 237–242.
9. Trimble MR, Ring HA, Schmitz B. Neuropsychiatric aspects of epilepsy. In: Fogel BS, Schiffer RB, Rao SM, eds. *Neuropsychiatry.* Baltimore: Williams & Wilkins, 1996: 771–803.
10. Kendler KS, Gallagher TJ, Abelson JM, et al. Lifetime prevalence, demographic risk factors, and diagnostic validity of nonaffective psychosis as assessed in a US community sample. The National Comorbidity Survey. *Arch Gen Psychiatry* 1996;53:1022–1031.
11. Poole R, Brabbins C. Drug induced psychosis [editorial] [see comments]. *Br J Psychiatry* 1996;168:135–138.

7

Management and Treatment of the Acute Phase of Schizophrenia

The acute phase of schizophrenia is characterized by severe positive symptoms that may be accompanied by negative symptoms, neurocognitive impairments, and mood symptoms. Acutely ill patients usually display greatly impaired reality testing, disorganized speech and grossly impaired judgment, along with an inability to care for themselves. During this phase there may be an increased potential for harm to self or others with poor impulse control and labile affect. Goals of treatment are to reduce psychotic symptomatology, control disturbed behavior, especially that which may be harmful to self or others, and provide structure, protection, and support for the patient.

CHOICE OF SITE OF TREATMENT

After the initial evaluation has been completed, the clinician's task is to determine the optimal treatment setting for the patient. The choice whether or not to hospitalize will depend on a number of factors, including the clinical status of the patient, the availability of alternative treatment programs, social supports, and adequate living arrangements in the community, and the wishes of the patient and family members. The patient should be treated in the least restrictive environment that offers the greatest potential for a positive outcome of the acute episode.

When patients are considered to be a serious threat to themselves or others and/or are unable to care for themselves without constant supervision, hospitalization is almost always indicated. There are many other possible indications for hospitalization of acutely psychotic patients, but these must be weighed against reasons for treatment in alternative settings, such as day hospitals, crisis residencies, home care, crisis family intervention, and the PACT Program, including assertive outreach (1). In fact, results of controlled studies have shown that outcome regarding symptom resolution, role functioning, and rehospitalization is at least as good and often better for patients treated in alternative settings instead of hospitals. For example, there have been many studies of day hospitalization as an alternative to inpatient care for acutely ill patients showing positive results in all of these areas for patients treated in day hospitals (2–13).

EXAMPLES OF SITUATIONS WHERE HOSPITALIZATION SHOULD BE STRONGLY CONSIDERED

Case 1

Bill is a 32-year-old single unemployed male who lives alone in a small apartment. He was diagnosed with schizophrenia about 6 years ago and with diabetes about 3 years ago. Until 2 months ago he could care for himself and was cooperative with treatment at a local mental health clinic. He followed his diabetic diet, injected himself with insulin daily, and was monitored for his diabetes by a visiting nurse service. It is not clear what precipitated his psychotic decompensation. He became increasingly delusional about the walls of his apartment being wired, believed he was being observed, and heard voices telling him to be watchful. He stopped going to the clinic and, despite outreach efforts, rarely took his antipsychotic medication, didn't follow his diabetic diet, and missed taking his insulin injections. The visiting nurses were alarmed because he was losing weight and had a very high serum glucose level. They had a good relationship with him and convinced him to go to the local hospital emergency room, where it was decided that it was imperative to gain control of his diabetes and vigorously treat his increasingly severe psychotic symptoms. In the hospital, treatment compliance could be ensured, he could be monitored closely for both his psychosis and diabetes, and his diet could be controlled.

Case 2

April is a 25-year-old single female who lives with her family, which has become very worried about her because in the past 2 weeks she has been going out in the evening and staying out all night. Two days ago, she returned home in the morning with her face bruised and her watch missing. Yesterday she was picked up by the police because she was walking around in a fringe neighborhood frequented by drug dealers and prostitutes, and began to take her clothes off. Later, it was discovered that she had been responding to voices telling her to do so. She had a history of occasional marijuana and cocaine abuse but never took heroin. Family members noted that she was becoming increasingly disorganized in her speech, were worried about her poor judgment, and observed her apparently responding to voices and complaining that the police were persecuting her. She said that she had special powers but would not discuss them. Her treatment compliance was sporadic at best. She and her family were told that if she was willing to be admitted to a psychiatric hospital, charges for disrobing in public would be dropped. She was admitted to the local psychiatric unit of a general hospital.

Case 3

Robert is a 28-year-old male who lives with his family. For the past week he has been staying up all night pacing back and forth in his room with his radio blaring and cursing at the neighbors. He believes they want to harm him, and he has heard voices that told him his family is against him. He has frequent loud arguments with his mother and father about his noncooperation with taking his medication and his behavior at night, which not only keeps them all awake but disturbs the neighbors. The local mental health center attempted to intervene with frequent home visits, aiming to improve family functioning, but this was of little help. He refuses intramuscular, long-acting medication and is adamant about continuing his disruptive behavior. His father has missed a good deal of work because of lack of sleep and concern about the patient. The mother seems very depressed and has frequent crying spells. Despite the therapeutic intervention, the tension in the family continues to mount and the family appears to be at the breaking point. Finally, it was decided to admit the patient to the hospital to decompress the high stress level in the family. In the hospital, medication compliance would be ensured, leading to a reduction of psychotic symptoms and disruptive behavior.

Discussion

Conceivably, alternatives to hospitalization would have been feasible in these situations, but they would have required heroic efforts on the part of the treatment teams and family members. All these patients improved considerably within a few weeks and were discharged from the hospital. They made reasonably satisfactory adjustments in the community while receiving treatment at their community mental health centers. Although alternatives to hospitalization are effective in many acute situations, hospitalization should not be avoided at all costs.

If a patient has some ability and willingness to cooperate in treatment, is not a lethality risk, and has adequate housing and social support, alternatives to hospitalization should be considered.

EXAMPLES OF ACUTE SITUATIONS WHERE ALTERNATIVES TO HOSPITALIZATION MIGHT BE PREFERABLE TO HOSPITALIZATION

Case 1

Tom is a 29-year-old single white male diagnosed with schizophrenia 8 years ago who lives with his family. Three months ago he started a relationship with a young woman at his sheltered workshop, but it ended abruptly when she said that she was not attracted to him. Since that time he has been secluding himself in his room, rarely leaving it. He sits in front of the TV, usually staring into space. At times he appears to be responding to voices; he talks out loud with no one else in the room. His speech has become more and more disorganized. His parents are worried that he is going into "a dream world," and each day it becomes more difficult to understand what he is saying. He refuses to leave the house and won't even consider going to the hospital. Because he has missed appointments at his community mental health center (CMHC), their outreach team began making frequent home visits. Since it was unlikely that he was taking his medication, they encouraged him to begin intramuscular decanoate medication and he finally agreed. The team had regular family meetings, offering support for the family in dealing with the patient. Over time, he began to admit to feelings that he was not worthwhile and that he would never have a girlfriend. He showed gradual improvement over 3 to 4 weeks and finally started attending a therapeutic social club and going to his outpatient appointments at the CMHC.

Discussion

In this situation the family was given a good deal of support, communication was facilitated between family members and the patient, the patient became compliant with medication, and it was unnecessary to hospitalize him against his will.

Case 2

Betty is a 35-year-old single female who lives in a supervised group home and receives outpatient treatment monthly. About 2 months ago she was dismissed from a clerical job after working there for 6 months. She had considerable difficulty finding a job before obtaining the one she was dismissed from. Since leaving the job she stopped socializing with her friends, seemed angry and irritable, and heard voices that told her she was a bad person. Betty talked back to the voices and argued with them. She then started to believe that a famous movie star was in love with her and that she should go to see him in Hollywood. During the day she would walk the streets aimlessly but did return to her apartment. Her therapist had increased the frequency of therapy visits but the patient's condition continued to deteriorate, leading the therapist to recommend day hospitalization to arrest the psychotic decompensation and facilitate recovery. The feeling of treatment team members was that a structured day hospital program guaranteed compliance with medication and that opportunities to socialize would be helpful. She attended the day hospital regularly. At first, the day hospital provided a case manager who drove her to the program, but after a few weeks she attended on her own. Her psychotic symptoms resolved completely in 1 month and she has gone on to regular outpatient visits and appears to be compliant with medication.

Discussion

This was a case in which the patient's psychotic decompensation was arrested by attendance at a day hospital. Her outpatient clinic treatment was not effective. It became clear that the patient needed a more structured therapeutic program to stabilize her symptomatology.

Studies have shown that patients who are treated in community settings do as well or better on follow-up than hospitalized patients with regard to resolution of psychotic symptoms, improved role functioning, and relapse and rehospitalization rates.

ADVANTAGES OF HOSPITALIZATION

What are the relative advantages and disadvantages of hospitalization versus community treatment programs for acutely psychotic patients?

When there is concern about the ability of a patient to control aggressive or self-destructive behaviors, the hospital provides the greatest protection against acting on these impulses. Often when patients recover from an acute episode they may tell you that they felt relieved about being in a hospital where they would not be in danger of hurting themselves or others.

Families often undergo severe stress when living with acutely psychotic patients and feel very relieved when the patient is admitted to the hospital, thus reducing the tension level and family burden.

When the patient is in the hospital, the staff can observe changes in symptomatology and behavior, evaluate reactions to medication and dose changes, and manage such medical conditions as diabetes that have been neglected because of the psychosis.

It is easier to monitor for compliance with medication while patients are on the inpatient service.

Where there is lack of availability of adequate housing or accessibility to community treatment, as is the case in many rural areas, and where community treatment programs are not equipped to deal with acutely psychotic patients, hospitalization is necessary to ensure that the patient receives needed treatment. Community treatment programs should have the capability to provide assertive outreach for patients who refuse to comply with care, since a substantial percentage of acute patients are not compliant with treatment. When outreach is unavailable, hospitalization is usually necessary for noncompliant patients.

ADVANTAGES OF COMMUNITY TREATMENT
ALTERNATIVES TO HOSPITALIZATION

Community treatment alternatives offer less restrictive environments than the hospital, and many patients experience them as less stigmatizing and as a result have improved self-esteem. The message is communicated to the patient that he is not so deranged that he needs to be "put away" in a hospital. There is an expectation of healthier functioning, which may lead to less regression than might be expected on an inpatient service. Patients are motivated to build on whatever healthy functioning is available to them.

There is no separation from family and friends, which can be helpful, since many families offer a great deal of emotional support. Patients often feel more secure and comfortable at home than in a hospital setting.

Patients treated in the community can maintain some social and instrumental roles, even if they are limited. On the positive side, it avoids the trauma of separation of children from a parent, but that must be weighed against the potential negative effects on children of interacting with a psychotic parent.

Many individuals with schizophrenia have severe problems in managing their dependent and passive needs. Once a patient is hospitalized and subjected to a regressive environment, the likelihood may increase that he or she will regress in the face of a subsequent life stress. A related issue is that patients who have been hospitalized are more likely to be rehospitalized because emergency room psychiatrists more readily admit previously hospitalized patients.

Of practical importance, patients treated in the community continue to receive public assistance, whereas inpatient admission may lead to termination of income assistance, with the hassle of reapplying later.

Thus the choice of site of treatment for an acutely psychotic patient may be obvious in many cases, such as danger to himself or others, but in some situations the clinician must weigh the benefits and risks of inpatient care versus community care. If hospitalization is considered necessary, then every attempt should be made to obtain the patient's consent. Family members and friends can often be helpful in persuading patients of the need for hospitalization. If the patient refuses hospital admission and is judged to be a danger to himself or others or if the patient cannot remain in the community because of an inability to care for himself, then involuntary hospitalization according to state and local laws should be arranged.

HOSPITALIZATION

If the decision is made to hospitalize acutely psychotic patients, then the issues are the following:

What are the goals of hospitalization?
How long should hospitalization last?
What is the optimal hospital milieu that will facilitate achieving the goals?

In recent years there has been a trend toward decreasing the length of inpatient hospitalization. Contributing factors have been use of antipsychotic medications; recognition that hospital treatment is but one modality in the treatment of an acute episode, with patients moving to a lesser intensity of care during the process of recovery; and stringent limitations placed upon length of hospitalization by third-party payers.

Is the shortening of inpatient stay justified by results of controlled research studies, or is it just an expedient way to save money? A related issue is whether adequate community programs are in place to offer comprehensive and continuous care for patients who are discharged after brief hospitalization. A number of controlled studies have compared brief with longer hospitalization (4,14–22). In the United States, the study by Herz et al. had the shortest stay brief hospitalization, comparing an 11-day stay with a 60-day stay (14). Despite differences in lengths of hospitalization, all these studies lead to the same conclusions: A lengthier hospital stay has no advantage over a brief hospital stay for most patients when outcome after 2 years is measured by symptomatology, role functioning, and readmission rates. Results of studies by Herz et al. and Caffey et al. showed that ensuring adequate posthospital aftercare treatment is probably more important than the length of hospital stay in determining outcome, since patients discharged from brief hospital treatment are often highly symptomatic (14,15). Furthermore, after resolution of the acute episode, it is the quality of ambulatory treatment that determines long-term outcome. Arrangements for community treatment programs should be worked out while the patient is in the hospital, with follow-up necessary to ensure that the patient follows through with the appropriate ambulatory treatment facility. A seamless system should be in place to ensure that patients do not fall between the cracks and became lost to treatment. The system should facilitate the patient's movement to the next level of care rather than having bureaucratic barriers in place, such as the requirement for a patient to apply and be interviewed for the community treatment program after hospitalization. Many patients lack insight and motivation for treatment and will not make any effort to obtain it if impediments are put in their way. If there is no ambulatory treatment program or it is inaccessible, then the patient's hospital stay should be extended until symptoms have sufficiently resolved to enable the patient to function adequately with minimal care and support. This principle also applies for patients who are known to be noncompliant with ambulatory treatment and would not be expected to follow through after hospital discharge.

THE OPTIMAL MILIEU FOR SHORT-TERM INPATIENT UNITS

Since the major goal of hospitalization for most patients is the rapid resolution of acute psychotic symptoms, the hospital milieu should be organized to achieve that goal (23). In the past, most studies of hospital milieu were carried out on longer-stay inpatient units that focused not only on resolution of acute symptomatology, but also on providing an environment for psychotherapeutic intervention, development of social skills, and rehabilitation that are dealt with largely on an outpatient basis today. The aim should be to provide a safe, low-stress, highly structured, and well-organized environment. Patients need a clear, well-defined external structure, since they are suffering from severe thought disorganization, greatly impaired reality testing, autistic thinking, cognitive impairment, and perceptual distortions.

To provide structure and a well-defined external reality, staff should wear name tags, and calendars, clocks, ward schedules, and regulations should be posted in frequently traveled areas. Newly admitted patients should be oriented to the ward as soon as possible and should be given an informational booklet that can be referred to at the patient's leisure. A well-organized activity and recreational program is often beneficial and enables patients to utilize whatever abilities are available to them. Extrapolating from the findings of Linn et al., patients should spend time being involved in activities that anchor them to external reality and take them out of focusing on their internal psychotic and disorganized thinking (24). If therapy groups are provided they should be supportive, focused, structured, and nonconfrontational, and generally consist of not more than 8 to 10 patients. For example, groups should focus on discharge planning, including problems and situations that patients may face upon discharge from the hospital.

Large, unstructured community meetings can be antitherapeutic, sometimes becoming disorganizing and confrontational, with expression of high levels of anger and aggression that can be damaging to a patient's recovery process. Community meetings were designed for long-term inpatient units that treated patients with severe character disorders to facilitate improved communication between patients and staff. The aim was to facilitate social learning of cognitively intact patients as a component of the functioning therapeutic community. With the advent of short-term hospitalization for acutely psychotic patients, that approach has little or no value. It is important to remember that the way the milieu of the hospital is organized can have positive effects on facilitating a patient's recovery but can also be toxic, particularly for patients with acute disorganization, severely impaired reality testing, and severe cognitive defects.

INDIVIDUAL PSYCHOTHERAPY

The clinician should use a supportive psychotherapeutic approach aimed at establishing a therapeutic alliance with the patient. As much as possible the approach should be collaborative and undemanding, aiming to reduce stress, overstimulation, and tension and anxiety. Therapists should display empathy, warmth, and genuineness while promoting compliance with medication, providing reality testing, setting limits, and giving positive reinforcement for healthy behaviors. As the patient shows some improvement and appears able to assimilate the information, the therapist can begin to provide information about the nature and management of the schizophrenia. Since education of patients during therapy is an ongoing process, the extent of education during the acute phase depends on the wishes and receptivity of the patient and the clinical judgment of the psychiatrist. If a patient has severely impaired reality testing and/or cognitive impairment, that patient will probably not profit from extensive education about the illness. For patients who have extreme denial of illness, spending a good deal of time attempting to convince the patient about the diagnosis might be counterproductive and stressful for both patient and psychiatrist. Instead the clinician can emphasize that treatment will be aimed at reducing any discomfort the patient may be experiencing (e.g., insomnia, tension, and anxiety).

ENGAGEMENT WITH FAMILIES AND PSYCHOEDUCATION

It is important to attempt to engage the family in a collaborative effort as soon as possible. Families of patients who are acutely psychotic are usually under a great deal of stress and highly receptive and grateful for any therapeutic intervention. Especially for first- or second-break patients, families are very anxious to learn about diagnosis, prognosis, and what they can do to help a patient. Educational meetings both individually and in groups (survival workshops) that teach the family how to cope with schizophrenia and referral to local chapters of the Alliance for The Mentally Ill may be helpful. Family members can also profit by reading books and pamphlets that provide useful information about schizophrenia. It is important to recognize that family members need support and guidance during this time of crisis. This is a time for establishing a collaborative ongoing relationship.

MANAGEMENT AND TREATMENT OF ACUTE PSYCHOTIC EPISODES

Importance of Early Treatment

Nearly every acute psychotic episode should be managed with an antipsychotic medication. Moreover, antipsychotics should be introduced as early as possible when there is evidence of psychosis. Early and definitive intervention with medication is important because patients can do substantial damage to their lives when they are psychotic. The potential is obvious for a patient who tends to become violent or self-destructive when hallucinations or delusions emerge. But more subtle damage can also occur. Individuals can harm their reputations by inappropriate remarks or behavior when they are psychotic. Also, work and school performance frequently deteriorates during exacerbation of schizophrenia. Moreover, prolonged psychotic episodes may be associated with enduring damage. (See the review by Richard Wyatt in ref. 25.) Among the studies he cited is one by Philip R.A. May and his associates, who assigned recent-onset patients with schizophrenia to a number of conditions, including an antipsychotic or a placebo (26). Patients assigned to an antipsychotic were more likely to be discharged. When May followed the course of patients 5 years later, nearly all were receiving an antipsychotic. Individuals who had received a placebo 5 years earlier had a greater need for hospitalization and a worse social and vocational outcome. This suggested that the 6 months during which the patients did not receive an antipsychotic may have resulted in a worsening of the course of their illness. (See Chapter 4, "Early-Intervention Prevention Programs," for a more complete discussion of the issue.)

Although these studies can be faulted for their lack of adequate controls and other methodological issues, it is unlikely that definitive experiments comparing early intervention with delayed intervention will ever occur. Studies in delayed initiation of treatment with antipsychotic medication lasted months and years, and present no evidence that delaying pharmacotherapy for hours or days has lasting effects.

There are certain circumstances where it is probably justifiable to delay treatment for a brief time. The most obvious example is when the diagnosis is unclear. Symptoms resembling schizophrenia may occur during certain medical conditions (described earlier) or as a result of taking a number of drugs, including steroids, stimulants, and LSD. An appropriate medical evaluation that includes blood or urine toxicologies may lead the clinician to conclude that the psychotic symptoms are likely to improve with supportive care. When patients experience a psychotic episode under very stressful conditions, it may also be reasonable to delay treatment while alleviating the stress, including removing the individual from the stressful conditions. For example, patients who are agitated and psychotic may improve in the safe environment of a psychiatric hospital. A brief delay of pharmacotherapy until the patient is hospitalized may result in a more accurate baseline evaluation.

Preparing Patients for Treatment

Under most circumstances, patients should receive a physical examination and laboratory evaluation before beginning drug treatment. However, sometimes an adequate examination is impossible because the patient is agitated or uncooperative, or the need for treatment is urgent. Fortunately, most antipsychotics (with the exception of clozapine) are safe enough to administer without an examination (although it is important to confirm that the patient has not had allergic reactions to the selected agent). When the patient improves, the medical evaluation can be completed.

It is also important to attempt to explain the plan to the patient before beginning drug treatment. It is usually helpful to thoroughly explain the justification for drug treatment as well as likely side effects. This step may help address the mistrust many patients with schizophrenia experience during psychotic episodes. If the patient was previously treated with antipsychotics, it is often helpful to inquire about drug preferences and the patient's subjective experiences when different agents were administered. There is evidence that patient reports of their preference for a particular antipsychotic can be helpful in drug selection (26). Patients who felt they had a poor response to an antipsychotic tended to do poorly on that agent. Poor subjective responses were usually related to side effects, often akathisia (or restlessness). The poor symptomatic responses were probably related to the patient's inability to tolerate an effective dose or to poor compliance.

The manner in which drug treatment is explained to the patient will vary according to the patient's psychopathology. Patients who are suspicious may require a thorough explanation of what to expect during drug treatment, particularly when they are drug reluctant. Individuals who are plagued by psychotic ambivalence may become anxious if they believe they can decide themselves whether to accept drug treatment. These patients may feel relieved when the clinician asserts that the treatment provider has decided that pharmacotherapy is appropriate and the patient needs only to agree.

SELECTING AN ANTIPSYCHOTIC DRUG

At present, no particular antipsychotic agent is best for all patients with schizophrenia. Rather, an important art in pharmacotherapy is matching a patient with an antipsychotic that is likely to be effective and to have an acceptable side effect profile. The introduction of the newer second-generation antipsychotics (SGAs) during the past several years has made decision making about drug treatment much easier than it was in the past. A number of considerations should guide the selection of a drug—usually in the following order:

1. Will the patient require a drug that is in a short-acting, injectable form or one in a long-acting depot formulation?
2. What experiences has the patient had with different antipsychotics?
3. Which side effects are likely to be most troubling to this patient?
4. Will formulary or cost considerations guide decision making?

Although all the antipsychotics are available in an oral formulation, only a few are available as injectables. The clinician may choose to administer an injectable drug if a patient is agitated and will benefit from a drug that can achieve a plasma level in a briefer period of time. For example, most intramuscular antipsychotics reach a maximum plasma level within 30 to 60 minutes. Patients usually experience substantial calming within 15 minutes. In contrast, an orally administered drug reaches a maximum plasma level within 1 to 4 hours. An injectable drug may also be the choice for patients who refuse to take oral medication and are being treated involuntarily. In selecting among available short-acting injectables, the best choice is probably a high-potency agent such as haloperidol or fluphenazine. Low-potency injectables such as chlorpromazine have the advantage of being sedating, but these drugs can also cause severe hypotension. Haloperidol and fluphenazine have the advantage of being calming without being sedating, but they can cause severe extrapyramidal side effects (EPS), particularly akathisia and dystonia.

A clinician may also decide that a patient is a candidate for a long-acting depot medication. Such a medication may be used with patients who fail to take their oral medication regularly or who prefer the convenience of depot injections. These patients should be started on the oral form of the depot agent for acute therapy and then gradually changed to the depot as they stabilize. Since the only two depot antipsychotics that are currently available in the United States are haloperidol and fluphenazine, the oral forms of these drugs represent the logical choice.

In most cases, the decision will be to administer an oral antipsychotic. A number of considerations can be used to select among the large number of effective drugs. The information for making this decision will come from a history of prior responses to antipsychotic treatment. If a patient responded well or poorly to a particular antipsychotic, it is likely that this response will be repeated. As mentioned in Chapter 5, one of the most valuable predictors of a response to an antipsychotic is a patient's subjective response to that drug. Therefore the clinician's interpretation of a prior drug response should be supplemented by a patient's subjective response to that drug.

Patients who had a poor symptomatic response to a conventional antipsychotic (or dopamine receptor antagonist) are likely to respond poorly to other conventional agents. This is supported by studies indicating that responsiveness to one conventional drug is likely to predict responsiveness to others (27). Therefore a history of refractoriness to even a single conventional agent should encourage the choice of a newer agent. Evidence indicates that patients who were refractory to conventional agents are more likely to respond to a newer antipsychotic (SGAs). For example, studies that compared risperidone and olanzapine to haloperidol in refractory patients found that the newer drugs were more effective (28,29). As noted in Chapter 5, patients who have failed both conventional and newer agents should be considered candidates for clozapine treatment.

Overall, the differences in antipsychotic effectiveness between older and newer drugs are rather small. For example, a meta-analysis by Leucht of studies comparing risperidone or olanzapine to haloperidol found that the newer drugs were significantly more effective (30). However, the size of the effects were small and the differences were statistically significant because the studies had very large sample sizes. Although the differences in effectiveness may be small, the differences in side effects are large. In other words, the clearest differences between older and newer drugs are in their side effects, particularly EPS. As a result, patients who have a history of susceptibility to EPS should receive a newer drug.

Other side effects should also guide the selection of an antipsychotic. These include weight gain, sedation, anticholinergic effects, and prolactin elevation. As noted in Table 5.3, substantial differences exist among the newer and older drugs in these side effects. Concerns about these side effects should guide drug selection. For example, patients who are very concerned about weight gain may be candidates for ziprasidone or risperidone rather than olanzapine, whereas women with a history of menstrual irregularities may do better on olanzapine or quetiapine.

All these concerns about efficacy make the decision about an antipsychotic appear unusually complicated. In most cases, the newer antipsychotics, with the exception of clozapine, are the agents of first choice. The side effects of these agents are much easier to tolerate, particularly during the acute phase of treatment, when doses tend to be higher. In first-episode patients, it may be particularly important to select an agent with a mild side-effect profile, since these patients are often reluctant to accept their need for an antipsychotic. An unpleasant or even frightening first experience with an antipsychotic, particularly akathisia or dystonia, may affect the patient's long-term attitude toward antipsychotic drug treatment. For those who can tolerate a conventional agent—but at the cost of mild subjective akathisia or mild parkinsonism—a newer drug may improve that individual's quality of life. On the other hand, patients who require a depot antipsychotic or those who have difficulty with weight gain on a newer drug may be candidates for conventional agents.

INITIATING DRUG TREATMENT

The procedures for starting patients on antipsychotics will differ among the antipsychotics. However, two principles (see Chapter 5) should guide the clinician in developing a treatment strategy. The goal of the first weeks of treatment is to begin the patient on a dose of an antipsychotic that is likely to be effective, based on experiences of populations of patients or on prior experiences with the individual being treated. Once the patient has achieved a steady-state drug level, he or she should remain on the drug dose for 2 to 6 weeks, since this is the time period that may be necessary for a drug response to emerge. It is usually best to avoid the temptation to increase the dose during this time, since the increased dose is likely to increase side effects and unlikely to be more effective.

It is usually best to start with a relatively low initial dose of a drug that the patient has never received previously and to inquire about the patient's subjective response an hour or two afterward. A patient's early subjective response to an antipsychotic is almost always determined by its side effects rather than by its therapeutic effect. For example, if patients report that they feel calmer it is likely to be a result of a sedative side effect of a drug such as clozapine or a hypokinetic effect of a dopamine receptor antagonist such as haloperidol. Patients who claim that an antipsychotic makes them feel anxious may be experiencing antipsychotic-induced akathisia. Although these effects may be unrelated to whether the drug will be effective, these initial experiences are important, since they determine a patient's attitude about a drug. For this reason it may be helpful to begin the patient on low divided doses, such as 1 mg bid of risperidone, 5 mg bid of olanzapine, or 25 mg tid of quetiapine. As the patient demonstrates tolerance of these low doses, the dose can be gradually escalated to the therapeutic range. This strategy may add a day or two to the time it takes before a patient receives an adequate dose, but it may contribute toward a better attitude toward antipsychotic treatment.

When patients have been titrated to their target dose, they should remain at this dose unless they have adverse side effects. Most will respond to an antipsychotic within 2 to 6 weeks, although some will take longer. It is usually best to avoid the temptation to increase the antipsychotic dose during this period, even if the patient is not improving. If the patient improves after the dose is increased, it will be difficult to know whether the response resulted from the dose change or from the additional days on the drug. As a result, if clinicians titrate dose against clinical response during the early days of treatment, they are likely to treat patients with higher doses of antipsychotic medications than patients require.

Managing Anxiety and Depression in Acute Psychosis

During the acute treatment period, patients may experience periods of anxiety or depression, or they may demonstrate excited or agitated behavior. Although increasing the amount of antipsychotic may reduce anxiety, these agents may cause EPS and other side effects. Moreover, increasing the antipsychotic dose may cause agitation that is secondary to akathisia. In some cases, patients may experience subjective akathisia that is difficult for the clinician to diagnose, particularly in inarticulate patients who have difficulty describing their internal experiences. Studies indicate that adding benzodiazepines to an antipsychotic can reduce anxiety and agitation as well as psychosis in some patients (31). Not all studies have found that benzodiazepines are effective for anxiety, and some have found that these agents are useful only for the first 4 weeks of treatment (32).

Despite these limitations, benzodiazepines—particularly lorazepam and clonazepam—are commonly prescribed when patients with schizophrenia are anxious. These agents are usually preferable to increasing the dose of an antipsychotic but should be prescribed very cautiously in patients with a history of substance dependence, since they have a clear potential for abuse. Moreover, patients who discontinue these agents abruptly are vulnerable to seizures and other withdrawal symptoms. Also, there is no indication that any particular benzodiazepine is superior to any other. Lorazepam is commonly prescribed since it is well absorbed orally or intramuscularly and is less likely to lead to respiratory arrest.

Patients who are experiencing a psychotic episode frequently experience depression as well. Often symptoms of depressed mood fulfill diagnostic criteria for major depressive disorder except for the symptoms being related to the patient's acute schizophrenia. In evaluating these patients it is important to determine whether the mood symptoms are secondary to other factors such as parkinsonism and akinesia, which can be experienced as depression. Knight and Hirsch evaluated the course of depression in schizophrenia by following patients as they recovered from psychosis (33). For the most part, depression improved as patients recovered from psychosis when patients were treated with antipsychotics only. This suggests that antipsychotics alone are usually sufficient for treating depression in acute schizophrenia. If depression fails to improve after the psychosis has improved, it is probably time to introduce an antidepressant. An exception to this strategy would be if the patient is seriously suicidal and severely depressed. In this case an antidepressant should be prescribed immediately, along with the antipsychotic medication. The management of depression in schizophrenia is discussed in Chapter 5.

MANAGEMENT OF SUICIDAL PATIENTS

After a thorough evaluation taking into account major risk factors (listed in Chapter 6), patients who are considered seriously suicidal should be hospitalized, and precautions against suicide should be instituted immediately. These precautions should be stringent since many completed suicides occur within the first days of hospitalization. It is impossible to predict accurately which patients with high-risk indicators will make serious attempts that result in completed suicide. However, patients with these risk factors should be treated aggressively with antipsychotic medication and antidepressants if they are seriously depressed. The clinician should attempt to establish a positive therapeutic relationship with the patient using a supportive, empathic approach. There should be no hesitation about talking to the patient directly about suicidal thoughts, ideas, preoccupations, and intent. Many patients willingly discuss their thoughts and feelings as well as plans about suicide. For those who are closed to such discussions it is important to obtain information from family members or friends wherever possible. Patients who have made suicidal attempts in the past should especially be considered serious risks. The clinician should evaluate the patient on a regular basis to evaluate suicidality, taking into account changes in such variables as the extent of the patients guilt if depressed, the severity of the depression, the intensity of command hallucinations telling the patient to kill himself and the patient's perceived ability to resist the voices, severe paranoid delusions that frighten the patient (e.g., warning of terrible torture), and any severe discomfort could be related to akathisia. If the patient is experiencing akathisia, it should be treated vigorously with antiparkinson medication.

Another period of high vulnerability to suicide is the time just before discharge or soon after release from the hospital. As the intensity of the psychosis diminishes, the patient may begin to develop more insight and recognize the seriousness of his psychiatric condition. Patients who have been high achievers who had great expectations about their future accomplishments before developing schizophrenia may experience feelings of hopelessness and demoralization about their futures. Some of these individuals may feel that the answer is to commit suicide and not face the future. Other possible scenarios are patients having to face unresolved life events that may have precipitated the acute episode (e.g., the loss of a loved one and the prospect of returning home without that person). Another situation might involve an individual such as a college graduate facing the prospect of returning to a sheltered workshop, which he finds degrading. At times, patients face the loss of their therapists who treated them before hospitalization and having to face the prospect of relating to a new therapist. These issues should be discussed before hospital discharge and followed up after the patient has been discharged. Every attempt should be made to instill hope in demoralized patients as well as to help them deal with reality problems. There are situations when an unexpected life event can precipitate suicide.

Case Example of an Unexpected Life Event

Phillip is a 32-year-old male who has been diagnosed with schizophrenia and has had two previous hospitalizations. After each episode he returned to fairly normal functioning, including working at a mid-level job in a local company. He and his wife have had some marital difficulties, which appeared to be resolving. A few days before his planned discharge, he went to the hospital gift shop and bought a newspaper; then he called his wife. During that conversation his wife told him that she was having second thoughts about his returning home and that she was not happy with their relationship. After he asked her to reconsider, she said that they could discuss it the following day. Phillip immediately went up to the roof of the hospital and jumped off, killing himself. This is an example of an intervening unexpected life event that led to the patient's suicide.

Before a patient's discharge from the hospital, there should be education for family members and others who are close to the patient about indicators of suicide risk, learning how to identify these warning signs and what to do if they occur. This is especially important for patients who continue to have risk factors for suicide and have made attempts in the past.

MANAGEMENT OF AGGRESSIVE AND ASSAULTIVE PATIENTS

In managing aggressive or assaultive behavior in psychotic patients it is important to understand the underlying cause of these behaviors. For example, patients can become violent in response to delusional experiences such as paranoid fears or when command hallucinations implore them to commit a particular act. Other patients may become agitated when they experience severely discomforting akathisia. Patients with schizoaffective or bipolar illnesses may experience psychotic excitement with severe agitation and irritability. Similar psychotic excitement may result from stimulant drugs such as cocaine or amphetamines. The most useful pharmacologic strategy depends upon the cause of the agitation. For all these causes of aggressive behavior, there are principles of clinical management that are likely to be helpful. These include placing the patient in an environment that is safe for both the patient and those who will manage him or her. The management should be supportive as well as relatively unintrusive. Staff members should be experienced in behavioral treatment methods and limit setting. If restraint and or seclusion are necessary, they should be carried out in a skilled and nonjudgmental manner.

If aggressive and psychotic patients have not been treated with an antipsychotic, this should be initiated. Under certain circumstances when rapid control is important, 5 to 10 mg intramuscular doses of haloperidol, olanzapine, ziprasidone, and droperidol can decrease excitement relatively rapidly. Although droperidol has the advantage of more rapid onset and more reliable sedation, it has the disadvantage of causing more severe hypotension and respiratory depression. If patients have recently received an antipsychotic or if they are already stabilized on an antipsychotic, it may be helpful to sedate the patient with 1 to 2 mg of intramuscular lorazepam. Lorazepam can also be administered hourly as oral or intramuscular doses when patients remain agitated.

MANAGEMENT OF SIDE EFFECTS DURING ACUTE TREATMENT

The first experience a patient has with a new drug is almost invariably a side effect. In most cases, the antipsychotic effect will be delayed for days or weeks, whereas side effects are likely to appear almost immediately. Moreover, when patients experience discomfort from an antipsychotic, they are less likely to take it regularly and are more likely to refuse it (26). For this reason it is important to forewarn patients about what they can expect from a new medication and to emphasize that the clinician is interested in hearing about the patient's experiences. Certain experiences should be closely monitored during the first days of treatment. Although akathisia (characterized by a subjective feeling of motor restlessness and/or restless movements of the legs) is most common on high-potency conventional agents, it can occur with nearly all the newer second-generation antipsychotics. The diagnosis of akathisia can be missed when patients are poor describers of their internal experience or when restlessness is experienced as agitation or irritability. Also, patients may experience akathisia that is purely subjective. If the clinician depends on observing restless motor behavior, cases of subjective akathisia will be missed. If akathisia is diagnosed, it can usually be managed by decreasing the dose of antipsychotic, adding an anticholinergic antiparkinson medication, or adding a beta blocker such as 30 to 90 mg daily of propranolol administered in divided doses. Although there are very little data comparing the effectiveness of propranolol and anticholinergics in akathisia, it is our opinion that beta blockers are somewhat more effective.

Dystonias (which consist of spastic contractions of certain muscular groups, particularly the neck, eye muscles, and torso) usually arise within the first 3 days of drug treatment and can be extremely distressing. Moreover, dystonias leading to laryngospasm can be life-threatening. Patients, and often family members, should be instructed to contact their physician if they experience any type of muscular paralysis. Dystonias tend to be more common among younger patients, particularly young men. If a dystonia is present, the clinician should treat it aggressively. Most patients respond rapidly to an anticholinergic (e.g., benztropine 2 mg) or an antihistaminic (e.g., Benadryl 50 mg) administered intramuscularly or intravenously.

Medication-induced parkinsonism (consisting of tremor, rigidity, impaired gait) tends to be more common in elderly patients, although it can occur in any group. Akinesia—a form of medication-induced parkinsonism—can be characterized by decreased expressive gestures, less spontaneous speech, diminished interest in the patient's environment, and depression. As with subjective akathisia, it is a drug side effect that can easily be missed.

Other side effects can also interfere with early treatment. All the antipsychotics can cause sedation, although this is less common with high-potency compounds. In most cases, patients will gradually develop tolerance to sedation. The effects of serious sedation can often be managed by having patients take all or most of their medication near bedtime. This may not be possible with quetiapine or clozapine, which should be dosed more than once daily.

The course of hypotension during acute treatment is often similar to that of sedation in that patients usually develop tolerance over time. However, hypotension can be a serious side effect for some patients, particularly the elderly. These patients may be vulnerable to falls that can lead to fractures.

Other, less common side effects during acute treatment include seizures that can occur, especially with clozapine at higher doses. Anticholinergic effects, including constipation, blurred vision, dry mouth, and urinary retention, can be due to antipsychotics themselves—particularly clozapine, chlorpromazine, or olanzapine—or to anticholinergic antiparkinson agents. Anticholinergic drug effects can also impair memory. This can be a particular concern for elderly patients. Side effects such as weight gain and those affecting sexual function are more commonly a concern during maintenance treatment and are discussed in Chapter 9.

EVALUATING A POOR RESPONSE

A substantial proportion of patients with schizophrenia fail to demonstrate an adequate response to an antipsychotic. Estimates of the proportion of patients who respond poorly vary according to how rigorously treatment response is defined. For example, if the focus is on remission of positive symptoms, approximately 60% will improve to the extent that they will achieve a complete remission or experience only mild symptoms; the remaining 40% will improve but will demonstrate variable levels of positive symptoms resistant to medication. If treatment failure also includes remission of negative, neurocognitive, and mood symptoms, the rate of poor response is likely to be considerably higher. However, since the goals of treating acute psychosis in schizophrenia usually focus on positive symptoms, most clinicians define drug response in terms of positive symptom improvement.

A failure to respond may occur for a number of reasons. Some individuals may have a form of illness in which positive symptoms such as hallucinations and delusions do not respond adequately to antipsychotic medications. These patients comprise the group that is usually called "treatment resistant." However, other common reasons exist for patients not responding adequately. Some cannot tolerate the doses of antipsychotic necessary to treat psychotic symptoms. This failure to respond usually results from EPS when a high-potency conventional antipsychotic drug is prescribed but could also result from sedation or dizziness with a newer antipsychotic.

Before considering a patient a poor responder to a particular drug it is important to ensure that he or she received an adequate trial of the medication. A 6-week trial on an adequate dose of an antipsychotic represents a reasonable period for most patients. If patients demonstrate even a mild amount of improvement during this period, it may be reasonable to wait, since data from groups of patients indicate that patients may improve at a steady rate for 3 to 6 months.

It is also important to confirm that the patient is receiving an adequate amount of the drug. Patients often fail to respond to an antipsychotic because they are not adhering to their treatment schedule. Some patients openly acknowledge noncompliance with a treatment regimen but others may be surreptitious. Even when patients are being carefully observed in a hospital setting, a proportion of highly determined patients will manage to not take their antipsychotics. Under some conditions it may be helpful to confirm that the patient is receiving an adequate amount of the drug by monitoring the plasma concentration. Therapeutic plasma level monitoring is not available for all antipsychotics and may not be available in all settings. However, if the patient is receiving one of a number of antipsychotics, including haloperidol, clozapine, fluphenazine, trifluoperazine, and perphenazine, therapeutic plasma levels may be helpful. A very low plasma concentration may indicate that the patient has been noncompliant or, more commonly, only partially compliant. It may also suggest that the patient is a rapid metabolizer of the antipsychotic or that the drug is not being adequately absorbed. Under these conditions raising the dose may be helpful. If the level is relatively high, clinicians should consider whether side effects might be interfering with therapeutic response.

If the patient is responding poorly, many clinicians will consider raising the dose above the usual therapeutic level or changing the patient to a different antipsychotic. The use of high doses in those who respond poorly to medication has been studied under a number of circumstances. Nearly all studies found that higher doses were not associated with greater improvement than conventional doses (34). Other studies indicate that changing from one conventional antipsychotic to another is also unlikely to be successful (27). These observations suggest that changing to a newer agent is more likely to be successful.

Substantial evidence indicates that clozapine is effective for patients who respond poorly to conventional antipsychotics. Double-blind studies comparing clozapine with other antipsychotics indicated that clozapine had the clearest advantages over conventional drugs in patients with the most severe psychotic symptoms as well as those who had previously responded poorly to other antipsychotics. The most definitive evidence of clozapine's advantages in this population comes from a multicenter trial in which clozapine was compared with chlorpromazine (35). Subjects in this study were a severely psychotic group of patients who had failed in trials with at least three antipsychotics. Clozapine was significantly more effective than chlorpromazine in nearly every dimension of psychopathology, including both positive symptoms and negative symptoms. This study found that 30% of patients treated with clozapine met improvement criteria by the end of the 6-week trial. Studies with a longer duration indicate that 60% of patients are likely to meet these same improvement criteria when patients are maintained on clozapine for 6 months (36).

Evidence also suggests that risperidone and olanzapine may be helpful when a conventional antipsychotic is only partially effective (see Fig. 5.1). A Swiss study found that clozapine and risperidone were equally effective in a treatment-resistant population, but risperidone's side effects were more easily tolerated (37). Another study found that risperidone was somewhat more effective than haloperidol in a similar population and that risperidone was better tolerated (28). A multicenter comparison of olanzapine and haloperidol in a largely treatment-resistant group of patients found that olanzapine was more effective for both positive and negative symptoms, and resulted in fewer side effects (29). These findings conflict with a study by Conley and co-workers, who found that olanzapine and chlorpromazine resulted in similar and low response rates in a treatment-resistant population (38). However, the Conley study consisted of patients who had failed to improve on both older antipsychotics and newer ones, including clozapine. Nevertheless, this study supports the experiences of the authors that clozapine may be more effective than other new drugs for the most severely ill treatment-refractory patients. Given the difficulties associated with clozapine, a reasonable strategy for refractory patients is to first administer an adequate trial of a newer drug, such as risperidone, olanzapine, or quetiapine. If the patient continues to demonstrate disturbing psychotic symptoms, the clinician should consider changing to another new drug or moving directly to clozapine.

Some patients have failed to respond to all the newer drugs, including clozapine. Virtually no empirical data exist to aid the clinician faced with these very difficult patients. It is common practice in Europe and the United States to add a high-potency antipsychotic to clozapine when patients have resistant-positive symptoms. Although this adjunctive agent has traditionally been a high-potency conventional agent such as haloperidol or fluphenazine, many clinicians added other new agents to clozapine. For example, if a patient has a limited tolerance for clozapine because of sedation or seizures, it is reasonable to attempt adding another SGA and lowering the clozapine dose. Risperidone may be helpful under these conditions, since it does not add to the sedation or anticholinergic effects of clozapine. Although there are reports of clinicians using other combinations, there is no evidence that these strategies are helpful.

Patients who show little or no response to trials of antipsychotic medications and who remain grossly psychotic may be candidates for electroconvulsive therapy (ECT), especially if affective features are present (39). A trial of ECT may be from eight to 20 treatments. It is recommended that antipsychotic medication be continued during and after ECT when used for patients with schizophrenia. ECT is often very helpful for severely catatonic patients who do not respond to a trial of lorazepam 1 to 2 mg IV or IM, or 2 to 4 mg PO repeated as needed over 48 to 72 hours.

Long-term hospitalization should be considered for treatment-refractory patients who cannot function adequately or safely in the community because of severe psychotic symptoms, usually involving severe thought disorganization and inability to care for themselves, which is often accompanied by bizarre behavior. Long-term inpatient units using behavioral approaches with token economies have been successful in improving patients' functioning and allowing some to be discharged to highly structured supportive living programs in the community (40–44).

REFERENCES

1. Warner R, Wolleson C. Alternative acute treatment settings. In: Vaccaro JV, Clark GH, eds. *Practicing psychiatry in the community: a manual.* Washington, DC: American Psychiatric Press, 1996:89–115.
2. Wilder JF, Levin G, Zwerling I. A two-year follow-up evaluation of acute psychotic patients treated in a day hospital. *Am J Psychiatry* 1966.;122:1095–1101.
3. Herz MI, Endicott J, Spitzer RL, et al. A. Day versus inpatient hospitalization: a controlled study. *Am J Psychiatry* 1971;71:1371–1382.
4. Hirsch SR, Platt S, Knight A, et al. Shortening hospital stay for psychiatric care: effect on patients and their families. *Br Med J* 1979;1:442–446.
5. Herz MI, Endicott J, Gibbon M. Brief hospitalization: two-year follow-up. *Arch Gen Psychiatry* 1979;36:701–705.
6. Washburn S, Vannicelli ML, Longabaugh R, et al. A controlled comparison of psychiatric day treatment and inpatient hospitalization. *J Consult Clin Psychol* 1976;44:665–676.
7. Creed F, Black D, Anthony P. Day-hospital and community treatment for acute psychiatric illness: a critical appraisal. *Br J Psychiatry* 1989;154:300–310.
8. Creed F, Black D, Anthony P, et al. Randomised controlled trial of day patient versus inpatient psychiatric treatment. *BMJ* 1990;300:1033–1037.
9. Creed F, Black D, Anthony P, et al. Randomised controlled trial of day and in-patient psychiatric treatment. 2: Comparison of two hospitals. *Br J Psychiatry* 1991;158:183–189.

10. Dick P, Cameron L, Cohen D, et al. A. Day and full time psychiatric treatment: a controlled comparison. *Br J Psychiatry* 1985;147:246–249.
11. Gudeman JE, Dickey B, Evans A, et al. Four-year assessment of a day hospital–inn program as an alternative to inpatient hospitalization. *Am J Psychiatry* 1985;142:1330–1333.
12. Gudeman JE, Shore MF, Dickey B. Day hospitalization and an inn instead of inpatient care for psychiatric patients. *N Engl J Med* 1983;308:749–753.
13. Schene AH, van Wijngaarden B, Poelijoe NW, et al. The Utrecht comparative study on psychiatric day treatment and inpatient treatment. *Acta Psychiatr Scand* 1993;87:427–436.
14. Herz MI, Endicott J, Spitzer RL. Brief hospitalization: a two-year follow-up. *Am J Psychiatry* 1977;77:502–507.
15. Caffey EM, Jones RD, Diamond LS, et al. Brief hospital treatment of schizophrenia: early results of a multiple-hospital study. *Hosp Community Psychiatry* 1986;19:282–287.
16. Caffey EM, Galbrecht CR, Klett CJ. Brief hospitalization and aftercare in the treatment of schizophrenia. *Arch Gen Psychiatry* 1971;24:81–86.
17. Glick ID, Hargreaves WA, Raskin M, et al. Short vs. long hospitalization: a prospective controlled study, II. Results for schizophrenic inpatients. *Arch Gen Psychiatry* 1975;132:385–390.
18. Hargreaves WA, Glick ID, Drues J, et al. Short vs. long hospitalization: a prospective controlled study, VI. Two-year follow-up results for schizophrenics. *Arch Gen Psychiatry* 1977;20:305–311.
19. Rosen B, Katzoff A, Carillo C, et al. Comparison of the clinical effectiveness of "short" versus "long" stay psychiatric hospitalization, I. Inpatient results. *Arch Gen Psychiatry* 1976;33:1316–1322.
20. Mattes JA, Rosen B, Klein DF. Comparison of the clinical effectiveness of "short" versus "long" stay psychiatric hospitalization. II. Results of a 3-year posthospital follow-up. *J Nerv Ment Dis* 1977;165:387–394.
21. Mattes JA, Rosen B, Klein DF, et al. Comparison of the clinical effectiveness of "short" versus "long" stay psychiatric hospitalization. III. Further results of a 3-year posthospital follow-up. *J Nerv Ment Dis* 1977;165:395–402.
22. Mattes JA, Klein DF, Millan D, et al. Comparison of the clinical effectiveness of "short" versus "long" stay psychiatric hospitalization, IV. Predictors of differential benefit. *J Nerv Ment Dis* 1979;167:175–181.
23. Herz MI. Short-term hospitalization and the medical model. *Hosp Community Psychiatry* 1979;79:117–121.
24. Linn MW, Caffey EM, Klett CJ, et al. Day treatment and psychotropic drugs in the aftercare of schizophrenic patients. *Arch Gen Psychiatry* 1979;36:1055–1066.
25. Wyatt RJ. Neuroleptics and the natural course of schizophrenia. *Schizophr Bull* 1992;17:325–351.
26. Van Putten T, May PR, Marder SR. Response to antipsychotic medication: the doctor's and the consumer's view. *Am J Psychiatry* 1984;141:16–19.
27. Kolakowska T, Williams AO, Ardern M, et al. Schizophrenia with good and poor outcome. I: Early clinical features, response to neuroleptics and signs of organic dysfunction. *Br J Psychiatry* 1985;146:229–239.
28. Wirshing DA, Marshall BD Jr, Green MF, et al. Risperidone in treatment-refractory schizophrenia. *Am J Psychiatry* 1999;156:1374–1379.
29. Breier A, Hamilton SH. Comparative efficacy of olanzapine and haloperidol for patients with treatment-resistant schizophrenia [see comments]. *Biol Psychiatry* 1999;45:403–411.
30. Leucht S, Pitschel-Walz G, Abraham D, et al. Efficacy and extrapyramidal side-effects of the new antipsychotics olanzapine, quetiapine, risperidone, and sertindole compared to conventional antipsychotics and placebo: a meta-analysis of randomized controlled trials. *Schizophr Res* 1999;(35)??:51–68.

31. Wolkowitz OM, Pickar, D. Benzodiazepines in the treatment of schizophrenia: a review and reappraisal [see comments]. *Am J Psychiatry* 1991;148:714–726.
32. Csernansky JG, Riney SJ, Lombrozo L, et al. Double-blind comparison of alprazolam, diazepam, and placebo for the treatment of negative schizophrenic symptoms. *Arch Gen Psychiatry* 1988;45:655–659.
33. Knight A, Hirsch SR. Revealed depression and drug treatment of schizophrenia. *Arch Gen Psychiatry* 2001;40:893–896.
34. Marder SR. An approach to treatment resistance in schizophrenia. *Br J Psychiatry Suppl* 1999;17:19–22.
35. Kane JM., Honigfeld G, Singer J, et al. Clozapine for the treatment-resistant schizophrenic: a double-blind comparison versus chlorpromazine/benztropine. *Arch Gen Psychiatry* 1988;45:789–796.
36. Kane JM, Marder SR, Schooler NR, et al. Clozapine and haloperidol in moderately refractory schizophrenia: a six month randomized and double blind comparison. *Arch Gen Psychiatry* 2001;58:965–972.
37. Bondolfi G, Dufour H, Patris M, et al. Risperidone versus clozapine in treatment-resistant chronic schizophrenia: a randomized double-blind study. The Risperidone Study Group [see comments]. *Am J Psychiatry* 1998;155:499–504.
38. Conley RR, Kelly DL, Gale EA. Olanzapine response in treatment-refractory schizophrenic patients with a history of substance abuse. *Schizophr Res* 1998;33:95–101.
39. American Psychiatric Association. Practice guidelines for treatment of schizophrenia. *Am J Psychiatry* 1997;154[Suppl4]:1–63.
40. Paul GL. Lentz RJ. Psychological treatment of chronic mental patients: milieu versus social-learning programs. Cambridge, MA: Harvard University Press, 1977:214.
41. Glynn SM. Token economy approaches for psychiatric patients: progress and pitfalls over 25 years. *Behav Modif* 1990;14:383–407.
42. Liberman RP. Behavior modification of schizophrenia: a review. *Schizophr Bull* 1972;6:537–548.
43. Medotta A, Valdes LA, Beck NC. Implementing a comprehensive social learning program within a forensic psychiatric service of Fulton State Hospital. In: Corrigan PW, Liberman RP. *Behavior therapy in psychiatric hospitals*. New York: Springer, 1994:61–78.
44. Wong SE, Flanagan SG, Kuehnel TLG, et al. Training chronic mental patients to independently practice personal grooming skills. *Hosp Community Psychiatry* 1988;39:874–879.

8

Stabilization Phase

STRATEGIES FOR TREATMENT-RESPONSIVE PATIENTS

The stabilization phase begins when the patient shows some improvement in positive, negative, and disorganized symptomatology. There is no sharp demarcation or boundary between the acute phase and the stabilization phase or between the stabilization phase and the stable phase. During the stabilization phase—which may last up to about 6 months after the onset of the acute episode—patients are highly vulnerable to relapse. Thus a major aim during this phase is to provide support for patients and their families, minimize stress on the patient, foster the patient's adaptation to life in the community, and continue antipsychotic medication to reduce and if possible eliminate psychotic symptomatology.

Unfortunately, treatment research has focused on patients who are either acutely ill or in a stable state. As a result, recommendations for management during this phase are based mainly on the authors' clinical observations and expert consensus rather than on data from controlled studies (1). Nevertheless a number of management principles are self-evident for this phase. As stated previously (see Chapter 3, p. 143), clinical management should focus on ensuring that the transition from a more to a less intensive form of treatment is smoothly carried out. Often this transition coincides with discharge from inpatient hospitalization to partial hospitalization or outpatient treatment. This transition often includes a change in the patient's treatment team. In public settings it may also include a change from one governmental agency to another or from one therapist to another. These transitions may interrupt continuity of care, which is extremely important for patients at this stage. A seamless system of care should be in place so that patients do not fall between the cracks and become lost to treatment. Not infrequently, there are delays in patients following up outpatient appointments, or patients may be unable or unwilling to make an appointment and thus fail to receive follow-up outpatient treatment. Ensuring that the patient adheres to the treatment plan and makes the first appointment should be one of the priorities of discharge planning. A successful transition is more likely if the treatment teams are linked and the patient attends his or her first outpatient appointment while still in the hospital. It is also critical for the outpatient team to utilize assertive outreach involving telephone calls, home visits, or other means to ensure that patients are retained in treatment when they do not appear for their first and subsequent appointments.

Since most patients discharged from the hospital are not fully recovered from their psychotic symptomatology, transitional day hospitalization can be effective in fostering the stabilization process through the provision of a structured therapeutic environment. In the study by Herz et al. of brief hospitalization, approximately one-half of the patients profited from day hospitalization after hospital discharge (2). The group that was offered day hospitalization had better outcomes in terms of symptomatology and role functioning than the group whose members were randomly assigned to a brief hospital group without transitional day hospitalization. Both groups received outpatient clinic treatment.

Case Example of Transitional Day Hospitalization

After a 12-day hospitalization for an acute psychotic episode characterized by severe paranoid delusions, hallucinations, and thought disorganization, a 43-year-old man with schizophrenia was discharged to the community. At the time of discharge he had shown a partial response to olanzapine 15 mg daily. He was less fearful that there was a plot to kill him, his hallucinatory voices were less threatening, and his thinking was better organized. Transitional day hospitalization was arranged for the patient to facilitate his continuing recovery from the acute psychotic episode by providing a structured therapeutic environment that ensured 5 days of treatment per week, monitoring of clinical status, and compliance with medications. After 2 months in the day hospital his symptoms and functioning had substantially returned to baseline with no evidence of delusions, hallucinations, or thought disorganization, although he remained suspicious of the motives of other people. At that time he was discharged for follow-up in the outpatient clinic.

MEDICATION MANAGEMENT DURING
THE STABILIZATION PHASE

As stated earlier, controlled studies have not specifically focused on the stabilization phase of treatment. As a result, our recommendations are based upon our clinical judgment, clinical consensus, and inferences from research that did not directly address treatment issues for the stabilization phase. Since the goal for the clinician is to prevent the patient from having a recurrence of psychotic symptoms and subsequent relapse, and to ensure that the stabilization process continue, it is recommended that the patient continue the same medication and dosage for the 6 months subsequent to hospital discharge. It is likely that antipsychotic medications are actively suppressing psychotic symptoms during the stabilization phase. As a result, patients who have their medications lowered too rapidly may experience a recurrence of psychotic symptoms. This observation provides the rationale for clinicians to continue the same medication and dose as the patient received during treatment of the acute psychotic episode.

There may be pressures during this phase to lower the dose of antipsychotic medication or to change to another medication. This pressure may emerge because side effects such as sedation or restlessness that were tolerated when the patient was acutely psychotic may be difficult to tolerate when the patient returns to community life. If a decision is made to lower the medication dose, this should be done gradually, balancing the risk of psychotic relapse against the important goal of reintegrating the patient into community life. Experienced clinicians will also be guided by the knowledge that even mild side effects can lead patients to reduce their dose or discontinue their medication without consulting their physician. In practical terms, the more conservative strategy of small reductions in dose will usually be preferable to changing to a different antipsychotic, since it is difficult for physicians to predict a patient's response to another drug. The agent that resulted in improvement during the acute phase is likely to be effective in sustaining that improvement.

Clinicians should also be cautious about concluding that the persistence of psychotic symptoms indicates that the patient is receiving the wrong antipsychotic drug. Patients who receive an antipsychotic may continue to demonstrate gradual improvement for months after the initial episode is treated. For example, a patient may demonstrate substantial improvement in hallucinations 8 weeks following treatment for an acute episode. This improvement may be manifest in reports from the patient that the voices are quieter and less persistent. In evaluating this response, the clinician may be concerned that auditory hallucinations have not been completely eradicated. A reasonable strategy at this stage is to continue the current regimen to determine whether a longer duration of the current treatment will result in continuing improvement.

Case Example of Premature Dose Reduction of Antipsychotic Medication

A 21-year-old college student was treated for the first episode of schizophrenia as an outpatient. She initially complained of suspicious ideas about her friends and teachers for more than 3 months and then developed frank delusions about a group of her friends. She believed that they were witches, and voices told her they could read her mind and take control of her. At the same time she became remote, she was socially inappropriate with her friends, and her speech was disorganized and hard to follow. She was treated with quetiapine and eventually improved on 500 mg, 200 mg in the morning and 300 mg at night. When she returned to college 4 months after beginning treatment, she complained of significant daytime sedation as well as difficulty arising in the morning. Although she continued to develop some tolerance to the sedative side effect, her family and friends noted that she seemed tired and less animated than before she became ill. Her dose was lowered to 300 mg/day at her next visit, but 2 weeks later her delusions and hallucinations began to reappear. The dose was immediately raised back to 500 mg/day, her original dose. After 2 months of being essentially asymptomatic, her psychiatrist lowered her quetiapine during each weekly visit by 50 mg until she was receiving 300 mg/day. Her sedation improved on this dose and she remained stable. The clinical plan was to continue her on this dose and to consider a further reduction in dose in 4 to 6 months. This case demonstrates that clinicians should be cautious about lowering the dose of antipsychotic medication during the stabilization phase. This clinician weighed the importance of minimizing sedation against the risk of relapse associated with dosage reduction and lowered dosage too abruptly at first. Later, the decision was to lower the drug dose gradually but to maintain it in the range that is usually effective for acute treatment.

Under some circumstances the clinician and the patient may agree that a change in antipsychotic drugs is necessary because of unmanageable side effects or insufficient efficacy. The changeover from one drug to another should be carried out using a cross-titration. That is, at the same time that the newer drug is being started, the current medication is being gradually discontinued. If the patient is being started on a newer agent that requires a gradual titration such as clozapine or quetiapine, it may require days or weeks to reach a dose that is likely to be effective. Under these circumstances the physician may choose to continue the patient on his or her current drug dose and gradually titrate the newer drug to a dose that may have some antipsychotic effectiveness such as 250 to 300 mg of clozapine or 200 to 300 mg of quetiapine. When it is clear that the newer drug is being tolerated, the older drug can be gradually reduced. This change commonly requires a month or more. The switch is relatively easy if both drugs are high-potency agents such as haloperidol, olanzapine, or risperidone. But even when this less complex change is being instituted, a gradual change over 2 to 4 weeks may be appropriate.

The stabilization phase may also be a good time to change patients to a long-acting depot antipsychotic. These agents are an obvious choice for patients who have a history of being unreliable pill takers. Other suitable patients may be those who have a history of dangerous behavior while psychotic. Prescribing a depot antipsychotic can ensure that patients maintain a therapeutic level. In changing from an oral to a depot formulation, a number of considerations should guide the rate of the change (3). These considerations (described in Chapter 9) suggest that the changeover from an oral to a depot compound should be done over 3 or more months. If this occurs during the stabilization phase, the dose of the oral drug should be gradually decreased over a 3-month period as the depot formulation gradually reaches a steady state.

The relative absence of positive symptoms may lead patients to minimize the need for an adequate dose of antipsychotic. As a result, it is important to educate and sometimes to reeducate patients—and sometimes their families—about the importance of adhering to a medication regimen. Patients who are recovering from a first episode of schizophrenia or who have a history of not taking their medication reliably may benefit from being seen more often (e.g., weekly) than those who understand the importance of continuing their medication.

Monitoring side effects is also important during this phase. Although the emergence of tardive dyskinesia is uncommon during the first months of antipsychotic drug treatment, early emergence of dyskinetic symptoms may be evidence that the patient should be changed to another antipsychotic. Before the introduction of agents such as clozapine and quetiapine that have relatively low D_2 affinities and therefore a probable reduced risk of tardive dyskinesia, there was less of an incentive for early monitoring. This has changed with the introduction of these drugs. Similarly, patients who experience even mild extrapyramidal side effects such as rigidity, akinesia, or akathisia should have these side effects assessed regularly. Again the introduction of newer agents provides a number of suitable alternative options for patients who develop these side effects.

Other side effects, such as weight gain and sexual problems, should also be assessed regularly. All the newer antipsychotics, with the possible exception of ziprasidone, can be associated with substantial weight gain. It is important to identify patients who are gaining weight and to intervene quickly, before the weight gain becomes a serious problem. The intervention can consist of changing to an agent that is less likely to cause weight gain (see Chapter 5, "Pharmacologic Treatment"), reducing the drug dose, or managing weight with strategies such as nutritional counseling. Weight gain on agents such as clozapine or olanzapine can be severe and can interfere with a patient's social adjustment. Attending to this side effect during the stabilization period can prevent the impact of weight gain on social adjustment, self-esteem, and overall health.

Clinical Example of Switching Antipsychotic Medication Because of Weight Gain

GL, a 25-year-old, was treated with 15 mg of olanzapine for an acute psychotic episode. After discharge from the hospital it was noted that she had gained 6 pounds while in the hospital. GL was of normal weight and had never had difficulty controlling her weight. She was aware of an increase in appetite and expressed concern that she no longer felt able to control her weight. A decision was made to change her to quetiapine. She was started on 25 mg of quetiapine twice daily, and the dose was increased by 50 mg every other day until she reached 150 mg, when the dose of olanzapine was reduced to 10 mg. Because of sedation, the rate of increasing quetiapine was slowed to 50 mg every 4 days. When she reached 300 mg, the olanzapine dose was decreased to 5 mg, and at 400 mg of quetiapine olanzapine was discontinued. The patient later confirmed that the change was associated with a decrease in appetite and weight loss.

As patients return to the community, the sexual side effects of medication may also become a concern. In men, symptoms such as erectile or ejaculatory dysfunction can lead to patients stopping their medication. Women may also be concerned about the effects of medication on libido or about menstrual disturbances. Clinicians are often unaware of these symptoms unless they specifically inquire about them. As with weight gain, detecting these side effects and changing medications or dose during the stabilization phase can prevent more serious effects, such as noncompliance, at a later stage of treatment.

PSYCHOSOCIAL TREATMENT

Psychotherapeutic interventions continue to be supportive with major aims to reduce stress and establish a therapeutic alliance involving an active collaboration between the patient and therapist. As the psychosis begins to resolve, patients are more amenable and accessible to education about schizophrenia, its course, and outcome. The importance of treatment compliance should be emphasized to both patients and family members. Psychoeducation should enable them to develop realistic expectations about the effects of the disorder on functioning, goals, and aspirations of the patient. Efforts to improve problem solving and communication between patients and families can help minimize any stress that may occur in families during this time of crisis. Educational programs during this phase have been effective in teaching patients about medication self-management (e.g., what the benefits of maintenance medication are, how to deal with side effects, and communicating with the psychiatrist about any problems associated with taking the medication). Also, symptom self-management training should include recognition of stressful life situations, how to cope with stress, identification of early-warning signs of relapse, and avoidance of any involvement with illicit drugs or alcohol. Case managers should be available to ensure that patients' basic living needs are met, including adequate housing and income supplementation as well as the support that some patients need in activities of daily living.

REFERENCES

1. American Psychiatric Association. Practice guidelines for treatment of patients with schizophrenia. *Am J Psychiatry* 1997;154[Suppl 4]:1–63.
2. Herz MI, Endicott J, Spitzer RL. Brief hospitalization: a two-year follow-up. *Am J Psychiatry* 1977;77:502–507.
3. Marder SR, Hubbard JW, Van Putten T, et al. Pharmacokinetics of long-acting injectable neuroleptic drugs: clinical implications. *Psychopharmacology (Berl)* 1989;98:433–439.

9

Stable Phase

Patients enter the stable phase when their clinical status has plateaued after stabilization has occurred. The degree of resolution of symptomatology after an acute episode varies greatly. Some achieve complete remission of positive and negative symptoms, whereas others may achieve only partial remission. Cognitive deficits of varying severity occur in most patients and are relatively independent of psychotic symptomatology. Not infrequently, individuals evidence nonpsychotic dysphoric symptoms such as tension, anxiety, depression, and insomnia. Levels of functioning range from being fully capable of independent living to needing a great deal of support to carry out the necessary activities of daily living. In fact, although some patients with schizophrenia can function well as doctors, lawyers, and university professors, others are almost completely nonfunctional and require continued hospital care.

Goals of treatment during the stable phase are to decrease or if possible eliminate positive and negative symptoms and side effects of medication; improve cognitive, social, and vocational functioning; decrease the patient's vulnerability to stress through improving coping skills and ability to manage and control dysphoric affects; educate patients to recognize the appearance of prodromal symptoms of relapse; decrease relapse and rehospitalization rates; and educate patients and families about characteristics of schizophrenia, its prognosis and course.

Treatment in the stable phase should involve an integration of psychopharmacologic, psychosocial, and rehabilitative approaches. In view of the wide variation in clinical characteristics and motivations of individuals with schizophrenia, it is very important that treatment approaches be individualized according to the specific needs of a particular patient at a particular time. Following is a discussion of psychopharmacologic and psychosocial treatment approaches for individuals with schizophrenia in the stable phase that may begin in the stabilization phase.

MEDICATION MANAGEMENT

Antipsychotic drugs are highly effective in preventing psychotic relapse in stable patients. The effectiveness of these agents has been demonstrated in studies in which stable patients are either continued on an antipsychotic or changed to a placebo. In these studies, relapse rates are invariably higher in the group of patients who have not remained on an antipsychotic. Although studies differ somewhat, most indicate that approximately 70% of the patients who are switched to a placebo will relapse. In contrast, only about 30% of drug-maintained patients relapse (1). Moreover, relapse rates are even lower when medication delivery is ensured through long-acting antipsychotics. This large advantage of antipsychotics for stable patients is why nearly all patients in a stable state should continue on their antipsychotics.

Patients who have been well and stable for years may inquire whether they should still continue on maintenance medication. Unfortunately, studies indicate that patients who have had prolonged stable periods still have a high relapse risk if their medications are discontinued (2). This observation is reinforced by a review by Kane (3), which found that well-stabilized patients whose medications were discontinued had relapse rates of 75% within 6 to 24 months. As will be discussed in a later section of this chapter, the duration of antipsychotic maintenance during the stable phase of schizophrenia needs to be balanced against the adverse effects of these drugs and the reality that many people resist taking medication when they feel well.

The clinician's and the patient's dilemma can be particularly difficult when the patient is recovering from a first episode of schizophrenia. These patients often resist the notion that they maintain a vulnerability to subsequent psychotic episodes; as a result, many try to have their medications discontinued as soon as possible. Since first-episode patients are more likely to return to work or school than multiepisode patients, the pressure to stop medication may be compelling. In either case, the side effects—particularly extrapyramidal side effects—associated with conventional antipsychotics may interfere with a return to normal community life. However, the pressure to withdraw medication should be balanced against the reality that 40% to 60% of these patients suffer a psychotic relapse in a year without it (3,4).

A group developed consensus guidelines for the duration of long-term maintenance therapy for relapse prevention (5). These guidelines recommend that first-episode patients receive 1 to 2 years of antipsychotic maintenance and that patients who have had multiple episodes receive at least 5 years of maintenance. Patients with severe or dangerous episodes should probably receive antipsychotics indefinitely.

DRUG SELECTION FOR THE STABLE PHASE

Before the introduction of the newer antipsychotics, drug selection was relatively straightforward. Patients were usually continued on the antipsychotic they responded to during earlier phases of treatment. If a decision was made to change the patient to a long-acting depot and the patient was not receiving an agent that was available as a depot, the patient would first be switched to the oral form of the depot and then gradually changed to the depot. The introduction of newer antipsychotics (including risperidone, clozapine, olanzapine, quetiapine, ziprasidone, and others) added new considerations to the decision-making process. That is, improvements in pharmacotherapy resulted in a change in expectations regarding pharmacotherapy. Patients anticipate living with fewer side effects of antipsychotics and expect medication to improve their social and vocational outcomes. We will review the evidence regarding the advantages of these drugs.

NEWER ANTIPSYCHOTICS AND NEGATIVE SYMPTOMS

As mentioned earlier, the first suggestion that a new agent was more effective than older agents in managing negative symptoms comes from the comparison of clozapine and chlorpromazine (6). In that study, negative symptoms were not specifically monitored. However, a cluster of items from the Brief Psychiatric Rating Scale (BPRS) that included emotional withdrawal, affective blunting, and motor retardation demonstrated significantly greater improvement on clozapine. Clozapine-treated patients also demonstrated greater improvements in social behaviors that were documented on nurse's rating scales. Similar advantages were associated with risperidone treatment and olanzapine treatment (7–9). Results from studies of quetiapine are less clear. However, the results of these studies are somewhat suspect. All the studies were carried out in acutely ill patients who demonstrated improvement in positive symptoms, negative symptoms, and other areas such as mood and anxiety. It is conceivable that the improvements in negative symptoms are secondary to other improvements. For example, as patients become less suspicious they may become less withdrawn and isolated. Patients who are demonstrating improvements in mood may demonstrate a more lively affect.

The advantages of the newer agents could also be related to their well-established property of causing minimal extrapyramidal side effects (EPS). Patients with EPS from conventional drugs may show minimal rigidity or tremor, but may have mild forms of akinesia. This EPS variant can appear as decreased speech, diminished gestures, or even decreased interest in environment. As a result, akinesia can result in negative symptoms that are secondary to EPS. Since newer agents are associated with a much lower tendency to cause EPS, it is not surprising when studies suggest that these agents are better treatments for negative symptoms. These issues have been addressed using statistical methods such as path analysis and have indicated that these agents have direct effects on negative symptoms (8–10).

However, other evidence also casts doubt on whether newer agents are more effective for negative symptoms. A well-done meta-analysis by Luecht and co-workers reviewed double-blind studies that compared risperidone, olanzapine, quetiapine, and sertindole to a placebo or to haloperidol (11). Although newer drugs were more effective for negative symptoms when compared with a placebo, when compared with haloperidol the effect sizes (i.e., the magnitude of the difference in effectiveness between the two types of agents) were trivial. A VA Cooperative Study compared clozapine to haloperidol during a 1-year trial and did not find an advantage for clozapine in negative symptoms (12). Buchanan and his co-workers also failed to find an advantage for clozapine in negative symptoms during a long-term study (13). However, the ambiguity regarding an effect on negative symptoms could be related to problems in measuring negative symptoms, since the scales may not be sensitive to changes that occur in patient populations. In addition, most studies were relatively brief, lasting only 2 to 6 months. If there are improvements in motivation or social behaviors, these may take many months to emerge and may be manifest in better social outcomes.

Other strategies for managing negative symptoms include the use of antidepressants, particularly serotonin-specific reuptake inhibitors (SSRIs) (14). However, the evidence supporting the effectiveness of these treatments is relatively weak. Recently, researchers have focused on agents that affect the glutamate system, including glycine and d-cycloserine. Although there are a number of negative studies, most were relatively small trials and used inadequate doses of glycine. One study found that supplementing antipsychotic treatment with 60 mg of glycine daily led to greater improvement in negative symptoms than placebo supplementation (15). The evidence supporting the effectiveness of d-cycloserine is also ambiguous. However, a well-done double-blind comparison by Goff and co-workers found that 50 mg daily of d-cycloserine was more effective than placebo as an adjunctive agent for managing negative symptoms (16). Although the data supporting these agents are interesting, this area is still confusing, since studies have found conflicting results. As a result, it is probably premature to prescribe either of these agents until larger studies have adequately proven their effectiveness.

NEUROCOGNITION AND SCHIZOPHRENIA

Individuals with schizophrenia often have one or more of a variety of neurocognitive symptoms, including impaired memory, attention, concentration, motor performance, and executive functions. These impairments are common, affecting as many as 70% of individuals with schizophrenia, and they are often severe (17). One study estimated that patients with schizophrenia performed one to three standard deviations below normative standards on most cognitive tests (18). It is interesting to note that these cognitive impairments have minimal or no effects on the intelligence quotient (19). Nevertheless, these impairments have important consequences. Evidence suggests that these impairments have a stronger relationship to the long-term functional outcome of schizophrenia than positive psychotic symptoms (20). As a result, clinicians should evaluate the severity of neurocognitive symptoms and should consider this dimension of psychopathology as a treatment target.

The neurocognitive deficits do not appear to be secondary to psychotic symptoms. Individuals may demonstrate these deficits before the onset of psychotic symptoms, and these symptoms may persist after patients have recovered from a psychotic episode. These impairments in cognition appear to be related to negative symptoms, since both occupy a different dimension of psychopathology compared with positive symptoms. Moreover, negative and neurocognitive deficits are often correlated (21).

Unfortunately, the examination administered by most clinicians is relatively insensitive to the cognitive deficits associated with schizophrenia. Harvey has pointed out that tests that focus on a patient's fund of knowledge are unlikely to reveal deficits (19). Some patients may be excellent reporters of memory or attention problems. They may describe problems in concentration, sustained attention, or manipulation of items in working memory. For example, a student may describe new problems that make studying or reading more difficult. This might include finding it difficult to learn from reading because the patient forgets the information at the top of the page before reaching the end of that page. Although typical neuropsychological testing may not be helpful, neuropsychologists familiar with the deficits that are common in schizophrenia may be able to focus on these areas. It is hoped that neuropsychologists will provide further guidance to clinicians interested in office strategies for monitoring cognition.

Conventional antipsychotics have relatively little effect on the neurocognitive deficits in schizophrenia. Recent evidence suggests that newer drugs, including risperidone and olanzapine, appear to improve certain aspects of cognition, including working memory, verbal memory, verbal fluency, and other cognitive domains (22). Clozapine has been reported to improve verbal fluency, although it can impair memory. Although these improvements are encouraging, studies have not yet provided information that can be used to determine whether the amount of improvement is sufficient to affect the lives of patients. Cognitive rehabilitation strategies have been developed that focus on these deficits, although these strategies (which are discussed in greater detail in Chapter 10) are unproven.

NEWER ANTIPSYCHOTICS AND FUNCTIONAL OUTCOMES

Although symptom rating scales are ambiguous with regard to the advantages of newer agents, other evidence indicates that these agents do have advantages over older antipsychotics. Perhaps the most dramatic evidence does not come from carefully designed controlled trials but from clinician observations. A proportion of patients—probably a small proportion—demonstrated dramatic improvements when they were changed from older drugs to clozapine and other new drugs. Some of these patients who appeared to be destined to a life of chronic mental illness demonstrated remarkable recoveries and returned to work or school. These individuals experienced a drug-induced improvement that was more than just a decrease in positive symptoms. They reported an increase in motivation and a tendency to think more clearly. Some also found that the newer drug was associated with improved mood as well.

A number of controlled studies support the advantages of newer agents in improving functional outcomes and quality of life. One study found that individuals who were treated with risperidone or clozapine experienced a better quality of life when they were compared with individuals receiving a conventional antipsychotic (23). Hamilton and co-workers (24) evaluated quality of life in patients who received one of three dose ranges of olanzapine (2.5 to 7.5, 7.5 to 12.5, or 12.5 to 17.5 mg/day), placebo, or haloperidol. Using the Quality of Life Scale (QLS) (25) the authors found that total QLS was significantly improved on the medium ($p =.009$) and higher ($p =.037$) doses of olanzapine than with placebo. Haloperidol did not lead to significant improvement. The most convincing study is probably the VA Cooperative Study that compared haloperidol and clozapine for patients who were treated for a year (12). The authors found that patients who received clozapine were more likely to participate in psychosocial or rehabilitation programs. Participation in these programs was associated with a better social outcome. This study suggests that clozapine interacts with psychosocial treatment to result in an improved social outcome.

If newer drugs have an advantage, it will be important to understand why. The evidence that this difference is related to a negative or neurocognitive symptom advantage for newer drugs is ambiguous. An alternative explanation is that the advantage is related to a difference in side effects. Patients who receive newer drugs may feel less constrained by extrapyramidal side effects and therefore demonstrate improved involvement in community activities. Also, patients who experience milder side effects may be more likely to continue taking their medications. The resulting reduction of the risk of exacerbations of psychosis may be associated with better functioning in the community.

LONG-ACTING MEDICATIONS

Long-acting medications are an important alternative for patients who are in the stable phase of treatment. Comparisons between older oral drugs and long-acting agents indicated that long-acting agents had advantages in preventing psychotic relapse. Open-label studies (i.e., studies where patients and clinicians were aware of the drug that the patient received) found much larger differences favoring depot over oral treatment. The difference probably results from the types of patients who enter these studies and the treatment conditions. Open-label studies usually take place in normal clinical settings and include typical patients who may be unreliable pill takers. Double-blind studies usually include individuals selected because they are cooperative and compliant. Also, these studies tend to have enriched staffs and to provide a higher quality of clinical care. As a likely result of these differences, double-blind studies are less conclusive. In a review of six studies, Davis found that the results favored depot in five (26). When the results were weighted for sample size, depot was favored by a significant amount. In addition, the comparison that lasted the longest found an advantage for depot (2).

Depot drugs may have other advantages. Hogarty and co-workers found that patients who received a depot rather than an oral drug derived the most benefit from a psychosocial treatment strategy (2). This difference could have been related to the reduced risk of relapse in the depot group that led to this group having a greater likelihood of benefiting from the psychosocial treatment. In addition, depot drugs may have milder side effects at their effective doses. Although this has not been proven, patients who benefit from low or moderate doses of a long-acting depot compound may have less of a plasma level peak than those who receive an oral compound. Since evidence suggests that this peak is associated with the severity of EPS, patients treated with depot drugs may experience milder EPS.

These advantages of depot therapy should be considered when clinicians are deciding between depot conventional agents and newer oral agents. At this time, no studies compare these two forms of long-term therapy. Moreover, there is a tendency in the United States to reserve long-acting drugs for patients with a clear history of noncompliance or uncooperativeness. This may result in an underutilization of these agents, since it has been estimated that 60% or more of patients with schizophrenia cannot be relied upon to take their medication as prescribed. Although it is reasonable to predict that the reduced EPS associated with newer drugs will lead to improved rates of compliance, no evidence supports this.

DRUG TREATMENT STRATEGIES FOR MAINTENANCE THERAPY

Decision making about the best dose and drug for stable phase treatment can be problematic. During this stage some patients demonstrate relatively few symptoms of schizophrenia; others are nearly completely asymptomatic. The most important role of the antipsychotic is to prevent a recurrence of psychotic symptoms. Without a clear target of treatment it is nearly impossible to titrate dose against clinical response.

Before the introduction of newer drugs, concerns about antipsychotic side effects—particularly acute EPS and tardive dyskinesia (TD) —led to the development of strategies aimed at reducing the amount of drug that patients received. A number of studies evaluated the usefulness of substantially reducing the amount of antipsychotic that patients received (27,28). Nearly all these studies evaluated long-acting antipsychotics, particularly fluphenazine decanoate, and found that patients did relatively well on these lower doses, although there was a slightly increased risk of mild symptomatic exacerbations that could usually be managed with medication adjustments. The Treatment Strategies in Schizophrenia multicenter study supported these results. In this study, lower doses led to relapse levels that were slightly higher than more conventional doses but that were in an acceptable range (29). Moreover, these studies suggest that there are advantages to dosage reductions, in that patients experienced milder side effects and better compliance.

Other studies focused on a strategy called *intermittent* or *targeted* treatment. In this strategy, patients who were in the stable phase had their antipsychotic drug dose lowered and eventually discontinued. Patients were subsequently monitored closely and antipsychotics were reinstated when patients demonstrated prodromal symptoms and behaviors that were considered early-warning signs of relapse. Nearly all the studies of this strategy indicated that intermittent treatment was associated with a substantially higher risk of relapse (29–33). There is evidence that some patients—estimated at 40% to 64% in one review—are able to remain stable with this strategy (34). This probably indicates that a subgroup of patients—perhaps those who refuse maintenance and can recognize their early signs of relapse or who have relatively mild psychotic symptoms during relapse—can be managed with this strategy.

Another strategy uses features of both low- and targeted-dose strategies. Patients are treated with low doses of a depot drug similar to those used in the low-dose studies. Patients are monitored for early prodromal signs of relapse. When these symptoms appear, patients are treated with oral medication. Results with this method suggest that this is an effective strategy for making low-dose treatment safer (35).

Most of the studies of low-dose treatment were justified by the importance of reducing EPS and TD. Since newer-generation medications are associated with a lower risk of these side effects but have other side effects, it is unclear what role low-dose strategies will play in the future.

SIDE EFFECTS OF ANTIPSYCHOTICS

Neurologic Symptoms

Acute EPS and its management are discussed in Chapters 5 and 7. These symptoms, including parkinsonism and tremor, are often less apparent during the stable phase of treatment. However, even mild EPS can have an important effect during maintenance. For example, mild akathisia may be experienced as a subjective experience of restlessness that occurs in the absence of motor restlessness. Although the symptom may be mild, patients often describe this side effect as difficult to tolerate for prolonged periods of time. Mild parkinsonism can result in akinesia, which had been described as a state with decreased speech, decreased motivation, and decreased spontaneous gestures (36). These symptoms can resemble negative symptoms and can adversely affect a patient's likelihood of participating in rehabilitation.

Patients who are in the stable phase of treatment should continue to receive a regular evaluation for acute EPS. The evaluation for parkinsonism consists of an examination for rigidity and tremor, and an observation of the patient's gait. Observing the patient's gait can be particularly useful, since a decrease in the normal arm swing can be a sign of mild parkinsonism. The evaluation for akathisia consists of observing for restlessness movements and asking whether the patient has difficulty sitting or standing still.

Both parkinsonism and akathisia can be managed by reducing the dose of antipsychotic medication. In some cases, patients may experience these side effects at the doses that are needed to maintain the patient in a stable state. If the clinician is reluctant to lower the drug dose, there is also the option of adding medications for EPS. As noted in Chapter 5, parkinsonism can usually be effectively managed with an anticholinergic medication such as benztropine. Akathisia can be managed with either an anticholinergic medication or a beta blocker.

The second-generation antipsychotics offer another alternative for patients who experience EPS. All the newer agents are associated with less EPS, although there are differences among them in their liabilities. For example, quetiapine and clozapine are almost never associated with EPS, whereas risperidone and to a lesser degree olanzapine can cause EPS in some patients. The introduction of the newer medications has changed what clinicians and patients should expect during stable-phase treatment. Before these medications some patients had to endure EPS or the side effects of antiparkinson medication. Newer drugs should eliminate these side effects during this phase of treatment.

Tardive Dyskinesia

Patients who receive long-term treatment with an antipsychotic medication are at risk for developing a chronic EPS known as tardive dyskinesia (TD). (Discussion of this side effect has been deferred to this chapter, since it is usually not a consideration during acute treatment.) A number of different movements are characteristic of TD. The most common are mouth and tongue movements, such as lip smacking, sucking, and puckering, as well as facial grimacing. Other movements may include irregular movements of the limbs, particularly choreoathetoid movements of the fingers and toes and slow, writhing movements of the trunk. Most patients with TD have relatively mild forms that may be disfiguring but have a minimal impact on the patient's quality of life. For a number of unfortunate patients, TD can affect breathing, speech, walking, and even the ability to eat. Also, long-term dyskinesias can take other forms. Tardive dystonias, which are among the most disabling forms of TD, consist of sustained contractions of muscles, most commonly in the face and neck. Other patients experience chronic restlessness movements, which have been called *tardive akathisia.*

Approximately 5% of patients who do not have TD and who receive a conventional antipsychotic will develop this disorder each year. Among the elderly, the proportion of patients who develop TD each year is substantially higher. Moreover, TD in the elderly is less likely to remit when antipsychotics are discontinued. Evidence suggests that patients who received higher doses of an antipsychotic are at greater risk for developing TD. Evidence also indicates that patients who developed EPS at some point in treatment are more likely to develop TD. This suggests that the process that causes acute EPS is related to the process that leads to TD. This evidence is consistent with the most widely held theory of the etiology of TD, which contends that when D2 receptors are chronically occupied, there is an increase in the sensitivity of dopamine receptors, and this increased sensitivity is characterized by abnormal movements. This theory also suggests that minimizing EPS may have long-term benefits in decreasing the risk of TD.

Newer antipsychotics are less likely to cause TD than older drugs. The best evidence is for clozapine. Kane et al. evaluated clozapine's risk for causing TD using survival analysis (37). They found that clozapine was associated with a substantially lower risk of causing TD than conventional antipsychotics studied in the same setting. The two individuals who had positive ratings for TD at the end of the study had borderline TD at the start of the study. The authors concluded that it was unclear if clozapine was associated with any risk of TD. This report, as well as a lack of reports of individuals developing TD on clozapine alone, indicates that the risk of developing TD with clozapine is very low. Moreover, clozapine's antipsychotic effect with relatively low D_2 receptor occupancy is consistent with the dopamine theory of TD. That is, drugs that have lower affinities for D_2 receptors are less likely to upregulate these receptors and less likely to cause TD.

The evidence is less clear for the other new antipsychotics. In contrast to clozapine, risperidone and olanzapine require much higher D_2 receptor occupancy to be effective. As a result, these agents appear to be just as likely as older agents to cause TD. However, they are much less likely to cause EPS at their clinically effective doses; this indicates that they may have different effects on striatal dopamine receptors when compared with older drugs. This relationship is supported by data indicating that risperidone and olanzapine have a substantially lower risk of causing TD than conventional dopamine receptor antagonists such as haloperidol (38). In both studies, there were fewer new cases of TD on the newer drug. Other evidence indicates that elderly patients, a group much more vulnerable to developing TD, are less likely to develop TD on risperidone (39).

The newer drugs will need to be in use for a longer time before we can decide whether they are definitely associated with a lower risk of TD. If this difference is substantiated in well-controlled studies, it may be difficult to justify selecting an older over a newer drug. It will also be important to know if there is an important difference in TD risk between newer agents with low D_2 receptor affinity such as clozapine and quetiapine and agents with higher affinity such as risperidone and olanzapine. This is of obvious importance since it may influence decision making about which drug a patient should receive. With the currently available information, we believe that there are advantages to newer drugs and that low-affinity D_2 agents may have a small advantage if clinicians are very concerned about TD risk.

Management of Tardive Dyskinesia

At this time there are no definitive treatments for TD. Rather, certain management strategies may be effective. The selection of a strategy is likely to depend on the characteristics of the movement disorder, its severity, the patient's age, and the patient's drug history. For some patients with mild dyskinesia, the management strategy may only involve regular monitoring and treating the patient with the lowest dose of an antipsychotic. Other patients may require a change to another antipsychotic.

An important part of management requires educating patients and families about TD. Some patients may fear that all forms of TD will progress to a serious disorder. However, fewer than 10% of patients with TD have a moderately severe or severe form (40). It is much more common for patients to continue to have only mild symptoms (41). Moreover, many patients experience a substantial improvement over time even when antipsychotics are continued.

Discontinuing antipsychotics may be effective for some patients with TD. Not all patients will have a reliable response to discontinuing antipsychotics, and some may show only a very gradual improvement. One study (42) found improvement in only 13 of 22 patients. In individuals with mild TD and without akathisia, five out of eight achieved complete remission in 2 to 4 years. Another study (43) found that only 2% of TD patients achieved remission and only 20% actually improved. Patients who are younger and those who have been treated with an antipsychotic for a briefer period time are most likely to improve (44).

Discontinuing antipsychotics is not an option for most patients. As mentioned earlier, patients with schizophrenia are at a very high risk for relapse when they are not receiving an antipsychotic. Although treatments such as vitamin E and selegeline have been used for TD, the effectiveness of these agents remains controversial. For example, a number of double-blind studies have found that vitamin E is effective as a treatment for TD (45,46). However, a large VA cooperative study failed to find an effect (47). Since vitamin E is a relatively benign agent, it may be reasonable to administer a therapeutic trial of up to 1,600 IU daily to patients with relatively mild TD.

Another approach to the management of TD is to change patients to a second-generation antipsychotic. As mentioned earlier, substantial evidence indicates that these agents are less likely to result in the development of TD. There is less information regarding the ability of these agents to decrease abnormal movements in patients who have already developed the disorder. The best data are from studies of clozapine (48), all of which were relatively small. However, taken together, they suggest that clozapine is a reasonable treatment choice for patients with TD. Anecdotal reports suggest that risperidone, olanzapine, and quetiapine may also be effective for TD (48).

Weight Gain

Obesity is a serious problem for many patients with schizophrenia. A recent study found that women with schizophrenia had a higher body mass index (BMI) than controls, although BMIs in men with schizophrenia were similar to those of controls (49). Others have found that individuals with schizophrenia are likely to have diets higher in fat and are less likely to exercise than controls (50). This life-style may contribute to the increased mortality associated with schizophrenia.

Unfortunately, evidence indicates that newer agents are associated with a greater risk of weight gain than older drugs. A meta-analysis by Allison found that weight gain over a 10-week trial was 4.45 kg on clozapine, 4.15 kg on olanzapine, 2.10 kg on risperidone, and 0.04 kg on ziprasidone (49). There was insufficient information to estimate weight gain on quetiapine. Other studies have found similar weight gain on newer drugs (51). Weight gain of more than 4 kg (or 8.8 pounds) may represent more than a 5% increase in weight. This amount has been associated with increases in morbidity and mortality (49). Moreover, it is not uncommon for patients to gain as much as 50 to 100 pounds during treatment with newer drugs.

Substantial weight gain can be a serious medical problem and can lead to increased morbidity and mortality. Case reports have indicated that patients who experience weight gain on newer antipsychotics are also vulnerable to diabetes (51,52). In addition, studies suggest that clozapine and olanzapine can increase cholesterol and triglycerides (53,54). Moreover, obesity can impair self-esteem and may interfere with attempts to reintegrate patients into normal community life.

The increased problem of weight gain with newer agents should affect how these agents are prescribed. Patients who will be started on an agent associated with substantial weight gain should be warned about this side effect before treatment begins. Clinicians should monitor weight routinely during each stage of treatment. If weight gain is a concern during the stable phase, clinicians may advise nutritional counseling and exercise. This problem can be extremely frustrating to clinicians in some patients who appear indifferent to their obesity or who find that negative symptoms impair their ability to exercise or alter their diet. Individuals who live in residential facilities may have few alternatives to the high-calorie and high-fat diet at their facility. In these circumstances clinicians may consider changing the patient to a drug that is associated with minimal weight gain.

Sexual Side Effects

Sexual side effects of antipsychotics can be difficult to distinguish from the sexual dysfunction that is common in schizophrenia. Individuals with schizophrenia, particularly men, report decreases in libido and sexual thoughts whether or not they are drug-free or treated with antipsychotic medication (55). Male patients who receive an antipsychotic are more likely to experience disturbances in erectile or ejaculatory function, suggesting that these effects are related to the drugs. At this time, the prevalence of sexual side effects in women has not been carefully studied. Sexual side effects in both men and women could be related to a number of factors, including dopamine blockade, prolactin elevation, decreased testosterone, or alpha-adrenergic blockade (56). It is unclear if there are differences among newer and older drugs in their tendency to cause these side effects. As a result, clinicians should regularly inquire about sexual dysfunction, since many patients fail to complain unless they are prompted. Lowering the dose of antipsychotic or changing drugs may be helpful, although empirical studies provide little guidance regarding which drugs are least likely to impair sexual functioning. A number of case reports have reported that sildenafil (Viagra) can be effective.

Prolactin Elevation

Prolactin secretion from the anterior pituitary is tonically inhibited by dopamine. As a result, dopamine receptor antagonists can cause elevation of serum prolactin (57). This elevation is common with risperidone and conventional antipsychotics. Other agents—including olanzapine, quetiapine, and clozapine—result in little or no prolactin elevation (58). Although tolerance to the elevated prolactin resulting from antipsychotics may develop over several months, patients frequently maintain a chronically elevated prolactin. These elevations can lead to amenorrhea and galactorrhea in women and to gynecomastia in men.

It is uncertain whether elevated prolactin from antipsychotics can lead to more serious problems. Hyperprolactinemia from pituitary tumors can lead to hypogonadism with deficiencies in estrogen in women and testosterone in men. In women this can result in decreased fertility, decreased libido, and decreased bone mineral density. In men hypogonadism can lead to decreased libido, erectile or ejaculatory dysfunction, and decreased spermatogenesis. However, it is unclear if hyperprolactinemia from antipsychotics is associated with these more serious side effects. Until more information is available, reasonable clinical practice should include the regular monitoring of sexual side effects in men and women as well as symptoms such as irregular menstruation and galactorrhea in women. If there is a suggestion of these side effects, a prolactin level should be monitored. If the levels are elevated, the clinicians should consider reducing the antipsychotic dose or changing to an agent that is less likely to cause prolactin. If the levels are very high (e.g., greater than 200), an endocrinologist should be consulted since other causes of hyperprolactinemia should be considered.

Other Important Side Effects During the Stable Phase

Sedation is a relatively common side effect of antipsychotics during the stable phase of treatment. Individuals who tolerated this side effect during recovery from a psychotic episode may find that even mild daytime sedation may impair adjustment as patients return to work, school, or family responsibilities. Sedation is most prominent on low-potency agents such as thioridazine, quetiapine, and clozapine, although some patients may feel tired or drowsy on high-potency drugs. Administering the total dose of drug at bedtime or changing to a medication associated with less sedation can usually resolve this problem.

TREATMENT ADHERENCE

Individuals with schizophrenia frequently miss scheduled appointments or fail to take their medications as directed. This nonadherence with treatment plans (often referred to as *noncompliance*, a term that some patients object to) is associated with a high rate of relapse as well as increased rates of suicide and violent behavior (59–64). Rates of nonadherence as high as 74% have been reported in groups of outpatients with schizophrenia who are followed for 2 years after hospital discharge (65–67). It has been estimated that 40% of the costs of rehospitalization in schizophrenia are related to the failure of patients to continue their medication. As a result, monitoring and improving treatment adherence is a vital component of the management of schizophrenia during the stable phase.

Nonadherence with treatment in schizophrenia or any medical illness cannot be explained by any single factor. Also, the degree of severity of nonadherence can vary. For example, some patients may miss doses of medication occasionally or reduce their dosages, whereas others are completely noncompliant and stop their medication entirely. Weiden and his colleagues have provided a structure for evaluating the domains of nonadherence in schizophrenia (66). In this model, nonadherence to treatment interventions can be related to the disease features (e.g., suspiciousness regarding the treatment team), the treatment system (e.g., the use of appointment reminders), the treatment itself (e.g., unpleasant side effects of medications), interactions between the patient and therapist, patient characteristics (e.g., substance abuse), psychosocial factors (e.g., the family's attitude), and psychological factors (e.g., the role of stigma). There is a substantial literature indicating the role of these factors. A recent meta-analysis by Kampman and Lehtinen found that nonadherence with antipsychotic medications was associated with medication side effects, the patient's attitudes toward medication, delusions, substance abuse, diminished insight, and lack of family support (67).

Detection of nonadherence is evident when patients do not appear for therapy visits or medication monitoring. It is more difficult to detect when patients comply with clinic visits but have stopped their medication. Clinician interviews consistently underestimate the magnitude of noncompliance

(66,68). If patients have frequent exacerbations of psychotic symptoms, non-compliance should be suspected. Plasma antipsychotic and prolactin levels can be measured. Pill counts have been used when there is concern about a patient's compliance but are not foolproof, since patients can feign compliance by emptying the pills out of the container before the appointment (66,69). Information from family members and other informants can be very useful regarding a patient's compliance with medication. Blackwell has suggested that clinicians inquire about treatment adherence in a manner that is unlikely to elicit defensive responses from patients (70). For example, asking patients if they have difficulty remembering to take their medications every day may lead to patients talking more openly about the difficulties of taking medications every day for an indefinite period of time. This may result in a useful dialogue about strategies to improve treatment adherence.

Various instruments have been devised to evaluate noncompliance, including the Rating of Medication Influences Scale (ROMI), which found the following clinical indicators correlating with nonadherence with medication (66):

- Denial of mental illness
- Lack of benefit from treatment (the patient perceives a poor therapeutic relationship and a lack of ongoing benefit from medication)
- Environmental obstacles (patients have difficulty accessing treatment or having a lack of family support with treatment)
- Rejection of mental illness (patients feeling embarrassed about having a mental illness)
- Financial obstacles (finances making it difficult for the patients to pay for medication)

Nearly every study of adherence to treatment has found that drug side effects are among the most common causes of failure to comply with medication. For conventional antipsychotics, akathisia and akinesia can lead to personal discomfort that leads to poor adherence (71,72). Patients who have experienced frightening dystonic reactions are also less likely to comply with medication in the future.

Lack of understanding regarding the goals of drug treatment can also lead to failures in compliance. This can be particularly important in maintenance treatment, where for many patients the medication is prophylactic in preventing relapse. For example, Herz and Melville found that many patients believed that their medication was not helping them (73). They had not been made aware that the medication was prophylactic in helping to prevent relapse. Patients may fail to understand that medications may not improve symptoms or make them feel better during the stable phase. If patients believe that they are not at risk for psychotic relapse if they stop taking their medication, they may perceive no benefit from the medication and may decide to decrease the amount of drug or stop medication completely (74).

Patient characteristics or particular forms of psychopathology can influence cooperation with treatment plans. Patients who are paranoid and hostile to authority figures often do not accept medication. On the other hand, those who experience grandiose delusions while psychotic may prefer their psychotic world in comparison to the real world (75). Patients who are abusing drugs are frequently noncompliant with antipsychotic medication (76). It may be necessary to deal appropriately with the patient's substance use disorder before the psychotic illness can be managed properly.

Preventing and Dealing with Noncompliance

Establishing a therapeutic alliance can be very helpful in ensuring compliance with treatment. This is best accomplished by entering into a collaborative relationship with the patient that encourages the patient's input regarding the medication's positive and negative effects, encouraging the patient to share feelings about taking the medication and having continuity of care that over time helps develop a trusting relationship with the psychiatrist. It is important to deal with drug side effects aggressively. Usually this entails warning patients about side effects before they occur and assuring them that discomforting drug experiences will be dealt with immediately. Managing these effects includes lowering the dose of antipsychotic medication, adding an antiparkinson medication, or switching to another medication, especially to a newer-generation medication, if there are neurologic side effects.

One of the most effective methods for dealing with patients who are unable to take their medication reliably is to prescribe a long-acting medication. Long-term studies indicate that patients who receive depot medications have lower relapse rates than those who receive oral antipsychotics (2,77). Although it is difficult to prove, this difference is likely to be related to the difference in treatment adherence between the two different forms of treatment. This form of pharmacotherapy is clearly preferable for some groups of patients, such as those who are unreliable pill takers or who refuse medication but have had a legal determination that they are dangerous when they are not receiving an antipsychotic. At this time, none of the newer agents are available in a long-acting form, although a risperidine microspheres long-acting formulation may be introduced in late 2002. This forces clinicians and patients to weigh the advantages of newer agents against the controlled drug delivery of depot conventional antipsychotic medication.

One of the most effective methods for improving treatment adherence involves educating patients and their families about schizophrenia and its treatments. Psychoeducation is discussed in Chapter 8. It is important to note that recently introduced approaches to psychoeducation focus on improving adherence to drug and other treatments by explaining their rationale (78,79). An educational environment provides a means for engaging family members and others in close contact with the patient. This can be helpful in overcoming any family resistance to medication and enlisting them to become allies in the treatment process.

It is also important for clinicians to recognize that many patients lack the capacity to make informed decisions about participation in treatment. For these individuals, refusal of medication or failure to attend therapy sessions may be the result of an inadequately managed illness. Therefore these refusals may require assertive outreach on the part of the treatment team. As stated previously, treatment of an individual with schizophrenia in the community should not be limited to office visits.

If an individual denies having a mental illness and therefore any need for medication, it is best not to tell the individual that he or she is sick and therefore must take the medication. This approach rarely is beneficial. In most cases it is best to enlist the family and friends as allies to convince the patient to continue the medication. Clinicians can encourage the patient to take the medication because it has other beneficial effects such as alleviating anxiety, insomnia, or other dysphoric symptoms. It can also be pointed out that taking the medication will help to prevent any future hospitalizations, which many patients fear, even though they deny the illness. They can be told that it can prevent disruptions in their educational or vocational training programs, jobs, and social relationships.

PSYCHOSOCIAL APPROACHES

Although pharmacotherapy is effective in controlling symptomatology and to some extent improving cognitive functioning, a variety of psychosocial treatments can be beneficial to patients in such areas as improving coping skills to decrease vulnerability to stress, preventing relapse, improving social and vocational functioning and quality of life, and coping with residual schizophrenic symptomatology. The following is a discussion of psychosocial treatment approaches.

Individual Therapy

To conduct individual therapy most effectively it is desirable for the therapist to gain a comprehensive understanding of the patient, including the individual's strengths and vulnerabilities, intrapsychic conflicts, defenses, coping skills, cognitive deficits, social support system, and cultural background. Effective treatment requires a trusting, collaborative relationship with the patient leading to a therapeutic alliance. This can occur only if there is continuity of care with the same therapist over a prolonged period of time.

In recent years there has been a great controversy over the relative efficacy of psychodynamically oriented psychotherapy versus supportive therapy. Many psychiatrists reported success in treating schizophrenic patients utilizing psychodynamic therapy. However, the weight of evidence of controlled studies has not born out the efficacy of this treatment as a primary approach for most individuals with schizophrenia. In fact, probably because psychodynamic therapy can be stressful and elicit highly charged affects such as anger, anxiety, and depression in those prone to affective dyscontrol, it has been found to be antitherapeutic for many (80). Probably the most definitive study (81,82) to date was carried out by comparing exploratory insight-oriented (EIO) psychotherapy provided three times a week to a reality-adaptive supportive (RAS) psychotherapy in which patients were seen up to once a week. The objective of EIO treatment was self-understanding. The interview focus was on the relationship to the therapist and significant others. It looked for current meanings, searched for hidden motivation, and examined present and past while offering support and emphasizing interpretation. RAS, on the other hand, emphasized symptom relief through drug management and strengthening of existing defenses. It dealt mainly in the present and offered support, reassurance, clarification, direction, and suggestions for utilization of environmental and community resources. The patient sample was intended to be a mid-range prognostic group of clearly schizophrenic patients. To be included, patients must have functioned outside of the hospital and been off medication in some major role for at least 4 consecutive months in the preceding 2 years. Standardized research criteria for the diagnosis of schizophrenia that had evolved out of the International Pilot Study for Schizophrenia were utilized. The initial sample consisted of 164 hospitalized patients. Fifty percent of the sample was never previously hospitalized and two-thirds had no prior exposure to individual psychotherapy. Eighty-one experienced therapists provided the treatment that began during hospitalization and continued for up to 2 years. Because the investigators believed that the effects of psychotherapy could not be expected to occur before a minimum of 6 months in treatment, this duration was set as a cutoff for inclusion in the project.

Results showed that of the 164 patients who entered the study, 69 (42%) dropped out before qualifying as study patients (less than 6 months of treatment). By the end of year 2 only 31% of patients had completed 2 years of treatment. The study was initiated in three different hospitals; the analytically oriented hospital had a lower dropout rate than the others. The patients in the latter hospital had a much longer initial hospitalization.

According to the investigators, the results failed to confirm either the strength or the breadth of favorable effects that were hypothesized to be associated with the EIO as opposed to the RAS treatment. Rather, the data suggest that in the areas of recidivism and role performance (occupational functioning and to a lesser extent social adaptation), RAS exerts a preferential and specific action compared with EIO therapy. In contrast, EIO therapy appears to have exerted a preferential, albeit more modest action in the areas of ego functioning and cognition. These advantages of EIO were not statistically significant. There were no differences between groups in number of days on antipsychotic medication, but RAS patients spent significantly more days on lithium in the second year. The investigators had postulated a lessened need for medication in the EIO group.

Unfortunately, the large attrition rate of this study limits the generalizability of the findings. However, the high dropout rate itself seems to indicate that most schizophrenic patients were not interested in participating in the one-to-one psychotherapy offered. Furthermore, it is evident from the results that insight-oriented therapy is clearly not indicated for the great majority of patients. A problem in determining the efficacy of psychotherapeutic treatment in schizophrenia is that the likelihood that a single approach over time is most effective is probably not great. Since the patient has different needs over time, a flexible, pragmatic approach seems justifiable. Following is a discussion of individual therapeutic approaches, including supportive psychotherapy, enhancing coping skills, and cognitive behavioral therapy, that should be employed flexibly and pragmatically to deal with specific issues facing a particular patient at a particular time.

SUPPORTIVE PSYCHOTHERAPY

Studies have demonstrated that a supportive problem-solving approach differentially reduced relapse and enhanced social and occupational functioning when combined with pharmacotherapy for schizophrenic outpatients (83–86). As stated earlier, the foundation of supportive psychotherapy is the therapeutic relationship that develops over time when there is continuity of care with a therapist who engages in a collaborative relationship with the patient. Generally, therapists who are empathic, warm, and genuine enhance development of this relationship. When a positive therapeutic relationship is in place it has been associated with improved outcome among schizophrenic patients. Concrete survival issues should be addressed in order for therapy to be effective (87,88). Attention should be paid to housing needs, income maintenance, and general medical care, along with education about schizophrenia, compliance with medication, reality testing, help in solving day-to-day problems, and positive reinforcement for healthy behavior. At times, therapists should give practical advice and guidance, set limits on regressive behaviors when appropriate, and collaborate with family members and others in the patient's support system. Part of the task for the therapist is to help the patient make realistic decisions about future goals and to assess the individual's ability and readiness for educational and vocational rehabilitation. At times it may be useful for the therapist to conduct home visits and other types of outreach. As stated in Chapter 4, it is important for patients to attempt to determine whether particular types of stress have led to relapse in the past, to learn to connect the occurrence of stressful situations with the development of prodromal symptoms, and to learn to identify the onset of prodromal symptoms and what steps to take if they occur.

IMPROVING COPING SKILLS AND COGNITIVE BEHAVIORAL THERAPY

In contrast to a generic supportive therapy approach, training in coping skills and cognitive behavioral therapy is more disorder specific. These approaches enable patients to gain a sense of control over their symptoms and lessen the likelihood of relapse. The locus of control can shift from the individual's feeling of being totally helpless in influencing the course of the illness to gaining a sense that he or she can control the course and outcome of the illness. This feeling of mastery and control can be very helpful in improving the morale of individuals with schizophrenia. With the locus of control shifting from external to internal (within the individual), the individual can take an active rather than a passive role in dealing with the illness and its effects and develop feelings of empowerment.

A newer strategy for relapse prevention and improvement in functioning is the Personal Therapy (PT) approach described by Hogarty et al. (89). PT focuses on improving the specific deficits associated with schizophrenia by graduated staged interventions. It postulates that stress can precipitate affective dysregulation in vulnerable patients. Over time patients are taught to recognize and effectively cope with their feelings without totally denying them. There are three phases of the treatment, which are clearly defined with corresponding interventions. As the patients achieve a goal at one level they are moved onto the next level.

PT encompasses several treatment approaches. Patients participate in social skills training to help them control and express their feelings, understand the effects of their behavior on others, and learn relaxation techniques and such traditional behavioral techniques as modeling, rehearsal practice, feedback, and homework assignments. All therapies are individualized and sequenced according to the patient's level of clinical recovery and ability to learn new behaviors. Family members are also encouraged to participate in the patient's recovery.

Results after 3 years showed that patients living with their families who received PT have fewer relapses. Those who lived alone experienced a greater relapse rate than control patients. Patients who lived alone tended to live in more unstable environments. Social adjustment was better in patients receiving Personal Therapy after 3 years in contrast to those receiving supportive and family therapy alone. It is important to remember that Personal Therapy is not a tightly prescriptive, manualized treatment; rather, it contains a set of principles and priorities that leave considerable room for individualization.

Herz et al. used a cognitive behavioral therapy approach in a relapse prevention study aimed at improving coping skills (90). There was an attempt to teach patients about the relationship between stress and relapse, recognition of prodromal symptoms, and learning to cope with the stressor more effectively and the symptoms that followed if patients began to relapse. It attempted to help patients recognize their emotional reactions to stressful life events and manage the emotions effectively. The aim was to prevent the buildup of these emotions to a point of affective dyscontrol. The program was carried out in both individual and group therapy.

Based on the vulnerability-stress model, we postulate that the likelihood of relapse occurring after the appearance of prodromal symptoms depends on the complex interaction of a number of personal and environmental factors. These include the magnitude and duration of the stressor, the individual's perception of that stressor, the individual's ability to control and regulate dysphoric affects, the individual's coping skills, the presence of social supports, and the promptness and effectiveness of psychiatric intervention.

The role of personal, environmental, and therapeutic factors in the process of relapse is illustrated in Fig. 9.1, in which a stressor initiates the process. The degree to which a vulnerable individual is affected by a stressor depends on how that individual perceives it. This perception may result in the emergence of such prodromal-type symptoms as tension, insomnia, and difficulty concentrating. In the absence of protective factors, or if stress continues or increases in intensity, such symptoms are likely to progress to relapse. If protective factors are sufficient, however, progression of the relapse process is halted.

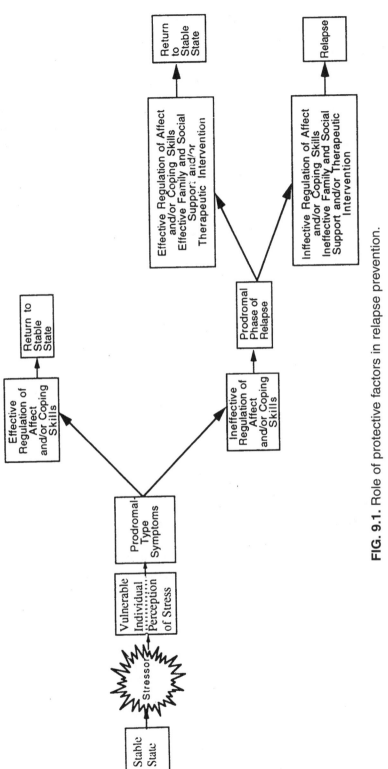

FIG. 9.1. Role of protective factors in relapse prevention.

Case Example

Jim, a young single male in his early 20s, had recovered after a second psychotic episode. He was a shy, reclusive, and socially awkward individual who had few friends and never dated the opposite sex. He met an attractive young woman in his rehabilitation program who was friendly to him. The second time he saw her, he asked her to be his girlfriend. She was taken aback and told him that she already had a boyfriend and left him abruptly. Jim did not sleep that night and the next day he told an acquaintance that the girl meant nothing to him, but he appeared depressed and withdrawn. He developed insomnia that worsened every day. He was tense and irritable and called his rehabilitation program to let them know that he would not be attending. He called his therapist to cancel his session. The therapist was concerned that Jim was entering the prodromal phase of relapse and arranged a home visit. Jim said he didn't feel well. He hardly slept and was tense and nervous but didn't know why. The therapist asked him to recount any events that happened during the past week that could have upset him. Jim said nothing upset him, but in recounting the events of the week he did mention his encounter with the young woman, but said that he really didn't care and that it had no effect on him. The therapist recognized that Jim had taken a big chance in approaching this young woman, which resulted in a great blow to his self-esteem when she turned him down. He asked Jim, "What do you think other men feel when a girl turns them down?" Jim replied, "I guess if they liked the girl they might be upset if they were turned down." The therapist agreed that most people are upset at a rejection. After some discussion, Jim acknowledged that his immediate reaction was to become depressed, but he later consoled himself that he didn't really care about the girl anyway. The therapist offered reassurance and stated that depressive feelings were a normal reaction and emphasized that he was progressing very well in the rehabilitation program. Another session was scheduled for 2 days later. Jim came in and said that he was sleeping a little better but that this was probably due to the increase in his medication. He said that he thought it over and probably was more upset than he realized about the girl turning him down. As the session progressed, he realized that the rejection made him feel both sad and angry. He felt worthless but also was angry with the girl for turning him down. Again the therapist said that these were feelings that many men would experience in similar circumstances. During the next session the therapist asked whether Jim could have handled the situation differently since he hardly knew her. Jim began to realize that he would have had a much better chance of gaining a positive response from the young woman if he had gotten to know her better, spent more time with her, and over time had a better idea of whether he wanted this girl to be his girlfriend and whether she appeared to want to be involved with him. In subsequent sessions the therapist emphasized the important link between the stressful event (being turned down), Jim's initial shock and subsequent depression, and other prodromal signs that if not dealt with could have led to relapse. The therapist then reassured Jim that most people experience depression, shame, anger, and loss of self-esteem and self-confidence when rejected by another person. These are normal feelings but the important issue is how one deals with them. One needs to recognize the difference between thoughts, feelings, and behavior. It is important to attempt to recognize how you feel. You can be effective handling the feeling if you recognize that you have the feeling. Having an angry thought or feeling does not automatically lead to lashing out. One can examine alternative ways of handling it. The therapist also emphasized that there were ways to avoid such situations in the future. After Jim's dysphoric feelings resulting from the incident resolved, the therapist reiterated the importance of recognizing stress leading to prodromal symptoms, the importance of attempting to recognize the impact of the stress on the person, the methods of avoiding the stress and dealing with affects that arise as a result of the stress. After these sessions it was agreed that social skills training would be very helpful for Jim.

There is a need to repeat these principles from time to time in the course of therapy in order to change behavior. Repetition is very important in the learning process. If these issues were brought up in a group therapy situation, other members of the group could describe their own reactions to rejection, thus making it more acceptable for the patient to examine how he reacted. They could also share some of the methods they used in coping with their own situations (Table 9.1 for therapist's probes to improve patient's coping with stressful situations and emerging prodromal symptoms). In summary, this cognitive behavioral therapeutic approach dealing with stress and coping seemed to be helpful for many patients in the Program for Relapse Prevention study, but its efficacy could not be parceled out from other components of the treatment program. Further research is needed.

TABLE 9.1. *Coping strategies to deal with stressful situations and emerging prodromal symptoms*

1. Strategies for self-awareness
Self-examination: *"What do I feel?"*
                      "Did anything happen that led to those feelings?"
Problem solving: *"What might someone else feel in this situation?"*
Introspection: *"Am I missing something? Should I be having more or different feelings?"*

2. Coping strategies for patients
Emotionally based
Talking it out (expressing emotional reactions) with a friend
Talking it out with a family member
Talking it out with a therapist
Cognitively based
Self-reassurance: *Telling oneself that it is OK to feel these feelings.*
Thought-stopping: *Thinking about something else to avoid the "troubling thoughts."*
Problem-solving: *"Was this event due to anything I did? If so, what could have been done differently? If it was out of my control, could I have handled it differently or avoided it? Just because I have a feeling does not mean I have to act on it."*
Action based
Planning an effective course of action to handle the situation.
Arranging for pleasurable activities and diversions to divert attention from negative feelings.
Planning a program to put the effects of the stressful situation behind and move on with goals and aspirations.

3. Coping strategies for families/support persons
Encouraging patient to express feelings.
Advising and helping patient to get in touch with treatment team.
Maintaining a close collaboration with treatment team.
Developing and implementing an emergency plan for crisis situations.
Using local groups (e.g., National Alliance for the Mentally Ill) for advice.

4. Using the treatment team
Seeing a therapist for crisis assessment and treatment.
Seeing a therapist with a focus on dealing with stress and prodromal symptoms.
Seeing a psychiatrist for medication adjustment.
Participating in peer support groups.

COGNITIVE BEHAVIORAL THERAPY FOR MEDICATION-RESISTANT PSYCHOTIC SYMPTOMS

During the stable phase 25% to 50% of individuals with schizophrenia continue to experience persistent psychotic symptoms despite adequate treatment with antipsychotic medications (91). These positive psychotic symptoms can be disturbing to the individual and impair ability to function both socially and vocationally. Investigators in the United Kingdom have led the way in attempting to utilize cognitive behavioral approaches of Beck in an attempt to reduce the stress and impairment in functioning due to these symptoms (92,93). Therapists attempt to develop a therapeutic alliance through working collaboratively with patients in setting agendas and goals of therapy. They take an active inquiring stance toward the client's accounts of their experiences. The content of therapy involves identifying thoughts and beliefs, reviewing evidence for these beliefs, encouraging self-monitoring of cognitions, relating thoughts to mood and behavior, and identifying thinking biases. However, the standard cognitive therapy approach must be modified to effectively address the particular problems of psychosis, including the special difficulties of establishing a therapeutic relationship, the complexity and severity of the problems presented, the need to take account of neurocognitive deficits, and the importance of working on the subject of understanding the psychosis (94). It is postulated that the role of emotions such as depression and anxiety in the onset of psychosis leads to direct application of cognitive therapy techniques (95,96).

Cognitive therapy is structured and time limited, with the duration and frequency of sessions varying according to the nature and severity of the patient's problem and ability to profit from the approach as the therapy progresses. The range of duration of treatment has varied from 12 to 30 sessions over 6 months to more than a year. Booster sessions can be offered after the initial program has been terminated. Fowler (91,96) conceptualizes therapy as a series of six components or stages that can be applied flexibly:

1. Building and maintaining a therapeutic relationship, collaboration, engagement, and assessment.
2. Improving coping strategies using a range of cognitive and behavioral strategies, including activity scheduling, anxiety reduction, and attention control.
3. Developing a new understanding of the experience of psychosis. This involves constructing a new model of psychosis, starting with an exploration of the client's current understanding of the disease and building on that acknowledgment, however tentative, the experience of personal dysfunction.
4. Working on delusions and hallucinations. The central work involves identifying and changing distressing and disabling delusions and hallucinations by a systematic process of reviewing the evidence and generating alternatives that draw on standard cognitive approaches.
5. Addressing negative self-evaluations, anxiety, and depression. Many individuals with schizophrenia have low self-esteem with negative self-evaluations after they have been identified. Standard cognitive therapy approaches are often applicable with review of the history of the development of these ideas over the lifespan and reevaluation of the evidence. The impact of the experience of psychosis is also relevant not only to the specific evaluations but also more generally to depression and anxiety.

6. Managing risk of relapse and social disability. The final stage of therapy involves reviewing the work done and looking to the future. The understanding clients have of psychosis influences their engagement with services and supports their attitudes toward medication. This issue is reviewed and discussed further in refs. 91 and 97–99.

Controlled clinical trials appear to indicate that cognitive therapy can reduce symptoms of psychosis and possibly reduce the risk of relapse (100–103). It appears that only about 50% to 60% of individuals receiving cognitive behavioral therapy benefit significantly. Those who report distress as a result of their symptoms and who show what has been called "A chink of insight" (i.e., admitting that there may be another explanation for their delusions) may engage more readily and benefit more quickly and to a greater extent. Generally, individuals who present only with negative symptoms show a poor outcome.

It is becoming clear that individual treatment of schizophrenia should be flexibly applied by therapists who are trained not only in supportive therapy but in cognitive behavioral approaches and those that improve coping skills and stress management. Unfortunately, it is difficult to conduct what is considered a scientifically valid controlled study of a flexible approach to individual psychotherapy when the approach is multifaceted and employs various therapeutic techniques. However, despite these problems, research is needed in this area to establish the efficacy of positive psychotherapeutic approaches when employed in conjunction with antipsychotic medication.

GROUP THERAPY

A review of the literature suggests that group psychotherapy is at least as effective and possibly more effective than individual psychotherapy for many individuals with schizophrenia (104–109). Although there have been differences between studies in methods of group therapy and flaws in research designs, the weight of evidence from the results of controlled clinical trials supports this conclusion (108). Furthermore, group therapy is much more cost-effective than individual therapy. This is an important issue since most patients benefit from longer-term psychosocial treatment rather than time-limited psychosocial interventions. As with pharmacotherapy, the benefits of psychosocial treatment tend to diminish with discontinuation over time. Possible advantages of group psychotherapy compared with individual psychotherapy include reduced rehospitalization rates, improved compliance with treatment, enhanced social effectiveness, and improved staff morale and efficiency. In general, we recommend that the patient be seen individually for at least a few months to establish a beginning therapeutic alliance with the therapist and then be offered the opportunity to participate in a group with periodic individual sessions scheduled on an as-needed basis.

A group format may be used to carry out a number of therapeutic approaches, including supportive therapy, psychoeducation, improvement of patients' skills in dealing with stress and psychotic symptoms, and social skills training (110–112). Group therapy on a weekly basis can be used to educate patients to identify prodromal symptoms of relapse and the relationship of prodromal symptoms to stress. It enables the therapist to monitor patients for the onset of prodromal symptoms in a timely fashion. In the Program for Relapse Prevention Study (90), patients were asked to fill out the Brief Early Signs Questionnaire before the beginning of the group session (Fig. 9.2). Therapists reviewed the responses and then focused on patients who indicated that they had experienced a particular stressor during the prior week, especially those who were developing prodromal symptoms. These patients were seen individually after the group if clinically indicated for further evaluation and treatment. As a result, patients developed a sense of better control and mastery over the course of the illness, with an increased feeling of confidence in their ability to prevent future relapses.

Generally, group therapy sessions should deal with "here and now" issues. Efforts should be made to establish a supportive social network for patients to enhance free communication among members. Group members are encouraged to discuss stressful situations they have experienced during the prior week with an emphasis on problem solving, using input from other patients in the group. Other group members can offer suggestions and advice, and share their own experiences in dealing with similar stressors and methods they used to cope with this stress. Group cohesion can also be fostered by encouraging patients to share positive experiences and interests (e.g., current events and sporting events). Depending on the needs of group members and their levels of functioning, modules of social skills training, cognitive behavioral therapy, and coping skills strategies can be introduced. However, in any particular session precedence should be given to important "here-and-now" issues before moving on to the modules. According to May and Simpson (107), groups should address the social and interpersonal deficits of schizophrenia and focus on problem solving, goal planning, social interactions, and medication and side effect management. Methods and goals should be adjusted according to the level of chronicity and interpersonal capacities of the group members. A well-controlled 2-year outcome study by Malm demonstrated significantly more improvement in symptomatology and social functioning in patients receiving a combination of communication-oriented group therapy, depot neuroleptics, and living skills instruction than occurred with patients receiving depot neuroleptics and living skills instruction alone (112,113). In addition to illustrating the advantages of a multi-

Early Signs Questionnaire
WEEKLY PROBLEMS FORM

NAME _____   DATE _____

Compared to last week, has there been an increase in any of the following symptoms?

	YES	NO
1. Problems with sleep?..	_____	_____
2. Problems with appetite?.....................................	_____	_____
3. Depression?...	_____	_____
4. Problems with concentration?.............................	_____	_____
5. Restlessness?..	_____	_____
6. Tension or worry?...	_____	_____
7. Use of Alcohol...	_____	_____
8. Use of street drugs (incl. Marijuana)?.....................	_____	_____
9. Hearing voices or seeing things others can't hear or see?...	_____	_____
10. Less pleasure gained from things you usually enjoy?...	_____	_____
11. Feeling people were watching you, were against you, or were talking about you?...............................	_____	_____
12. Preference for being alone and/or been spending less time with other people?...................................	_____	_____
13. Irritable and angry at little things?...........................	_____	_____
14. Inability to get your mind off of one or two things?.......	_____	_____

Have you had any symptoms other than those mentioned above?
If so, what were they?_____

_____

_____

Did anything specific happen last week which upset you?
If so, what was it?_____

_____

_____

Have you been taking your medication as it is prescribed for you?....   YES   NO

FIG. 9.2. Brief early signs questionnaire.

faceted treatment approach, the study demonstrated the efficacy of long-term group psychotherapy with schizophrenic patients. Research results have demonstrated that an intensive insight-oriented group approach is not indicated for the great majority of individuals with schizophrenia (114).

It is most desirable to select patients who are similar symptomatically and functionally for entry into a group. Patients in the stable phase are most suitable for this treatment, although those in the later phase of stabilization can be appropriate for the group therapy experience. Ordinarily, it is best to exclude patients who have poor impulse control and/or severe psychotic symptoms that interfere with their ability to participate meaningfully in the group (e.g., patients who are actively responding to frequent auditory hallucinations or are grossly paranoid or severely thought disordered). Patients with prominent negative symptoms can benefit from group participation. In conducting group therapy for individuals with schizophrenia, therapists should be active in structuring the group. They should provide modeling and encourage behavioral rehearsal, role playing, and active feedback. As stated previously, it is important to foster group cohesion. Direct confrontation should be discouraged, especially strong displays of anger and hostility, thereby creating a feeling of safety among members of the group.

Optimal size of a group is approximately six to eight patients and should include members of each sex and be diagnostically homogeneous (i.e., schizophrenia). Depending on the compliance rate of members and to ensure adequate attendance at each session, the roster of a group can be as high as 15 patients (115). Groups should be open-ended (i.e., new patients can enter the group during its progress), and it usually is useful for patients to reenter the group following recovery from a relapse. Group members should be encouraged to notify the group leader in advance if unable to attend a session, and if feasible, group members should call those members who failed to notify the group before missing a session. If possible, patients should be seated in a circle without a table separating them and the same room should be used for each session. Groups generally meet for 60-minute sessions on a weekly basis and should begin with any "here-and-now" issues, including medication-related concerns. Compared with psychoanalytically oriented groups of nonpsychotic patients, flexibility is indicated in conducting groups with schizophrenic patients. For example, contacts among group members outside the session is not discouraged, since many have been socially isolated and confrontations should be kept to a minimum (108). Although initial frequency of sessions should be once a week, if the group remains relatively stable in membership, over time it may meet less frequently, depending on the wishes and needs of the members.

As with individual therapy, we are recommending a multifaceted group treatment approach. It should include supportive therapy techniques, psychoeducation, and efforts to improve group cohesion and communication among members. Monitoring for the appearance of prodromal symptoms is an important component of group treatment. The treatment program can benefit from introduction of social skills and cognitive behavioral training modules and coping skills training. Group treatment should be part of an overall treatment approach, which includes maintenance antipsychotic medication and arrangements to provide adequate economic and housing support for the members. With regard to therapists for the groups, it has been our experience that some therapists who are well trained in individual therapy are reluctant to conduct groups. It is especially important for beginning therapists of groups to obtain training both in techniques of conducting groups and in the specialized therapeutic approaches described earlier.

FAMILY INTERVENTIONS

Family approaches to managing schizophrenia have evolved considerably during the past decades. Early approaches were based on psychodynamic theories and focused on repairing relationships that were thought to have caused the illness. These approaches have been largely discredited. More recent studies have focused on the family as an important element in the patient's environment that can support the individual's recovery. Approaches to assisting families have included strategies for improving interactions between patients and family members, providing supports for families who are experiencing a burden associated with the care of a member with a serious mental illness, and educational programs that improve the families' understanding of schizophrenia and its treatment.

The strategy of improving the emotional climate in the families of patients with schizophrenia originated in the United Kingdom, where Vaughn and Leff (116) noted that relapse rates were higher when patients returned to families that were high in expressed emotion (EE). In their definition, high EE was characterized by critical comments, hostility, and emotional overinvolvement. It also fits with the stress vulnerability model, since increased tension among family members, including the patient, is but one of many possible stressors that may lead to relapse (117). These observations are consistent with the common observation that patients with schizophrenia are often more sensitive to criticism than their siblings. Family members and advocacy groups have criticized studies of EE since they imply that parents could be blamed for a poor outcome of the illness. In addition, the method of categorizing families into high or low categories ignores the many positive influences the family may have on the patient. These criticisms are valid, especially since the attitudes of family members may result from understandable responses to the patient. For example, patients with severe negative symptoms may engender overinvolvement in family members, and individuals who are hostile and suspicious may require limit setting that may be interpreted as criticism. Nevertheless, this group of studies indicates that understanding the nature of schizophrenia should be helpful in guiding the responses of family members.

The relationship of expressed emotion and relapse has led to the development of interventions that were aimed at reducing the amount of EE in families. An educational strategy developed by Falloon and co-workers consists of highly structured educational sessions for family members (118). These sessions are commonly held in the patient's home as a means for promoting generalization and providing treatment in a manner that would lead to families being more receptive. The elements of the intervention included education about schizophrenia, training in communications, and training in family problem solving. The communication training emphasized listening skills for family members as well as the importance of clear statements. Falloon found that this method was more effective than a control condition in reducing relapse rates.

A number of studies have reinforced the usefulness of similar approaches (119–121). Each of these approaches has interesting features. For example, the educational strategy in the Leff et al. study delivers four didactic lectures to relatives and provides opportunities for questions (120). In addition, this strategy combined families that were both high and low in EE. This encouraged discussion of different approaches to coping with family issues and provided a source of support for relatives. Research in these strategies has demonstrated that they are more effective than usual clinical care. There is no indication that any family strategy is more effective than any other.

A study of treatment strategies in schizophrenia sponsored by the National Institute of Mental Health compared an intensive family management strategy based on the technique of Falloon with a family psychoeducation strategy (29). All study participants participated in an educational workshop for families and subsequent monthly support groups that included both patients and family members. The more intensive family strategy consisted of group meetings and home visits by therapists who taught communication and problem-solving skills. The study found no difference in clinical outcomes between the two forms of family treatment. Although this study did not find an advantage for the more intensive form of management, this does not mean that this treatment was ineffective. An alternative explanation was that the supportive form of treatment, with its emphasis on education and building of a mutual support group among family members, was equally effective. Therefore implementing family and patient education in conjunction with supportive groups may be sufficient for many patients and their families.

Other strategies have also demonstrated the effectiveness of strategies that emphasize psychoeducation. The strategy developed by Anderson and Hogarty emphasizes a survival skills education workshop that provides information about schizophrenia and its treatments (122). The authors emphasize that the program is not family therapy, but a program of education about the disorder and strategies for improving its management. The advantage of this definition is that family members are considered by the treatment team to be allies in the treatment process, rather than a problem for the patient. The treatment is initially delivered in an educational workshop; this is followed by regular group sessions. McFarlane et al. used a multifamily psychoeducation and support approach, comparing it with a single-family approach, and found a lower relapse rate for the multifamily approach (121). Most of the patients were chronically ill. The lowered relapse rate was most evident for patients who had only partially remitted for their psychotic symptoms at hospital discharge. On the other hand, Leff et al. found no difference in outcome when comparing multifamily and single-family interventions (119).

These studies, when taken together, provide a compelling argument for including family psychoeducation as part of routine practice for patients with schizophrenia. These methods were recognized by the schizophrenia PORT (patient outcomes research team), which concluded that family interventions were effective in preventing or delaying psychotic relapses (123). Nevertheless, the clinician is forced to choose among different strategies with different levels of intensity. Fortunately, there are important similarities among the different techniques: They all include formal education in schizophrenia, and all focus on methods for improving the emotional climate in the patient's family. Although initial studies suggested that brief family treatment was effective, most authorities have emphasized that treatment should be continued for at least several months. Although studies of more intensive family management such as the work of Falloon suggest that these strategies are effective, it is unclear if they are more effective than less intensive methods such as those used in the Treatment Strategies in Schizophrenia study. In that study, families participated in an educational workshop followed by monthly multifamily groups. This strategy is relatively inexpensive and can be implemented at many clinical sites.

The PORT study found that effective family strategies were seldom implemented in actual clinical practice. This failure of the field to provide patients with an effective and relatively inexpensive intervention may explain why family members and other advocates for the seriously mentally ill developed the National Alliance for the Mentally Ill (NAMI) Family to Family Educations and the Journey of Hope Program. These programs provide psychoeducation as well as support for family members. An important distinction of these programs is that family members who have received substantial training lead the groups. Moreover, these programs stress the well-being of family members as well as the management of the family member with schizophrenia. In addition, family members can receive this form of education and support even if the patient with schizophrenia is not participating in a treatment program. (Information for family members can be obtained at the NAMI website, www.nami.org.)

REFERENCES

1. Davis JM. Overview: maintenance therapy in psychiatry. I: Schizophrenia. *Am J Psychiatry* 1975;132:1237–1245.
2. Hogarty GE, Ulrich RF, Mussare F, et al. Drug discontinuation among long term, successfully maintained schizophrenic outpatients. *Dis Nerv Syst* 1976;37:494–500.
3. Kane JM, Rabiner CJ. Studies of maintenance pharmacotherapy in schizophrenia: the Hillside Series. *Psychiatr Hosp* 1982;13:47–49.
4. Crow TJ, Macmillan JF, Johnson AL, et al. A randomised controlled trial of prophylactic neuroleptic treatment. *Br J Psychiatry* 1986;148:120–127.
5. Kissling WJ, Kane JM, Barnes TRE, et al. Guidelines for neuroleptic relapse prevention in schizophrenia: towards a consensus view. In: Kissling W, ed. *Guidelines for neuroleptic relapse prevention in schizophrenia.* Berlin: Springer-Verlag, 1991:155–163.
6. Kane JM, Honigfeld G, Singer J, et al. Clozapine for the treatment-resistant schizophrenic: a double-blind comparison versus chlorpromazine/benztropine. *Arch Gen Psychiatry* 1988;45:789–796.
7. Marder SR, Meibach RC. Risperidone in the treatment of schizophrenia. *Am J Psychiatry* 1994;151:825–835.
8. Marder SR, Davis JM, Chouinard G. The effects of risperidone on the five dimensions of schizophrenia derived by factor analysis: combined results of the North American trials. *J Clin Psychiatry* 1997;58:538–546.
9. Tollefson GD, Beasley CM Jr, Tran PV, et al. Olanzapine versus haloperidol in the treatment of schizophrenia and schizoaffective and schizophreniform disorders: results of an international collaborative trial. *Am J Psychiatry* 1997;154:457–465.
10. Muller MJ, Grunder G, Wetzel H, et al. Antipsychotic effects and tolerability of the sigma ligand EMD 57445 (panamesine) and its metabolites in acute schizophrenia: an open clinical trial. *Psychiatry Res* 1999; 89:275–280.
11. Leucht S, Pitschel-Walz G, Abraham D, et al. Efficacy and extrapyramidal side-effects of the new antipsychotics olanzapine, quetiapine, risperidone, and sertindole compared to conventional antipsychotics and placebo. A meta-analysis of randomized controlled trials. *Schizophr Res* 1999;35:51–68.
12. Rosenheck R, Tekell J, Peters J, et al. Does participation in psychosocial treatment augment the benefit of clozapine? *Arch Gen Psychiatry* 1998;55:618–625.
13. Buchanan RW, Breier A, Kirkpatrick B, et al. Positive and negative symptom response to clozapine in schizophrenic patients with and without the deficit syndrome. *Am J Psychiatry* 1998;155:751–760.
14. Buchanan RW, Brandes M, Breier A. Pharmacological strategies for treating negative symptoms. In: Breier A, ed. *The new pharmacotherapy of schizophrenia.* Washington, DC: American Psychiatric Press, 1996:179–204.
15. Heresco-Levy U, Javitt DC, Ermilov M, et al. Efficacy of high-dose glycine in the treatment of enduring negative symptoms of schizophrenia. *Arch Gen Psychiatry* 1999;56: 29–36.
16. Goff DC, Tsai G, Levitt J, et al. A placebo-controlled trial of d-cycloserine added to conventional neuroleptics in patients with schizophrenia. *Arch Gen Psychiatry* 1999;56: 21–27.
17. Palmer BW, Heaton RK, Paulsen JS, et al. Is it possible to be schizophrenic and neuropsychologically impaired? *Neuropsychology* 1997;11:437–477.
18. Saykin AJ, Gur RC, Gur RE, et al. Neuropsychological deficits in neuroleptic naive patients with first-episode schizophrenia. *Arch Gen Psychiatry* 1994;51:124–131.

19. Harvey PD. Management of schizophrenia with cognitive impairment. *Psychiatr Ann* 2000;30:53–58.
20. Green MF. What are the functional consequences of neurocognitive deficits in schizophrenia. *Am J Psychiatry* 1996;153:321–330.
21. Nuechterlein KH, Edell WS, Norris M, et al. Attentional vulnerability indicators, thought disorder, and negative symptoms. *Schizophr Bull* 1986;12:408–426.
22. Keefe RS, Silva SG, Perkins DO, et al. The effects of atypical antipsychotic drugs on neurocognitive impairment in schizophrenia: a review and meta-analysis. *Schizophr Bull* 1999;25:201–222.
23. Franz M, Lis S, Pluddemann K, et al. Conventional versus atypical neuroleptics: subjective quality of life in schizophrenic patients. *Br J Psychiatry* 1997;170:422–425.
24. Hamilton SH, Revicki DA, Genduso LA, et al. Olanzapine versus placebo and haloperidol: quality of life and efficacy results of the North American double-blind trial. *Neuropsychopharmacology* 1998;18:41–49.
25. Heinrichs DW, Hanlon TE, Carpenter WT Jr. The Quality of Life Scale: an instrument for rating the schizophrenic deficit syndrome. *Schizophr Bull* 1984;10:388–398.
26. Davis JM, Janicak PG, Singla A, et al. Maintenance and antipsychotic medication. In: Barnes TRE, ed. *Antipsychotic drugs and their side effects.* New York: Academic Press, 1993.
27. Marder SR, Van Putten T, Mintz J, et al. Low and conventional dose maintenance therapy with fluphenazine decanoate: two-year outcome. *Arch Gen Psychiatry* 1987;44:518–521.
28. Hogarty GE, McEvoy JP, Munetz M, et al. Dose of fluphenazine, familial expressed emotion, and outcome in schizophrenia: results of a two-year controlled study. *Arch Gen Psychiatry* 1988;45:797–805.
29. Schooler NR, Keith SJ, Severe JB, et al. Relapse and rehospitalization during maintenance treatment of schizophrenia: the effects of dose reduction and family treatment. *Arch Gen Psychiatry* 1997;54:453–463.
30. Herz MI, Glazer WM, Mostert MA, et al. Intermittent vs maintenance medication in schizophrenia: two-year results. *Arch Gen Psychiatry* 1991;48:333–339.
31. Carpenter WT, Heinrichs DW, Hanlon TE. A comparative trial of pharmacologic strategies in schizophrenia. *Am J Psychiatry* 1987;144:1466–1470.
32. Jolley AG, Hirsch SR, Morrison E, et al. Trial of brief intermittent neuroleptic prophylaxis for selected schizophrenic outpatients: clinical and social outcome at two years. *BMJ* 1990;301:837–842.
33. Pietzcker A, Gaebel W, Kopcke W, et al. Intermittent versus maintenance neuroleptic long-term treatment in schizophrenia: two-year results of a German multicenter study. *J Psychiatr Res* 1993;27:321–339.
34. Hirsch SR, Kohen D. Recent neuroleptic maintenance strategies in the management of schizophrenia. In: Shriqui CL, Nasrallah HA, eds. *Contemporary issues in the treatment of schizophrenia.* Washington, DC: American Psychiatric Press, 1995:247–261.
35. Marder SR, Wirshing WC, Van Putten T, et al. Fluphenazine versus placebo supplementation for prodromal signs of relapse in schizophrenia. *Arch Gen Psychiatry* 1994; 51:280–287.
36. Rifkin A, Doddi S, Karajgi B, et al. Dosage of haloperidol for mania. *Br J Psychiatry* 1994;165:113–116.
37. Kane JM, Woerner MG, Pollack S, et al. Does clozapine cause tardive dyskinesia? *J Clin Psychiatry* 1993;54:327–330.
38. Casey DE. Will the new antipsychotics bring hope of reducing the risk of developing extrapyramidal syndromes and tardive dyskinesia. *Int Clin Psychopharmacol* 1997;[12 Suppl]:S19–S27.
39. Jeste DV, Lacro JP, Bailey A, et al. Lower incidence of tardive dyskinesia with risperidone in older patients. *J Am Geriatr Soc* 1999;47:716–719.
40. Kane JM, Woerner M, Lieberman J. Tardive dyskinesia: prevalence, incidence, and risk factors. *J Clin Psychopharmacol* 1988;8:52S–56S.

41. Egan MF, Apud J, Wyatt RJ. Treatment of tardive dyskinesia. *Schizophr Bull* 1997;23: 583–609.

42. Fahn SA. A therapeutic approach to tardive dyskinesia. *J Clin Psychiatry* 1985;464:19–24.

43. Glazer WM, Hafez HM. A comparison of masking effects of haloperidol versus molindone in tardive dyskinesia. *Schizophr Res* 1990;3:315–320.

44. Smith JM, Baldessarini RJ. Changes in prevalence, severity and recovery in tardive dyskinesia. *Arch Gen Psychiatry* 1980;37:1368–1373.

45. Lohr JB, Caligiuri MP. A double-blind placebo-controlled study of vitamin E treatment of tardive dyskinesia. *J Clin Psychiatry* 1996;57:167–173.

46. Adler LA, Edson R, Lavori P, et al. Long-term treatment effects of vitamin E for tardive dyskinesia. *Biol Psychiatry* 1998;43:868–872.

47. Adler LA, Rotrosen J, Edson R, et al. Vitamin E for tardive dyskinesia. *Arch Gen Psychiatry* 1999;56:836–841.

48. Simpson GM. The treatment of tardive dyskinesia and tardive dystonia. *J Clin Psychiatry* 2000;61[Suppl 4]:39–44.

49. Allison DB, Mentore JL, Moonseong H, et al. Antipsychotic-induced weight gain: a comprehensive research synthesis *Am J Psychiatry* 1999;156:1686–1696.

50. Brown S, Birtwistle J, Roe L, et al. The unhealthy lifestyle of people with schizophrenia. *Psychol Med* 1999;29:697–701.

51. Wirshing DA, Spellberg BJ, Erhart SM, et al. Novel antipsychotics and new onset diabetes. *Biol Psychiatry* 1998;44:778–783.

52. Hägg S, Joelsson L, Mjörndal T, et al. Prevalence of diabetes and impaired glucose tolerance in patients treated with clozapine compared with patients treated with conventional depot neuroleptic medications. *J Clin Psychiatry* 1998;59:294–299.

53. Gaulin BD, Markowitz JS, Caley CF, et al. Clozapine-associated elevation in serum triglycerides. *Am J Psychiatry* 1999;156:1270–1272.

54. Osser DN, Najarian DM, Dufresne RL. Olanzapine increases weight and serum triglyceride levels. *J Clin Psychiatry* 1999; 60:767–770.

55. Aizenberg D, Zemishlany Z, Dorfman-Etrog P, et al. Sexual dysfunction in male schizophrenic patients. *J Clin Psychiatry* 1995; 56:137–141.

56. Rojansky N, Wang K, Halbriech U. Reproductive and sexual adverse effects of psychotropic drugs. In: Kane JM, Lieberman JA, eds. *Adverse effects of psychotropic drugs.* New York: Guilford, 1992:356–375.

57. Petty RG. Prolactin and antipsychotic medications: mechanism of action. *Schizophr Res* 1999;35:S67–S73.

58. Dickson RA, Glazer WM. Neuroleptic-induced hyperprolactinemia. *Schizophr Res* 1999;35:S75–S86.

59. Cohen S, Leonard CV, Faberbrow AC, et al. Tranquilizers and suicide in schizophrenic patients. *Arch Gen Psychiatry* 1964;11:312–321.

60. Planansky K, Johnston R. Clinical setting and motivation in suicidal attempts of schizophrenics. *Acta Psychiatr Scand* 1973;49:680–690.

61. Virkkunen M. Suicides in schizophrenia and paranoid psychoses. *Acta Psychiatr Scand Suppl* 1974;250:1–305.

62. Tanay E. Homicidal behavior in schizophrenics. *J Forensic Sci* 1987;32:1382–1388.

63. Weider PJ, Dixon L, Frances A, et al. Neuroleptic noncompliance in schizophrenia. In: Tamminga CA, Schulz SC, eds. *Advances in neuropsychology and psychopharmacology.* New York: Raven, 1991, 285–296.

64. Allgulander C. Psychoactive drug use in a general population sample, Sweden: correlates with perceived health, psychiatric diagnoses, and mortality in an automated record. *Am J Public Health* 1989;79:1006–1009.

65. Serban G, Thomas A. Attitudes and behaviors of acute and chronic schizophrenic patients regarding ambulatory treatment. *Am J Psychiatry* 1974;136:991–995.

66. Weiden P, Rapkin B, Mott T, et al. Rating of medication influences (ROMI) scale in schizophrenia. *Schizophr Bull* 1994;20:297–310.

67. Kampman O, Lehtinen K. Compliance in psychoses. *Acta Psychiatr Scand* 1999;100: 167–175.
68. Kapur S, Ganguli R, Ulrich R. Use of random-sequence riboflavin as a marker of medication compliance in chronic schizophrenics. *Schizophr Res* 1992;6:49–53.
69. Rudd P, Byyny RL, Zachary V, et al. The natural history of medication compliance in a drug trial: limitations of pill counts [see comments]. *Clin Pharmacol Ther* 1989;46: 169–176.
70. Blackwell B. The drug defaulter. *Clin Pharmacol Ther* 1972;13:841–848.
71. Van Putten T, May PR, Marder SR. Akathisia with haloperidol and thiothixene. *Arch Gen Psychiatry* 1984;41:1036–1039.
72. Weiden PJ, Mann JJ, Dixon L, et al. Is neuroleptic dysphoria a healthy response? *Compr Psychiatry* 1989;30:546–552.
73. Herz MI, Melville C. Relapse in schizophrenia. *Am J Psychiatry* 1980;80:801–805.
74. Adams J, Scott J. Predicting medication adherence in severe mental disorders. *Acta Psychiatr Scand* 2000;101:119–124.
75. Van Putten T, Crumpton E, Yale C. Drug refusal in schizophrenia and the wish to be crazy. *Arch Gen Psychiatry* 1976;33:1443–1446.
76. Olfson M, Mechanic D, Hansell S, et al. Predicting medication noncompliance after hospital discharge among patients with schizophrenia. *Psychiatr Serv* 2000;51:216–222.
77. Davis JM, Kane JM, Marder SR, et al. Dose response of prophylactic antipsychotics. *J Clin Psychiatry* 1993;54[Suppl]:24–30.
78. Keith SJ, Bellack AS, Frances A, et al. The influence of diagnosis and family treatment on acute treatment response and the short-term outcome in schizophrenia. *Psychopharmacol Bull* 1991;25:336–339.
79. Eckman TA, Liberman RP, Phipps CC, et al. Teaching medication management skills to schizophrenic patients. *J Clin Psychopharmacol* 1990;10:33–38.
80. Mueser KT, Berenbaum H. Psychodynamic treatment of schizophrenia: is there a future? *Psychol Med* 1990;20:253–262.
81. Stanton AH, Gunderson JG, Knapp PH, et al. Effects of psychotherapy in schizophrenia: I. Design and implementation of a controlled study. *Schizophr Bull* 1984;10:520–563.
82. Gunderson JG, Frank AF, Katz HM, et al. Effects of psychotherapy in schizophrenia. II: Comparative outcome of two forms of treatment. *Schizophr Bull* 1984;10:564–598.
83. Hogarty GE, Goldberg SC. Drug and sociotherapy in the aftercare of schizophrenic patients. *Arch Gen Psychiatry* 1973;28:54–64.
84. Hogarty GE, Ulrich RF, Mussare F, et al. Drug discontinuation among long term, successfully maintained schizophrenic outpatients. *Dis Nerv Syst* 1976;37:494–500.
85. Hogarty GE, Goldberg SC, Schooler NR, et al. Drug and sociotherapy in the aftercare of schizophrenic patients. II. Two-year relapse rates. *Arch Gen Psychiatry* 1974;31:603–608.
86. Hogarty GE, Goldberg SC, Schooler NR. Drug and sociotherapy in the aftercare of schizophrenic patients. III. Adjustment of nonrelapsed patients. *Arch Gen Psychiatry* 1974;31:609–618.
87. Frank AF, Gunderson JG. The role of the therapeutic alliance in the treatment of schizophrenia: relationship to course and outcome. *Arch Gen Psychiatry* 1990;47:228–236.
88. Herz MI, Lamberti JS. *Psychotherapy, relapse prevention, and management of relapse in schizophrenia in schizophrenia,* vol. I. New York: John Wiley, 1996.
89. Hogarty GE, Kornblith SJ, Greenwald D, et al. Three years trials of Personal Therapy among schizophrenic patients living with or independent of family. I: Description of study and effects on relapse rates. *Am J Psychiatry* 1997;154:1504–1513.
90. Herz MI, Lamberti JS, Mintz J, et al. A program for relapse prevention in schizophrenia: a controlled study. *Arch Gen Psychiatry* 2000;57:277–283.
91. Fowler D, Garety P, Kuipers E. *Cognitive behavior therapy for people with psychosis.* New York: John Wiley, 1995.
92. Beck AT, Rush AJ, Shaw BF, et al. *Cognitive therapy of depression.* New York: Guilford, 1979.

93. Beck AT, Rector NA. Cognitive therapy of schizophrenia: a new therapy for the new millennium. *Am J Psychother* 2000;54:291–300.
94. Birchwood M, Iqbal Z. Depression and suicidal thinking in psychosis: a cognitive approach. In: Wykes T, Tarrier N, Lewis S, eds. *Outcome and innovation in psychological treatment of schizophrenia.* New York: John Wiley, 1998.
95. Freeman D, Garety PA. Worry, worry processes and dimensions of delusions: an exploratory investigation of a role for anxiety processes in the maintenance of delusional distress. *Behav Cogn Psychother* 1999;27:47–62.
96. Fowler D, Morley S. The cognitive-behavioral treatment of hallucinations and delusions: a preliminary study. *Behav Psychother* 1989;17:267–282.
97. Tarrier N. Management and modification of residual positive psychotic symptoms. In: Birchwood M, Tarrier N, eds. *Innovations in the psychological management of schizophrenia.* New York: John Wiley, 1992.
98. Tarrier N, Yusupoff L. Coping strategy enhancement for persistent hallucinations and delusions. In: Haddock G, Slade P, eds. *Cognitive-behavioral interventions with psychotic disorders.* London: Routledge, 1996.
99. Tarrier N, Beckett R, Harwood S, et al. A trial of two cognitive-behavioural methods of treating drug-resistant residual psychotic symptoms in schizophrenic patients. I: Outcome. *Br J Psychiatry* 1993;165:524–532.
100. Garety PA, Kuipers E, Fowler D, et al. Cognitive behavioral therapy for drug-resistant psychosis. *Br J Med Psychol* 1994;67:259–271.
101. Kuipers E, Garety P, Fowler D, et al. London-East Anglia randomized controlled trial of cognitive-behavioural therapy for psychosis. *Br J Psychiatry* 1997;171:319–327.
102. Kuipers E, Garety P, Fowler D, et al. London-East Anglia randomised controlled trial of cognitive-behavioural therapy for psychosis. III. Follow-up and economic evaluation at 18 months. *Br J Psychiatry* 1998;173:61–68.
103. Tarrier N, Uusupoff L, Kinney C, et al. Randomised controlled trial of intensive cognitive behaviour therapy for chronic schizophrenia. *Br Med J* 1998;317:303–307.
104. O'Brien CP. Group psychotherapy for schizophrenia: a practical approach. *Schizophr Bull* 1975;13:119–130.
105. Luborsky L, Singer B. Comparative studies of psychotherapies: Is it true that "everybody has won and all must have prizes"? *Proc Am Psychopathol Assoc* 1976;64:3–22.
106. Parloff MB, Dies R. Group psychotherapy outcome research. *Int J Group Psychiatry* 1977;21:281–319.
107. May PR, Simpson G. Schizophrenia: evaluation of treatment methods. In: Kaplan HI, Freedman AM, Sadock BJ, eds. *Comprehensive textbook of psychiatry*, vol. 2. Baltimore: Williams & Wilkins, 1980.
108. Kanas N. Group psychotherapy with schizophrenia. In: Kaplan HI, Sadock BJ, eds. *Comprehensive group psychotherapy.* Baltimore: Williams & Wilkins, 1993.
109. Herz MI, Spitzer RL, Gibbon M, et al. Individual versus group aftercare treatment. *Am J Psychiatry* 1974;74:808–812.
110. Andres K, Pfammatter M, Garst F, et al. Effects of a coping-orientated group therapy for schizophrenia and schizoaffective patients: a pilot study [In Process Citation]. *Acta Psychiatr Scand* 2000;101:318–322.
111. Wykes T, Parr AM, Landau S. Group treatment of auditory hallucinations: exploratory study of effectiveness. *Br J Psychiatry* 1999;175:180–185.
112. Malm U. The influence of group therapy on schizophrenia. *Acta Psychiatr Scand* 1982;65(Suppl 297).
113. Malm U. Group therapy. In: Herz MI, Keith SJ, Docherty JP, eds. *Handbook of schizophrenia* Vol. IV. New York: Elsevier Science Publishers, 1990:191–211.
114. Group for the Advancement of Psychiatry (GAP). *Implications for psychosocial interventions in patients with schizophrenia.* Washington, DC: American Psychiatric Press, 1992:134, 59–78.
115. Stone WN. Group therapy for seriously mentally ill patients in a managed care system,

In: Mackenzie KR, ed. *Effective use of group therapy in managed care.* Washington, DC: American Psychiatric Press, 1995.

116. Vaughn CE, Leff JP. The measurement of expressed emotion in the families of psychiatric patients. *Br J Clin Soc Psychol* 1976;15:157–165.

117. Zubin J, Spring B. Vulnerability: a new view of schizophrenia. *J Abnorm Psychol* 1977; 86:103–126.

118. Falloon IRH, Boyd JL, McGill CW, et al. Family management in the prevention of morbidity of schizophrenia. I: Clinical outcome of a two-year longitudinal study. *Arch Gen Psychiatry* 1985;42:887–896.

119. Leff J, Berkowitz R, Shavit N, et al. A trial of family therapy v. a relatives group for schizophrenia. *Br J Psychiatry* 1989;154:58–66.

120. Leff J, Wig NN, Bedi H, et al. Relatives' expressed emotion and the course of schizophrenia in Chandigarh: a two-year follow-up of a first-contact sample. *Br J Psychiatry* 1990;156:351–356.

121. McFarlane WR, Lukens E, Link B, et al. Multiple-family groups and psychoeducation in the treatment of schizophrenia. *Arch Gen Psychiatry* 1995;52:679–687.

122. Anderson CM, Hogarty GE, Reiss DJ. *Schizophrenia in the family.* New York: Guilford Press, 1986.

123. Dixon L, Adams C, Lucksted A. Update on family psychoeducation for schizophrenia (see comments). *Schizophr Bull* 2000;26:5–20.

10

Rehabilitative Approaches

SOCIAL SKILLS TRAINING

Social skills training (SST) was developed as a means for addressing the deficits in social functioning that are common in schizophrenia and that can interfere with a patient's community adjustment. Nearly all forms of SST are based on learning theory and address a number of issues, including problem solving, interpersonal skills, management of stress, and leisure skills. The social problem-solving approach to SST is based on the finding that individuals with schizophrenia have deficits in their abilities to perceive social information and to use it in developing appropriate social responses. The difficulties in social perception involve impairments in ability to interpret the affective and cognitive cues essential for communication. Social skills training also recognizes deficits that patients may have in choosing among available behavioral approaches to solving problems in social situations. SST methods usually include active teaching with didactic instruction, behavioral rehearsal, social reinforcement, and homework assignments. Moreover, the teaching methods are adjusted to accommodate to the cognitive deficits common in schizophrenia. In most SST strategies, treatment occurs in a group setting.

Research during the past two decades has addressed a number of the important issues in skills training: (a) Can patients with schizophrenia learn social skills using SST methods? (b) If they do learn the skills, do they retain the information? (c) Does learning these skills result in patients actually practicing these skills in the community? (d) Do patients who receive SST and practice these skills show demonstrable improvements in social adjustment and quality of life?

Compelling evidence demonstrates that patients who receive SST can learn new skills. A number of studies have shown that patients can learn relatively simple social skills such as making appropriate eye contact as well as more complex behaviors such as conversation skills or medication self-management (1). When learning criteria are set, patients with relatively severe positive and negative symptoms can learn these skills and retain them over many months. In the study by Eckman et al., skills were well retained at a 1-year follow-up (2).

The generalizability of benefits derived from skills training programs is sometimes limited, however. For example, in a recent meta-analysis of 27 social skills training studies of individuals with schizophrenia, Benton and Schroeder reported these interventions had consistently positive effects on actual skill level and inpatient discharge rates but seemed to be less effective at improving overall functioning and reducing subsequent relapse (3). On the other hand, there is evidence that patients who receive skills training demonstrate improvement in social areas that are related to independent living skills learned in a clinical setting (4,5). A recent study by Blair et al. found that supplementing SST with training that occurs in the patient's natural community setting results in improvement over SST that is confined to a clinical setting (6).

A number of studies provide strong support for the effectiveness of SST in improving the outcome for stable patients with schizophrenia who are living in the community (7,8,1). Hogarty and his co-workers compared SST to a control condition during a 2-year trial (9). During the first year, patients who received SST demonstrated lower relapse rates when compared with patients who did not receive it. However, during the second year of the study, when there was a reduction in the intensity of the treatment from weekly to biweekly, some of the effects of the treatment were lost (10). The Hogarty study suggested that SST improved relapse rates without improving social adjustment. A subsequent study by Marder et al. compared a form of SST and an equally intense form of supportive group therapy (11). This study found the opposite. At 2 years, relapse rates and psychopathology were similar for both treatments, but patients who received SST demonstrated improvement in social adjustment, whereas the supportive group therapy patients did not. These and other studies support the use of forms of SST for outpatients with schizophrenia.

Other studies have demonstrated that briefer forms of SST may be useful for patients who are recovering from psychotic episodes. Mueser and his co-workers evaluated a 2-week training program for acutely ill inpatients that focused on improving communication skills (12). Patients who received a version of SST modified for inpatients demonstrated improvements. Smith and his co-workers evaluated a brief SST program called the Community Reentry Module that focused on assisting inpatients to comply with medication and outpatient treatment following inpatient hospitalization (13). The program focuses on such issues as planning discharge, identifying symptoms, understanding antipsychotic effects, and adhering to outpatient appointments. Patients who received this program had fewer symptoms and higher rates of compliance. Kopelowicz et al. carried out a randomized comparison between the Community Reentry Module and Occupational Therapy (14). Patients who received the module were more likely to attend their first outpatient appointment. Although the studies of these brief methods of SST are only preliminary, they suggest that this form of treatment has promise for acute settings.

The preceding results provide strong support for the use of SST for outpatients with schizophrenia. For these individuals, skills training is effective for shaping behavior change and improving social adjustment. The evidence supporting SST strategies for acutely ill inpatients is less convincing, but promising. Among the advantages of SST is that it can be administered by a wide range of mental health practitioners, including paraprofessionals. For example, the program developed by UCLA faculty includes a number of modules for medication management, symptom management, community reentry, basic conversation, recreation and leisure, and others. Each includes materials for trainers as well as patient workbooks and videotapes. As a result, these programs can be easily implemented in nearly any psychiatric setting. Periodic booster sessions after the initial presentation of the modules will probably enhance the retention and application of learned skills. (See Appendix 1 for a description of modules.)

STRATEGIES TO IMPROVE VOCATIONAL ADJUSTMENT

During the past several years there has been renewed interest in strategies for assisting patients interested in vocational rehabilitation. Past experiences suggested that patients with schizophrenia who were receiving disability seldom returned to work. Until recently nearly all vocational rehabilitation strategies depended on programs such as long-term sheltered workshops or transitional employment programs that emphasized lengthy periods of prevocational training. Unfortunately, evidence suggests that these programs were seldom successful. For example, studies have found that the longer a person remained in prevocational training and preparation, the less likely that person would be to enter gainful employment (15). Other studies found that programs that focused on teaching patients how to obtain jobs had only limited success (16). These attitudes may explain the finding that vocational services are seldom included in the services provided to patients with schizophrenia (17).

A number of factors may explain a recent change in attitude regarding vocational programs. The introduction of the second generation of antipsychotic drugs has resulted in renewed interest in psychosocial treatments. The milder side effects of these agents as well as evidence that they may result in improvements in negative and neurocognitive symptoms could result in patients showing a greater interest in work. In addition, legislation, including the Americans with Disabilities Act, has encouraged employers to hire patients with disabilities. These federal laws have required that employers make reasonable accommodations for individuals with psychiatric disabilities (18).

This change in attitude may have resulted from a body of research that questioned assumptions of traditional vocational rehabilitation. One of these assumptions was that individuals with serious mental disorders would demonstrate better work outcomes if they were employed in sheltered workshops or other environments that were segregated from competitive employment settings. However, a number of studies indicate that placing patients in competitive employment settings was more effective than placing them in alternative settings (19). A study by Robert Drake and co-workers compared traditional vocational rehabilitation that included sheltered workshops with a supported employment program that utilized jobs in competitive settings (20). The outcomes were better in the supported employment programs.

Another assumption in traditional programs was that patients should have experiences in protected environments such as sheltered workshops as preparation for competitive employment. Research indicates that there is an advantage to placing patients as rapidly as possible into a competitive employment setting. This was demonstrated by Bond et al., who found that patients who were assigned to jobs immediately had better vocational outcomes than those who received prevocational services before job placement (21). Other studies reinforced this finding. They indicated that even when the severity of illness and the amount of functional impairment was statistically controlled, those who participated in sheltered workshops were less likely to obtain competitive jobs (19).

The vocational strategy of supported employment has challenged these assumptions and has shown success in improving vocational outcomes and the overall quality of life in individuals with schizophrenia. The strategy was modeled after programs developed for the developmentally disabled. In that case, supported employment provided individuals who assisted patients in adjusting to the workplace. This strategy was modified to develop methods for assisting patients with serious mental illnesses to adapt to the workplace. The criteria for supported employment are displayed in Table 10.1. It is important to note that participants in supported employment work at the prevailing wage alongside nondisabled workers. Although the job coach may assist patients to obtain jobs, the expectation is that the patient—with appropriate assistance—can complete the job. Another important principle is that the job coach works with the mental health team. In other words, this individual may be associated not with traditional vocational rehabilitation programs but with the clinical team.

A number of studies have evaluated the effectiveness of supported employment and nearly all have found substantial gains in work outcomes. A re-

TABLE 10.1. *Criteria for supported employment*

- Clients work for pay at the prevailing wage rate.
- Clients are regular employees, integrated on the job with nondisabled workers.
- Clients receive ongoing support from a job coach or employment specialist.
- Jobs are developed for clients based on the latter's preferences, deficits, and assets.
- The job developer also serves as a job coach, offering time-unlimited support services to the worker.
- Close liaison is maintained between the job coach and the mental health team providing psychiatric services.
- Liaison is also provided by the job coach with the employer or supervisor to ensure that the job gets done.

view by Bond and co-workers found that those who received supported employment were twice as likely to be employed as individuals in control groups (22). It is unclear at this stage if the improvements in patients receiving supported employment are limited to work outcomes or if other domains such as negative symptoms and quality of life are affected. At least one study (23) indicates that patients who are competitively employed have better overall clinical outcomes than those who are not. Moreover, individuals who work tend to have better self-esteem, even if work is only part-time.

The approach to supported employment that has received the most attention by researchers is the Individual Placement and Support (IPS) model of Deborah Becker and Robert Drake at Dartmouth (24). The critical components of IPS include placing patients in a job immediately, without extensive evaluation or training, using patient preferences in the job search, integrating employment specialists into the mental health team, and providing long-term support (25). There is no indication that patients are adversely affected by a strategy that moves them into competitive jobs in a relatively brief period of time.

Unfortunately, patients who find jobs in supported employment programs are often unable to keep them. Studies indicate that 41% to 77% of clients terminate a supported employment job within 6 months, many with negative experiences (22). Not surprisingly, the most common reasons for job terminations among persons with schizophrenia or other serious psychiatric illnesses are difficulties with medication and distrust of other people or interpersonal difficulties and "mental illness" (26,27). It is clear that, although some with serious psychiatric illnesses lose positions because their work abilities are poor, others are impeded by deficiencies in illness management and/or interpersonal skills. These observations suggest that employment outcomes are likely to be improved if patients can adapt better to the social environment of the workplace. Strategies such as combining supported employment with social skills training that focuses on the work environment appear promising, although there is no indication at this time that these strategies improve work outcomes (28). It is also important to emphasize to patients that the process of finding a job setting that is a good fit for a particular individual may require some trial and error. Also, each job placement may be an opportunity to improve the patient's ability to adjust to work.

Although sheltered workshops may not be the placement of choice if the aim is to progress to competitive employment, they can be useful for very severely impaired individuals. Another approach, transitional employment, based on the Fountain House psychosocial clubhouse model can be successful in enabling individuals to obtain employment, but not to remain competitively employed for very long (29–31). According to this model, clients are asked to choose one of the many in-house jobs at the clubhouse, such as kitchen work, cleaning, and clerical or simple work tasks, similar to those in sheltered workshops. As stated previously, the most efficient model for helping the mentally ill obtain and retain competitive employment appears to be the supported employment approach, in which the individual proceeds directly to competitive employment without transitional stages.

COGNITIVE REHABILITATION

Cognitive rehabilitation (which is also termed *cognitive remediation*) has the objective of improving deficits in cognitive functions such as memory, executive function, social perception, concentration, and vigilance. It is important to distinguish this form of treatment from cognitive therapy that is aimed at modifying the content of thoughts and beliefs (25). Although, as described later, there are relatively few data to support the use of cognitive rehabilitation, it has captured substantial interest for a number of reasons. The most important reason probably stems from a recent appreciation that the social and functional outcomes of schizophrenia are strongly influenced by the severity of the cognitive impairments (32). In addition, antipsychotics are frequently ineffective in treating cognitive disturbances in schizophrenia. As a result, nonpharmacologic interventions, if effective, would be likely to be the only effective treatment strategy. And finally, evidence suggests that the severity of these impairments can be modified by interventions. These observations have led to an increased interest in approaches to improving cognition in the substantial proportion of patients who suffer from substantial cognitive deficits.

There are a number of important challenges for developers of cognitive rehabilitation. Patients with schizophrenia may have widespread deficits in cognitive function. That is, patients may have deficits in memory but have relative preservation of functions such as sustained attention or executive function. The challenge is to focus on the deficits that have the most important effects on a particular individual. Also, if patients have deficits in multiple areas, cognitive remediation is likely to be effective if the treatment improves more than a single deficit. Even if a particular function can be improved, the improvement must be sufficient to influence important outcome dimensions. Moreover, any learning that occurs in a laboratory must be maintained in the patient's community life and must be sustained for a prolonged period of time. As will be noted later, recent studies have addressed these questions to some extent.

Brenner and his co-workers developed a strategy termed *Integrated Psychological Therapy* (IPT), which focused on enhancing basic social and cognitive skills (33). The treatment is delivered in small groups using published manuals. Their results were encouraging in that patients demonstrated improvements in attention, abstraction, and concept formation. However, patients still performed below the normal range. More important, they have been unable thus far to demonstrate that improvements in these cognitive domains led to improvements in social functioning. Nevertheless, Brenner's findings encouraged others to develop treatment strategies based on cognitive rehabilitation.

Spaulding and his colleagues found that stabilized patients with schizophrenia can show improvements in cognitive functioning over time (34). These changes tended to occur in higher areas of executive functioning. Moreover, these investigators compared IPT to a form of supportive psychotherapy (35). Patients in IPT showed improvements in a number of areas, including problem-solving skills and measures of psychosis. They also demonstrated improvements in a number of tests of cognitive functioning, including verbal learning, memory, and executive functioning. The findings suggest that this form of cognitive remediation improves patients' cognitive abilities, which in turn leads to improved social skills and symptoms.

Wykes and co-workers recently compared what they termed *neurocognitive rehabilitation* with a form of intensive occupational therapy (36). They based their experimental method on the work of Delahunty and Morice (37). The method includes modules for cognitive flexibility, working memory, and planning. In each module patients are given graded tasks beginning with very simple ones. For example, a task may begin with patients being asked to cross off odd numbers from a page and then may shift to even numbers. Similar tasks are included in the other modules. The progression is gradual, ensuring that patients learn without making errors. Moreover, evidence from studies using SPECT imaging suggests that patients can change cognitive strategies as they learn to master these cognitive tasks (38). Using 1-hour sessions that lasted up to 3 months, the authors found greater improvement in the patients who received cognitive remediation for memory and cognitive flexibility. There was a trend suggesting that patients who received second-generation antipsychotics were more likely to benefit from the experimental treatment. There were no clear effects of cognitive remediation on social adjustment, although patients who received this treatment may have been more likely to improve. This study, although it was limited to only 33 patients, certainly lends support to the belief that cognitive remediation may be a reasonable intervention for some patients with schizophrenia.

In summary, intriguing but very preliminary evidence indicates that cognitive remediation may be helpful in schizophrenia. Interventions may affect cognitive functions, which in turn affect social outcomes. Green and Nuechterlein, and Hogarty and Flesher have proposed that the deficits in social perception in schizophrenia may be managed by improving the cognitive functions that underlie social cognition (39,40). As a result, cognitive remediation may be an important component of a long-term rehabilitation strategy.

REFERENCES

1. Heinssen RK, Liberman RP, Kopelowicz A. Psychosocial skills training for schizophrenia: lessons from the laboratory. *Schizophr Bull* 2000;26:21–46.
2. Eckman TA, Wirshing WC, Marder SR, et al. Technique for training schizophrenic patients in illness self-management: a controlled trial. *Am J Psychiatry* 1992;149:1549–1555.
3. Benton MK, Schroeder HE. Social skills training with schizophrenics: a meta-analytic evaluation. *J Consult Clin Psychol* 1990;58:741–747.
4. Liberman RP, Wallace CJ, Blackwell G, et al. Skills training versus psychosocial occupational therapy for persons with persistent schizophrenia [see comments]. *Am J Psychiatry* 1998;155:1087–1091.
5. Dobson DJ, McDougall G, Busheikin J, et al. Effects of social skills training and social milieu treatment on symptoms of schizophrenia. *Psychiatr Serv* 1995;46:376–380.
6. Liberman RP, Blair KE, Glynn SM, et al. Generalization of skills training to the natural environment. In: Brenner HD, Boker W, Genner R (eds). *The treatment of schizophrenia: Status and emerging trends.* Seattle: Hogrefe & Huber, 1951:104–120.
7. Bellack AS, Mueser KT. Psychosocial treatment for schizophrenia. *Schizophr Bull* 1993;19:317–336.
8. Lauriello J, Bustillo J, Keith SJ. A critical review of research on psychosocial treatment of schizophrenia. *Biol Psychiatry* 1999;46:1409–1417.
9. Hogarty GE, Anderson CM, Reiss DJ, et al. Family psychoeducation, social skills training, and maintenance chemotherapy in the aftercare treatment of schizophrenia. I: One-year effects of a controlled study on relapse and expressed emotion. *Arch Gen Psychiatry* 1986;43:633–642.
10. Hogarty GE, Anderson CM, Reiss DJ, et al. Family psychoeducation, social skills training, and maintenance chemotherapy in the aftercare treatment of schizophrenia. II: Two-year effects of a controlled study on relapse and adjustment. *Arch Gen Psychiatry* 1991;48:340–347.
11. Marder SR, Wirshing WC, Mintz J, et al. Behavioral skills training versus group psychotherapy for outpatients with schizophrenia: two-year outcome. *Am J Psychiatry* 1996;153:1585–1592.
12. Mueser KT, Levine S, Bellack AS, et al. Social skills training for acute psychiatric inpatients. *Hosp Community Psychiatry* 1990;41:1249–1251.
13. Smith TE, Hull JW, MacKain SJ, et al. Training hospitalized patients with schizophrenia in community reintegration skills. *Psychiatr Serv* 1996;47:1099–1103.

14. Kopelowicz A, Wallace CJ, Zarate R. Teaching psychiatric inpatients to re-enter the community: a brief method of improving the continuity of care [see comments]. *Psychiatr Serv* 1998;49:1313–1316.
15. Bond GR, Friedmeyer MH. Predictive validity of situational assessment at a psychiatric rehabilitation center. *Psychosoc Rehab* 1987;11:61–77.
16. Jacobs HE, Wissusik D, Collier R, et al. Correlations between psychiatric disabilities and vocational outcome. *Hosp Community Psychiatry* 1992;43:365–369.
17. Lehman AF, Steinwachs DM. Patterns of usual care for schizophrenia: initial results from the Schizophrenia Patient Outcomes Research Team (PORT) Client Survey. *Schizophr Bull* 1998;24:11–20.
18. Cook JA, Razzano L. Vocational rehabilitation for persons with schizophrenia: recent research and implications for practice [see comments]. *Schizophr Bull* 2000;26:87–103. 2000.
19. Cook JA, Razzano L. Discriminant function analysis of competitive employment outcomes in transitional employment program. 1995;5:127–139.
20. Drake RE, Becker DR, Biesanz JC, et al. Rehabilitative day treatment vs. supported employment. I. Vocational outcomes. *Community Ment Health J* 1994;30:519–532.
21. Bond GR, Dietzen L, McGrew J, et al. Accelerating entry into supported employment for persons with severe psychiatric disabilities. *Rehab Psychol* 1995;40:75–94.
22. Bond GR, Drake RE, Mueser KT, et al. An update on supported employment for people with severe mental illness. *Psychiatr Serv* 1997;48:335–346.
23. Bell MD, Lysaker PH, Milstein RM. Clinical benefits of paid work activity in schizophrenia. *Schizophr Bull* 1996;22:51–67.
24. Drake RE, Becker DR, Clark RE, et al. Research on the individual placement and support model of supported employment. *Psychiatr Q* 1999;70:289–301.
25. Mueser KT, Bond GR, Drake RE, et al. Models of community care for severe mental illness: a review of research on case management. *Schizophr Bull* 1998;24:37–74.
26. Harrow M, Westermeyer JF. Process-reactive dimension and outcome for narrow concepts of schizophrenia. *Schizophr Bull* 1987;13:361–368.
27. Becker DR, Drake RE, Bond GR, et al. Job terminations among persons with severe mental illness participating in supported employment. *Community Ment Health J* 1998;34:71–82.
28. Wallace CJ, Tauber R, Wilde J. Teaching fundamental workplace skills to persons with serious mental illness. *Psychiatr Serv* 1999;50:1147–1149, 1153.
29. Bond GR. Psychiatric vocational programs: a meta-analysis. Presented at the annual meeting of the International Association of Psychosocial Rehabilitation Services. 1986. Cleveland.
30. Cook JA, Solomon M, Mock L. What happens after the first job placement? *Programming Adolesc Behav Disord* 1989;4:71–93.
31. Rutman I, Armstrong K. A comprehensive evaluation of transitional employment programs in the rehabilitation of chronically mentally disabled clients. Unpublished manuscript. 1985.
32. Green MF. What are the functional consequences of neurocognitive deficits in schizophrenia? [see comments]. *Am J Psychiatry* 1996;153:321–330.
33. Brenner HD, Hodel B, Rodel V, et al. Treatment of cognitive dysfunctions and behavioral deficits in schizophrenia. *Schizophr Bull* 1992;18:21–26.
34. Spaulding WD, Fleming SK, Reed D, et al. Cognitive functioning in schizophrenia: implications for psychiatric rehabilitation. *Schizophr Bull* 1999;25:275–289.
35. Spaulding WD, Reed D, Storzback D, et al. The effects of remediational approach to cognitive therapy for schizophrenia. In: Wykes T, ed. *Outcome and innovation in psychological treatment of schizophrenia*. New York: John Wiley, 1998:145–160.
36. Wykes T, Reeder C, Corner J, et al. The effects of neurocognitive remediation on executive processing in patients with schizophrenia. *Schizophr Bull* 1999;25:291–307.
37. Morice R, Delahunty A. Integrated psychological therapy for schizophrenia [letter; comment]. *Br J Psychiatry* 1993;163:414–415.

38. Wykes T. What are we changing with neurocognitive rehabilitation? Illustrations from two single cases of changes in neuropsychological performance and brain systems as measured by SPECT. *Schizophr Res* 1998;34:77–86.
39. Green MF, Nuechterlein KH. Should schizophrenia be treated as a neurocognitive disorder? *Schizophr Bull* 1999;25:309–319.
40. Hogarty GE, Flesher S. Developmental theory for a cognitive enhancement therapy of schizophrenia. *Schizophr Bull* 1999;25:677–692.

11

Community Intervention and Support

In the 1960s, after the process of deinstitutionalization was inaugurated and seriously mentally ill patients were discharged to the community, it became evident that traditional medical-psychiatric services were not adequate to meet the many needs of these patients. It was recognized that many chronically ill patients were severely disabled because of varying degrees of deficits in reality testing and cognition, negative symptomatology, the deleterious effects of prolonged custodial hospitalization, and demoralization. Many of these deinstitutionalized individuals were found to be without the resources necessary for successful survival in the community, including receiving little or no psychiatric and medical care, lack of income support, and inadequate or absent housing (homelessness). To deal with these problems, in 1978 the National Institute of Mental Health developed guidelines for community support programs (1). They specified that there should be an adequate system for the severely mentally disabled in place that fixes responsibilities and provides staff and resources to perform the following functions:

1. Identification of a target population and outreach to offer appropriate services to those in need
2. Assistance in applying for entitlements
3. Crisis stabilization services in the least restrictive setting, with hospitalization available when other options are insufficient
4. Psychosocial rehabilitation services, including but not limited to goal-oriented rehabilitation evaluation, training in community living skills in the natural setting wherever possible, opportunities to improve employability, appropriate living arrangements in an atmosphere that encourages improvements in functioning, opportunities to develop social skills, interests and leisure-time activities to provide a sense of participation and worth
5. Supportive services of an indefinite duration, including supportive living and working arrangements and other such services for as long as they are needed

6. Medical and mental health care
7. Backup support to families, friends, and community members
8. Involvement of concerned community members in planning and offering housing or working opportunities
9. Protection of patient's rights both in hospitals and in the community
10. Case management to ensure continuous coordinated availability of appropriate forms of assistance

The guidelines recommended that a core service agency exist within the community that is committed to helping severely mentally disabled people improve their lives. In the agency a single person (or team) at the patient level should be responsible for remaining in touch with the patient on a continuous basis regardless of how many other agencies become involved. It presumed that the institution of community support programs in conjunction with specific treatment programs would greatly benefit patients, families, and communities in which they reside.

CASE MANAGEMENT

To carry out the preceding functions, case management programs have been established at community support programs. Case managers' responsibilities included the following (1):

1. *Mental health treatment*—ensure that mental health treatment consistent with the patient's needs and desires was provided.
2. *Crisis response*—provide early intervention and 24-hour response by familiar staff in times of crisis.
3. *Health/dental health care*—coordinate with health providers and ensure compliance, since it was recognized that many chronically mentally ill patients were not receiving adequate medical/dental care.
4. *Rehabilitation*—ensure that rehabilitation services are provided consistent with the patient's goals.
5. *Peer support*—ensure involvement with club/consumer activities or other social networks.
6. *Housing*—arrange housing based on patient choice and needs, assist the patient in adjusting to a housing situation.
7. *Income maintenance*—assist in arranging for financial support and entitlements. Financial management as needed, since some patients need assistance in managing their finances.
8. *Family/community support*—ensure that family members are supported in dealing with the patients and attempt to enlarge and strengthen community supports.

9. *Advocacy protection*—ensure a reasonably safe environment for the individual and advocate for that person as needed.
10. *Outreach*—engage the patient as needed in community settings to ensure adequate services are provided.

To accomplish these manifold goals and tasks, either several members of a team or one individual can be assigned to be the case manager, ensuring that patients receive coordinated, continuous, and comprehensive services. A variety of models of case management have been developed (2):

1. *Full-Support Model*—the model is based on the Program for Assertive Community Treatment (PACT) or Training in Community Living Model developed by Stein and Test (3). This model is described in the next section of this chapter.
2. *Personal-Strengths Model*—called the Developmental Acquisition Model, emphasizing individual strengths, self-determination, and aggressive outreach and resource acquisition in the community (4).
3. *Rehabilitation Model*—this model emphasizes principles of psychiatric rehabilitation, providing case management in the context of an individualized rehabilitation plan (5).
4. *The Expanded Broker Model*—in this model a case manager assesses needs and links patients to various resources but does not provide much direct clinical intervention (6).

Hargreaves et al. described five core case management functions: assessing, planning, linking, monitoring, and advocacy (7). All these functions emphasize the need to help patients navigate a complex array of community programs. Some programs use case managers as direct service providers, especially providing crisis intervention during psychiatric emergencies (8). Examples of a case manager's tasks may be to accompany a patient to a welfare agency to ensure receipt of benefits, making a home visit if a clinical appointment is missed, or convening a meeting of workers from different agencies serving the patient to formulate an overall treatment plan in conjunction with the psychiatrist and other team members (9).

Problems that may arise in planning for case management services include the following: (a) Some public programs have emphasized the development of case management services but have not provided adequate treatment and other community support resources. (b) Case managers may not have a clear role definition vis-à-vis other members of the treatment team. They may function independently without core integration into the treatment team, creating conflict and confusion among team members.

Results of controlled studies of the effects of case management have yielded inconsistent findings, probably related to methodological problems in design, including (10)

1. Lack of specification of the case management intervention
2. Poor characterization of the patient population
3. Inadequacy of outcome measures
4. Inadequate length of the program
5. Lack of specification of the community context

Evidence for the impact of the different case management models on reduction in use of psychiatric inpatient care suggests that intensive case management programs may reduce utilization of inpatient care. However, many of the results cited by reviewers were not statistically significant. Although several studies have demonstrated significant reductions in the mean number of rehospitalizations, other studies have reported no differences in the average number of readmissions (11). In fact, reducing the patient load of mental health case managers was shown not to be sufficient to improve the clinical or social outcomes of mental health patients in the United Kingdom and Europe (12). In this study, caseloads were reduced from 30 to 35 patients per case manager to only 10 to 15 patients. Results showed that intensive case management neither improved clinical or social functioning of patients nor affected the rate of hospitalizations compared with standard case management over the 2-year period.

Although the results of studies of the effects of case management on hospitalization and functioning are not conclusive, it is evident that many of the functions ascribed to case management need to be in place in a comprehensive system of health care for schizophrenic patients. These results may also indicate that case management services may be necessary but not sufficient in the care of this population. Other treatment and rehabilitation services described elsewhere in this volume are clearly indicated in the care of individuals with schizophrenia.

PROGRAM FOR ASSERTIVE COMMUNITY TREATMENT

The Program for Assertive Community Treatment (PACT) includes many elements of the case management function but also offers active treatment interventions by a clinical team that is based in the community using a highly integrated approach. The team offers many treatment services but in addition collaborates with other treatment programs to obtain high-quality care for the patients. This program is designed specifically for marginally adjusted, severely impaired, and poorly functioning individuals. Also, it focuses on patients who are noncompliant with treatment, including substance abusers, who constitute the group of patients that are continually admitted and readmitted to hospitals (revolving-door patients). A key component of PACT is having a very high staff-to-patient ratio, one staff member for every 10 patients. The aims of the program are to help prevent relapse and maximize social and vocational functioning using an individually tailored treatment program in the community based on an assessment of each person's deficits and coping skills, assets, and requirements for community living (3,10,13).

Stein et al. described PACT clinical principles of treatment (13). They state that effective treatment of the person with schizophrenia must include working with both the patient and the community in which that patient lives. Even the most innovative and potentially effective treatment will fail if the treatment process does not actively involve the community. Principles of working with the patients include the following:

1. *Assertive approach.* Since many patients lack motivation for treatment and even refuse it, programs should be assertive in keeping patients involved. For example, if an individual doesn't appear for an appointment, an attempt will be made to find that person either in the home or elsewhere in the community. The attempt is made to try to explain how treatment can be helpful to him/her, and the effort needs to be persistent and repetitive, thereby reducing dropouts.
2. *Individually tailored programming.* Since patients have a wide variety of needs, treatment plans must be individualized after a comprehensive assessment. Efforts are made to design a program to ensure that the patient is receiving what he or she actually needs to make a stable adjustment in the community (14–17).
3. *Ongoing monitoring.* It is necessary to monitor patients' functioning and symptomatology in the community and to change the treatment plan to meet patients' changing needs.
4. *Titered support.* Most patients need to be dependent on the treatment team to a greater or lesser extent. It is important not to give too much support or too little.
5. In vivo *services.* Since many with schizophrenia have difficulty transferring learning from one situation to another, training should take place in environments close to the natural environment the patient is living in. For example, for some patients, if the aim is to try to help them to shop and cook, the teaching should take place in their homes and neighborhoods rather than in a location in or near the hospital or mental health center.
6. *Capitalizing on the patient's strengths.* The aim here is to enhance the individual's strengths rather than to spend all the time remediating pathology.

7. *Relating to patients as responsible citizens.* It is extremely important to have an attitude of respect for the individual, who has a right to function in the community with dignity. For example, patients who are not compliant with medication should be dealt with as responsible individuals and attempts should be made to collaborate with them, including negotiations about dosage and willingness to set a range within which patients can control their own dosages according to their needs.

8. *Crisis resolution available 24 hours a day.* Since patients do not limit their crises to 9:00 a.m. through 5:00 p.m., Monday through Friday, staff must be available to deal with emergencies 24 hours a day, 7 days a week. With this approach, more effective clinical treatment is offered that appears to markedly reduce the use of hospitals, according to the authors.

Working with the Community

1. *Use an assertive approach.* An assertive approach is necessary not only in working with patients but also in working in the community. For example, working with a landlord who might be ready to evict the patient; early intervention can often alleviate the problem.

2. *Use a wide variety of community resources.* Many public agencies in the community have dealt only marginally or not at all with the mentally ill. For example, the visiting nurse service in the local community may have had almost no psychiatric patients but when approached and given on-the-job training to deal with the mentally ill, have begun to administer depot neuroleptic medications on a regular basis.

3. *Provide support and education to community members.* It is obviously important to provide support and education to families, landlords, shopkeepers, employers, and anyone else with whom patients come into significant contact. Rather than attempting to mount a mass education program, Stein et al. decided to educate and support community members every time there was a problem between a patient and community member.

4. *Retain responsibility for patient care.* Since individuals with serious mental illness require a wide variety of different services usually not provided by a single agency, there should be coordination among the various providers, and someone in the PACT team needs to take responsibility in maintaining coordination and continuity of care for the patient.

5. *Work with the family.* The program believes that it is important to help educate families and relieve the great burden placed upon them.

Results of Studies of PACT

Many controlled studies of PACT have demonstrated that this program reduces the rate and duration of psychiatric hospitalization and improves living conditions (3,18–21). Bond et al. concluded that assertive outreach programs for frequent users of hospitals can be expected to reduce inpatient days by about 50% (22). Scott and Dixon (11) point out that the reduction in the use of psychiatric hospitalization may be partially offset by an increased use of other community-based alternative services such as 24-hour crisis intervention and residential services and that this reduction would probably not be as pronounced if these other services were unavailable. Second, the effectiveness in reducing hospitalization may be a function of the PACT team's capacity to control hospital admissions, length of stay, and discharge. Third, reductions in hospital use have tended to cease after PACT treatment is discontinued (3,23,24). Scott and Dixon point out that fidelity to the original PACT Program model appears to be an important determinant of reduction in psychiatric inpatient utilization, including a patient-to-staff ratio of approximately 10:1.

It is important to mention that many of the research studies of outcome reviewed earlier dealt with the broader category of persons with severe mental illness, not limited to a diagnosis of schizophrenia. Exceptions include studies by Test et al. and Hornstra et al. (25,26). It should be emphasized that PACT was designed for the most seriously ill, poorly functioning patients who were noncompliant with treatment. Many individuals with schizophrenia have better functional ability and do collaborate in treatment. These individuals are not in need of such extensive and expensive services. Furthermore, it is unclear which elements of the PACT program are most essential for positive outcomes.

SUPPORTIVE HOUSING AND HOMELESSNESS

With the advent of deinstitutionalization in the 1960s, as a matter of expediency many patients were discharged from state hospitals to nursing homes, single room occupancy hotels (SROs), or board and care homes. The transfer to nursing homes was inappropriate for most patients, since these facilities were geared to the physically disabled or those suffering from senile dementia and were not prepared to treat individuals with schizophrenia and often could not provide optimal care. Board and care homes are generally proprietary rooming houses, as are SROs. Often these facilities are in blighted urban areas where the crime rate is high and substance abuse is common. Close collaboration between community mental health programs with owners and managers of rooming houses involving case management and other services is necessary to ensure that patients receive adequate support wherever they reside. Working with managers of rooming houses can alleviate problems they may have in dealing with problematic behavior of residents. Often these facilities do not provide a good quality of life and frequently residents complain of loneliness.

According to Budson the most common types of residential facilities currently in use are the following (27):

1. *Transitional halfway houses.* These are defined as a residential facility providing room and board and promoting socialization until suitable housing is available (28). They are used as transitional facilities between the hospital and the community for recovering patients. A review of 109 studies indicated that the effectiveness of transitional halfway houses in reducing recidivism, increasing economic self-sufficiency, and improving community adjustment is highly suspect (29). According to Carling, transitional residential programs may in fact be preferable to institutional care, but they fall short of helping people achieve community integration (30).

2. *Long-term group residences.* These facilities have onsite staff and are used for chronically functionally disabled individuals. Length of stay is indefinite, in contrast to the halfway house, where stays are usually 6 to 8 months.

3. *Cooperative apartments.* No onsite staff are present in cooperative apartments, but there are regular visits by staff for oversight and guidance of residents.

4. *Intensive care crisis community residences.* These facilities can be used to prevent hospitalization or shorten the length of a hospital stay. Usually there are onsite nursing personnel and counseling staff.

5. *Foster or family care.* Patients are placed in foster or family care in private homes. Although in some cases they can provide a positive environment, in others they may be antitherapeutic, with only a custodial atmosphere (31). As with board and care homes, it is important that the mental health facility work closely with foster care families to provide them with ongoing guidance and support to ensure an optimal living experience.

Supportive living arrangements are usually preferable for patients who need assistance in managing their self-care, since they provide professional supervision and care. Studies have indicated that these programs can decrease rehospitalization and homelessness and increase social and vocational functioning and quality of life (32–34).

A substantial number of individuals with schizophrenia live with their families. For some this arrangement is optimal, providing mutual satisfaction and benefit for family members as well as the individual with schizophrenia. However, for others there may be problems either for family members and/or the individual with schizophrenia or both. Family interventions by mental health professionals can provide education and attempt to improve communication and reduce any family burden. However, mental health professionals should also help the family and the individual with schizophrenia to evaluate whether it is best for that person to continue to live with the family or to move out. If the determination is to move out, arrangements can be made for a supportive living program or an unsupervised apartment, depending on the wishes and needs of the individual. Indicators for the patient not to live at home include the following (35):

- The presence of a stressful or a tense home environment
- Other family members such as children who are frightened of the patient
- Inability of the patient to follow household rules
- Persistent problems with setting limits or adhering to them
- Extremely disruptive behavior at home such as frequent angry outbursts, violent or threatening behavior
- Persistent problematic behavior such as waking family members at night, grossly inappropriate behavior such as walking around the house naked, severe substance abuse, consistent noncompliance with medication
- Inability of family members to set realistic expectations for the patients
- Substantial ongoing conflict between other family members such as issues between parents regarding the patient
- Lack of meaningful structure for the patient
- In addition, we would add the situation where patients feel the need for independence because they feel stifled by what they perceive as parental overprotection.

Homelessness

Homelessness is a serious problem for those with severe mental illness. Estimates of the extent vary, ranging from 20% to 35% of homeless persons suffering from severe and persistent mental illness (SPMI) (36,37). For those with schizophrenia, it has been estimated that the prevalence ranges up to 12% of homeless individuals. Factors associated with homelessness in individuals with schizophrenia have been attributed to issues external to the individual as well as their personal characteristics.

Factors external to individuals with schizophrenia include poorly implemented deinstitutionalization, limitations of public funding, problems in service integration, and lack of low-cost housing (38,39). Lack of adequate discharge planning for living arrangements, aftercare, and finances is a serious contributing factor to low utilization of mental health services among homeless men with schizophrenia (40). A comparison of characteristics of male schizophrenic patients that compared those who were homeless with those who were not homeless found that the homeless were much more likely to have concurrent substance abuse and a diagnosis of antisocial personality disorder (41). Findings were similar for female individuals with schizophrenia. They were also more likely to have the diagnosis of alcohol abuse. Also, homeless women had less adequate family supports (42). The co-occurrence of substance abuse and antisocial personality makes it less likely that these individuals will be accepted or retained in housing programs (39). Problems with the housing authorities may occur for individuals who are severely disorganized with disruptive behaviors (43). Many homeless individuals lack care for their physical health as well as social and income supports.

Studies of programs to reduce homelessness in this population have demonstrated positive results. Lehman et al. found that a program of Assertive Community Treatment (ACT) compared with usual care in the community resulted in significantly fewer psychiatric inpatient days, fewer emergency department visits, and more psychiatric outpatient visits than comparison subjects (44). The ACT subjects also spent significantly more days in stable community housing and experienced significantly greater improvements in symptoms, life satisfaction, and perceived health status. Rosenheck et al. evaluated the hypothesis that greater integration and coordination between agencies within service systems can be associated with greater accessibility of services and improved client housing outcomes for homeless persons with severe mental illness (45). Results showed that service integration among agencies was associated with superior housing outcomes at 12 months, and this relationship was mediated through greater access to housing agencies. The authors conclude that service system integration is related to improved access to housing services and better housing outcomes among homeless people with mental illness. Shern et al. found that service integration and providing accessible and desirable housing led to a great decrease in homelessness (46).

Goldfinger et al. examined the influence of group or individual housing placement and consumer characteristics on the number of days of subsequent homelessness among formerly homeless mentally ill persons (47). Results showed that 76% of the study participants were housed at the end of the 18-month follow-up period, although 27% had experienced at least one episode of homelessness during the period. The number of days homeless was greater for those assigned to independent apartments than for those placed in staffed group homes, but only for members of minority groups. Substance abuse was the strongest single predictor of days of homelessness. Individuals whom clinicians identified as needing group living experienced more days of homeless regardless of the type of housing they received. Consumers who stated a strong preference for independent living had more days of homelessness than those who were amenable to staff group homes. The authors conclude that although consumers frequently prefer independent living, placement in staffed group housing resulted in somewhat fewer days of homelessness for some groups of consumers. Furthermore, individuals with substance abuse need effective treatment to remain in housing.

Another program attempted to reach severely mentally ill persons who were so impaired they were unable to recognize their basic needs or avoid personal dangers (48). The program Homeless Emergency Liaison Project (HELP) used a mobile treatment team that arranged involuntary psychiatric emergency room evaluation of high-risk homeless patients. Involuntary hospitalization resulted from 93% of such evaluations, and 80% of all patients received the diagnosis of schizophrenia. At 2-year follow-up of 298 patients initially evaluated during the project only 12% were found to be living back on the streets.

Goldfinger outlined four basic stages in working with this homeless population (43):

1. Introduction of services into the community
2. Outreach
3. Provision of treatment and other services during homelessness
4. Support in a transition to housing

Psychiatrists and other mental health professionals must be prepared to work with homeless patients in nonclinical environments, including streets, shelters, subways, bus terminals, and other public spaces. Active outreach is usually necessary to engage the homeless schizophrenic patient and is often performed by case managers. Goldfinger stressed the importance of engagement of homeless schizophrenic patients, who are often fearful and distrustful of the mental health system (43). They can require a combination of patience, persistence, and understanding. Depending on the needs and wants of a particular patient, provision of food, clothing, medical attention, or simply company can be indispensable in developing a therapeutic relationship. He notes that through these efforts the individual may recognize the concern of the mental health worker as well as demonstrate reliability in helping that individual achieve his goals and needs.

Results of studies summarized earlier indicate that homelessness among individuals with schizophrenia can be greatly reduced through such programs as ACT, which offer comprehensive, integrated, continuous involvement with the homeless population and which implement outreach efforts to meet the homeless in the community and deal with comorbid problems of substance abuse and impaired physical health. Integration with other public agencies, especially housing, is necessary to provide decent and acceptable housing alternatives for this population.

OTHER COMMUNITY SUPPORTS

Mental health professionals should inform patients and their families about programs and organizations in the community that could be of great benefit to them. Patients and families have become increasingly involved in organizations that enable them to feel some mastery in dealing with the many problems associated with having an individual with schizophrenia in the family. Goals of consumer organizations, in addition to providing a feeling of empowerment and a social support network, include becoming less dependent on professionals, decreasing the stigma associated with mental illness, and working to achieve adequate support for treatment and research in mental illness. These organizations fall into three major categories, each with its own membership, purpose, and philosophy (49):

1. *Patient organizations.* These are independent organizations founded by patients themselves. Often many of the members take a critical attitude toward standard psychiatric treatment based on negative personal experiences. The National Alliance of Mental Patients (NAMP) is an example of this type of organization. Their principal goal is to advocate and work for the patient's right to exercise choice in the selection of treatment, including the possible choice of no treatment at all. This group has operated patient-run services in some communities. In these and other communities patients have developed drop-in centers for socialization and support.

2. *Self-help treatment organizations.* An example of such an organization is Recovery, Incorporated, which uses an educational and cognitive model based on the writings of the late Dr. Abraham A. Lowe, a psychiatrist. Groups meet weekly to discuss issues in their daily lives and apply Dr. Lowe's principles in dealing with them. Tactics for managing symptoms include spotting irrational fears or symptomatic experiences such as hallucinations or depressive thoughts, identifying them as neither dangerous nor life-threatening, and choosing a strategy for bearing the discomfort, such as thinking about or doing something constructive.

The organization welcomes professionals to attend its meetings, and members are encouraged to follow professional direction concerning medication and other therapy.

3. *Organizations of relatives.* The largest organization of relatives is the National Alliance for the Mentally Ill (NAMI). This is a national organization with local affiliates. Members are mainly parents of individuals with major mental illness, including schizophrenia. They function as an advocacy group to improve psychiatric services and lobby for better third-party coverage of mental health care and increased research funding for major mental illness. NAMI affiliates provide education for consumers and their families about understanding and managing major mental illness, including schizophrenia. As part of the educational process local groups have regular meetings for education and discussion of major issues regarding mental illness. Books are recommended to further the knowledge of the membership, including *Families of Mentally Ill: Coping and Adaptation* by A. B. Hatfield and H. P. Lefley (50), *Coping with Schizophrenia: A Guide for Families* by K. T. Mueser and S. Gingerich (51), and *Surviving Schizophrenia: A Manual for Families, Consumers and Providers,* 3rd ed., by E. Fuller Torrey (52). Studies have suggested that helping families educate and empower themselves and helping them become more involved in service delivery result in better outcomes for the mentally ill family members (53,54). (See Appendix 2 for an example of a consumer and family guide distributed by NAMI, which is available on the internet, www.NAMI.org.

Another major resource for patients and their families is the National Mental Health Association. Local chapters are located in most metropolitan areas.

REFERENCES

1. Turner JC, Ten Hoor WJ. The NIMH Community Support Program: pilot approach to a needed social reform. *Schizophr Bull* 1978;4:319.
2. Robinson G. Choices in case management. *Community Support News* 1991;7:11–12.
3. Stein LI, Test MA. Alternative to mental hospital treatment. I: Conceptual model, treatment program, and clinical evaluation. *Arch Gen Psychiatry* 1980;37:392–397.
4. Modrcin M, Rapp C, Chamberlain R. Case management with psychiatrically disabled individuals: curriculum and training program. 1985. The University of Kansas School of Social Welfare.
5. Goering PN, Wasylenki DA, Farkas M, et al. What difference does case management make? *Hosp Community Psychiatry* 1988;39:272–276.
6. Johnson P, Rubin A. Case management in mental health: a social work domain? *Soc Work* 1983;28:49–55.
7. Hargreaves WA, Shaw RE, Shadoan R, et al. Measuring case management activity. *J Nerv Ment Dis* 1984;172:296–300.
8. Wasylenki DA, Goering PN, Humphrey BC, et al. Components of care for patients with schizophrenia. *Psychiatr J Univ Ott* 1989;14:287–295.

9. Practice guideline for the treatment of patients with schizophrenia. *Am J Psychiatry Suppl* 1997;154:1–63.

10. Baker F, Intagliata J. Case management. In: Liberman RP. *Handbook of schizophrenia.* Boston: Allyn & Bacon, 1992:213–243.

11. Scott JE, Dixon LB. Assertive community treatment and case management for schizophrenia. *Schizophr Bull* 1995;21:657–668.

12. Burns I, Creed F, Fahy T, et al. Intensive versus standard case management for severe psychotic illness: a randomized trial. *Lancet* 1999;353:2185–2189.

13. Stein LI, Diamond RJ, Factor RM. A system approach to the care of persons with schizophrenia. In: Herz MI, Keith SJ, Docherty JP, et al., eds. *Handbook of schizophrenia,* vol. IV. New York: Elsevier, 1990:213–246.

14. Harris M, Bergman HC. Differential treatment planning for young adult chronic patients. *Hosp Community Psychiatry* 1987;38:638.

15. Anthony WA. The rehabilitative approach to diagnosis. *New Dir Ment Health Serv* 1979; 2:25.

16. Freddolino PP, Moxley DP, Fleishman JA. Daily living needs at time of discharge: implications for advocacy. *Psychosoc Rehab* 1988;11:33.

17. Liberman RP. Assessment of social skills. *Schizophr Bull* 1982;8:62.

18. Scott JE, Dixon, LB. Psychological interventions for schizophrenia. *Schizophr Bull* 1995; 21:621–630.

19. Group for the Advancement of Psychiatry (GAP). *Implications for psychosocial interventions in patients with schizophrenia.* In: *Beyond symptom suppression: improving long-term outcomes of schizophrenia.* Report #134. Washington, DC: American Psychiatric Press, 1992:59–78.

20. Burns BJ, Santos AB. Assertive community treatment: an update of randomized trials. *Psychiatr Serv* 1995;46:669–675.

21. Weisbrod BA, Test MA, Stein LI. Alternative to mental hospital treatment. II: Economic benefit-cost analysis. *Arch Gen Psychiatry* 1980;37:400–405.

22. Bond GR, Witheridge TF, Wasmer D, et al. A comparison of two crisis housing alternatives to psychiatric hospitalization. *Hosp Community Psychiatry* 1989;40:177–183.

23. Steinwachs DM, Cullum HM, Dorwart RA, et al. Service systems research. *Schizophr Bull* 1992;18:627–668.

24. Audini B, Marks IM, Lawrence RE, et al. Home-based versus out-patient/in-patient care for people with serious mental illness. Phase II of a controlled study [see comments]. *Br J Psychiatry* 1994;165:204–210.

25. Test MA, Knoedler WH, Allness DJ, et al. Characteristics of young adults with schizophrenic disorders treated in the community. *Hosp Community Psychiatry* 1985;36: 853–858.

26. Hornstra RK, Bruce-Wolfe V, Sagduyu K, et al. The effect of intensive case management on hospitalization of patients with schizophrenia. *Hosp Community Psychiatry* 1993;44: 844–847.

27. Budson RD. Models of supportive living: community residential care. In: Herz MI, Keith SJ, Docherty JP, eds. *Handbook of schizophrenia,* vol. IV. New York: Elsevier, 1990:317–338.

28. Campbell RJ. *Psychiatric dictionary.* New York: Oxford University Press, 1996:212, 311.

29. Cometa MS, Morrison JK, Ziskoven M. Halfway to where? A critique of research on psychiatric halfway houses. *J Community Psychol* 1979;7:23–27.

30. Carling PJ. Housing and supports for persons with mental illness: emerging approaches to research and practice. *Hosp Community Psychiatry* 1993;44:439–449.

31. Murphy HB, Engelsmann F. The influence of foster-home care on psychiatric patients. *Arch Gen Psychiatry* 1976;33:179–183.

32. Okin RL, Pearsall D. Patient's perceptions of their quality of life 11 years after discharge from a state hospital. *Hosp Community Psychiatry* 1993;44:236–240.

33. Okin RL, Borus JF, Baer L, et al. Long-term outcome of state hospital patients discharged into structured community residential settings. *Psychiatr Serv* 1995;46:73–78.

34. Hawthorne WB, Fals-Stewart W, Lohr JB. A treatment outcome study of community-based residential care. *Hosp Community Psychiatry* 1994;45:152–155.
35. Mueser KT, Rojcewicz SJ, Peele R. *Clinical manual of supportive psychotherapy.* Washington, DC: American Psychiatric Press, 1993.
36. Lamb HR. *The homeless mentally ill.* Washington, DC: American Psychiatric Press, 1984.
37. Lehman AF, Cordray DS. Prevalence of alcohol, drug and mental disorders among the homeless: one more time. *Contemp Drug Prob* 1993;20:355–383.
38. Bachrach LL. What we know about homelessness among mentally ill persons: an analytical review and commentary. *Hosp Community Psychiatry* 1992;43:453–464.
39. Schlenger WE, Kroutil LA, Roland EJ. Case management as a mechanism for linking drug abuse treatment and primary care: preliminary evidence from the ADAMHA/HRSA linkage demonstration. *NIDA Res Monogr* 1992;127:316–330.
40. Caton CL. Mental health service use among homeless and never-homeless men with schizophrenia. *Psychiatr Serv* 1995;46:1139–1143.
41. Caton CL, Shrout PE, Eagle PF, et al. Correlates of codisorders in homeless and never homeless indigent schizophrenic men. *Psychol Med* 1994;24:681–688.
42. Caton CL, Shrout PE, Dominguez B, et al. Risk factors for homelessness among women with schizophrenia. *Am J Public Health* 1995;85:1153–1156.
43. Goldfinger SM. Homelessness and schizophrenia: a psychosocial approach. In: Herz MI, Docherty JP, Keith SJ. *Handbook of schizophrenia,* vol. IV. Amsterdam: Elsevier, 1990: 355–386
44. Lehman AF, Dixon LB, Kernan E, et al. A randomized trial of assertive community treatment for homeless persons with severe mental illness. *Arch Gen Psychiatry* 1997;54: 1038–1043.
45. Rosenheck R, Morrissey J, Lam J, et al. Service system integration, access to services, and housing outcomes in a program for homeless persons with severe mental illness. *Am J Pub Health* 1998;88:1610–1615.
46. Shern DL, Felton CJ, Hough RL, et al. Housing outcomes for homeless adults with mental illness: results from the second-round McKinney program. *Psychiatr Serv* 1997;48: 239–241.
47. Goldfinger SM, Schutt RK, Tolomiczenko GS, et al. Housing placement and subsequent days homeless among formerly homeless adults with mental illness. *Psychiatr Serv* 1999;50:674–679.
48. Cohen NL. Outreach intervention models for the homeless mentally ill. In: *Treating the homeless mentally ill: a report of the Task Force on the Homeless Mentally Ill.* Washington, DC: American Psychiatric Association, 1992:141–157.
49. Vine P, Beels CC. Psychosocial treatment of schizophrenia—support and advocacy groups for the mentally ill. In: Herz MI, Keith SJ, Docherty JP, eds. *Handbook of schizophrenia,* vol. IV. New York: Elsevier, 1990:387–405.
50. Hatfield A, Lefley H. *Families of the mentally ill: coping and adaptation.* New York: Guilford Press, 1987.
51. Mueser KT, Gingerich S. *Coping with schizophrenia: a guide for families.* Oakland, CA: New Harbinger Publications, 1994.
52. Torrey EF. *Surviving schizophrenia: a manual for families.* New York: Harper Collins, 1995.
53. Lam DH. Psychosocial family intervention in schizophrenia: a review of empirical studies. *Psychol Med* 1991;21:423–441.
54. Strachan A. Family intervention. In: Liberman RP. *Handbook of psychiatric rehabilitation.* Needham, MA: Allyn & Bacon, 1992.

SECTION III

Special Issues in Treating and Managing Schizophrenia

12

Management of First-Episode Psychosis Patients

It is advantageous to attempt to intervene therapeutically as early as possible in the first episode of diagnosed schizophrenia. Early intervention is helpful in relieving the pain and suffering of patients and family members that is associated with an untreated psychotic disorder. Another potential advantage of early intervention is the possibility that it may have positive effects on the long-term course and outcome of the disorder. In a review article, McGlashan states that evidence from research studies suggests that early intervention in first-episode patients may slow or stop deterioration (1). Similarly, Wyatt et al. conclude that there is increasing evidence that untreated schizophrenia is associated with a worse prognosis, implying that something related to psychosis itself may produce long-term changes in the brain (2). The latter is a hypothesis since there is no conclusive evidence about long-term changes in the brain. It is possible that decreasing the severity and duration of psychosis that a person experiences early in the illness and preventing relapses is not only of immediate importance but may alter the long-term morbidity of the illness.

Studies of first-break patients from which this evidence is based can be classified into three types: (a) those comparing outcomes of hospitalized patients before and after the introduction of antipsychotic medications; (b) those reporting duration of untreated psychosis (DUP) in first-episode patients; and (c) controlled studies that compare treatment with and without antipsychotic medication in first-break patients (3). The latter studies were usually carried out during the immediate period after antipsychotic medications were introduced.

COMPARING OUTCOMES OF FIRST HOSPITALIZED PATIENTS BEFORE AND AFTER THE INTRODUCTION OF ANTIPSYCHOTIC MEDICATIONS

Wyatt found that five studies showed statistically significant improved long-term outcomes for patients treated with antipsychotic medications

(3,4). One study showed a trend in that direction and one had nonsignificant results. These studies of first-break patients are suggestive of a better outcome with antipsychotic medication but have methodological shortcomings. They were not controlled studies with random assignment, and they did not study patients simultaneously. They were studies comparing the outcomes before and after the introduction of antipsychotic medications. Problems associated with interpretation of the data are as follows: Some investigators believe that schizophrenic symptomatology has become less severe over the course of this century, including Odegard, Grinker, Romano, and Bleuler (5–8). Diagnostic criteria for schizophrenia have changed considerably over the years so that the samples may not have been comparable diagnostically. Psychosocial treatment has improved, with a greater emphasis on comprehensive community care rather than definitive treatment in long-term hospitalization. Long stays were more common in the pre-antipsychotic medication years and led to regression in many patients (9). Also, patients who received antipsychotic medication initially in the hospital may have continued to receive ambulatory maintenance antipsychotic medication that improved their long-term course rather than medication received while in the hospital.

DURATION OF UNTREATED PSYCHOSIS

Numerous retrospective studies have provided suggestive evidence that the longer the duration of untreated psychosis (DUP), the worse the longitudinal course of the illness (10–12).These studies had many methodological problems, but they point in the same direction: Results are better when untreated psychosis is short. Two were prospective studies that offered more conclusive evidence that prolonged untreated psychosis is associated with worse outcome. Johnstone et al. found that patients with a longer duration of illness relapsed more frequently over the 2-year follow-up period (13). Loebel et al. studied 70 first-episode patients diagnosed with schizophrenia or schizoaffective disorder, mostly schizophrenia, according to the Research Diagnostic Criteria (RDC) (14). Patients were followed for 2 years with the independent variables, duration of untreated psychosis (DUP) and duration of untreated illness, prodrome plus psychosis (DUI). Interestingly, the independent variables showed a mean DUI of 151 weeks and a mean DUP of 52 weeks. These studies showed that a longer duration of untreated psychosis predicted a longer time to remission and a lower level of remission. Although some prognostic variables such as premorbid functioning, age at onset, and type of onset were not predictive of time to remission, better premorbid functioning and older age at onset did relate to better levels of remission. However, a more recent prospective study found no relationship between duration of untreated psychosis and quality of life, symptom severity, and remission of positive symptoms at 6 months after the initial hospitalization (15). Thus only two of the three prospective studies reinforced the conclusions from retrospective studies that the longer the DUP, the worse the treatment response and long-term outcome. Further research is needed to clarify the importance of length of duration of untreated psychosis on outcome.

CONTEMPORANEOUS CONTROL GROUP STUDIES

Most of these studies were conducted around the time of the introduction of antipsychotic medications, when their efficacy was unknown when compared with psychosocial treatment approaches. Almost all these studies suffered from major methodological flaws. The largest and most carefully controlled of these studies, May et al., evaluated recent-onset patients who were treated for 6 to 12 months with or without antipsychotic medications (16). After the study was concluded, all the patients received antipsychotic medication. Interestingly, those who were initially assigned to the group that did not receive medication had more days in the hospital during subsequent years and a worse social adjustment. These findings suggest that not being treated with an antipsychotic during the study period had long-lasting effects.

A MODEL PROGRAM FOR EARLY INTERVENTION IN FIRST-EPISODE PATIENTS WITH SCHIZOPHRENIA

McGorry et al., in Melbourne, Australia, have described a model early-intervention program for first-episode psychotic patients (17). The Early Psychosis Prevention and Intervention Centre (EPPIC) began operation in 1992, providing a community-based service to older adolescents and young adults experiencing the first onset of a psychotic illness through the critical early years of psychosis. The center's comprehensive aims were early detection to prevent secondary morbidity and to maintain social and occupational functioning during this early critical period (2 years after entering into treatment). This model has two fundamental aims: (a) to identify patients at the early stage of onset of psychosis and (b) to provide intensive phase-specific treatment for up to 2 years thereafter.

Program Components

The following are components of the program:

1. Through networking and carefully targeted community education activities, the assessment team sought to raise community awareness of psy-

chosis in young people and to promote recognition and early referral. The team conducted assessments in the least threatening environment (i.e., the home, school, or local doctor's office).

2. An outpatient case management system was developed with a therapist case manager as a centerpiece who serves as a coordinator for all aspects of treatment and ensures continuity of care.

3. The inpatient unit focuses on symptom reduction and containment, and rapid transition to outpatient case management services with mobile support if required. Low-dose neuroleptics are standard practice in the acute phase.

4. The day program provides a range of group and individual experiences for individuals referred during the recovery phase of the initial episode. Involvement is time limited, with the patient setting goals and working toward rejoining mainstream society, with most returning to education, work, or other vocational rehabilitation programs.

5. Family work is another crucial element. The family is included in the treatment process wherever possible.

6. Cognitively oriented psychotherapy aims to help each patient adapt to the onset of a psychotic illness and its effects on self-concept, identity development, and self-esteem.

Results showed that there were better levels and rates of recovery with the shorter duration of untreated psychosis, as was found in other studies. However, it was determined that the more severe the illness, with such features as persecutory ideation or social withdrawal, which could lead to delayed presentation, the poorer the outcome. Further analysis led McGorry et al. to conclude that duration could be a relatively independent and important influence on short-term outcome. Although results have been encouraging regarding symptomatology and functional outcome, there was no concurrent control group. Rather, a historical sample was used and the follow-up period at the time of this report was only 12 months.

Although not conclusive, the weight of evidence indicates that the longer the duration of untreated psychosis, the less favorable the outcome. Efforts should be made to increase public awareness about the symptoms of schizophrenia and what to do when the symptoms are recognized. The EPPIC program has demonstrated that it is useful to concentrate educational efforts on teachers, guidance counselors, family practitioners, and others who come into frequent contact with adolescents and young adults. Our recommendation would be to ensure that first-break patients are not undertreated. If psychotic symptoms persist after resolution of the acute episode, there should be vigorous efforts to eliminate them. (See Chapter 7 on treatment of refractory patients.)

The following section discusses the special considerations in the psychosocial treatment of first-break individuals.

The Patient

It is preferable for the psychiatrist to wait until there are the beginnings of a positive therapeutic relationship with the patient before discussing the diagnosis of schizophrenia and its implications. Ordinarily, this discussion should not begin until the patient has recovered substantially from the acute psychotic episode and has good reality testing. It is important to separate fact from fiction about the course of the disorder, outcome, and treatment. Many believe that there is a universally poor outcome and that they have no control over the course of the illness. This is especially true since it is widely recognized and publicized that schizophrenia is a brain disorder (i.e., the individual has a damaged brain). The clinician should emphasize that the patient does have a good deal of control over the course of the illness and point out the strengths the individual possesses that will improve the possibility of a positive outcome. Psychoeducation should include information that the course of schizophrenia can be quite variable, with a favorable outcome for many patients.

The patient should learn about the stress-vulnerability hypothesis, which states that individuals with schizophrenia have an increased vulnerability to stress that can lead to relapse. This implies that the patient may need to modify but not abandon most goals for the future so that stress can be kept at a reasonable level. If a patient is educated about prodromal symptoms of relapse and stressors that might precipitate relapse, the individual can gain some hope that relapse can be prevented through his or her active collaboration with the treatment team in recognizing prodromal symptoms. Increased hope for the future can also be conveyed by discussing the potential for the development of newer, more effective medications for the disorder through ongoing research. While discussing schizophrenia, diagnosis, treatment, and outcome, the clinician should be alert for potential feelings of disappointment, anger, depression with low self-esteem and self-worth, and fears for the future that may occur in many patients. If they do occur the psychiatrist needs to deal with them in a realistic, supportive manner. If an individual patient displays massive denial about any of these feelings, it is probably best for the therapist not to pursue them by confronting the patient. Patients are well aware of the stigma attached to a diagnosis of schizophrenia and sometimes overcompensate by volunteering their diagnosis to others even when not asked. Therapists should discourage this behavior, emphasizing that the individual has a right to privacy while exploring the patient's own feeling about having the diagnosis of schizophrenia.

The Family

Families of individuals who are hospitalized with acute psychotic episodes are in great need of professional involvement and engagement as soon as possible. The psychiatrist and members of the treatment team should make every effort to engage with families soon after the patient is hospitalized. Family members often experience shock, disappointment, fear for the future, anger, and shame as an initial reaction to the acute psychotic episode. If a strong collaborative relationship is established with family members from the very beginning, when they are most in need, it can be invaluable for both patients and family members. Many of the same principles described for the patient, including psychoeducation and a supportive therapeutic relationship in dealing with distressing feelings, should be followed. Special efforts should be made to emphasize that the family members did not cause the illness through psychoeducation about the importance of genetics in the etiology and recognition that schizophrenia has an underlying brain pathophysiology. On the other hand, it is useful to emphasize that the patient has an increased vulnerability to stress, helping families understand why it is important for the patient sometimes to modify goals and aspirations for the future. Family members themselves often are disappointed by the need to modify goals of the patient. If it appears that the family environment is very stressful, techniques such as those described in Chapter 9 can be used to improve communication among family members and thereby reduce stress. Families can be encouraged to collaborate in recognizing the appearance of prodromal symptoms of relapse, since it has been reported that family members often recognize these early symptoms before the patients themselves do (18). It is well recognized that many families endure a great deal of burden in living with an individual with schizophrenia; thus therapists should provide support and help them to deal with reality problems that arise with the patient. Since many families, because of stigma, often retreat from friends and relatives, involvement in multifamily groups can be very helpful in sharing mutual feelings, problems and concerns, and methods of coping, and in providing a supportive social network. Both patients and family members should be made aware of self-help and peer organizations, which are listed in Chapter 9.

ANTIPSYCHOTIC MEDICATIONS IN FIRST-EPISODE PATIENTS

When and How Long to Treat

The psychiatrist who is prescribing medication for a patient experiencing a first episode faces a number of problems. Patients and their families may be having difficulty accepting a diagnosis of schizophrenia; this may result in reluctance to start an antipsychotic. If they are ready to start medication, they may have unrealistic expectations about when patients will begin to improve and how long it may take for the individual to recover. In addition, there may be no clinical history regarding drug responses, leaving the clinician to guess at the right drug and the right dose. On a positive note, patients who are experiencing a first episode usually have a better prognosis for recovery than patients who have experienced multiple episodes (19,20). For example, the study by Robinson and co-workers found that 87% of patients had a good response to treatment (20). Comparable studies in multiepisode patients have found much lower response rates. On the other hand, the median time to response in this study was 9 weeks, indicating that the rate of improvement was relatively gradual. A similar study by Lieberman found that the mean time to remission was 36 weeks and the median time was 8 weeks (21). These figures suggest that patients should be cautioned to exercise patience during this recovery period. This may be frustrating for patients who feel pressure to return to work or school.

Maintaining first-episode patients on their medications is also important. Relapse rates are relatively high during the first 5 years following an initial episode when medications are discontinued (22). In the Crow et al. study, 62% of patients receiving placebo and 46% of patients receiving drug relapsed over a 2-year period (22). These observations led an expert consensus group to recommend that first-episode patients continue to receive antipsychotics for at least 1 year (23).

However, following these recommendations may be insufficient for many individuals. There is a body of evidence that, when taken together, supports the view that relapses early in the course of schizophrenia may be particularly damaging. As mentioned earlier, patients tend to have a better outcome in terms of recovery following an initial episode. Each subsequent psychotic episode appears to be less responsive to drug treatment than the prior episode in terms of the likelihood of recovery and the amount of time it takes the patient to recover (24). In other words, each episode may result in a biological process that makes subsequent psychotic episodes more serious. This observation suggests that patients should receive maintenance treatment for longer periods of time—perhaps 1 to 2 years—and that medications should be gradually withdrawn with frequent monitoring for the appearance of prodromal symptoms.

SELECTION OF AN ANTIPSYCHOTIC

There is no hard evidence to indicate that any antipsychotic is more effective for first-episode patients than any other. Nevertheless, three principles are probably useful for drug and dose selection. First-episode patients

1. Have high response rates to antipsychotics.
2. Are more sensitive to antipsychotic side effects than multiepisode patients.
3. Tend to respond well to lower doses of antipsychotic (14,20,25).

The issue of side effects is particularly important, since the initial subjective experience from an antipsychotic is usually a side effect rather than a therapeutic effect. For a conventional antipsychotic this is often akathisia and is manifest as a feeling of restlessness. For second-generation drugs this may be sedation. If patients assume that medication will make them feel better, they will probably be disappointed. If a patient is suspicious, an unexpected side effect may undermine the patient's trust in the psychiatrist and other members of the treatment team. Moreover, an extremely unpleasant side effect such as a dystonia can have a long-lasting effect on a patient's attitude toward antipsychotics. Also, first-episode patients are often actively involved in community life when they become ill. If medication side effects affect their ability to attend school, to work, or to fulfill family responsibilities, these individuals may elect not to take their drugs. These concerns encourage a very cautious approach toward the selection of drug and dose for first-episode patients.

There is some evidence that first-episode patients do well on lower doses of antipsychotic when compared with multiepisode patients. An interesting study by McEvoy et al. found that the mean haloperidol dose for first-episode patients—as determined by a neuroleptic threshold strategy—was only 2.1 mg/day (26). Studies with risperidone (noted later) also found that first-episode patients tended to respond to lower doses than multiple-episode patients. The advantage of lower doses may stem from the sensitivity of these individuals to the neurologic side effects of antipsychotics.

This sensitivity to side-effect advantages has led to the suggestion that newer antipsychotics are preferable for first-episode patients. A number of studies—usually industry-sponsored—have supported this view. A large international study randomized 183 patients to either risperidone or haloperidol and found that response rates were high on both drugs (27). Risperidone was better tolerated and led to fewer dropouts due to side effects. The mean dose of risperidone was 6.1 mg/day, which is higher than doses that are currently prescribed. As a result, the study may have underestimated the advantage of risperidone in reducing side effects. A recent study that gradually titrated the dose of risperidone at a rate of 1 mg/week found that 76% of patients had an optimal response at a dose of 3 mg/day or less.

There is also evidence that olanzapine has advantages over conventional antipsychotics for first-episode patients. In a large multicenter study that compared olanzapine and haloperidol, a subpopulation of 83 patients was recovering from a first episode (28). These recent-onset patients demonstrated a better response to olanzapine for both positive and negative symptoms. Moreover, patients on olanzapine demonstrated improvements in extrapyramidal symptoms, whereas patients on haloperidol worsened. Although we are unaware of controlled studies of quetiapine in first-episode patients, its side-effect profile indicates that it may also have advantages for these individuals.

Taken together, these findings suggest a strategy for first-episode patients. It is clear that pharmacologic intervention should occur relatively soon after the diagnosis is confirmed. There are important advantages associated with beginning treatment relatively early in the first episode. In selecting an antipsychotic, there are advantages to choosing a second-generation drug. Since this is the patient's first experience with an antipsychotic, newer agents are likely to have advantages in subjective response when compared with older drugs. We concur with both the Texas Medication Algorithm and the Expert Consensus panel recommendation that newer drugs should be first line for first episodes of schizophrenia.

The selection among the newer drugs should be guided by a number of considerations such as side-effect profiles and convenience in taking the medication. For example, if patients are very concerned about weight gain, the clinician may choose to prescribe ziprasidone. Patients who may have difficulty conforming to twice daily-dosing may be poor candidates for quetiapine. Each of the newer agents has its own side-effect liabilities that should guide drug selection. For each drug it is likely that patients will respond to somewhat lower doses than those that are usually prescribed for multiepisode patients.

REFERENCES

1. McGlashan TH. Early detection and intervention in schizophrenia: research. *Schizophr Bull* 1996;22:327–345.
2. Wyatt RJ, Apud JA, Potkin S. New directions in the prevention and treatment of schizophrenia: a biological perspective. *Psychiatry* 1996;59:357–370.
3. Wyatt RJ. Neuroleptics and the natural course of schizophrenia. *Schizophr Bull* 1992; 17:325–351.
4. Wyatt RJ. Early intervention for schizophrenia: Can the course of the illness be altered? [editorial]. *Biological Psychiatry* 1995;38:1–3.
5. Odegard O. Changes in the prognosis of functional psychoses since the days of Kraepelin. The forty-first Maudsley Lecture, delivered before the Royal Medico-Psychological Association, 18th November, 1966. *Br J Psychiatry* 1967;113:813–822.
6. Grinker RR Sr, Holzman PS. Schizophrenic pathology in young adults. a clinical study. *Arch Gen Psychiatry* 1973;28:168–175.
7. Romano J. Requiem or reveille: psychiatry's choice. *Bull NY Acad Med* 1977;53: 787–805.
8. Bleuler M. Schizophrenic deterioration. *Br J Psychiatry* 1983;143:78–79.
9. The role of hospitalization. In: Herz MI, Keith SJ, Docherty JP, eds. *Handbook of schizophrenia,* vol. 4. New York: Elsevier, 1990:269–295.

10. Fenton WS, McGlashan TH. Prognostic scale for chronic schizophrenia. *Schizophr Bull* 1987;13:277–286.
11. Coryell W, Tsuang MT. *DSM-III* schizophreniform disorder: comparisons with schizophrenia and affective disorder. *Arch Gen Psychiatry* 1982;39:66–69.
12. Birchwood M. Early intervention in schizophrenia: theoretical background and clinical strategies [review]. *Br J Clin Psychol* 1992;31:257–278.
13. Johnstone EC, Crow TJ, Johnson AL, et al. The Northwick Park Study of first episodes of schizophrenia. I: Presentation of the illness and problems relating to admission. *Br J Psychiatry* 1986;148:115–120.
14. Loebel AD, Lieberman JA, Alvir JM, et al. Duration of psychosis and outcome in first-episode schizophrenia. *Am J Psychiatry* 1992;149:1183–1188.
15. Ho BC, Andreasen NC, Flaum M, et al. Untreated initial psychosis: its relation to quality of life and symptom remission in first-episode schizophrenia. *Am J Psychiatry* 2000; 157:808–815.
16. May PR, Tuma AH, Yale C, et al. Schizophrenia: a follow-up study of results of treatment. *Arch Gen Psychiatry* 1976;33:481–486.
17. McGorry PD, Edwards J, Mihalopoulos C, et al. EPPIC: an evolving system of early detection and optimal management. *Schizophr Bull* 1996;22:305–326.
18. Herz MI, Melville C. Relapse in schizophrenia. *Am J Psychiatry* 1980;80:801–805.
19. Szymanski SR, Cannon TD, Gallacher F, et al. Course of treatment response in first-episode and chronic schizophrenia. *Am J Psychiatry* 1996;96:519–525.
20. Robinson DG, Woerner MG, Alvir JM, et al. Predictors of treatment response from a first episode of schizophrenia or schizoaffective disorder [see comments]. *Am J Psychiatry* 1999;156:544–549.
21. Lieberman J, Jody D, Geisler S, et al. Time course and biologic correlates of treatment response in first-episode schizophrenia. *Arch Gen Psychiatry* 1993;50:369–376.
22. Crow TJ, Macmillan JF, Johnson AL, et al. A randomised controlled trial of prophylactic neuroleptic treatment. *Br J Psychiatry* 1986;148:120–127.
23. Kissling WJ, Kane JM, et al. Guidelines for neuroleptic relapse prevention in schizophrenia: towards a consensus view. In: Kissling W, ed. *Guidelines for neuroleptic relapse prevention in schizophrenia.* Berlin: Springer-Verlag, 1991:155–163.
24. Lieberman JA, Alvir JM, Koreen A, et al. Psychobiologic correlates of treatment response in schizophrenia. *Neuropsychopharmacology* 1996;14[3 Suppl]:13S–21S.
25. Remington G, Kapur S, Zipursky R. APA practice guideline for schizophrenia: risperidone equivalents. American Psychiatric Association [letter]. *Am J Psychiatry* 1998;155: 1301–1302.
26. McEvoy JP, Schooler NR, Wilson WH. Predictors of therapeutic response to haloperidol in acute schizophrenia. *Psychopharmacol Bull* 1991;27:97–101.
27. Emsley RA. Risperidone in the treatment of first-episode psychotic patients: a double-blind multicenter study. *Schizophr Bull* 1999;25:721–729.
28. Sanger TM, Lieberman JA, Tohen M, et al. Olanzapine versus haloperidol treatment in first-episode psychosis. *Am J Psychiatry* 1999;156:79–87.

13

Treatment and Management of Dual-Diagnosis Patients

COMORBIDITY WITH CHEMICAL ABUSE

Comorbidity with other disorders is common in individuals with schizophrenia. Results from the Epidemiologic Catchment Area Study of all individuals with a lifetime diagnosis of schizophrenia or schizophreniform disorder showed that 47% have met criteria for some form of substance abuse dependence, 33.7% met criteria for an alcohol disorder, and 27.5% qualified for another drug abuse disorder. The odds of having a substance abuse diagnosis are 4.6 times higher for those with schizophrenia than for the rest of the population. Odds for alcohol disorders are more than three times as high, whereas for other drug disorders they are six times higher (1). Other studies have reported that the incidence of concurrent substance abuse or dependence is as high as 40% among those with schizophrenia, and the lifetime incidence is even higher, 60% in some studies (2).

It has been established that individuals with co-occurring schizophrenia and substance abuse have a much worse prognosis and long-term outcome than those without substance abuse. Schizophrenic individuals with associated substance abuse are more likely to have increased relapses and hospitalizations, medication and other treatment noncompliance, violence, suicidal behaviors, and decreased social functioning (3,4). Other negative consequences to associated substance abuse include homelessness, incarceration, suicide, and HIV infection (5–7). A study by Owen and colleagues found that at 6-month follow-up, subjects with substance abuse were 8.1 times more likely to be noncompliant with their medications than those without substance abuse (8). Since compliance with treatment in individuals with schizophrenia is not high in general, it is obvious that those with comorbid substance abuse present a great challenge to engagement and retention in treatment. A major goal early in treatment is to engage these individuals and ensure their compliance with treatment. The goals of treatment for these patients are the same as those for treatment of schizophrenia without comorbidity but with the addition of the goals of substance abuse treatment (e.g., harm reduction, abstinence, relapse prevention, and rehabilitation) (9).

Not infrequently, psychiatrists fail to detect substance abuse in their patients with schizophrenia. Since substance abuse is so common, the evaluation of the patient with schizophrenia should include a comprehensive inquiry into substance use. Laboratory tests (e.g., liver function tests and urine and blood screens) for substances of abuse and screening instruments for substance disorders should be carried out (7,9–12). A variety of self-report screening instruments can be employed, including the Drug Abuse Screening Test, The Michigan Alcoholism Screening Test (MAST), The CAGE Questionnaire, The Dartmouth Assessment of Lifestyle Instrument, and The Addiction Severity Index (ASI) (13–19). Since many with substance abuse underreport or deny this condition, recommendations for improving self-report data include ensuring the sobriety and mental stability of the respondent when the assessment is being conducted, using interview approaches rather than paper-and-pencil self-report instruments, and using verification techniques comprising multiple sources of data, including that of case managers, family members, and friends. Establishing adequate rapport between the interviewer and the respondent and providing respondents with assurances of confidentiality can be very helpful in obtaining reliable data (3). A contributing factor to underreporting is that many with schizophrenia do not develop the full physiologic dependence syndrome associated with alcohol or substance dependence (6). Therefore the psychiatrist should be aware of other evidence of possible substance abuse, including homelessness, violence, medication noncompliance, frequent symptom exacerbations, financial problems, and family difficulties (10).

A major question regarding treatment of dual-diagnosis patients is whether they should be seen in one comprehensive integrated program or treated separately in substance abuse and mental health programs either in parallel or sequentially. There have been many studies dealing with this question, but most had problems in research design, including small numbers, lack of randomization, short follow-up periods, and lack of blindness, and some studies used only homeless patients in their samples. Despite these limitations the results generally provide encouraging evidence for the effectiveness of integrated treatment of dual disorders. Results of integrated treatment, especially when delivered for 18 months or longer, resulted in significant reductions of substance abuse and in some cases substantial rates of remission as well as reductions in hospital use and/or improvements in other outcomes (20).

In integrated treatment for patients with dual disorders, mental health and substance abuse treatments are brought together by the same clinician or team of clinicians in the same program to ensure that patients receive a consistent explanation of their illness and a coherent prescription for treatment rather than a contradictory set of messages from different providers. Integrated treatment aims to reduce conflicts between providers by eliminating the patient's burden of attending two programs and hearing potentially conflicting messages, and by removing financial and other barriers to access and retention (6,21).

Drake et al. have summarized current concepts of integrated treatment for dual disorders (Table 13.1) (20). There is general agreement that integrated treatment programs should be designed to provide continuous treatment interventions and support over long periods of time. They should include stage-wise motivational interventions and components of assertive outreach, case

TABLE 13.1. *Integrated treatment for dual disorders*

- The patient participates in one program that provides treatment for two disorders—severe mental disorder and substance use disorder.
- The patient's mental disorder and substance use disorder are treated by the same clinicians.
- The clinicians are trained in psychopathology, assessment, and treatment strategies for both mental disorders and substance use disorders.
- The clinicians offer substance abuse treatments tailored for patients who have severe mental illness. These tailored treatments differ from traditional substance abuse treatment.
    Focus on preventing increased anxiety rather than on breaking through denial
    Emphasis on trust, understanding, and learning rather than on confrontation, criticism, and expression
    Emphasis on reduction of harm from substance use rather than on immediate abstinence
    Slow pace and long-term perspective rather than rapid withdrawal and short-term treatment
    Provision of stage-wise and motivational counseling rather than confrontation and front-loaded treatment
    Supportive clinicians readily available in familiar settings rather than being available only during office hours and at clinics
    Twelve-step groups available to those who choose and can benefit rather than being mandated for all patients
    Neuroleptics and other pharmacotherapies indicated according to patients' psychiatric and medical needs rather than being contraindicated for all patients in substance abuse treatment
- Some program components specifically address substance use reduction as a central focus of programming.
- Components focus especially on integrated treatment.
    Substance abuse group interventions
    Specialized substance abuse assessment
    Case management
    Individual counseling
    Housing supports
    Medications and medication management
    Family psychoeducation
    Psychosocial rehabilitation

management, group interventions, individual counseling, and family interventions (22–24).

Future studies of effective treatment strategies should remedy the limitations of previous study research designs and especially attempt to differentiate homeless from nonhomeless dual-disorder patients, the differential needs
of male and female patients, and the differential treatment needs of patients
with and without antisocial personalities. It is important to note that women
who seek treatment for substance abuse disorder are more likely to report a
family history of instability and physical and sexual abuse than are men who
seek such treatment (25,26). Women with severe mental illness and substance use disorder are more likely to have experienced childhood physical
or sexual abuse than women with severe mental illness alone (27). Substance
use disorders are less likely to be detected among women than among men
because of their more solitary lifestyle and decreased likelihood of engaging
in antisocial behavior that would attract attention (28). Women admitted to
drug and alcohol treatment programs tend to have more severe symptoms of
substance abuse than males. Important treatment components for women
with dual disorders include screening for accompanying medical problems
and an approach that builds on safety and empowerment in the community,
education about sexuality and pregnancy prevention, and issues related to
victimization and homelessness (29–31). Groups for women only have been
reported to be both therapeutic and supportive because they provide a safe
place to talk about issues of violence and abuse (32). Some investigators
have argued that groups for women only are more beneficial (33–36).

Antipsychotic medications can be used in usual doses, and patients should
be informed that combining antipsychotic medication with alcohol or other
substances may increase sedation and lack of coordination (37). Psychiatrists
should take into account the potential for lowering the seizure threshold by
antipsychotic medications and the potential for abuse of such medications as
benzodiazepines and antiparkinson agents. Infrequently, antipsychotic medications can precipitate seizures during alcohol or benzodiazepine withdrawal (38). Use of disulfiram has several risks, since it can precipitate psychosis at high doses and has harmful physical effects when taken with
alcohol (39,40). Therefore it should be used only for patients with reasonably
good judgment, treatment compliance, and reality testing (10). Naltrexone is
being used to decrease desire for alcohol and opiates, and should be considered for individuals with schizophrenia. Studies are needed to evaluate the
differential effectiveness of the new atypical antipsychotic agents compared
with conventional antipsychotic medications for dual-diagnosis patients. It
appears that clozapine is helpful for these patients in reducing symptoms of
schizophrenia and reducing their substance abuse (41,42). It is unclear
whether clozapine, by reducing schizophrenic positive and negative symp-

toms, indirectly helps reduce substance abuse or whether it may have a direct effect on reducing substance abuse (20). Other, newer antipsychotics have also been found to be effective (43). Proper treatment of these patients requires that physicians and staff ensure compliance with medication and adequate response (44).

COMORBID DEPRESSION AND SCHIZOPHRENIA

Depressive symptoms are common in schizophrenia and can occur in every phase of the disorder. Estimates of frequency vary but appear to occur in approximately 25% of individuals with schizophrenia (45–49). When depressive symptoms are present there is increased likelihood of suicide (50,51).

Depressive symptoms occur frequently during the prodromal phase of relapse (see Chapter 4). It is very important to differentiate the onset of prodromal symptoms of relapse from symptoms of a depressive disorder, since introducing antidepressant medication during the prodromal phase may exacerbate schizophrenic symptomatology. Points to consider in the differential diagnosis include the following: During the prodromal phase of relapse the individual often displays the same symptomatology that occurred before previous relapses as well as idiosyncratic behaviors (e.g., females wearing excessive make-up, males wearing sunglasses at night, and so on). Therefore it is important to document which prodromal symptoms and behaviors occurred in prior episodes. In addition, in the prodromal phase individuals experience symptoms of anxiety, including difficulties in falling asleep and remaining asleep, rather than the typical early-morning awakening that occurs in depression. They may also experience referential ideas, feelings of impending doom, and a breakthrough of early psychotic symptoms such as beginning delusions and hallucinations that are not mood-congruent depressive symptoms.

Treatment of prodromal symptoms involves increasing antipsychotic medication and more frequent therapy visits that provide support, structure, and help in identifying and dealing with a stressful situation that may have precipitated the symptomatology. As stated earlier, antidepressant medication is contraindicated during this phase (52).

Depressive symptoms may present during the acute psychotic phase of schizophrenia and when present at the syndromal level may lead to a diagnosis of schizoaffective disorder. Some positive and negative symptoms of acute schizophrenia may resemble depressive symptomatology (e.g., agitation resembling psychomotor restlessness, catatonia or thought blocking resembling psychomotor retardation, thought disorder or distractibility resembling difficulty in concentrating, and excitability resembling sleep disturbances). Other symptoms of acute schizophrenia that may resemble depressive symptomatology include negative symptoms such as anergia, anhedonia, and reduced appetite and attention (53). In differentiating depression from flat affect, sadness is usually present in depression but is usually not present with flat affect.

Treatment of possible depressive symptoms in acute schizophrenia involves treating the psychosis first with antipsychotic medication. Introduction of antidepressant medication during an acute episode may retard the antipsychotic medication response (54). Evidence suggests that the newer antipsychotic medications, including clozapine, that affect both the dopamine and serotinergic systems may be more beneficial in reducing negative symptomatology than the earlier generation of conventional dopamine-blocking neuroleptics (55–59). The neurologic side effects of conventional antipsychotic medications, including akinesia and akathisia, can easily be mistaken for depressive symptomatology. A major benefit of the new antipsychotic agents is that they are not likely to cause these neurologic side effects when used at recommended dosages. They may have an independent antidepressant effect as well (60).

Depressive symptoms that persist after remission of the acute psychotic state or that develop during the stable state are termed "residual" or "secondary" (postpsychotic depressive symptoms). They have been shown to respond to antidepressant treatment (48). As in the acute state, negative symptoms of the deficit state may be confused with depressive symptomatology. Differential diagnosis of depression during the stable state includes other potentially etiologic conditions, such as general medical disorders and substance-induced conditions (61,62). Demoralization, which occurs frequently in individuals with schizophrenia, is often accompanied by subjective feelings of depressed mood, feelings of inadequacy, lack of hope for the future, and low self-esteem (63,64). Demoralization occurs frequently in younger adults with schizophrenia, especially those who have had high aspirations for the future before the development of schizophrenia. When symptoms of demoralization meet the criteria for major depressive disorder, they should be treated both with psychosocial treatment and antidepressant medication. However, when demoralization occurs without symptoms of major depression, vigorous psychosocial and rehabilitative efforts should be instituted, including reassuring and helping the individual achieve realistic academic and vocational aspirations consistent with the therapist's efforts to help the individual recognize an increased vulnerability to stress.

Treatment of major depressive symptoms in schizophrenia consists of psychosocial intervention plus antidepressant medication. It is important to recognize that selective serotonin reuptake inhibitors (SSRI) antidepressant medication may result in higher blood levels of antipsychotic medication and that blood levels of some antidepressants are elevated by the concomitant administration of antipsychotic medications. Therefore patients should be monitored closely for signs of toxicity, particularly during the dose titration phase (65). Generally, use of SSRIs may be preferential to tricyclic antidepressants because of their better side effect profiles.

COMORBIDITY WITH OBSESSIVE-COMPULSIVE DISORDER

Estimates of the prevalence of comorbid schizophrenia and obsessive-compulsive disorder vary widely, but this comorbidity is not infrequent and may be increasing (66,67). Obsessive-compulsive disorder may be present in some patients before the onset of schizophrenia or may appear during the course of schizophrenia. Hwang and Hollander compared the clinical and neuropsychological profiles of schizophrenic patients with and without obsessive-compulsive symptoms (68,69). They found that patients who had schizophrenia with obsessive-compulsive symptoms had significantly greater neuropsychological impairments (e.g., prefrontal executive functioning) and negative psychopathologic symptoms (68,69). The findings supported earlier reports regarding individuals with schizophrenia that noted a positive correlation between greater prefrontal lobe dysfunction and high negative symptomatology with a worse clinical course (70). Another study found that comorbid patients had cognitive deficits that were similar to those with patients with obsessive-compulsive disorder alone (71).

The prognosis of schizophrenic patients with comorbid obsessive-compulsive symptoms appears to be worse than that of those with schizophrenia alone. Global functioning has been found to be more impaired (71,72). These patients were found to have a more florid presentation of symptoms, an earlier age of onset of psychosis, and a greater number of hospitalizations than patients without obsessive-compulsive symptoms (73).

Effective pharmacologic treatment involves combining an antipsychotic agent with either clomipramine hydrochloride or SSRIs. Psychosocial treatment involves the use of cognitive behavioral treatment approaches (74). It is recommended that patients be in the stable remitted phase of schizophrenia before instituting specific pharmacologic treatment for the obsessive-compulsive symptoms, since antidepressant agents may exacerbate schizophrenic symptoms in acute patients. Clinicians should be aware of important interactions between antipsychotic medications and medications for obsessive-compulsive disorder (OCD). For example, the OCD medications may exacerbate akathisia and add to the anticholinergic effects of antipsychotic medication, including sedation and hypotension. SSRIs appear to increase the levels of atypical neuroleptic agents in the blood by as much as 25% to 30%, with a greater increase in the level of clozapine (75,76). Some patients on clozapine and other newer antipsychotic agents may develop obsessive-compulsive symptoms, or if they already have these symptoms, the symptoms may worsen with inauguration of these antipsychotic medications. If this occurs, the clinician should consider lowering the dose of the antipsychotic or switching to another.

COMORBID MEDICAL ILLNESS

Compared with the general population, there is approximately a twofold increase in natural death in individuals with schizophrenia (77). This higher natural mortality rate suggests that in this population some illnesses are more prevalent, more lethal, or both. Some studies suggest that cardiovascular and infectious diseases have led to increased mortality rates in individuals with schizophrenia (78–84). High rates of heavy smoking in these patients may lead to an increased incidence of pneumonia and emphysema (83,85). Paradoxically, there appears to be a reduced rate of lung cancer in these patients, although the incidence of breast cancer is higher (83–88). The latter finding may be related to increases in serum prolactin levels associated with antipsychotic medications (88). Prevalence of HIV infection is increased in individuals with schizophrenia (89).

Although there is a high prevalence of comorbid medical disorders in individuals with schizophrenia, these medical disorders are often unrecognized and if diagnosed are not treated adequately (90–93). These problems are related to a combination of patient, provider, and health care system factors (94). As summarized by Stroup et al., patient-related factors include the presence of positive and negative symptoms, neurocognitive abnormalities, and altered pain thresholds that interfere with symptoms recognition, symptom reporting, health seeking, and adherence to treatment recommendations (95). Provider-related factors in underdiagnosis and undertreatment may be associated with a lack of physical assessment skills and lack of interest in medical problems by psychiatrists. Of course, today individuals in allied mental health professions with no medical training often carry out much of the treatment of individuals with schizophrenia. In our own experience, physicians often have negative attitudes toward treating individuals with schizophrenia, who can be poorly dressed, appear odd, sometimes exhibit bizarre and occasionally frightening behavior, lack the ability to describe their symptomatology well, and are often noncompliant with treatment. Furthermore, because of negative symptoms, including flat affect and positive symptomatology, it may be difficult to establish rapport with some patients. As Stroup et al. point out, a key factor resulting in underdiagnosis and undertreatment of these patients is poor access to services (95). Many community mental health programs have little or no connection with general medical services and little or no communication or collaboration between the mental health care system and the general medical care system.

To remedy these problems it is important to have a well-integrated system of care with close collaboration and integration of mental health and general medical services. An example of such integration is the University of Rochester Community Support Program, where a general medical outpatient service has been established onsite. Mental health and general medical personnel are in close contact and communicate regularly about patient health issues. General internists have been recruited who have a special interest and training in working with the chronically mentally ill. Some of these internists have completed a combined medical/psychiatric residency program. Every new patient has a comprehensive medical and psychiatric evaluation upon admission and routine periodic follow-ups. Case managers are available to assist patients in verbalizing their medical concerns as well as to help ensure compliance with medical care, including accompanying patients to their medical care appointments. Therapists work with family members individually or in multifamily groups to engage their collaboration in the overall treatment program.

POLYDIPSIA

Some patients with severe schizophrenia develop compulsive water drinking, or polydipsia. Estimates of the prevalence of polydipsia vary. One estimate from a study of 360 state hospital patients found that 42% of patients had polydipsia diagnosed at one time and 5% had experienced water intoxication with hyponatremia (96). Another survey of 353 patients in a state hospital in France found that 11% experienced polydipsia and that a third of these were at risk for water intoxication (97). Studies that were carried out before the introduction of antipsychotics found a high prevalence of polydipsia (98). This suggests that this syndrome is related to psychosis and not to drug treatment. Individuals who are severely ill, are male, and smoke are at a higher risk for polydipsia. The pathophysiology of polydipsia and hyponatremia in schizophrenia is not well understood. Excessive drinking usually does not lead to hyponatremia, since the kidneys have the capacity to excrete large quantities of dilute urine. A number of medical illnesses, including malignancies, central nervous system illnesses, and pulmonary disorders, can lead to the syndrome of inappropriate antidiuretic hormone (SIADH) that is associated with hyponatremia and increases in ADH or ADH-like substances. However, the polydipsia in schizophrenia is not associated with elevations in ADH, suggesting a different mechanism.

Hyponatremia may be a medical emergency. In its early stages it may present to the clinician as lethargy, weakness, or drowsiness. In more severe cases it may be manifest in seizures or coma that can lead to death. The diagnosis of hyponatremia can be confirmed by a serum sodium concentration of 120 mEq/L or less.

The evaluation of patients with polydipsia includes ruling out medical causes of hyponatremia such as diabetes, renal failure, malignancy, pulmonary disease, hypocalcemia, and hypokalemia. These causes can usually be ruled out with routine laboratory work (including electrolytes, blood glucose, blood urea nitrogen (BUN), creatinine), chest radiograph, and a physical examination. Urinary sodium should also be evaluated when hyponatremia is present.

Acute water intoxication should be managed in collaboration with a medical specialist. The goal is to raise the serum sodium gradually to a normal level and to manage the central nervous system manifestations of hyponatremia. Management may include water restriction as well as sodium replacement.

The only well-established treatment for the long-term management of chronic polydipsia/hyponatremia is fluid restriction. This is effective but is not always practical. A number of studies suggest that clozapine may be effective in managing patients with this syndrome (99,100). Although these studies are open label with relatively small samples, clozapine appears to be promising. Case reports suggest that risperidone and olanzapine are helpful, but there are insufficient data to evaluate their effectiveness. Other treatments that have been considered include naltrexone and propranolol (101,102).

REFERENCES

1. Regier D, Farmer, M, Rae, et al. Comorbidity of mental disorders with alcohol and other drug abuse: results from the Epidemiologic Catchment Area (ECA) Study. *JAMA* 1990; 264:2511–2518.
2. Mueser KT, Yarnold PR, Levinson DF, et al. Prevalence of substance abuse in schizophrenia: demographic and clinical correlates. *Schizophr Bull* 1990;16:31–56.
3. RachBeisel J, Scott J, Dixon L. Co-occurring severe mental illness and substance use disorders: a review of recent research. *Psychiatr Serv* 1999;50:1427–1434.
4. Cuffel BJ. Violent and destructive behavior among the severely mentally ill in rural areas: evidence from Arkansas' community mental health system. *Community Ment Health J* 1994;30:495–504.
5. Drake RE, Osher FC, Wallach MA. Alcohol use and abuse in schizophrenia: a prospective community study. *J Nerv Ment Dis* 1989;177:408–414.
6. Drake RE, Osher FC, Noordsy DL, et al. Diagnosis of alcohol use disorders in schizophrenia. *Schizophr Bull* 1990;16:57–67.
7. Kivlahan DR, Heiman JR, Wright RC, et al. Treatment cost and rehospitalization rate in schizophrenic outpatients with a history of substance abuse. *Hosp Community Psychiatry* 1990;42:609–614.
8. Owen RR, Fischer EP, Booth BM, et al. Medication noncompliance and substance abuse among patients with schizophrenia. *Psychiatr Serv* 1996;47:853–858.
9. American Psychiatric Association. Practice guidelines for the treatment of patients with substance abuse disorders: alcohol, cocaine, opioids. *Am J Psychiatry* 1995;152[Nov. Supplement]:1–59.
10. American Psychiatric Association. Practice guidelines for treatment of patients with schizophrenia. *Am J Psychiatry* 1997;154[Suppl 4]:1–63.

11. Searles JS, Alterman AI, Purtill JJ. The detection of alcoholism in hospitalized schizophrenics: a comparison of the MAST and the MAC. *Alcohol Clin Exp Res* 1990;14: 557–560.

12. Brady K, Casto S, Lydiard RB, Malcolm R, Arana G. Substance abuse in an inpatient psychiatric sample. *Am J Drug Alcohol Abuse* 1991;17:389–397.

13. Gavin DR, Ross HE, Skinner HA. Diagnostic validity of the Drug Abuse Screening Test in the assessment of *DSM III* drug disorders. *Br J Addict* 1989;84:301–307.

14. Skinner HA. The Drug Abuse Screening Test. *Addict Behav* 1982;7:363–371.

15. Moore RA. The diagnosis of alcoholism in a psychiatric hospital: a trial of the Michigan Alcoholism Screening Test (MAST). *Am J Psychiatry* 1972;128:1565–1569.

16. Pokorny AD, Miller BA, Kaplan HB. The brief MAST: a shortened version of the Michigan Alcoholism Screening Test. *Am J Psychiatry* 1972;129:342–345.

17. Ewing JA. Detecting alcoholism: the CAGE questionnaire. *JAMA* 1984;252:1905–1907.

18. Rosenberg SD, Drake RE, Wolford GI, et al. The Dartmouth Assessment of Lifestyle Instrument (DALI): a substance use disorder screen for people with severe mental illness. *Am J Psychiatry* 1998;155:232–238.

19. McLellan AT, Kushner H, Metzger D, et al. The fifth edition of the Addiction Severity Index. *J Subst Abuse Treat* 1992;9:199–213.

20. Drake RE, Mercer-McFadden C, Mueser KT, et al. Review of integrated mental health and substance abuse treatment for patients with dual disorders. *Schizophr Bull* 1998; 24:589–608.

21. Minkoff K. An integrated treatment model for dual diagnosis of psychosis and addiction. *Hosp Community Psychiatry* 1989;40:1031–1036.

22. Lehman AF, Dixon L. *Double jeopardy: chronic mental illness and substance abuse.* New York: Harwood Academic Publishers, 1995.

23. Carey KB. Substance use reduction in the context of outpatient psychiatric treatment: a collaborative, motivational, harm reduction approach [see comments]. *Community Ment Health J* 1996;32:291–306.

24. Drake RE, Mueser KT, Clark RE, et al. The course, treatment, and outcome of substance disorder in persons with severe mental illness. *Am J Orthopsychiatry* 1996;66:42–51.

25. Gomberg ESL, Nirenberg TD. Antecedents and consequences. In: Gomberg ESL, Nirenberg TD, eds. *Women and substance abuse.* Norwood, CT: Ablex. 1993.

26. Lex BW. Women and illicit drugs: marijuana, heroin, and cocaine. In: Gomberg ESL, Nirenberg TD, eds. *Women and substance abuse.* Norwood, CT: Ablex, 1993.

27. Alexander MJ. Women with co-occurring addictive and mental disorders: an emerging profile of vulnerability. *Am J Orthopsychiatry* 1996;66:61–70.

28. Weisner C, Schmidt L. Gender disparities in treatment for alcohol problems. *JAMA* 1992;268:1872–1876.

29. Burman S. The disease concept of alcoholism: its impact on women's treatment. *J Subst Abuse Treat* 1994;11:121–126.

30. Hagan TA, Finnegan LP, Nelson-Zlupko L. Impediments to comprehensive treatment models for substance-dependent women: treatment and research questions. *J Psychoactive Drugs* 1994;26:163–171.

31. Harris M. Modifications in service delivery and clinical treatment for women diagnosed with severe mental illness who are also the survivors of sexual abuse trauma. *J Ment Health Adm* 1994;21:397–406.

32. Copeland J, Hall W. A comparison of predictors of treatment drop-out of women seeking drug and alcohol treatment in a specialist women's and two traditional mixed-sex treatment services. *Br J Addict* 1992;87:883–890.

33. Reed BG. Developing women-sensitive drug dependence treatment services: why so difficult? *J Psychoactive Drugs* 1987;19:151–164.

34. Schleibner CT. Gender-sensitive therapy: an alternative for women in substance abuse treatment. *J Subst Abuse Treat* 1994;11:511–515.

35. National Women's Resource Center for the Prevention and Treatment of Alcohol, To-

bacco, and Other Drug Abuse and Mental Illness. *Gender-specific substance abuse treatment.* Rockville, MD: Center for Substance Abuse Prevention., 1997.

36. Hodgins DC, el Guebaly N, Addington J. Treatment of substance abusers: single or mixed gender programs? *Addiction* 1997;92:805–812.
37. Seppala T. Effect of chlorpromazine or sulpiride and alcohol on psychomotor skills related to driving. *Arch Int Pharmacodyn Ther* 1976;223:311–323.
38. Janicak PG, Davis JM, Preskorn SH, et al. *Principles and practice of psychopharmacology.* Baltimore: Williams and Wilkins, 1993:527–529.
39. Kofoed L, Kania J, Walsh T, et al. Outpatient treatment of patients with substance abuse and coexisting psychiatric disorders. *Am J Psychiatry* 1986;143:867–872.
40. Kingsbury SJ, Salzman C. Disulfiram in the treatment of alcoholic patients with schizophrenia. *Hosp Community Psychiatry* 1990;41:133–134.
41. Albanese MJ, Khantzian EJ, Murphy SL, et al. Decreased substance use in chronically psychotic patients treated with clozapine. *Am J Psychiatry* 1994;151:780–781.
42. Marcus P, Snyder R. Reduction of comorbid substance abuse with clozapine [letter; comment]. *Am J Psychiatry* 1995;152:959.
43. Wilkins JN. Pharmacotherapy of schizophrenic patients with comorbid substance abuse. *Schizophr Bull* 1997;23:215–228.
44. Osher FC, Kofoed LL. Treatment of patients with psychiatric and psychoactive substance abuse disorders. *Hosp Community Psychiatry* 1989;40:1025–1030.
45. Siris SG. Depression and schizophrenia. In: Hirsch SR, Weinberger DR. *Schizophrenia.* Cambridge, MA: Blackwell Science, 1995:128–145.
46. Siris SG. Depression in the course of schizophrenia. In: Hwang MY, Bermanzohn PC, eds. *Management of schizophrenia with comorbid conditions.* Washington, DC: American Psychiatric Association, 2000.
47. McGlashan TH, Carpenter WT Jr. Postpsychotic depression in schizophrenia. *Arch Gen Psychiatry* 1976;33:231–239.
48. Siris SG. Diagnosis of secondary depression in schizophrenia: implications for *DSM-IV. Schizophr Bull* 1991;17:75–98.
49. Koreen AR, Siris SG, Chakos M, et al. Depression in first-episode schizophrenia [see comments]. *Am J Psychiatry* 1993;150:1643–1648.
50. Miles CP. Conditions predisposing to suicide: a review. *J Nerv Ment Dis* 1977;164: 231–246.
51. Caldwell CB, Gottesman II. Schizophrenics kill themselves too: a review of risk factors for suicide. *Schizophr Bull* 1990;16:571–589.
52. Herz MI, et al. A program for relapse prevention in schizophrenia: a controlled study. *Arch Gen Psychiatry* 2000;57:277–283.
53. Siris SG. Management of depression in schizophrenia. *Psychiatr Ann* 2000;30:13–19.
54. Kramer MS, Vogel WH, DiJohnson C, et al. Antidepressants in depressed schizophrenic inpatients: a controlled trial [see comments]. *Arch Gen Psychiatry* 1989;46:922–928.
55. Kane JM, Honigfeld G, Singer J, et al. Clozapine for the treatment-resistant schizophrenic: a double-blind comparison with chlorpromazine. *Arch Gen Psychiatry* 1988;45:789–796.
56. Marder SR, Meibach RC. Risperidone in the treatment of schizophrenia. *Am J Psychiatry* 1994;151:825–835.
57. Tollefson GD, Beasley CM Jr., Tran PV, et al. Olanzapine versus haloperidol in the treatment of schizophrenia and schizoaffective and schizophreniform disorders: results of an international collaborative trial [see comments]. *Am J Psychiatry* 1997;154:457–465.
58. Tandon R, Harrigan E, Zorn SH. Ziprasidone: a novel antipsychotic with unique pharmacology and therapeutic potential. *J Serotonin Res* 1997;4:159–177.
59. Buchanan RW. Clozapine: efficacy and safety. *Schizophr Bull* 1995;21:579–591.
60. Moller HJ, Muller H, Borison RL, et al. A path-analytical approach to differentiate between direct and indirect drug effects on negative symptoms in schizophrenic patients: a re-evaluation of the North American risperidone study. *Eur Arch Psychiatry Clin Neurosci* 1995;245:45–49.

61. Bartels SJ, Drake RE. Depressive symptoms in schizophrenia: comprehensive differential diagnosis. *Compr Psychiatry* 1988;29:467–483.
62. Siris SG. Akinesia and postpsychotic depression: a difficult differential diagnosis. *J Clin Psychiatry* 1987;48:240–243.
63. Klein DF. Endogenomorphic depression: a conceptual and terminological revision. *Arch Gen Psychiatry* 1974;31:447–454.
64. deFigueiredo JM. Depression and demoralization: phenomenologic differences and research perspectives. *Compr Psychiatry* 1993;34:308–311.
65. Siris SG, Rifkin AE, Reardon GT. Response of postpsychotic depression to adjunctive imipramine or amitriptyline. *J Clin Psychiatry* 1982;43:485–486.
66. Bland RC, Newman SC, Orn H. Schizophrenia: lifetime co-morbidity in a community sample. *Acta Psychiatr Scand* 1987;75:383–391.
67. Jahrreiss W. Obsessions during schizophrenia. *Arch Psychiatry* 1926;77:740–788.
68. Hwang MY, Hollander E. Schizophrenia with obsessive-compulsive features: clinical and neuropsychological study. Presented at the Annual Meeting of the American College of Neuropharmacology. 1992.
69. Hwang MY, Morgan JE, Losonzy MF. Clinical and neuropsychological profiles of OC schizophrenia. *J Neuropsychiatry Clin Neurosci* 2000.
70. Butler RW, Jenkins MA, Sprock J, Braff DL. Wisconsin Card Sorting Test deficits in chronic paranoid schizophrenia. Evidence for a relatively discrete subgroup? *Schizophr Res* 1992;7:169–176.
71. Berman J, Pappas D, Berman S. Obsessive-compulsive symptoms in schizophrenia: are they manifestations of a distinct subclass of schizophrenia? *CNS Spectrums* 1997;2: 45–48.
72. Fenton WS, McGlashan TH. The prognostic significance of obsessive-compulsive symptoms in schizophrenia. *Am.J Psychiatry* 1986;143:437–441.
73. Samuels J, Nestadt G, Wolyniec P, et al. Obsessive-compulsive symptoms in schizophrenia. *Schizophr Res* 1993;9:139.
74. Hwang MY, Opler LA. Management of schizophrenia with obsessive-compulsive disorder. *Psychiatr Ann* 2000;30:23–28.
75. Ciraulo DA, Shader RI. Fluoxetine drug-drug interactions. I: Antidepressants and antipsychotics. *J Clin Psychopharmacol* 1990;10:48–50.
76. Goff DC, Midha KK, Brotman AW, et al. Elevation of plasma concentrations of haloperidol after the addition of fluoxetine. *Am J Psychiatry* 1991;148:790–792.
77. Tsuang MT, Woolson RF. Mortality in patients with schizophrenia, mania, depression and surgical conditions: a comparison with general population mortality. *Br J Psychiatry* 1977;130:162–166.
78. Allebeck P, Wistedt B. Mortality in schizophrenia: a ten-year follow-up based on the Stockholm County inpatient register. *Arch Gen Psychiatry* 1986;43:650–653.
79. Black DW. Mortality in schizophrenia: the Iowa Record-Linkage Study: a comparison with general population mortality. *Psychosomatics* 1988;29:55–60.
80. Tsuang MT, Woolson RF, Fleming JA. Premature deaths in schizophrenia and affective disorders: an analysis of survival curves and variables affecting the shortened survival. *Arch Gen Psychiatry* 1980;37:979–983.
81. Hayward C. Psychiatric illness and cardiovascular disease risk. *Epidemiol Rev* 1995;17: 129–138.
82. Herrman HE, Baldwin JA, Christie D. A record-linkage study of mortality and general hospital discharge in patients diagnosed as schizophrenic. *Psychol Med* 1983;13: 581–593.
83. Mortensen PB, Juel K. Mortality and causes of death in first admitted schizophrenic patients. *Br J Psychiatry* 1993;163:183–189.
84. Baldwin JA. Schizophrenia and physical disease: a preliminary analysis of the data from the Oxford Record Linkage Study. In: Hemmings G. *The biochemistry of schizophrenia and addiction.* Lancaster, PA: MTP Press, 1980:297–318.

85. Masterson E, O'Shea B. Smoking and malignancy in schizophrenia. *Br J Psychiatry* 1984;145:429–432.
86. Soni SD, Gill J. Malignancies in schizophrenic patients. *Br J Psychiatry* 1979;134:448.
87. Tsuang MT, Perkins K, Simpson JC. Physical diseases in schizophrenia and affective disorder. *J Clin Psychiatry* 1983;44:42–46.
88. Ettigi P, Lal S, Friesen HG. Prolactin, phenothiazines, admission to mental hospital, and carcinoma of the breast. *Lancet* 1973;2:266–267.
89. Cournos F, Guido JR, Coomaraswamy S, et al. Sexual activity and risk of HIV infection among patients with schizophrenia. *Am J Psychiatry* 1994;151:228–232.
90. Barnes RF, Mason JC, Greer C, et al. Medical illness in chronic psychiatric outpatients. *Gen Hosp Psychiatry* 1983;5:191–195.
91. D'Ercole A, Skodol AE, Struening E, et al. Diagnosis of physical illness in psychiatric patients using axis III and a standardized medical history [published erratum appears in *Hosp Community Psychiatry* 1991;42:539]. *Hosp Community Psychiatry* 1991;42: 395–400.
92. Koran LM, Sox HC, Marton KL, et al. Medical evaluation of psychiatric outpatients. *Arch Gen Psychiatry* 1989;46:733–740.
93. Koranyi EK. Morbidity and rate of undiagnosed physical illnesses in a psychiatric clinic population. *Arch Gen Psychiatry* 1979;36:414–419.
94. Gilmore JH, Jarskog LF, Stroup TS. Recognition and management of medical and surgical illness in patients with schizophrenia. In: Hwang MY, *Management of medical and surgical illness in patients with schizophrenia.* Washington, DC: American Psychiatric Association, 2000.
95. Stroup TS, Gilmore JH, Jarskog LF. Management of medical illness in persons with schizophrenia. *Psychiatr Ann* 2000;30:35–40.
96. De Leon J, Dadvand M, Canuso C, et al. Polydipsia and water intoxication in a long-term hospital. *Biol Psychiatry* 1996;40:28–34.
97. Mercier-Guidez E, Loas G. Polydipsia and water intoxication in 353 psychiatric inpatients: an epidemiological and psychopathological study. *Eur Psychiatry* 2000;15: 306–311.
98. Verghese C, de Leon J, Josiassen RC. Problems and progress in the diagnosis and treatment of polydipsia and hyponatremia. *Schizophr Bull* 1996;22:455–464.
99. Spears NM, Leadbetter RA, et al. Clozapine treatment in polydipsia and intermittent hyponatremia. *J Clin Psychiatry* 1996;57:123–128.
100. Canuso DM, Goldman MB. Clozapine restores water balance in schizophrenic patients with polydipsia-hypoatremia syndrome. *J Neuropsychiatry Clini Neurosci* 1999;11: 86–90.
101. Becker JA, Goldman MB, Alam MY, et al. Effects of naltrexone on mannerisms and water imbalance in polydipsia schizophrenics: a pilot study. *Schizophr Res* 1995;17: 279–282.
102. Kishi Y, Kurosawa H, Endo S. Is propranolol effective in primary polydipsia? *Int J Psychiatry Med* 1998;28:315–325.

14

Special Populations

This chapter deals with specific populations of individuals with schizophrenia, which require special considerations in their evaluation and treatment. Children and developmentally disabled individuals are not covered in this volume.

GENDER

There are numerous differences in manifestations of schizophrenia between males and females, including presenting symptoms, response to treatment, course of illness, and outcome. Generally, males have an earlier onset of psychosis, poorer premorbid functioning, increased negative symptoms and cognitive deficits, and greater structural brain and neuropsychological abnormalities. Females display more affective symptoms, auditory hallucinations, and persecutory delusions with a more rapid and greater response to antipsychotic medications in the premenopausal period. They also generally require lower doses of antipsychotic medication than men, even after body weight is considered. The course of illness is more favorable in females in the short and middle term, and they are less likely to smoke or be substance abusers (1–6). It is interesting that a study found that the relative duration of the prodromal phase in first-episode patients was longer in women than in men, whereas the duration of untreated psychosis showed no difference between the sexes (7).

The many differences between males and females with schizophrenia probably arise from the interplay of biological factors such as sex hormones, neurodevelopmental factors, and psychosocial and behavioral variables. For example, if females present with less substance abuse, which is highly related to noncompliance and relapse, that factor alone would partially account for the better prognosis in females (1). A study of inpatient family treatment found that females had better responses to inpatient family intervention and better occupational functioning at follow-up than males (8). According to the authors, social and occupational role demands may result in unrealistic family expectations for male schizophrenic patients. This issue should be dealt with in family meetings. Furthermore, the authors noted that traditional socialization practices may allow greater dependence on the family and greater acceptance of family treatment among female schizophrenic patients.

Menstrual Cycle and Pregnancy Issues

When considering the choice of an antipsychotic medication for females, it is important to consider the issue of neuroleptic-induced hyperprolactinemia, which can cause menstrual disorders, impaired fertility, galactorrhea, and sexual dysfunction as well as hypoestrogenism secondary to disruption of the hypothalamic/pituitary/ovarian axis (9). If any of these problems are present with the use of conventional antipsychotic medication or risperidone, prolactin-sparing newer-generation antipsychotic drugs in therapeutic doses offer the possibility of prevention and resolution of these adverse reactions.

With the advent of deinstitutionalization there was an increased risk of unplanned pregnancy in females with schizophrenia. However, studies have shown that fertility rates for women with schizophrenia have only been between 30% and 80% of the rate of the general population (10). A major reason for the decrease in fertility appears to have been the increased prolactin levels that occurred with the conventional antipsychotic agents. Since most of the newer antipsychotic medications do not increase prolactin levels at therapeutic doses, there is an increased likelihood of unplanned pregnancies with their use. This is especially true since some patients who were on conventional antipsychotic medications may have believed that they could not become pregnant and were not in need of birth control measures. When starting a patient on an atypical antipsychotic medication, it is important to provide counseling regarding family planning, emphasizing the need for starting a birth control program (10). Women of childbearing age should have regularly scheduled pregnancy tests, since prenatal care is important for a healthy outcome of the pregnancy. With the high rates of noncompliance in individuals with comorbid substance abuse and homelessness, case management services with assertive outreach is an important component of treatment during pregnancy to ensure proper prenatal care. There should be close collaboration between mental health professionals, obstetricians, and pediatricians during pregnancy, delivery, and thereafter. Patients may stop their antipsychotic medication on their own either during pregnancy, delivery, or the neonatal period, resulting in an increased risk of relapse. Therefore they should be closely monitored for early signs of decompensation, which may occur at any time from conception through the neonatal period.

Females with schizophrenia have a high rate of loss of custody of their children. This is related to a number of factors, including problems in bonding with the child and misreading cues from the child (11,12). Furthermore many of these women are single parents with little or no family support who have problems in daily living skills and impaired reality testing (13). The needs of the child may be overwhelming for some mothers. Part of the management of the pregnancy should be planning for optimal care for the mother and child after delivery, often requiring ongoing in-home services. Direct observation of the mother/child interaction can be useful in determining the adequacy of mothering the child receives.

Medication management should consider the needs of the mother with schizophrenia balanced against those of the fetus and newborn child. Studies have shown only a minimal increase in congenital malformations (2.4% versus 2.0% for the overall population) when conventional antipsychotics were used. It appears that the use of low-potency phenothiazines, especially chlorpromiazine, was responsible for the malformations. No birth defects were associated with haloperidol or piperazine class medications (11). Use of antipsychotic medications during the first trimester should be minimized or avoided if possible, especially between weeks 6 and 10, with high-potency antipsychotic medications the treatment of choice for conventional antipsychotics (14). At this time there is not enough information regarding the effects on the fetus of newer-generation antipsychotics. If it is determined that medication is required during the first trimester, the lowest possible dose should be used (4,15). Antiparkinsonian medication should also be avoided, especially during the first trimester (16,17). Opinions differ about whether medications should be tapered during the weeks immediately before delivery to avoid withdrawal symptoms in infants. Because of vulnerability of the mother to decompensation during this period, some investigators believe that the medication should be continued (17). If the mother displays severe psychotic symptoms, hospitalization should be arranged until the time of delivery for the safety of the mother and child. Although there are advantages to breast-feeding, including nutrition and increased immunity to infections as well as helping to establish a bond between the mother and the child, we recommend against it (18). All antipsychotic medications pass into the mother's milk at low concentrations and the ingestion of these medications by the newborn should be avoided if possible. However, if the mother insists on breast-feeding after being informed of the possible deleterious effects, the psychiatrist should continue to prescribe the lowest possible dose of antipsychotic medication during the nursing period. The use of clozapine is contraindicated because of its potential to cause agranulocytosis or to build up to toxic levels because of the immaturity of the newborn's liver (11).

RACE AND ETHNICITY

Race and ethnicity are key factors to consider in the evaluation and treatment of individuals with schizophrenia. When conducting a diagnostic evaluation of patients, it is important to note that studies have shown that blacks are more likely than whites to be misdiagnosed as having schizophrenia when an affective disorder is present (4,19,20). One study reported that even when a semistructured *DSM-III-R* symptom checklist was used in addition to the usual hospital clinical diagnosis, blacks were still more likely to be diagnosed as schizophrenic (21). In another study of the association of race with diagnosis and disposition from a psychiatric emergency service, it was found that black patients were significantly more likely to be diagnosed with schizophrenia and substance abuse than similar white patients, although less likely to be diagnosed with personality disorder. Furthermore, black patients were significantly more likely to be hospitalized, particularly at a public hospital, although there were no significant differences in insurance coverage or measures of suicidal or homicidal ideation (22). A study by Trierweiler et al. found that psychotic symptoms not differentially attributed between whites and blacks seemed to correspond to higher rates of the diagnosis of schizophrenia for black patients (23). Attributions of negative symptoms showed the largest differences between black and nonblack patients in the rates of diagnosis of schizophrenia. That is, whites with negative symptoms were less likely to be diagnosed as schizophrenic than blacks with negative symptoms. Although it is unclear why blacks are more likely to be diagnosed as schizophrenic, it appears that lack of cultural sensitivity by white clinicians may play a role and that black patients may distrust white clinicians. It is evident that white psychiatrists need to take special care when interviewing blacks and arriving at a diagnosis of schizophrenia. Interviews with family and friends may be helpful in establishing a diagnosis, and certainly the course of the illness over time should be followed to help confirm the diagnosis. A British 18-year follow-up study of first-episode psychosis in Afro-Caribbean and white people had the following results: Diagnosis was established by direct interview using the Present State Examination at both first admission and follow-up (24). Ninety-seven percent of the original sample was traced. The study found no difference between the two groups in the consistency of diagnosis over the 18 years or in the proportion of patients considered psychotic, but Afro-Caribbean people tended to have fewer negative symptoms at follow-up. There were striking differences between the two groups in their experience of psychiatric care; Afro-Caribbean people were more likely to have been readmitted and to have experienced longer hospitalizations and to have undergone more involuntary admissions than their white counterparts. The author's conclusions were that Afro-Caribbean individuals who met clinical and research criteria for schizophrenia had less satisfactory experiences of psychiatric care over 18 years than their white counterparts (25). In a 5-year prospective study in England of an epidemiologic cohort of individuals diagnosed with schizophrenia, age-standardized rates for schizophrenia were higher for black and Asian people than for whites (26). Stability of diagnosis and course of illness were similar in all ethnic groups, suggesting at least in these two studies that the British were more accurate in the initial diagnosis of schizophrenia for blacks. During the fifth year of the study, blacks were more likely than others to be detained, brought to the hospital by the police, and given emergency injections. The investigators conclude that the nature and outcome of psychotic illness were similar in all ethnic groups, but black people experienced more adverse contacts with services later in the course of the illness.

Cultural, racial, and ethnic factors play other major roles in working with patients of diverse backgrounds. For example, it is useful to know attitudes toward mental illness, extent of stigma in the culture, and social support available. The greater the cultural sensitivity of a therapist, the greater the ability to be of benefit to patients and their families who come from various cultural and racial groups. For example, what are the attitudes toward alcoholism among particular groups of American Indians who have high rates of alcoholism? If some members of a particular group consider alcoholism acceptable, it can be more difficult to treat patients from that group. Since it is known that females with schizophrenia can be taken advantage of and sexually abused, it has been found that HIV infections are more prevalent in these females, as well as in segments of the gay male population and among the economically deprived black Hispanic populations, who have a high incidence of substance abuse and dependence (27).

It should be noted that wide generalizations about a particular group may not be accurate. For example, different subgroups of Hispanics (e.g., Puerto Ricans versus Cuban-Americans) may have very different attitudes about mental illness. Even among particular cultures, social class may play a differential role in determining attitudes toward mental illness, stigma, and social support available.

Pharmacotherapy

Pharmacotherapy of individuals with schizophrenia should take into account racial and ethnic differences. For example, some studies have suggested that Asian-American patients may require lower doses of haloperidol and have higher serum levels of haloperidol after oral administration than Caucasian patients (28). In a review of the literature, Frackiewicz et al. found that studies suggest that Asian-Americans may respond to lower doses of antipsychotics because of pharmacokinetic and pharmacodynamic differences (29). They also found that research relative to blacks is limited, but some studies suggest that differences reported in this group may be due to clinician biases and prescribing practices rather than to pharmacokinetic or pharmacodynamic variability. The authors point out that future studies should focus on homogeneous ethnic groups, use recent advances in pharmacogenetic testing, and control for such variables as observer bias, gender, disease chronicity, dietary and environmental factors, and exposure to enzyme-inducing and inhibiting agents. Such agents include other medications, smoking, and chemical abuse, which can have varied prevalence rates in different racial groups. A study by Ruiz et al. suggests that if weight is taken into consideration, black patients need the same doses of neuroleptics as white patients to obtain a similar response in the treatment of schizophrenia (30). However, it appears that Hispanic patients respond to lower doses of antipsychotic medications. Regarding ethnicity and medication side effects, schizophrenic patients of Jewish descent have been found to be at greater risk for clozapine-induced agranulocytosis than others with schizophrenia and therefore need to be monitored closely for these side effects during clozapine treatment (31).

FORENSIC ISSUES

With the advent of deinstitutionalization in the 1950s, large numbers of seriously mentally ill individuals were released into the community. In 1955 there were more than 559,000 persons in state psychiatric hospitals; by 1992 the total had fallen to 83,320. Taking account of the increase in the population of the United States, it appears that approximately 750,000 individuals are now living in the community who 40 years ago would have been inpatients in state psychiatric hospitals (32). With large numbers of severely mentally ill individuals residing in the community, they are at increased risk for arrest and incarceration. The percentage of individuals with severe mental illness who are in jails and prisons has been estimated at between 6% and 15%; while the rate for the general population is approximately 2.8% (33,34). Factors cited as causes for the large numbers of severely mentally ill individuals housed in jails and prisons are deinstitutionalization (since they are at risk for involvement with the criminal justice system), more rigid criteria for civil commitment, the difficulties involved in involuntary commitment, lack of adequate community support for persons with mental illness, difficulties that mentally ill offenders have in gaining access to community mental health treatment, violence at the time of arrest, and the attitudes of police officers and society (33,35–37). Other risk factors that have been identified include comorbid chemical abuse, treatment noncompliance, and homelessness (38,39). Rates of noncompliance with medication for seriously mentally individuals have been reported to be as high as 63%. For outpatients with schizophrenia at any given follow-up interval 30% to 40% of the individuals were noncompliant. A frequent and predictable consequence of noncompliance with medication is relapse and rehospitalization (32). Poor or absent discharge planning has been identified as a major cause of homelessness, which is associated with non-compliance with treatment and chemical abuse. All the latter factors are associated with involvement in the criminal justice system.

Studies have shown that individuals with severe mental illness are more likely to be jailed for misdemeanors than non–mentally ill individuals and are often held in jail for longer periods of time (40–42). A study in Madison, Wisconsin, found that the most common charges brought against the mentally ill who end up in jail were lewd and lascivious behavior (such as urinating on a street corner), defrauding a restaurant (eating a meal and not paying for it), disorderly conduct (such as being too loud), menacing, panhandling, criminal damage to property, loitering, and petty theft (41,43). Researchers often find a direct relationship between the person's mental illness and the behavior that led to arrest. E. F. Torrey's book *Out of the Shadows: Confronting America's Mental Illness*, provides the following examples: A woman with schizophrenia was arrested for assault when she entered a department store and began rearranging the shelves because of her delusion that she worked there; when she was asked to leave, she struck a store manager and a police officer (41). A man with schizophrenia who was behaving bizarrely on the street was arrested for assault after he struck a teenager who was making fun of him. Police frequently use a disorderly conduct charge to arrest a mentally ill person when no other charge is available. For example, an individual was arrested frequently for just wanting to talk to normal people in the malls and street. He would follow them and keep talking, and would not go away. His looked very unkempt, which added to their fear. The charges may be trespassing: For example, a mentally ill individual sleeping in a cemetery or local businesses exerting pressure on the police to get rid of "undesirables," including the mentally ill who loiter near their stores. The police also resort to "mercy bookings," trying to protect mentally ill individuals, especially women, who are easily victimized and raped. Thus jails and prisons have increasingly become surrogate mental hospitals for individuals with severe mental illnesses, who are often jailed for misdemeanors that are the direct result of the expression of their severe mental illness. For example, the Los Angeles County Jail, where approximately 3,300 of the 21,000 inmates require mental health services on a daily basis, is now *de facto* the largest mental institution in the country (44).

It is obvious that jails are inappropriate placements for many with severe mental illness. Most jails or prisons have inadequate psychiatric facilities, and a jail environment that emphasizes discipline and punishment can exacerbate psychotic symptoms. Factors related to exacerbation include the stress related to incarceration, removal from support systems, inadequate mental health services, a general disciplinary rather than a therapeutic approach, and threats of rape or violence by other inmates (4,41). It is not uncommon for jailed individuals with severe mental illness to commit suicide in jails. Studies have shown that 50% to 71% of suicides in jails have occurred in individuals with histories of hospitalization for mental disorder (45,46). Another study revealed that 75% of individuals who attempted suicide in jails had histories of previous mental health treatment (47). It is clear that jails are not the appropriate placement for the severely mentally ill who have not committed major crimes. If they are jailed they should receive appropriate treatment, including psychotropic medications and psychosocial rehabilitation (4).

Alternatives to Incarceration

For the large percentage of severely mentally ill who are inappropriately jailed there have been increasing attempts to find other solutions, including jail diversion programs, outpatient commitment, and for those who remain under the jurisdiction of the criminal justice system, probation by the court that includes a condition of mandatory outpatient treatment or mandatory referral for treatment by their parole officer, with the understanding that failure to comply may result in revocation of parole and return to custody (48). Jail diversion services are not common at present, but recent federal legislation will provide a strong impetus to a great expansion of these programs throughout the United States. Jail diversion services consist of two interlocking areas of intervention: (a) the diversion mechanism through which an individual is identified at some point in the arrest process and diverted into mental health services; (b) the system of integrated mental health and substance abuse services to which the client is diverted (49). What makes jail diversion unique is that the service positions itself within the criminal justice system as an immediate alternative to incarceration, providing opportunities for police officers to easily redirect an individual in custody into treatment rather than jail. Jail wardens have the opportunity and means to securely remove individuals from the stress of a jail environment into treatment, and jail diversion provides a probation officer with an alternative to a violation of parole hearing for troubled clients. Draine and Solomon described a model program in Montgomery County, Maryland (49). It provides for prebooking jail diversion when psychiatric treatment is provided in lieu of arrest or criminal incarceration, postbooking jail diversion through regular and direct communication with county jail personnel, and coterminous diversion, which occurs when an offender is taken into custody by the police and delivered directly into psychiatric treatment while charges are being filed. In these cases the offender has been arrested and a charge has been filed but the offender has been directed away from criminal incarceration. The program supports all three forms of diversion through several services and programs. It provides police training and support to members of the police force in Montgomery County. Emergency service staff members are available for consultation, and continued education about mental illness and substance abuse is provided. It provides the opportunity for police officers to learn to differentiate behaviors arising from psychiatric and substance abuse problems from criminally motivated behaviors. Emergency crisis services are available 24 hours a day, and staff case managers broker services for clients and link them to services. They also follow clients into the community after release. Another model program consists of a consortium of five community service agencies in Monroe County, New York (50). The consortium spans the healthcare system, social services, and criminal justice systems and features a mobile treatment team with a forensic psychiatrist, a dual-diagnosis treatment residence, and a multicultural staff. It incorporates the principles of assertive community treatment, and intensive case management. Preliminary results are encouraging, demonstrating a significant impact on decreasing the number of mentally ill individuals in jails and the number of persons admitted to psychiatric hospitals from jails. It has also reduced reliance on inpatient hospitalization in a high-risk consumer group. Unfortunately, however, there is little or no empirical research on the effectiveness of jail diversion for those with serious mental illness that has utilized a randomized controlled design. Anecdotal evidence appears to support the increased use of jail diversion programs.

In recognition of the problem of inappropriate incarceration of those with severe mental illness, the U.S. Congress has passed legislation to increase the number of jail diversion programs in the United States. In November 2000, President Clinton signed the bill that authorized funding to establish up to 100 mental health courts for nonviolent offenders who are mentally ill. Passage of S 1865 authorized $10 million in appropriations annually from 2001 through 2004 in an attempt to reduce the inappropriate conviction and jailing of severely mentally ill individuals for misdemeanors and nonviolent crimes. The lawmakers were impressed by the positive results that mental health courts had in Broward County, Florida, and King County, Washington, with this alternative for nonviolent mentally ill offenders. Special judges hear cases involving these individuals and decide whether the offenders should be placed in outpatient or inpatient treatment programs. The judges also require the offender to be monitored closely. Another provision of the legislation requires centralized case management for each mentally ill offender, including the coordination of their mental health treatment plans and social service needs such as housing placements, vocational training, education, job placement, health care, and relapse prevention (51). It will be important to conduct scientifically valid outcome studies to determine the effectiveness for these programs.

MANAGING SCHIZOPHRENIA IN THE ELDERLY

Early authorities on schizophrenia, including Kraepelin, believed that patients whose onset of symptoms occurred after the age of 45 had an illness that should be differentiated from schizophrenia. They used such terms as *paraphrenia, late-onset paraphrenia,* and *involutional psychosis* to designate this disease. Before the introduction of *DSM-IV*, the term *late-onset schizophrenia* was required when onset occurred before the age of 45. *DSM-IV* dropped the age-of-onset criteria after research found that individuals with a late onset had important similarities to those with early onset. These similarities include symptom patterns, responses to medication, neurocognitive impairments, and structural abnormalities in the brain. Approximately 90% of elderly patients with schizophrenia have the early-onset form. The remaining 10% have the late-onset form.

Individuals with late-onset schizophrenia are more likely to have persecutory delusions and less likely to have negative symptoms and conceptual disorganization. Studies by Jeste and his co-workers found that those with later onset were more likely to be women, were more often paranoid, and tended to have a better premorbid adjustment (52). Individuals who are socially isolated or hearing impaired are more likely to develop late-onset schizophrenia (53). It is unclear whether the differences between early and late onset indicate that late-onset schizophrenia results from a distinct disease process, but patients with late-onset disease have at least been spared some of the effects of a more chronic illness.

Diagnosis of Schizophrenia in Elderly Patients

A number of disorders can lead to psychosis in the elderly, including dementia with psychotic symptoms, late-onset schizophrenia, delusional disorder, early-onset schizophrenia, late-onset mood disorders, psychotic disorders caused by medical conditions or medications, and delirium. Making an accurate diagnosis can be difficult because of complicating factors such as comorbid medical illnesses and the effects of multiple medications. The diagnostic process is similar to that for younger patients: Schizophrenia is diagnosed in elderly patients after other illnesses or other possible causes of psychosis (such as medications) are excluded.

The diagnostic process should include a thorough review of the patient's medical and psychiatric history. All the medications the patient is taking, including over-the-counter medications, should be reviewed. This often requires asking outpatients to bring all their medications to the clinician's office. The clinician should also make direct inquiries about alcohol intake and the possible abuse of pain, antianxiety, and sleep medications.

If the patient demonstrates the recent onset of psychotic symptoms, it is important to assess if these symptoms are associated with delirium. Delirium usually has a rapid onset and is often associated with confusion and other mental status changes. Hallucinations during delirium tend to be visual and are often more frightening to the patient than the hallucinations present in schizophrenia. Common causes of delirium in the elderly include infections, electrolyte imbalances, cardiac events, and adverse drug reactions. In addition, withdrawal from a number of drugs such as alcohol and benzodiazepines can cause periods of delirium (54).

Pharmacotherapy of Schizophrenia in the Elderly

The treatment responses of elderly patients with schizophrenia are similar to those of younger patients. Studies reviewing response rates in both early- and late-onset schizophrenia have found that the patterns of response to antipsychotics are similar to those in younger patients in that positive symptoms respond more reliably than negative symptoms (51). Moreover, there is no indication that there are differences in response patterns between early- and late-onset patients. For this reason antipsychotics should be prescribed for nearly all individuals with schizophrenia in late life for both acute and maintenance treatment.

There is no indication that one antipsychotic is more effective than another for elderly patients with schizophrenia. The higher-potency conventional antipsychotics are clearly preferable over the lower-potency drugs because of the side effects of the latter. Low-potency agents have anticholinergic effects that can cause urinary retention, constipation, dry mouth, and memory impairments. All these effects can be serious in the elderly. Low-potency agents also tend to cause orthostatic hypotension because of their affinity for α-adrenergic receptors. This can contribute to falls, which are also a serious concern in this population. The side effects of low-potency drugs should be balanced against the tendency of high-potency conventional drugs to cause extrapyramidal side effects (EPS). Elderly patients are particularly vulnerable to parkinsonism as a side effect, although some may experience akathisia.

Second-generation antipsychotics have gained considerable popularity in the treatment of the elderly because of their tendency to cause milder side effects than conventional agents. However, there are relatively few data on the effectiveness and toxicity of newer drugs from controlled trials in elderly patients with schizophrenia. Most controlled studies have evaluated newer agents in patients with dementia or in populations that include different forms of psychosis. This makes it difficult to form conclusions about dosage and side effects of these agents in individuals with schizophrenia. On the other hand, there may be an important advantage for agents that cause fewer EPS. Second-generation antipsychotics can usually be prescribed without anticholinergic antiparkinson drugs, which can cause serious side effects of their own. In addition, newer agents appear to be associated with a lower risk of tardive dyskinesia (TD), another serious problem in the elderly that will be discussed later.

Because of its side effect profile, clozapine is usually reserved for patients who have failed to respond well to other antipsychotics. These side effects can be particularly difficult to manage in elderly patients. That is, anticholinergic effects, hypotension leading to falls, seizures, and sedation can be devastating in many patients who have coexisting medical conditions. There is also evidence that elderly patients are more likely to develop agranulocytosis when they receive clozapine (55). The side effects of clozapine may occur more frequently during the first weeks of treatment, when patients are vulnerable to severe sedation and falling (56). However, one literature search of 133 patients found that the great majority of patients could tolerate clozapine, particularly when they were treated with doses in the 100-mg range (57). When taken together, these findings indicate that clozapine can be effective in elderly patients with schizophrenia, especially when the dosing is very carefully titrated against the drug's side effects.

Risperidone's side effect profile has made it relatively popular for elderly patients with schizophrenia. An open-label study suggested that risperidone was effective and well tolerated in the elderly (58). Although the mean dose of risperidone was 3.7 mg daily, this may be higher than necessary for the elderly. Although responses in patients with dementia may not provide reliable information about dosage requirements in schizophrenia, a double-blind study found that 1 mg daily was effective for patients with an average age of 82.7 years (59).

The most common side effects of risperidone are likely to be hypotension, sedation, fatigue, and tachycardia. We agree with the recommendation of Zayas and Grossberg to start risperidone at a dose of 0.25 mg bid and to manage patients with 2 mg or less daily (54). Since risperidone can cause EPS, it is important to carefully evaluate patients for akathisia and parkinsonism.

Relatively little information is available on olanzapine for elderly patients with schizophrenia. Retrospective studies and a number of case reports indicate that olanzapine is relatively safe in this population (60,61). A study of olanzapine in elderly patients with Alzheimer's disease found that 5 to 10 mg daily was well tolerated (62). This dose range is consistent with the case report literature for schizophrenia (63). Advantages of olanzapine in the elderly include a very low risk for EPS as well as a mild degree of sedation. Common side effects of olanzapine include weight gain, sedation, and a possible association with type 2 diabetes. Since olanzapine is mildly anticholinergic, its effects on memory in older patients should be monitored.

Even less information is available about quetiapine for elderly patients, although initial reports are promising (64). An open-label study suggests that elderly patients respond to 100 mg daily of quetiapine and that the most common side effect is sedation (65). This is substantially less than the commonly prescribed dose of 300 to 600 mg for younger adults. This may be explained by quetiapine's metabolism, which is largely governed by CYP 3A4. This enzyme may decline with age, resulting in a lower dosage requirement for the elderly (66). An advantage of quetiapine is its very low liability for causing EPS.

Prescribing Antipsychotics in Elderly Patients

The pharmacokinetics of antipsychotics may change in the elderly because of a number of factors. Older patients frequently have altered absorption of drugs because of such factors as the use of antacids, changes in gastric emptying, and reductions in the rate of drug absorption. Once drugs are absorbed, age-related changes in liver function may substantially decrease the rate of drug metabolism. Similarly, decreases in renal clearance may also reduce the rate of drug clearance, which will increase drug levels in plasma. For example, one study of risperidone in elderly patients found that the clearance of risperidone and its active metabolite was reduced by 30% (67). The same study found reductions of about 50% in patients with renal disease. These observations may explain the evidence that elderly patients have higher plasma levels of antipsychotics when they are prescribed the same drug doses as younger patients (68). In addition, the elimination half-lives of drugs in the elderly tends to be longer.

Elderly patients are more vulnerable to drug/drug interactions because they frequently receive multiple medications. There is no evidence that cytochrome P450 systems are altered in the elderly. Nevertheless, patients with complex regimens often take agents that can have complex effects on their psychiatric condition and drug responses. For this reason, experienced clinicians often ask elderly patients to bring all their medications—both prescription and over-the-counter medications—to the physician's office.

These findings, as well as clinical experience, support the common clinical practice of beginning elderly patients at very low doses and increasing the dose gradually ("start low and go slow"). For example, starting elderly patients at 25% to 50% of the dose prescribed for younger patients has been recommended as a routine practice (66).

Side Effects in the Elderly

Acute Extrapyramidal Side Effects

Elderly patients are more vulnerable to developing EPS, particularly parkinsonism and, to a lesser degree, akathisia. Dystonia is less common in elderly patients. Parkinsonism can be easy to detect when patients have typical shuffling gait, rigidity, and tremor. However, milder forms of parkinsonism can cause more subtle effects of akinesia that include decreased spontaneous gestures, decreased energy, and decreased interest in activities. These symptoms can be easily missed in elderly patients if they are attributed to aging rather than to the patient's medications. EPS will usually respond either to anticholinergic antiparkinson medications such as biperiden or benztropine or to dosage reduction. The later is usually preferred, since anticholinergric drugs can impair cognition and cause other side effects (mentioned earlier). The other alternative is to change patients to agents that are less likely to cause parkinsonism. All the second-generation antipsychotics are associated with substantially reduced EPS at their effective doses. Quetiapine and clozapine are the least likely to cause EPS.

Tardive Dyskinesia in the Elderly

Elderly patients are much more vulnerable to developing TD than younger patients. One study found that the annual incidence of TD in patients more than 45 years of age was 46% (69). This compares with an incidence of about 5% for younger patients. Another study in patients older than 55 found that that 25% of patients developed TD after 1 year and 53% during 3 years of antipsychotic treatment (70). Moreover, elderly patients are more vulnerable to developing severe and disabling forms of TD. One study found that 22.9% of elderly patients had developed severe TD after 3 years (71).

These findings suggest that concerns about TD should be an important factor in selecting an antipsychotic drug in older patients. Recent findings indicate that newer antipsychotics are less likely to cause TD in this population. A study by Jeste and co-workers found that patients treated with risperidone had a much lower risk of TD (2.6% over 1 year versus 25% in a similar population) (72).

Other Side Effects in the Elderly

Elderly patients may have reduced cardiac reserve and are often more vulnerable to the cardiovascular side effects of antipsychotics. These can include orthostatic hypotension, tachycardia, and arrhythmias. Orthostatic hypotension is a serious concern in the elderly since it is a major contributor to falls and fractures. Also, elderly patients are more susceptible to developing hypotension because of an age-related decrease in their ability to vasoregulate. This problem can be compounded when patients receive other medications such as antidepressants, anticholinergics, and some antihypertensives. A number of agents, including clozapine and risperidone, can cause tachycardia, which can be a serious problem in elderly patients with reduced cardiac reserve. A number of antipsychotics can increase the QT interval on the cardiogram (or the heart-corrected QT_c). Excessive prolongation of this interval results in increased vulnerability to developing a potentially fatal ventricular arrhythmia called *torsades de pointes*. The risk is minimal with most antipsychotics, with the exception of thioridazine, mesoridazine, and to a lesser degree, ziprasidone.

The sedating side effects of antipsychotics can also contribute to falls as well as confusion. Although some of the newer antipsychotics (e.g., risperidone and ziprasidone) cause minimal sedation, these agents may increase the sedation caused by other drugs, including benzodiazepines, certain antidepressants, and antihypertensives.

SUMMARY AND RECOMMENDATIONS

The population of elderly individuals with schizophrenia continues to grow as life expectancy increases. Unfortunately, the literature on the pharmacologic treatment of this population is limited, and the literature on psychosocial treatments is almost nonexistent. Nevertheless, a few principles of treatment can be applied to the elderly. The diagnostic process is similar to that in younger patients. That is, other sources of psychotic symptoms should be ruled out before early- or late-onset schizophrenia is diagnosed. In the elderly medical illness and drug reactions should be given very serious consideration.

Antipsychotic medications are as effective for elderly patients with schizophrenia as they are for younger patients. However, these agents should be prescribed with more caution, since elderly patients often respond to much lower doses and have a greater sensitivity to side effects. In most cases, patients will respond to 25% to 50% of the dose used for younger patients. For example, haloperidol can be started at 0.25 mg; risperidone at 0.5 mg; olanzapine at 2.5 mg; or quetiapine at 12.5 mg. The dose of drug should be increased very slowly, since elderly patients tend to have a longer elimination half-life than younger patients.

All the conventional and second-generation agents appear effective in the elderly, although there are few controlled trials for either class of agents. The selection should be based on side effects that are a concern to the patient and the clinician. TD is extremely common in the elderly. Since evidence suggests that newer agents are less likely to cause TD, this should influence the use of one of the newer first-line agents. Clozapine's side effects can cause serious problems in the elderly. As a result, it should be reserved for use when other agents are ineffective.

REFERENCES

1. Leung A, Chue P. Sex differences in schizophrenia, a review of the literature. *Acta Psychiatr Scand Suppl* 2000;401:3–38.
2. Goldstein JM, Tsuang MT. Gender and schizophrenia: an introduction and synthesis of findings. *Schizophr Bull* 1990;16:179–183.
3. Szymanski S, Lieberman JA, Alvir JM, et al. Gender differences in onset of illness, treatment response, course, and biologic indexes in first-episode schizophrenic patients. *Am J Psychiatry* 1995;152:698–703.
4. APA Practice Guidelines for The Treatment of Patients with Schizophrenia. 1997.
5. Bardenstein KK, McGlashan TH. Gender differences in affective, schizoaffective, and schizophrenic disorders: a review. *Schizophr Res* 1990;3:159–172.
6. Kelly DL, Conley RR, Tamminga CA. Differential olanzapine plasma concentrations by sex in a fixed-dose study. *Schizophr Res* 1999;40:101–104.
7. Cohen RZ, Gotowiec A, Seeman MV. Duration of pretreatment phases in schizophrenia: women and men. *Can J Psychiatry* 2000;45:544–547.
8. Haas GL, Glick ID, Clarkin JF, et al. Gender and schizophrenia outcome: a clinical trial of an inpatient family intervention. *Schizophr Bull* 1990;16:277–292.
9. Dickson RA, Seeman MV, Corenblum B. Hormonal side effects in women: typical versus atypical antipsychotic treatment. *J Clin Psychiatry* 2000;61[Suppl 3]:10–15.
10. Nanko S, Moridaira J. Reproductive rates in schizophrenic outpatients. *Acta Psychiatr Scand* 1993;87:400–404.
11. Miller LJ. Sexuality, reproduction, and family planning in women with schizophrenia. *Schizophr Bull* 1997;23:623–635.
12. Appleby L, Dickens C. Mothering skills of women with mental illness [editorial] [see comments]. *BMJ* 1993;306:348–349.
13. White CL, Nicholson J, Fisher WH, et al. Mothers with severe mental illness caring for children. *J Nerv Ment Dis* 1995;183:398–403.
14. Canuso CM, Goldstein JM, Green AI. The evaluation of women with schizophrenia. *Psychopharmacol Bull* 1998;34:271–277.
15. Altshuler LL, Cohen L, Szuba MP, et al. Pharmacologic management of psychiatric illness during pregnancy: dilemmas and guidelines [see comments]. *Am J Psychiatry* 1996;153:592–606.
16. Altshuler LL, Szuba MP. Course of psychiatric disorders in pregnancy: dilemmas in pharmacologic management. *Neurol Clin* 1994;12:613–635.
17. Goldberg HL. Psychotropic drugs in pregnancy and lactation. *Int J Psychiatry Med* 1994; 24:129–147.
18. Mortola JF. The use of psychotropic agents in pregnancy and lactation. *Psychiatr Clin North Am* 1989;12:69–87.
19. Cheetham RW, Griffiths JA. Errors in the diagnosis of schizophrenia in black and Indian patients. *S Afr Med J* 1981;59:71–75.
20. Baker FM. A research agenda for the mental health concerns of African Americans. *J Assoc Acad Minor Phys* 1994;5:74–76.
21. Neighbors HW, Trierweiler SJ, Munday C, et al. Psychiatric diagnosis of African Americans: diagnostic divergence in clinician-structured and semistructured interviewing conditions. *J Natl Med Assoc* 1999;91:601–612.
22. Strakowski SM, Lonczak HS, Sax KW, et al. The effects of race on diagnosis and disposition from a psychiatric emergency service. *J Clin Psychiatry* 1995;56:101–107.
23. Trierweiler SJ, Neighbors HW, Munday C, et al. Clinician attributions associated with the diagnosis of schizophrenia in African American and non-African American patients. *J Consult Clin Psychol* 2000;68:171–175.
24. Wing JK, Cooper JE, Sartorious N. *The measurement of classification of psychiatric symptoms.* Cambridge: Cambridge University Press, 1974.
25. Takei N, Persaud R, Woodruff P, et al. First episodes of psychosis in Afro-Caribbean and

white people: an 18-year follow-up population-based study. *Br J Psychiatry* 1998;172: 147–153.

26. Goater N, King M, Cole E, et al. Ethnicity and outcome of psychosis [see comments]. *Br J Psychiatry* 1999;175:34–42.

27. Cournos F, Guido JR, Coomaraswamy S, et al. Sexual activity and risk of HIV infection among patients with schizophrenia. *Am J Psychiatry* 1994;151:228–232.

28. Chang WH, Hwu HG, Chen TY, et al. Plasma homovanillic acid and treatment response in a large group of schizophrenic patients. *Schizophr Res* 1993;10:259–265.

29. Frackiewicz EJ, Sramek JJ, Herrera JM, et al. Ethnicity and antipsychotic response. *Ann Pharmacother* 1997;31:1360–1369.

30. Ruiz P, Varner RV, Small DR, et al. Ethnic differences in the neuroleptic treatment of schizophrenia. *Psychiatr Q* 1999;70:163–172.

31. Lieberman JA, Yunis J, Egea E, et al. HLA-B38, DR4, DQw3 and clozapine-induced agranulocytosis in Jewish patients with schizophrenia. *Arch Gen Psychiatry* 1990;47:945–948.

32. Torrey EF, Kaplan RJ. A national survey of the use of outpatient commitment [see comments]. *Psychiatr Serv* 1995;46:778–784.

33. Lamb HR, Weinberger LE. Persons with severe mental illness in jails and prisons: a review [see comments]. *Psychiatr Serv* 1998;49:483–492.

34. Report of the National Advisory Mental Health Council. Health care reform for Americans with severe mental illness. *Am J Psychiatry* 1993;150:1447–1465.

35. Borzecki M, Wormith JS. The criminalization of psychiatrically ill people: a review with a Canadian perspective. *Psychiatr J Univ Ott* 1985;10:241–247.

36. Jemelka R, Trupin E, Chiles JA. The mentally ill in prisons: a review. *Hosp Community Psychiatry* 1989;40:481–491.

37. Robertson G, Pearson R, Gibb R. The entry of mentally disordered people to the criminal justice system. *Br J Psychiatry* 1996;169:172–180.

38. Abram KM, Teplin LA. Co-occurring disorders among mentally ill jail detainees: implications for public policy. *Am Psychol* 1991;46:1036–1045.

39. Belcher JR. Are jails replacing the mental health system for the homeless mentally ill? *Community Ment Health J* 1988;24:185–195.

40. Valdiserri EV, Carroll KR, Hartl AJ. A study of offenses committed by psychotic inmates in a county jail. *Hosp Community Psychiatry* 1986;37:163–166.

41. Torrey E.F. *Out of the shadows: confronting America's mental illness crisis.* New York: John Wiley and Sons, 1997.

42. Butterfield F. Prisons replace hospitals for the nation's mentally ill. *The New York Times* (CXL VII). 1998.

43. Mulhern B. Everyone's problem, no one's priority. *Capital Times,* 1990. Madison, Wisconsin.

44. Grinfeld MJ. Report focuses on jailed mentally ill. *Psychiatric Times,* 1–3, 1993.

45. Correctional Association of New York. Insane and in jail: the need for treatment options for the mentally ill in New York's county jails [mimeo]. 1989.

46. Tobar H. When jail is a mental institution. *Los Angeles Times.* 1991.

47. Jemelka R. The mentally ill in local jails: issues in admissions and booking. In: Steadman HJ, ed. *Jail diversion for the mentally ill.* Washington, DC: Department of Justice National Institute of Corrections, 1991; citing a study by L. Le Brun.

48. Lamb HR, Weinberger LE, Gross BH. Community treatment of severely mentally ill offenders under the jurisdiction of the criminal justice system: a review. *Psychiatr Serv* 1999;50:907–913.

49. Draine J, Solomon P. Describing and evaluating jail diversion services for persons with serious mental illness. *Psychiatr Serv* 1999;50:56–61.

50. Lamberti JS, et al. Prevention of jail and hospital recidivism among persons with severe mental illness. *Psychiatr Serv* 1999;50:1477–1480.

51. Sharfstein S. Congress agrees to fund test of mental health courts. *Psychiatr News* 2000; 35:2.

52. Jeste DV, Harris MJ, Krull A, et al. Clinical and neuropsychological characteristics of patients with late-onset schizophrenia. *Am J Psychiatry* 1995;152:722–730.
53. Almeida OP, Howard RJ, Levy R, et al. Psychotic states arising in late life (late paraphrenia): the role of risk factors. *Br J Psychiatry* 1995;166:215–228.
54. Zayas EM, Grossberg GT. The treatment of psychosis in late life. *J Clin Psychiatry* 1998;59[Suppl 1]:5–10; discussion, 11–12.
55. Herst L, Powell G. Is clozapine safe in the elderly? *Aust N Z J Psychiatry* 1997;31: 411–417.
56. Pitner JK, Mintzer JE, Pennypacker LC, et al. Efficacy and adverse effects of clozapine in four elderly psychotic patients [see comments]. *J Clin Psychiatry* 1995;56:180–185.
57. Barak Y, Wittenberg N, Naor S, et al. Clozapine in elderly psychiatric patients: tolerability, safety, and efficacy. *Compr Psychiatry* 1999;40:320–325.
58. Davidson M, Harvey PD, Vervarcke J, et al. A long-term, multicenter, open-label study of risperidone in elderly patients with psychosis. *Int J Geriatr Psychiatry* 2000; 15:506–514.
59. Katz IR, Jeste DV, Mintzer JE, et al. Comparison of risperidone and placebo for psychosis and behavioral disturbances associated with dementia: a randomized, double-blind trial. *J Clin Psychiatry* 1999;60:107–115.
60. Solomons K, Geiger O. Olanzapine use in the elderly: a retrospective analysis. *Can J Psychiatry* 2000;45:151–155.
61. Madhusoodanan S, Brenner R, Suresh P, et al. Efficacy and tolerability of olanzapine in elderly patients with psychotic disorders: a prospective study. *Ann Clin Psychiatry* 2000; 12:11–18.
62. Street JS, Clark WS, Gannon KS, et al. Olanzapine treatment of psychotic and behavioral symptoms in patients with Alzheimer disease in nursing care facilities: a double-blind, randomized, placebo-controlled trial. *Arch Gen Psychiatry* 2000;57:968–976.
63. Sajatovic M, Perez D, Brescan D, et al. Olanzapine therapy in elderly patients with schizophrenia. *Psychopharmacol Bull* 1998;34:819–823.
64. Madhusoodanan S, Brenner R, Alcantra A. Clinical experience with quetiapine in elderly patients with psychotic disorders. *J Geriatr Psychiatry Neurol* 2000;13:28–32.
65. McManus DQ, Arvanitis LA, Kowalcyk BB. Quetiapine, a novel antipsychotic: experience in elderly patients with psychotic disorders. *J Clin Psychiatry* 1999;60:292–298.
66. Tariot PN. The older patient: the ongoing challenge of efficacy and tolerability. *J Clin Psychiatry* 1999;60[Suppl 23]:29–33.
67. Snoeck E, Van Peer A, Sack M, et al. Influence of age, renal and liver impairment on the pharmacokinetics of risperidone in man. *Psychopharmacology* 1995;122:223–229.
68. Chang WH, Jann MW, Chiang TS, et al. Plasma haloperidol and reduced haloperidol concentrations in a geriatric population. *Neuropsychobiology* 1996;33:12–16.
69. Jeste DV, Eastham JH, Lacro JP, et al. Management of late-life psychosis. *J Clin Psychiatry* 1996;57[Suppl 3]:39–45; discussion, 49–50.
70. Woerner MG, Alvir JM, Saltz BL, et al. Prospective study of tardive dyskinesia in the elderly: rates and risk factors. *Am J Psychiatry* 1998;155:1521–1528.
71. Caligiuri MP, Lacro JP, Rockwell E, et al. Incidence and risk factors for severe tardive dyskinesia in older patients. *Br J Psychiatry* 1997;171:148–153.
72. Jeste DV, Okamoto A, Napolitano J, et al. Low incidence of persistent tardive dyskinesia in elderly patients with dementia treated with risperidone. *Am J Psychiatry* 2000;157: 1150–1155.

Appendixes

Appendix 1
Modules for Training Social and Independent Living Skills

Empirically validated, the modules are designed to teach those with serious and persistent mental disabilities the social and independent living skills necessary to improve their functioning and the quality of their lives. Each module provides a structured, user-friendly protocol that includes (a) a trainer's manual with step-by-step instructions; (b) 10 copies of the *Participant's Workbook,* which provides reinforcement for practicing the skills taught; (c) a demonstration videocassette that models the skills to be learned; and (d) a user's guide stating the administrative support and resources required to implement the module successfully. The modules are flexible in their implementation in that they can be used alone or as an entire program. They are suitable for treatment with individuals, groups, and families in a wide variety of mental health and rehabilitation settings.

SUBSTANCE ABUSE MANAGEMENT

Constructed to teach those who are abusing or dependent upon alcohol or drugs how to acquire the skills for relapse prevention and for living satisfying and sober lives, this module is suitable for all types of substance abusers and is specially organized to meet the needs of the dually diagnosed whose mental disorders are complicated by drug or alcohol abuse. The trainer's manual contains exercises and handouts for facilitating the development of required skills by participants.

INVOLVEMENT OF FAMILIES IN SERVICES FOR THE SERIOUSLY MENTALLY ILL

Using this program, clients, relatives, and professionals work together to learn about the nature and treatment of mental disorders, as well as services available in the community. The practitioner uses structured exercises for engaging the family and client in the educational process. Interventions for reducing the family's emotional burden include methods for learning communication skills and problem solving. The program can be used for single families or multifamily groups. A clinician's manual, consumer's guidebook, and demonstration video are used in a coordinated way to reinforce "learning while doing."

RECREATION FOR LEISURE

Suitable both for those with mental disorders and for those undergoing transitions in their lives, the module enables individuals to learn how to develop independent recreational activities. The skills involved in this module include locating, exploring, evaluating, and maintaining recreational activities.

BASIC CONVERSATION SKILLS

Those with poor social skills and restricted relationships learn, in this module, how to initiate, maintain, and conclude friendly conversations with acquaintances, co-workers, family members, and strangers. The skills learned in this module decrease social isolation and enlarge social networks.

FRIENDSHIP AND INTIMACY: A FOLLOW-UP TO BASIC CONVERSATION SKILLS

Using the skills learned in the Basic Conversation Skills module, clients learn in this module how to meet and develop friends, to begin and succeed at dating, and to gradually develop intimacy in relationships. Participants learn how to make decisions regarding sexual relationships and how to engage in responsible, safe, mutually satisfying sexual relations, as well as the use of birth control.

WORKPLACE FUNDAMENTALS

In this module, clients learn how to use problem-solving techniques to successfully adjust to work situations and challenges. The module addresses the pros and cons of working, work incentives offered by the Social Security Administration, workplace rules and expectations, and on-the-job stressors and dilemmas. Led by a mental health or rehabilitation professional, this module should be integrated with a job placement and supported employment program, as well as with the services of a psychiatric team.

MEDICATION MANAGEMENT

Designed for those with psychotic disorders who require medication for acute treatment and maintenance of improvement, this module can be adapted for those needing antidepressants and mood-stabilizing medicine for therapeutic and prophylactic purposes. The module covers the benefits of medication, including long-acting depot drugs, self-administration and self-monitoring of medication effects, ways of coping with side effects, and how to negotiate medication issues with healthcare providers. This module, when combined with those for symptom management, substance abuse management, and community reentry, comprises a total package for *disease self-management*. (This module is available in Spanish translation.)

SYMPTOM MANAGEMENT

The Symptom Management module can be used to solidify the clinician/client collaboration in preventing relapse and minimizing the intrusion of persisting symptoms in schizophrenia, bipolar disorder, obsessive-compulsive disorder, and recurrent depressions. Skills developed in the learning activities include identifying warning signs of relapse and seeking early intervention, devising a relapse-prevention plan, coping with persistent symptoms, and avoiding substance abuse. (This module is available in Spanish translation.)

COMMUNITY REENTRY

Suitable for individuals hospitalized briefly for acute flare-ups, for long-term clients in psychiatric hospitals or residential treatment centers, and for clients participating in day treatment programs, this module has 15 sessions that address key issues such as planning discharge, developing a stress management program for community life, making and keeping appointments, locating a residence, and connecting with community mental health services. The module can be used on a recurring basis in an inpatient setting where patients cycle through some of the sessions, then complete their learning with a community-based continuing-care psychiatric team.

VIDEOCASSETTES DEMONSTRATING MODULES IN ACTION

The set of four videocassettes that demonstrate modules in action provides an ideal way to orient staff to the modules. A panel of professionals explains the scope, purpose, and impact of the modules. Psychologists, nurses, social workers, and mental health technicians demonstrate learning activities clearly by teaching skills to the mentally disabled. The behavioral learning principles underlying the modules are presented, and the techniques used in training are illustrated. All levels of staff involved in implementing the modules should view the videocassettes as a means of gaining competence and confidence.

ADDITIONAL INFORMATION

To order and obtain additional information on modules, visit the following web site or telephone or fax the following numbers:

Web address: www.psychrehab.com
Phone: (805) 484-5663
Fax: (805) 484-0735

Appendix 2

NAMI Consumer and Family Guide to Schizophrenia Treatment

The *NAMI Consumer and Family Guide to Schizophrenia Treatment*[1] gives patients and families information about treatment that has been shown to work. Although other interventions may also be helpful, an extensive body of research, analyzed by leading experts in schizophrenia, shows that the treatments and services described here benefit patients.

The first step in identifying the best treatment for you or your loved one is getting the right diagnosis. These treatment recommendations presume an accurate diagnosis of schizophrenia.

1. The Appropriate and Careful Use of Antipsychotic Medication is Essential for the Treatment of Schizophrenia.

- You and your doctor should have a choice of all the available antipsychotic medications as first-line treatment. The only exception is clozapine.
- Clozapine should be an option if at least two other antipsychotic medications have failed or if they have produced intolerable side effects.
- Discuss which antipsychotic medication will likely be most effective in your situation and will have the fewest and most tolerable side effects.
- Make sure the lowest possible dose of the drug is prescribed to reduce the likelihood of side effects.
- Antipsychotic medication should be taken for at least a year or longer to prevent symptoms from recurring or getting worse.

---

[1]*The NAMI Consumer and Family Guide to Schizophrenia Treatment* is based on the Schizophrenia Patient Outcome Research Team (PORT) Treatment Recommendations (National Institute of Mental Health, *Schizophr Bull* 1998;24[1],), developed by Dr. Anthony F. Lehman and colleagues at the Center for Research on Services for Serious Mental Illness (at Johns Hopkins University and the University of Maryland), the University of Maryland Center for Mental Health Sciences Research, and the Maryland Psychiatric Research Center (at the University of Maryland). Funding for the schizophrenia PORT treatment recommendations was provided by the U.S. Agency for Health Care Policy and Research and the National Institute of Mental Health.

Antipsychotic Medications and Recommended Dosage (Mg/Day)

Medication	Use 6 to 8 weeks following initial psychotic symptoms or relapse	Ongoing use
Chlorpromazine	300–1,000 mg/day	300–600 mg/day
Triflupromazine	75–250	75–150
Mesoridazine	150–400	150–300
Thioridazine	300–800	300–600
Acetophenazine	60–200	60–120
Fluphenazine HCl	6–20	6–12
Perphenazine	30–100	30–60
Prochlorperazine	50–150	50–100
Trifluoperazine	15–50	15–30
Chlorprothixene	300–1,000	300–600
Thiothixene	15–50	15–30
Haloperidol	6–20	6–12
Loxapine	30–100	30–60
Molindone	30–100	30–60
Clozapine	200–600	200–800
Risperidone	4–10	4–10
Olanzapine	5–20	5–15
Quetiapine	150–750	150–450

- Going on and off antipsychotic medication can result in relapse and is not recommended.
- Discuss the use of long-lasting injections of antipsychotic medication if taking a pill every day presents difficulties or if there is a problem with medication compliance.
- *Never* give rapid injection of large doses of antipsychotic medications.
- Except when taking clozapine[2], obtain blood tests *only* if there is a concern about a lack of response to medication, worry about too much antipsychotic medication, or a question of compliance with treatment.

2. Other Medical Interventions Can Also Help.

- Discuss the use of antiparkinson medications to control side effects of antipsychotic medications resulting in uncontrollable muscle movements.
- Antidepressant medications, together with antipsychotic medications, can be helpful with symptoms of depression.
- Benzodiazepines or propranolol, together with antipsychotic medications, can be helpful with persistent feelings of anxiety and tension.
- The use of benzodiazepines, carbamazepine, or lithium, together with antipsychotic medications, should be discussed if serious disruptiveness, assaultiveness, irritability, or excitability persists.

---

[2]The U.S. Food and Drug Administration requires weekly or biweekly testing with clozapine.

- Electroconvulsive therapy (ECT) may help in the short term, if—and only if—an extremely severe episode of schizophrenia symptoms does not respond to medication. ECT is not a long-term treatment.

3. The Right Kind Of Psychotherapy, Together With Medication, Can Help You Better Understand And Manage Schizophrenia And Can Help Reduce Symptoms.

- Psychotherapy aimed at providing information about the illness, managing symptoms and treatment, providing support, and helping with problem-solving skills should be provided to all individuals with schizophrenia.
- Psychotherapy aimed at understanding unconscious drives or getting at the psychological roots of schizophrenia is *never* appropriate.
- Family members in regular contact with a patient as well as others who help the patient day to day should receive at least 9 months of education about schizophrenia, support, crisis intervention, and problem-solving skills.
- Family therapy based on the premise that family dysfunction caused schizophrenia should *never* occur.

4. Vocational Rehabilitation Is Essential For The Best Possible Recovery.

- Supported employment services can help most individuals with schizophrenia return to work, at least on a part-time basis, and thus should always be made available.
- Other types of vocational training and supports may also help.

5. Assertive Community Treatment (ACT) Is Essential For Individuals Who Suffer Repeated Relapse And Hospitalization, And Have Trouble Complying With Treatment.

- ACT is a form of treatment provided by a team of care providers, including doctors, nurses, social workers, and others, who reach out to individuals with schizophrenia where they live, on a 24-hour-per-day basis, to monitor symptoms and treatment and to provide treatment and support.
- ACT reduces relapse and hospitalization and improves treatment compliance and quality of life.
- ACT should be provided to individuals with the most severe forms of schizophrenia.

For information on serious mental illnesses and brain disorders or for a referral to your state and local affiliates, please contact the NAMI Helpline: (800) 950-NAMI (6264) / TDD: (703) 516-7227.

Subject Index

Note: Page numbers followed by f indicate figures; those followed by t indicate tables.